Managing Enterprise Projects

Using Microsoft Office Project Server 2003

2nd Edition

Gary L. Chefetz

Dale A. Howard

Managing Enterprise Projects
Using Microsoft Office Project Server 2003, 2nd Edition

Publisher: Soho Corp.
Authors: Gary L. Chefetz, Dale A. Howard
Cover Design: Tony Valenzuela
Cover Photo: Peter Hurley

ISBN 0-9759828-9-3

Library of Congress Control Number: 2006921169

EPM Learning™

EPM Learning is a complete series of role-based training manuals for professional trainers and corporate training programs. To learn more about the EPM Learning courseware series for Technical Administrators, PMO Administrators, Project Managers, Resource Managers, Executives and Team Members, or to obtain instructor companion products and materials, contact Soho Corp. by phone (646) 736-1688 or by email info@msprojectexperts.com.

Contents

Contents

Contents

About the Authors

Gary Chefetz is the founder and President of Soho Corp. and MSProjectExperts, which exist to support businesses and organizations that choose the Microsoft enterprise project management platform. Gary has worked with Microsoft Project since 1995 and has supported Microsoft Project users since the introduction of Project Central in early 2000. Gary continues to receive the prestigious Microsoft Project Most Valuable Professional (MVP) award for his contributions. As a long-time MVP, he works closely with the Microsoft Project product team and support organizations. Gary is dedicated to supporting Microsoft Project Server implementations through his business efforts with clients and through his contributions in the newsgroups. Contact Gary Chefetz online in one of the Microsoft Project newsgroups at msnews.microsoft.com or e-mail him at:

gary_chefetz@msprojectexperts.com

Dale Howard is an enterprise project management trainer/consultant and is Vice President of Educational Services of MSProjectExperts. Dale is a Certified Technical Trainer (CTT) who has more than 13 years of experience training and consulting in productivity software. He has worked with Microsoft Project since 1997 and volunteers many hours each week answering user questions in the various Microsoft Project communities. Dale received the prestigious Microsoft Project Most Valuable Professional (MVP) award in 2004 for his expertise with the software and for his contributions to the user communities. Dale is married to Mickey and lives in Denver, Colorado. Contact Dale online in one of the Microsoft Project newsgroups at msnews.microsoft.com or e-mail him at:

dale_howard@msprojectexperts.com

Introduction

Thank you for reading Managing Enterprise Projects Using Microsoft Office Project Server 2003. Herein find a complete learning guide and reference to managing projects using the Microsoft EPM platform. Our goal in writing this training/reference manual is to help you build on your knowledge of the stand-alone tool and bring you up to speed on the new enterprise features and concepts you will need to manage projects using the Microsoft EPM tool set.

We take a systematic approach to the topical ordering in this book beginning with an overview of Project Server. The next three modules teach you how to use Microsoft Project Professional to create an enterprise project, build an enterprise project team, and publish the project. We then dive into the project updating cycle where you learn how team members update progress in Project Web Access and in Outlook, and how you accept and update their progress into the project plan. The four modules that follow demonstrate how to set up important options in the Home page, along with how to use Risks, Issues, Documents, and Status Reports in Project Web Access. The final four modules teach you how to view information about your enterprise projects and resources across your organization's project portfolio.

Throughout each module, you get a generous amount of Notes, Warnings, and Best Practices. Notes call your attention to important additional information about a subject. Warnings help you to avoid the most common problems experienced by others and Best Practices provide tips for using the tool based on our field experience.

Because you have read this manual, we believe that you will be much more effective using Microsoft Enterprise Project Management tools. If you have questions about the book or are interested in our professional services, please contact us at our office. If you have questions about Microsoft Project or Project Server, contact us through the Microsoft public news groups.

Gary L. Chefetz, Microsoft Project MVP

Dale Λ. Howard, Microsoft Project MVP

MSProjectExperts

Module 01

Introducing Microsoft Project Server

Learning Objectives

After completing this module, you will be able to:

- Understand Project Server's enterprise project management terminology

- Describe the project communications life cycle used in Project Server

- Be familiar with Project Server team collaboration tools

- Understand the concept of publishing with Project Server

- Acquire an overview understanding of OLAP and Project Server analytical tools

- Be familiar with the Enterprise Global file and the Enterprise Resource Pool

- Open and close the Enterprise Resource Pool

- Understand custom and enterprise custom field and outline codes

- Understand how tracking methods impact progress reporting

What Is Microsoft Project Server?

Microsoft Project Server is an enterprise-capable project management automation system. It is designed to support business and industry-specific project management and tracking requirements. Microsoft Project Server is both an out-of-the-box project assignment tracking system and a platform for business-specific configuration and customization.

Project Server is Microsoft's second-generation, server-based project management solution. Its predecessor, Project Central, was introduced with Project 2000 and offered workgroup-style collaborative features. With Project Server, Microsoft introduces a more robust architecture that offers enterprise-wide deployment capabilities, lacking in Project Central, and has added a cadre of features to support its enterprise worthiness.

The combination of Microsoft Project Professional 2003 and Project Server 2003 provides a powerful enterprise portfolio management system that is rich in features but fraught with complexity and challenges. Our goal is to help you maximize the feature benefits and minimize the frustrations.

Applying Enterprise Project Management Terminology to Microsoft Project Server

In the world of enterprise project management, you hear terms like project, program, and portfolio. How do these terms apply to your organization's project management environment?

According to the Project Management Institute (PMI), a **project** is "a temporary endeavor undertaken to create a unique product or service." A project is temporary, meaning that it has a beginning and an end. A project is unique, meaning that it is something that your organization has not done before.

For the purposes of this course, a **program** is "a collection of related projects" and a **portfolio** is "a collection of programs and/or projects within a business unit or across an entire enterprise". Many companies have their own interpretation of these terms, reflecting their approach to project management. Sometimes the sheer size of the organization drives these definitions.

The concept of a portfolio is fairly flexible, depending on the size of the company. A smaller organization may have a single portfolio of projects, whereas a larger business may conceive of an enterprise portfolio made up of numerous departmental or line-of-business portfolios, each containing its own set of programs and projects. However a business conceives these terms, you can model them in Project Server 2003.

Understanding Project Server's Language

Two terms that you must understand in the context of the Project Server 2003 environment are "enterprise project" and "enterprise resource." Very specific criteria determine whether a project is an enterprise or non-enterprise project, and whether a resource is an enterprise or local resource.

Enterprise Project

A project is an **enterprise project** when one of the following two conditions is true:

- You create the project using the Project Professional 2003 client while connected to Project Server 2003 with Enterprise Features enabled.

- You import the project to the enterprise using the Import Project to Enterprise wizard in Project Professional 2003.

No other non-programmatic method of creating an enterprise project is possible because all enterprise projects are stored in the Project Server database. Any project not stored in the Project Server database, such as a project saved as an .mpp file, is termed a non-enterprise project or a local project.

Enterprise Resource

A resource is an **enterprise resource** when one of the following two conditions is true:

- You create the resource in the Enterprise Resource Pool using the Project Professional 2003 client while connected to Project Server 2003 with Enterprise Features enabled.

- You import the resource into the Enterprise Resource Pool using the Import Resource to Enterprise wizard in Project Professional 2003.

If a resource exists in an enterprise project, but does not exist in the Enterprise Resource Pool, then this resource is termed a local resource, meaning that it is local to the project only.

Check In and Check Out

The terms **check in** and **check out** apply to enterprise projects, enterprise resources, and to the Enterprise Global. A user must check out any of these before editing, so that others have read-only access to these until they are checked back in.

Using Project Server's Enterprise Resource Management Tools

A centralized **Enterprise Resource Pool** is vital to the advanced resource management functionality in Project Server 2003. The resource pool contains resources and resource attributes that drive functionality like matching people to tasks using skills or based on department or location. The system models these resource attributes in custom Enterprise resource outline codes in Project Professional 2003. These might describe practice groups, location, department, or other company-specific information that project and resource managers use to intelligently assign resources to task assignments and management can use to drive reporting and analysis. After defining custom outline codes for your organization, the Project Server 2003 administrator assigns values for these outline codes to each resource in the Enterprise Resource Pool.

As a project manager, after you complete the task planning process in Project Professional 2003, you begin the resource management process by building a team for your project using resources from the Enterprise Resource Pool. Initial resource management activities include assembling the project team and making specific task assignments. Through the use of manual team-building tools such as the **Build Team dialog** and the **Assign Resources dialog**, Project Server 2003 allows you to locate resources by both skill and availability, even if you are using a large resource pool. This simplifies the project staffing process not only by leveraging the custom attributes in the pool, but also by providing instant access to availability data enhanced with graphical representations.

In addition to manual staffing tools, Project Server 2003 also offers you an automated staffing tool called the **Resource Substitution wizard**. This wizard rapidly analyzes the resources in the Enterprise Resource Pool to identify skills and availability for staffing a single project or a group of projects. You can save the subsequent staffing results as a recommendation for input into manual team building or directly update the results into the working plan.

Understanding the Project Communications Life Cycle in Project Server

Project Server's core functionality provides a cyclical assignment and update process between project managers and team members. This cycle is the heart of the management system. Work assignments flow from the plan to resources performing the work and resources report progress data back to the plan. This project communication cycle flows through the following steps:

1. The project manager publishes the project plan in the Project Server database, as illustrated in Figure 1-1.

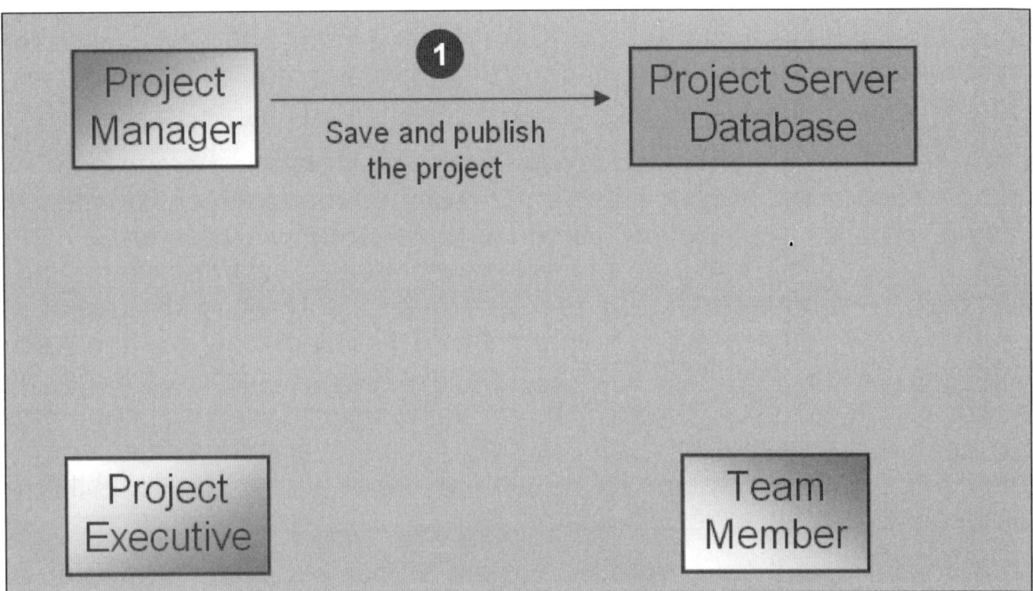

**Figure 1-1: Save and publish the project
in the Project Server database**

2. When the project manager publishes the project in the database, Project Server 2003 acts like a messaging service and sends an e-mail message to each resource notifying them of their new task assignments in the project. Using an embedded link in the e-mail message, team members can quickly click to view their task assignments in the project through Project Web Access, as illustrated in Figure 1-2.

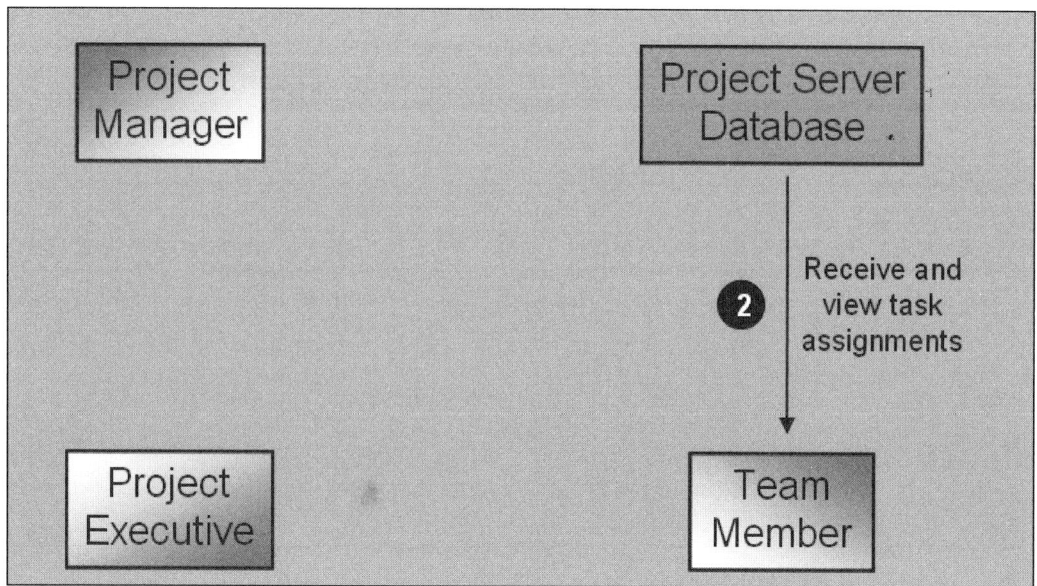

**Figure 1-2: Team members receive task
assignments in Project Web Access**

3. At the end of each reporting period, team members update their actual
    progress on the project to the Project Server database, as illustrated in
    Figure 1-3. Actual progress includes completion percentages and/or
    hours worked on each task, based on the organization's reporting
    method.

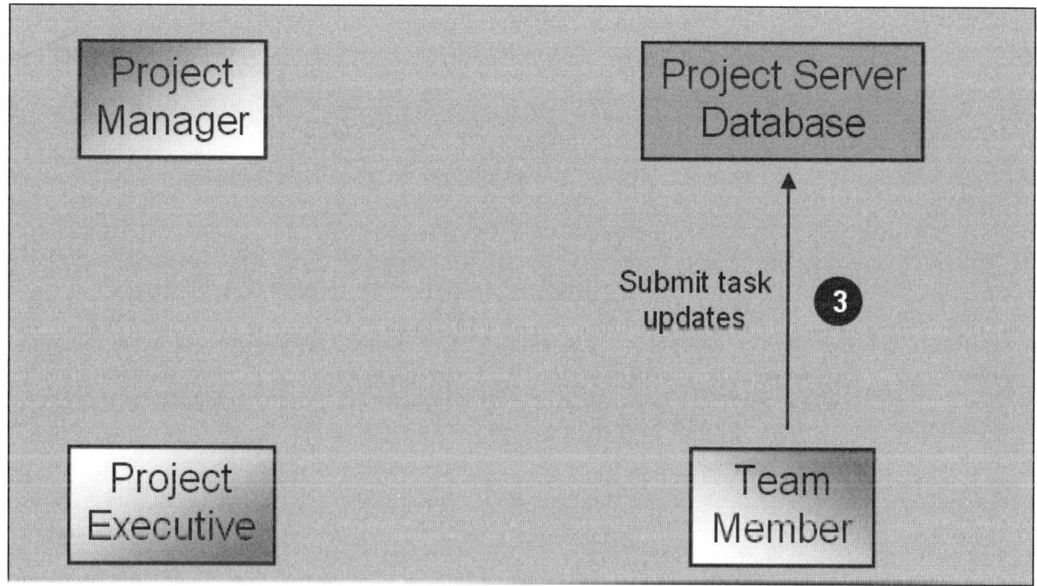

**Figure 1-3: Team members submit
actual progress for the project**

4. The project manager receives and reviews each set of task updates from project team members, as illustrated in Figure 1-4. The project manager can individually accept or reject each task update or process them in total or in batches using automation tools.

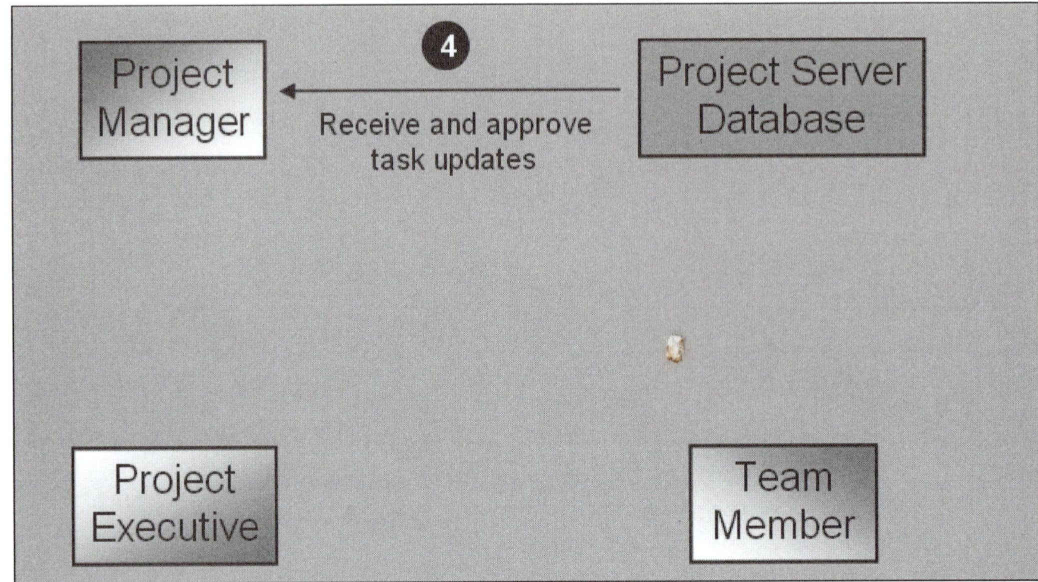

**Figure 1-4: Project manager
reviews updates from team members**

5. After accepting or rejecting each task update, the project manager publishes the latest project schedule changes to the Project Server database, as illustrated in Figure 1-5.

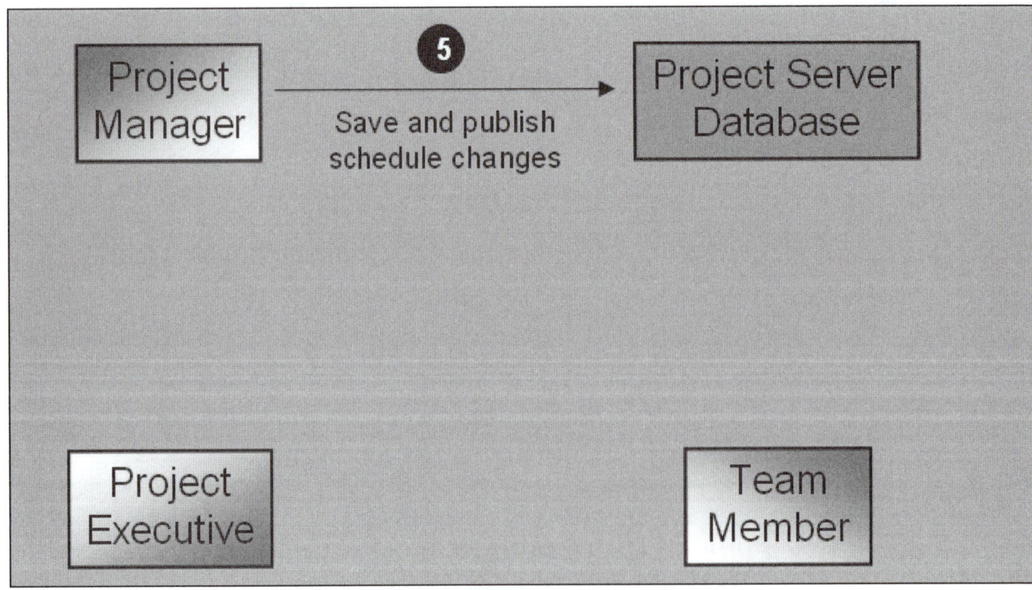

**Figure 1-5: Save and publish
schedule changes**

At any time throughout the life of the project, executives within the organization can view all projects or individual projects in the organization's portfolio, as illustrated in Figure 1-6.

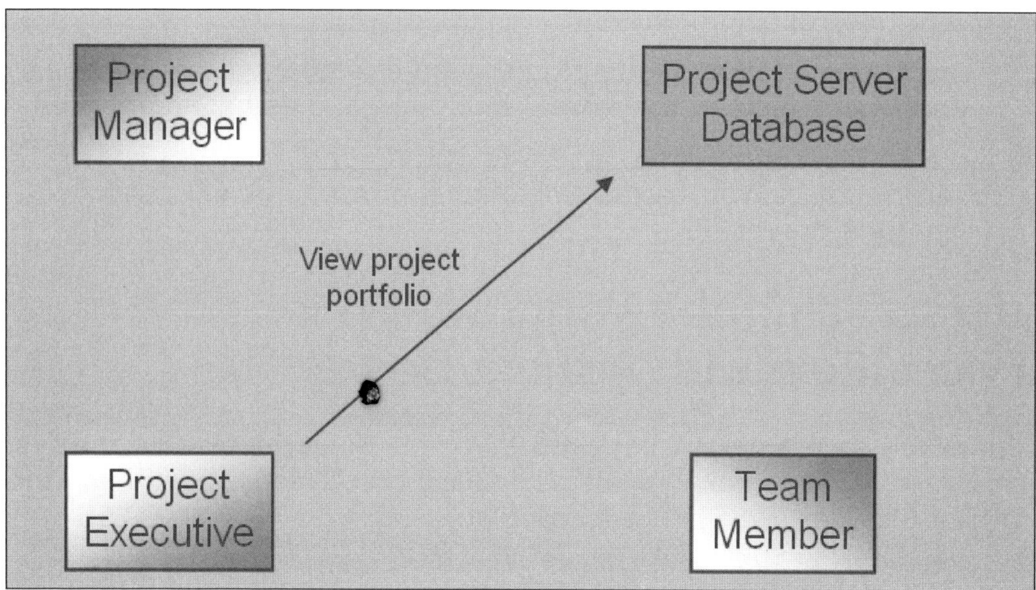

**Figure 1-6: Executives view the
organization's project portfolio**

Additional Collaboration and Management Tools

Beyond the core communication between project managers and project team members, Project Server 2003 provides additional features for project team collaboration. Some of these features are native to Project Server 2003, whereas others leverage integration with Windows SharePoint Services (WSS). The features that are native to Project Web Access include:

- **Status Reports** allow project managers, resource managers, and executives to establish single or periodic status reports to which team members must respond. Team members may also create their own unrequested reports and submit them at any time.

- **Automated Alerts and Reminders** generate e-mail notices for a variety of situations, including reminding team members of upcoming and overdue task work, and status reports that are due. All users have the ability to set their own alerts and reminders, and managers have the added ability to set reminders for their resources.

- **To-Do Lists** provide an alternative to formal project task tracking allowing all users to manage shared detail not represented in the project plan.

- **Outlook Integration** allows users to display Project Web Access components within the Outlook folder and shortcut framework. New functionality in 2003 allows users to push their project tasks to their calendar view in Outlook and report status on their tasks by opening the Outlook appointment.

- **Task Delegation** supports a team lead structure where functional leaders participate in the work distribution and management process.

- **Ad Hoc Reporting** allows users to quickly print information from data grids in Project Web Access selecting and ordering fields and formatting the results.

Understanding the Windows SharePoint Services Role with Project Server

Each time you save a new project in the Project Server database, the system optionally provisions a new Project workspace on the server running Windows SharePoint Services (WSS). The Project workspace contains the WSS features customized specifically for Project Server 2003, such as document libraries, issues and risks, which a user can access through the Project Web Access interface. When users access the Project workspace directly, they can avail themselves to a collection of other WSS tools that are part of the standard WSS Project workspace template, such as the following:

- **Document Libraries** are a core WSS tool that provides document management services such as automatic version control and document check-in and check-out. Users can upload project-related documents of all types to the appropriate project Document libraries. Project-specific customizations support linking documents to projects, project tasks, issues, and risks. These documents might include definition documents such as a Project Charter, change control documents, meeting minutes, checklists, etc.

- **Issues and Risk Management** is available through Project Web Access and through the native Project workspace interface. As the project progresses, users can add project-related issues and risks to the appropriate list and track these through resolution and closure.

- **Lists** include freeform custom list pages as well as specialized preconfigured templates for calendar events, links, picture libraries, contact lists, and announcements giving Project managers and team members the tools they need to communicate with each other in a shared web space.

- **Discussions and Surveys** round out the list of standard WSS tools. Collaborators can attach discussions to documents or establish discussion lists in the Project workspace.

Understanding Publishing in Project Server

There are four primary groups of tables in the Project Server database, with each group containing a specific type of data. The four groups of Tables contain the following types of data:

- **Project data** – The native data about any project is exposed in the Project Server database in a collection of tables labeled with the prefix "msp_." The system populates the project tables each time the project manager saves a project in the Project Server database.

- **Project Web Access data** – Once a project has been "published" to Project Web Access, the system stores the published data in a collection of tables labeled with the prefix "msp_web."

- **OLAP Cube data** – Each time the system processes the OLAP Cube, it stores the data in a collection of tables labeled with the prefix "msp_cube."

- **View data** – The system stores data used for the processing of business and presentation logic in Project Web Access in a collection of tables labeled with the prefix "msp_view."

In addition to the four main groups of Tables in the Project Server database, a nominal fifth group contains application settings for Project Server 2003 and its connections to its member services.

Warning: Saving a project in the Project Server database is not the same as publishing the project to Project Web Access. When you save a project in the Project Server database by clicking File ➢ Save, the project data remains local to the project tables, and is only partially visible in Project Web Access. When you publish the project by clicking Collaborate ➢ Publish, the system makes the project data completely visible in Project Web Access.

Understanding Analysis Tools

Project Server 2003 leverages SQL Server 2000's Analysis Services to provide browser-based access to dimensioned data in OLAP cubes. You can add additional dimensions to the data cubes through the Project interface by adding custom outline codes that group data in a way that is tailored to and meaningful to your business needs.

What Is OLAP?

The <u>On</u><u>L</u>ine <u>A</u>nalytical <u>P</u>rocessing (OLAP) technology relies on a multidimensional view of project and resource data. The relational database structure that underpins most transactional applications is two-dimensional. OLAP leverages data cubes based on relational fact sources, which contain preprocessed three-dimensional data typically time-phased and aggregated by business dimension. The advantages of employing OLAP technologies for business analytics include the performance advantages of using preprocessed data and, more important, the transparent enforcement of standardized analytical formulas.

Most portfolio analysis activities rely on custom Portfolio Analyzer views in Project Web Access. If you are familiar with PivotTables and PivotCharts in Excel, you already know how to work with Portfolio Analyzer views.

I created the Portfolio Analyzer view shown in Figure 1-7 by "dragging and dropping" five OLAP cube dimensions into the drop areas of the PivotTable in the view. The system automatically renders the PivotChart in the view based on the PivotTable data. Portfolio Analyzer views offer the full range of Excel charting capabilities in the Web browser, and you can view and manipulate both data and charting on the fly. The primary purpose of analyzer views is to analyze workforce usage, along with availability, project costs, and performance. Users can analyze project data across projects, programs, portfolios, and custom business dimensions which provide powerful insights into business trends and issues. In Figure 1-7, it is plain to see that the workload needs redistribution across the Africa team.

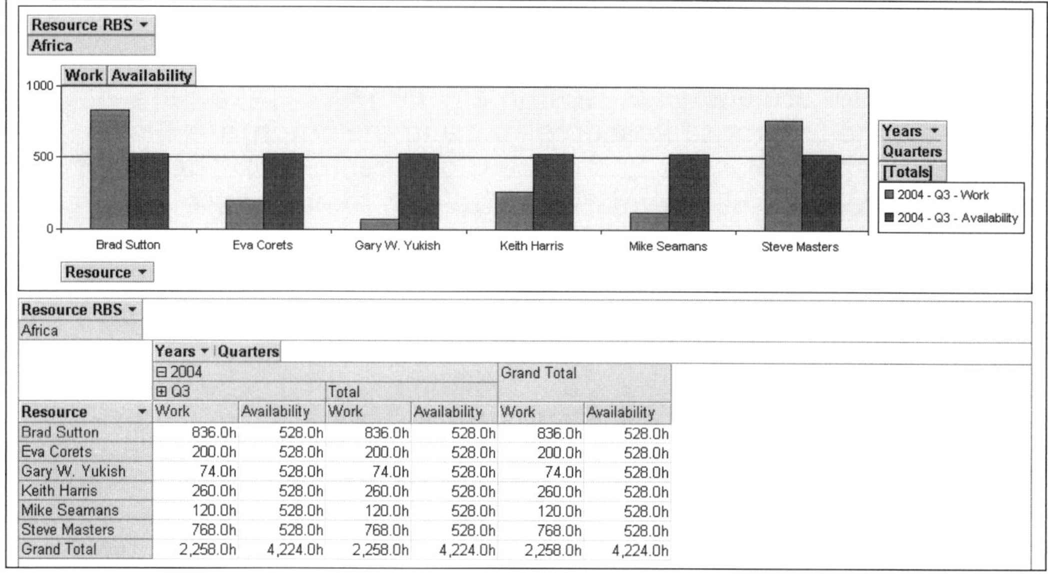

**Figure 1-7: Portfolio Analyzer view
displays resource work versus availability**

Portfolio Modeling

In addition to the Portfolio Analyzer, Project Server 2003 also offers you the
Portfolio Modeler tool for portfolio analysis that allows you to perform "what-
if" analysis on staffing changes in a single project or across a portfolio of
projects. Using this tool can help you improve resource utilization and
eliminate resource overallocation. The Portfolio Modeler provides only
rudimentary what-if analysis, but does not specify "how-to" feedback.
Because of this, it is the weaker of the two analysis arenas.

Understanding Enterprise Global Concepts

Two global entities are always present in any Project Server 2003 environment: the Enterprise Resource Pool and the Enterprise Global (sometimes referred to as the Enterprise Global template). The Enterprise Resource Pool contains all information pertaining to enterprise resources. The Enterprise Global contains all of your company's custom features, such as enterprise Views, Tables, Filters, Groups, Reports, Fields, etc. The system dynamically distributes these custom features to all project managers each time they connect to Project Server 2003 through Project Professional 2003.

Opening the Enterprise Resource Pool

In some environments, project managers may also function as resource managers. In situations like this, the Project Server administrator must grant Read/Write access to the Enterprise Resource Pool for project managers.

If you are a project manager who also functions as a resource manager, you can add and edit enterprise resources by completing the following steps:

1. Open Project Professional 2003 and log in to Project Server 2003.

2. Select Tools ➢ Enterprise Options ➢ Open Enterprise Resource Pool.

Figure 1-8 shows the Open Enterprise Resources dialog.

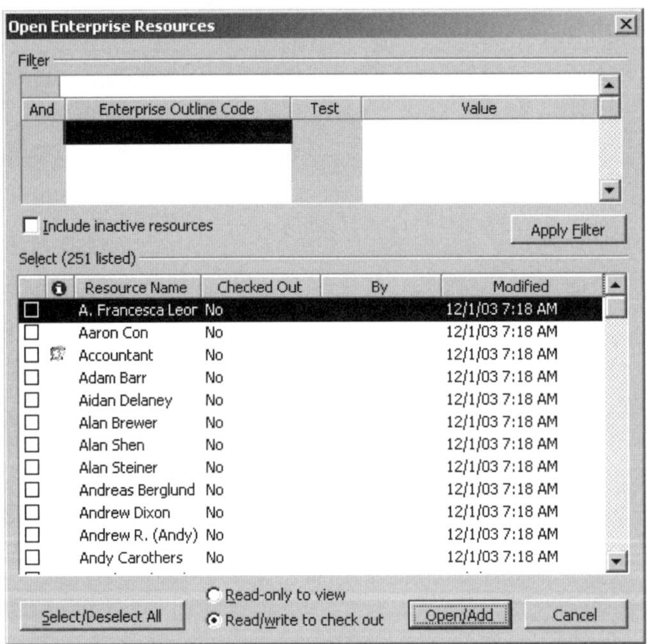

Figure 1-8: Open Enterprise Resources dialog

3. Select the resources that you want to check out by clicking the individual check box next to the resource name or by using the *Select/Deselect All* button.

4. Click the *Open/Add* button.

The resources open in the Resource Sheet view. The title bar across the top of the Project Professional 2003 screen displays "Microsoft Project – Checked-out Enterprise Resources," as shown in Figure 1-9.

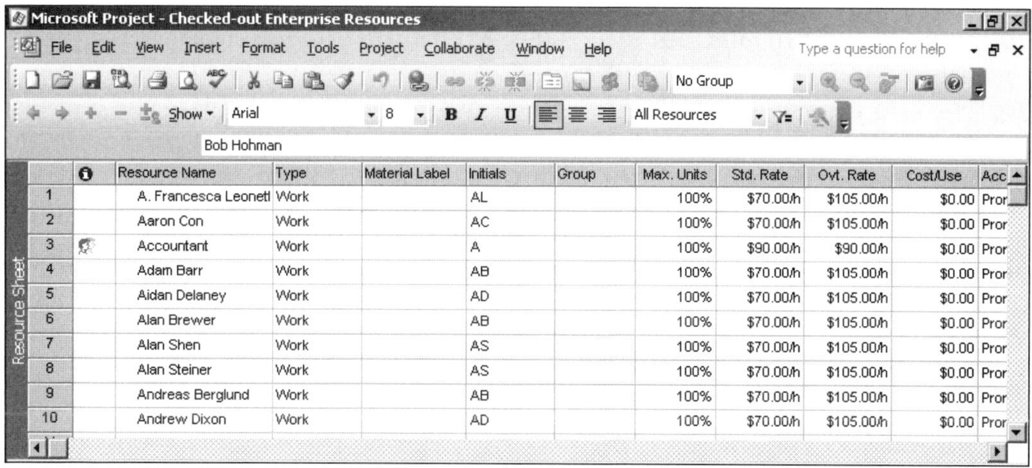

**Figure 1-9: Checked-out Enterprise Resources
Resource Sheet view**

5. You can now edit resource information for the checked-out resources. You can also add resources at this time; however it's better practice to add new resources by opening the resource pool without selecting any existing resources to check out.

6. Click File ➢ Save to save your changes.

7. Click File ➢ Close to close the file and check in your enterprise resources.

When opening the resource pool for adding and editing, you can select specific resources to check out, leaving other resources available for others to edit.

Understanding Custom Outline Codes and Custom Fields

Your implementation team must mold the raw functionality provided in Project Server 2003 to contour and channel information for your organization's specific requirements. Although the built-in generic information streams provide useful tracking and statistical data, implementers accomplish a more meaningful presentation by seeding the database with custom attributes. These exist in Project Server 2003 as custom fields and custom outline codes, which come in two flavors: enterprise and local. Those of you familiar with field customization will find that the process for customizing enterprise fields is the same as it is for local fields in prior versions of Project. The most striking difference is the lack of enterprise Start and Finish fields. These remain available as local fields only.

Administrators manage enterprise fields and outline code definitions centrally. Only administrators or users who are specifically granted permission can modify these. Project managers can modify local custom fields and outline codes on an individual project basis. Local fields and codes are not available across projects unless you embed them in templates and force everyone to initiate new projects from these templates or you move these from one project to another through the Organizer. Regardless of how you to choose to manage local fields, they are vulnerable to end-user changes. As a project manager, you may or may not participate in managing enterprise fields and outline codes in your organization.

Project Server 2003 configuration, to some degree, focuses on enterprise custom fields and outline codes. The most important distinction between a custom enterprise field and a custom enterprise outline code is that Project and Resource enterprise outline codes publish to the OLAP cube as dimensions. Thus, your ability to craft Analyzer output to meet specific requirements is dependent on enterprise outline codes. Consequently, outline codes should follow reporting vectors and you must use them judiciously in the portfolio design.

 A new feature of Project Server 2003 is the availability to define up to 10 multi-value enterprise resource outline code fields designed for skills matching. You can use these fields, for instance, to select multiple values for resource language proficiencies. Multi-value outline codes support expanded and more flexible skills matching between Generic resources and human resources in Project Server 2003. Multiple values are not available in enterprise task and enterprise project outline codes.

Traditionally, Project Professional 2003 offers a complement of fields and outline codes definable at the task/assignment and resource levels. Both remain available as local field sets, and as enterprise fields and outline codes. New with the Project Server 2003 generation are Project-level fields and outline codes, which facilitate flexible portfolio designs.

Why Enterprise Fields and Outline Codes Are Important to You

Project stakeholders and management often have difficulty accessing project facts traditionally buried in charter and scope documents. Project Web Access gives you the opportunity to capture and display this information in convenient views that can bring metadata associated with a project to the public eye. Information as mundane as what stage the project is at in the corporate approval process, to stakeholder names and contact information provided in a one-stop source adds value. Of course, you can accomplish the same effect by sharing the project charter document through WSS, but that might be too much clicking and searching for some.

In the Project Center view shown in Figure 1-10, the Project Server administrator added two custom project Text fields: Budget and Schedule, to detail the status of each project in the portfolio. A formula in the field detects the level of budget and schedule variance, respectively, and displays a graphic indicator based on the result. Using these indicators, project executives, and stakeholders can quickly ascertain both the budget status and the schedule status of each project in the portfolio.

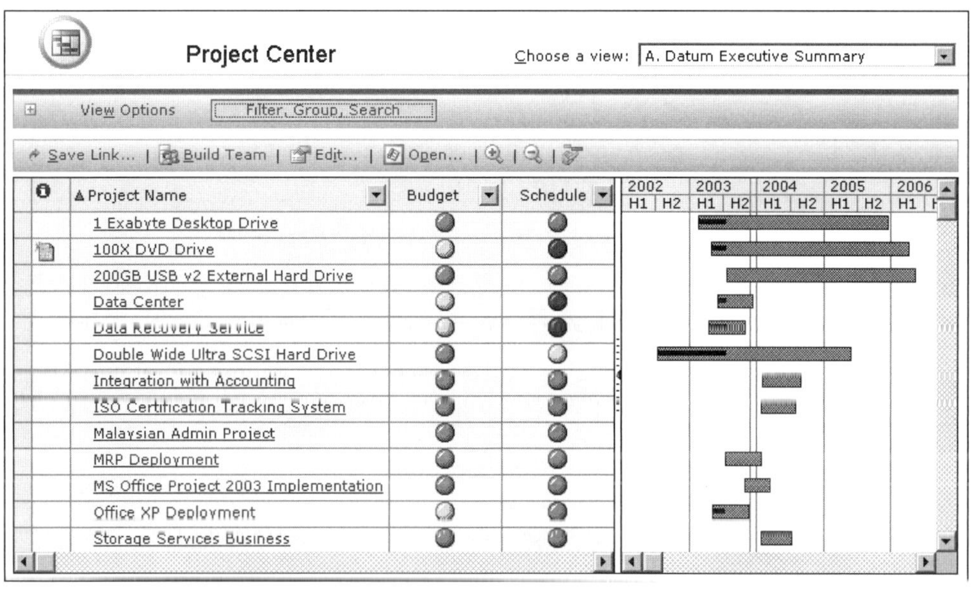

**Figure 1-10: Project Center view with
stoplight indicators in custom fields**

The Portfolio Analyzer view shown in Figure 1-11 demonstrates some of the power of outline codes when using OLAP cube data. Department is an enterprise resource outline code used to filter the resources in the view. Because of this, we can dimension the resource workload for a single department or across multiple departments. By expanding the dimensions we can drill down through the structure of the outline with the system quickly displaying data totals at all these levels.

By way of example, if you wanted to, you could expand the standard time dimension to quarters, months, or days. Without the use of data dimensioning this display would not be possible. The power of Project Server 2003's enterprise resource and enterprise project outline codes is their ability to add your organization's proprietary business dimensions to this very powerful data source.

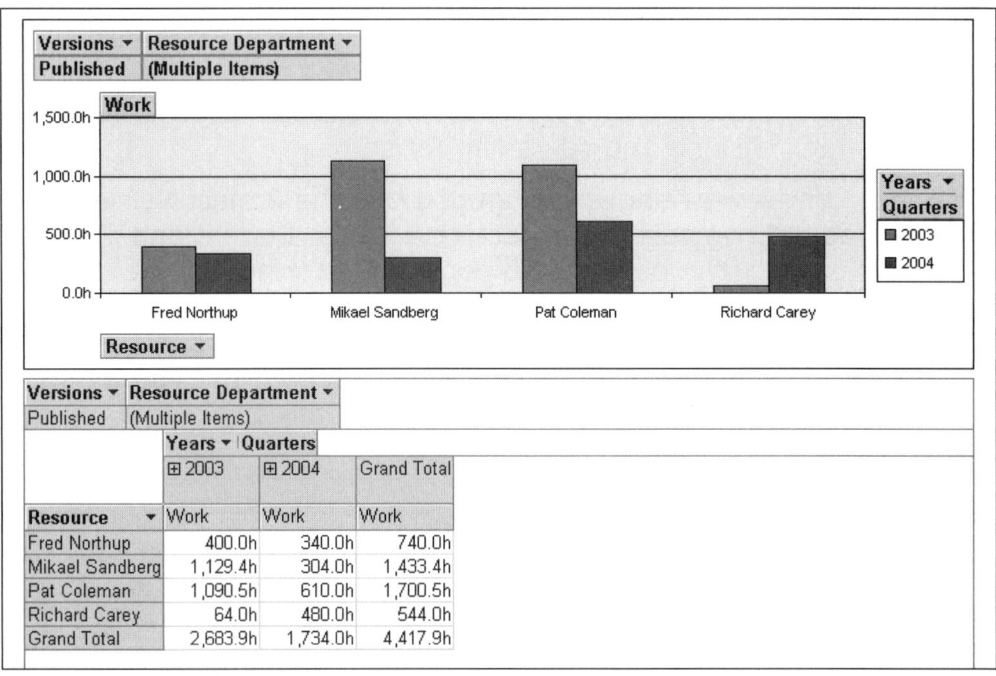

Versions ▼	Resource Department ▼		
Published	(Multiple Items)		
	Years ▼ Quarters		
	⊞ 2003	⊞ 2004	Grand Total
Resource ▼	Work	Work	Work
Fred Northup	400.0h	340.0h	740.0h
Mikael Sandberg	1,129.4h	304.0h	1,433.4h
Pat Coleman	1,090.5h	610.0h	1,700.5h
Richard Carey	64.0h	480.0h	544.0h
Grand Total	2,683.9h	1,734.0h	4,417.9h

Figure 1-11: Portfolio Analyzer view

Enterprise Field and Outline Code Types

There are six field types and one outline code type available at the task/assignment, resource, and project levels. At each level are fields of each of the following types and quantities:

- Enterprise **Cost** 1 through 10
- Enterprise **Date** 1 through 30
- Enterprise **Duration** 1 through 10
- Enterprise **Flag** 1 through 20

- Enterprise **Number** 1 through 40

- Enterprise **Text** 1 through 40

- Enterprise **Outline Codes** 1 through 30

Project Server 2003 reserves enterprise resource outline code fields 20-29 for use as multi-value fields and reserves enterprise outline code 30 for the RBS. You can select multiple entries in a multi-value field simply by clicking one or more checkboxes in that field. Figure 1-12 shows the multiple language proficiencies for Aaron Con in the Languages-MV field.

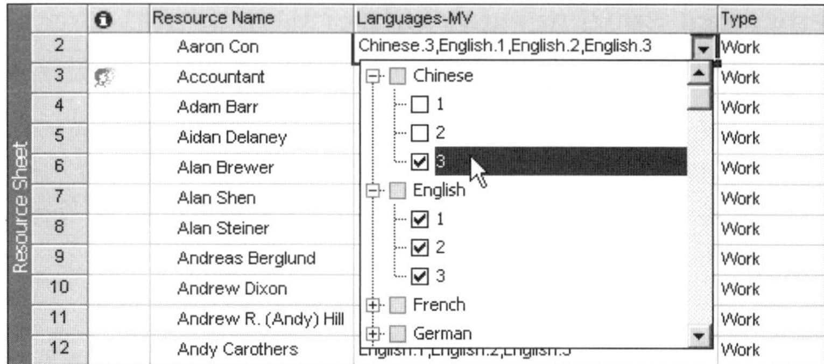

Figure 1-12: Select language proficiency
from a multi-value outline code field

Understanding Tracking Method Settings

The tracking method your organization chooses has a significant impact on project team members and their interaction with their timesheets. Not only do some of these options control what data a resource reports, but they also determine the appearance of the timesheet. You must understand the interface impact to decide on tracking method settings. Most importantly, your organization's choice of tracking settings determines the precision at which project data capture occurs.

As part of the Project Server 2003 implementation, your organization must make two decisions about tracking method settings:

- You must decide which method of tracking to set as the default.

- You must decide whether to "lock down" the default method of tracking, or to allow individual project managers to select their own method of tracking for each project.

Once you make these decisions, your Project Server 2003 implementer or administrator must set the method of tracking in Project Web Access.

Default Method for Reporting Progress

Project Server 2003 offers three default methods for tracking progress. The difference between each tracking method is the information collected and information precision level characteristic of each. These methods are:

- **Percent of work complete** – Resources enter the percent of work complete and work remaining.

- **Actual work done and work remaining** – Resources enter the actual work completed and the work remaining on a task.

- **Hours of work done per day or per week** – Resources enter hours by day or week and work remaining.

"Percent of work complete" is the system default method of tracking progress unless your organization selects another method.

Figure 1-13 shows the upper section of the Tracking Settings page in Project Web Access. The Project Server administrator displays this page by selecting Customize Microsoft Project Web Access from the *Admin* menu.

Tracking settings
Specify the default method for reporting progress on tasks
○ Percent of work complete: Resources report the percent of work complete, between 0 and 100%.
○ Actual work done and work remaining: Resources report the actual work done and the work remaining to be done on each task.
◉ Hours of work done per day or per week: Resources report the hours worked on each task during each time period.

**Figure 1-13: Tracking Settings page
in Project Web Access**

The Tracking Settings page is accessible only to those in your organization who have Administrator security permissions in Project Web Access.

Figure 1-14 shows the View My Tasks page for a team member when "Percent work complete" is the default tracking method. The % Work Complete and Remaining Work columns in the task list are the only columns available for user entry. With this method of tracking progress, the system displays a Gantt chart on the right side of the page. Although you can display a timesheet in place of the Gantt chart by clicking the *Timesheet* link in the actions pane, you will not be able to enter values in the cells in the timesheet.

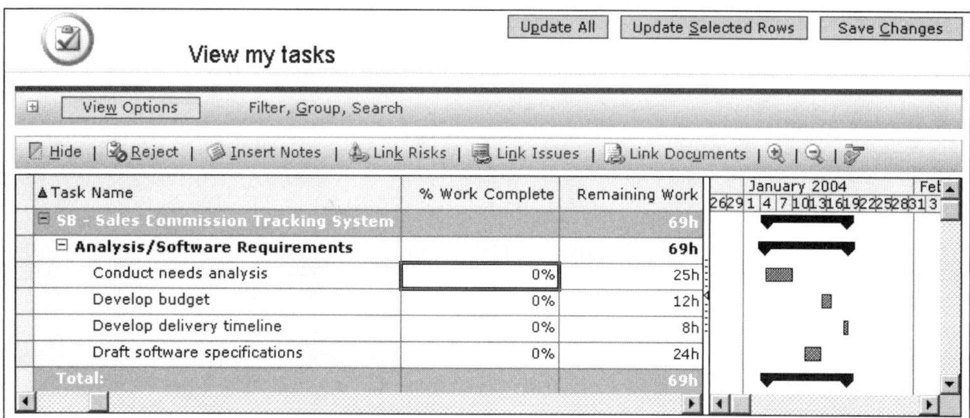

**Figure 1-14: View My Tasks page using
"Percent Work Complete" method**

Figure 1-15 shows the View My Tasks page for a team member with "Actual work done and work remaining" as the tracking method. The Actual Work and Remaining Work columns in the task sheet are the only columns available for entry of actual data. Again, a Gantt chart rather than a timesheet displays by default on the right side of the page.

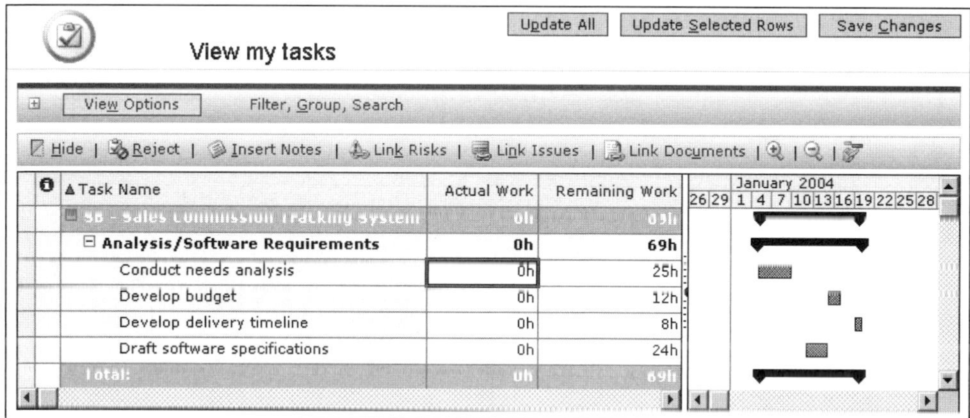

**Figure 1-15: View My Tasks page using
"Actual work done and work remaining" method**

Figure 1-16 shows the View My Tasks page for a team member with "Hours of work done per day or per week" as the tracking method, along with daily hour entry selected. The Remaining Work column in the task sheet and the Actual Work cells in the timesheet become available for the entry. When selecting this tracking method, a timesheet displays by default on the right side of the page.

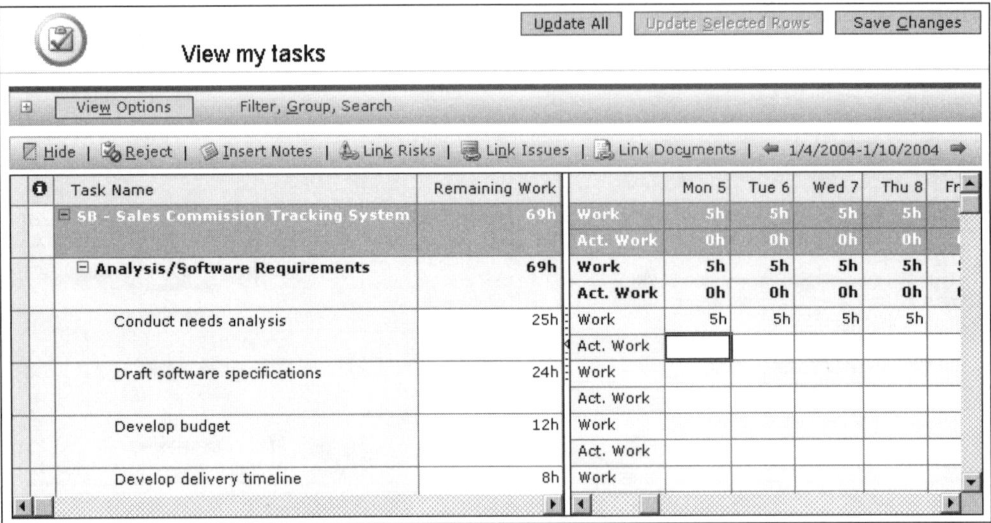

**Figure 1-16: View My Tasks page
with daily timesheet reporting**

Lock Down Defaults

As mentioned previously, an organization must decide whether to "lock down" the default method of tracking, or to allow individual project managers to select their own method of tracking for each project. In the Lock Down Defaults section of Figure 1-17, the method of tracking progress is "locked down" for every project in the organization.

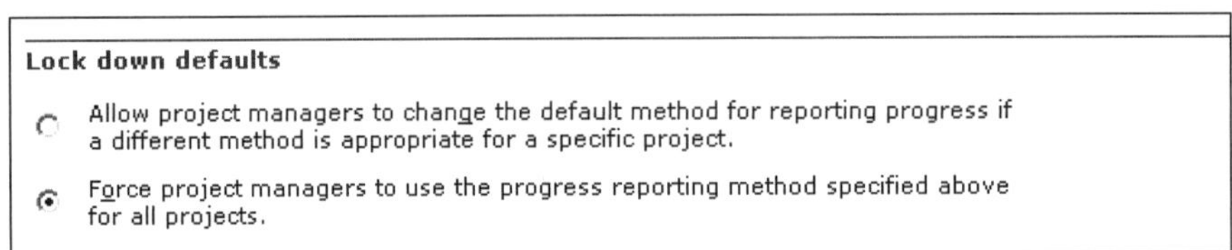

**Figure 1-17: Lock Down Defaults section
of Tracking Settings page**

Most organizations choose to force project managers to use the default tracking method in an enterprise implementation. The consequence of not locking this down is potential confusion in the minds of resources when their timesheets display tasks that use different tracking methods. Moreover, it's difficult to derive reliable performance indices with an assortment of tracking methods.

If your organization does not lock down the default tracking method, a resource must know how to report progress in as many as three or four different ways. Generally, simplicity and uniformity are more desirable. In certain implementations where project teams are static entities, multiple reporting methods may be a viable option.

When your organization does not lock down the default tracking, project managers can change the method of tracking for each of their individual projects by clicking Tools ➢ Customize ➢ Published Fields. Figure 1-18 shows the Customize Published Fields dialog. Select a different method of tracking progress in the Always Use a Specific Method of Progress Reporting for This Project section in the upper left corner of the dialog.

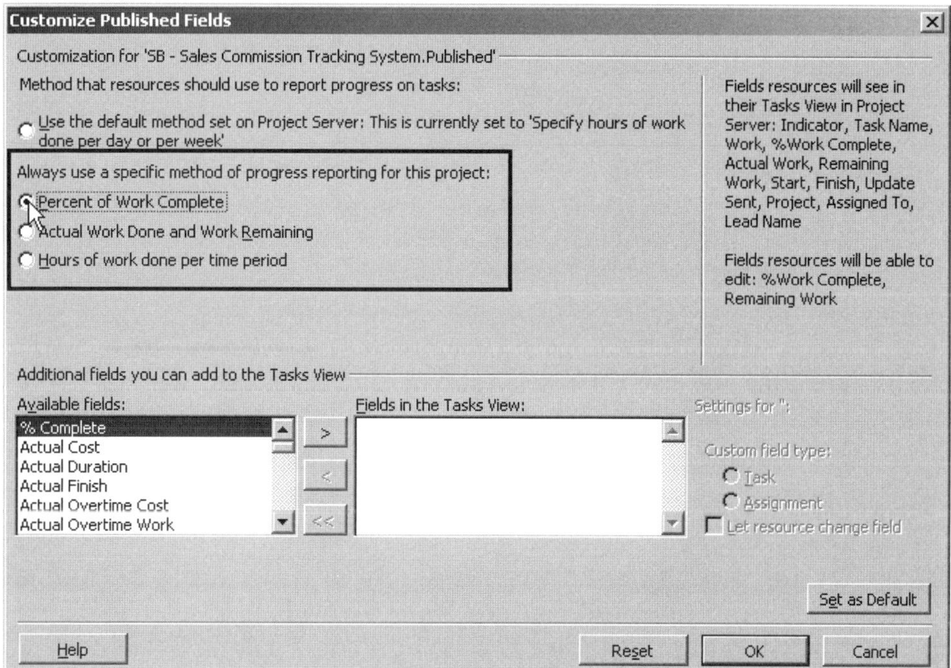

Figure 1-18: Customize Published Fields dialog

Managed vs. Non-Managed Time Periods

Project Server 2003 allows your organization to set time periods used for tracking progress as either managed or non-managed. You can determine these settings in the Time Period Settings section of the Tracking Settings page in Project Web Access. Non-managed time periods allow users of both Project Professional 2003 and Project Web Access to enter actual work values in any time period, whether in the past, present or future. The Managed time periods feature allows the organization to control the specific time periods in which users may and may not enter actual work values.

Notice in Figures 1-19 and 1-20 that I selected the *Non Managed Periods* option. The settings for non-managed time periods are based on a weekly or monthly frequency, and certain options change according to the frequency selected. Figure 1-19 shows the Time Period Settings section with the *Weekly* option selected and with the *Number of weeks spanned* option set to 2 weeks. The Project Server administrator can specify between one and four weeks for the number of weeks spanned on each user's timesheet.

**Figure 1-19: Time Period Settings section
with Weekly option selected**

In Figure 1-20, the *Monthly* option is set along with two time periods per month. These two monthly time periods span from the 1st to the 15th and from the 16th to the end of each month. When the Project Server administrator selects a monthly span, a semi-monthly reporting period is enforced by modeling up to three reporting periods and setting the From and To dates using the Period selection pick lists.

**Figure 1-20: Time Period Settings section
with Monthly option selected**

Remember that by using managed time periods, an organization allows team members to enter actuals only in open time periods, and forbids them from entering actuals in both closed time periods and future time periods. Figure 1-21 shows the Time Period Settings section with the *Managed Periods* option selected.

**Figure 1-21: Time Period Settings section
with Managed Periods option selected**

When selecting the *Managed Periods* option, you must also specify in which time periods users may enter actual work. You determine these in the Managed Timesheet Periods section of the Tracking Settings page, shown in Figure 1-22.

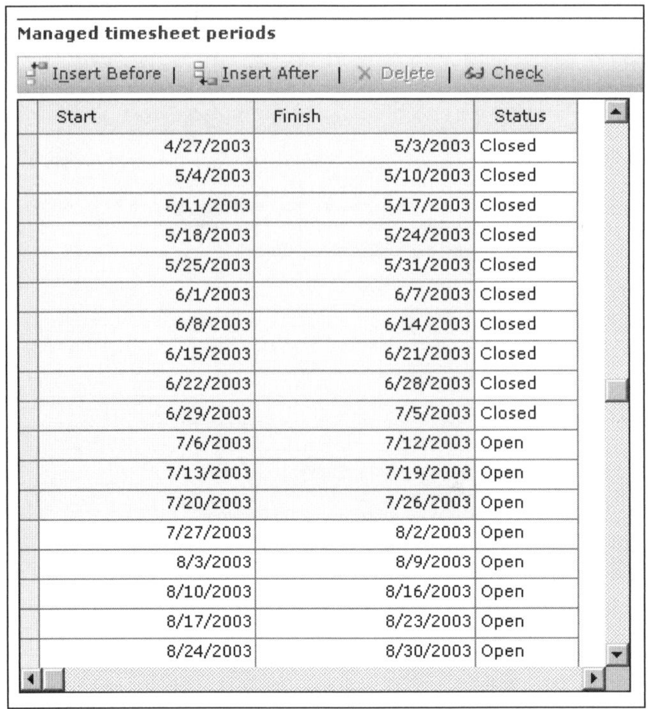

**Figure 1-22: Managed Timesheet Periods
section with open and closed periods**

Notice in Figure 1-22 that timesheet periods are designated as either Open or Closed. When a timesheet period is Open, team members may enter actuals in any cell during that time period. When a time period is Closed, users are forbidden from entering actuals anywhere in that time period. Closing a time period is how an organization "closes the books" on numbers submitted during a particular time period.

Whether your organization uses managed or non-managed time periods, your organization must also decide how each user's timesheet accepts the input of actuals. Figure 1-23 shows the lower half of the Time Period Settings section where this is determined in the system.

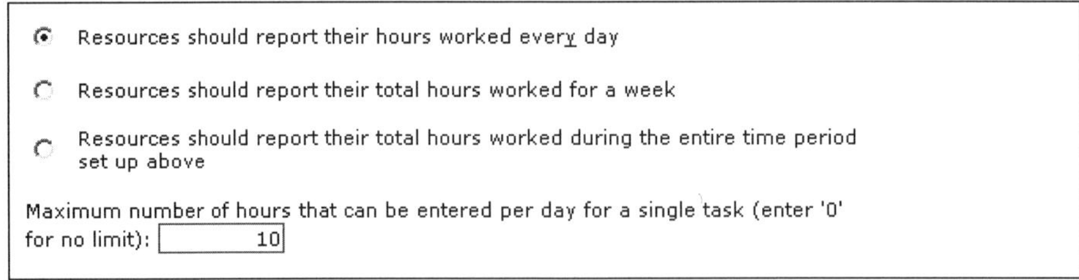

**Figure 1-23: Time period settings
options for entry of actuals**

Selecting the *Resources should report their hours worked every day* option causes the timesheet to provide daily input cells for time entry within the format specified by the span period and number of periods spanned. A weekly timesheet prepared for daily reporting over a one-week time span previously appeared in Figure 1-16.

Selecting the *Resources should report their total hours worked for a week* option opens weekly entry cells on the timesheet for resource hour entries. Figure 1-24 shows a weekly timesheet with a two-week span with weekly reporting selected.

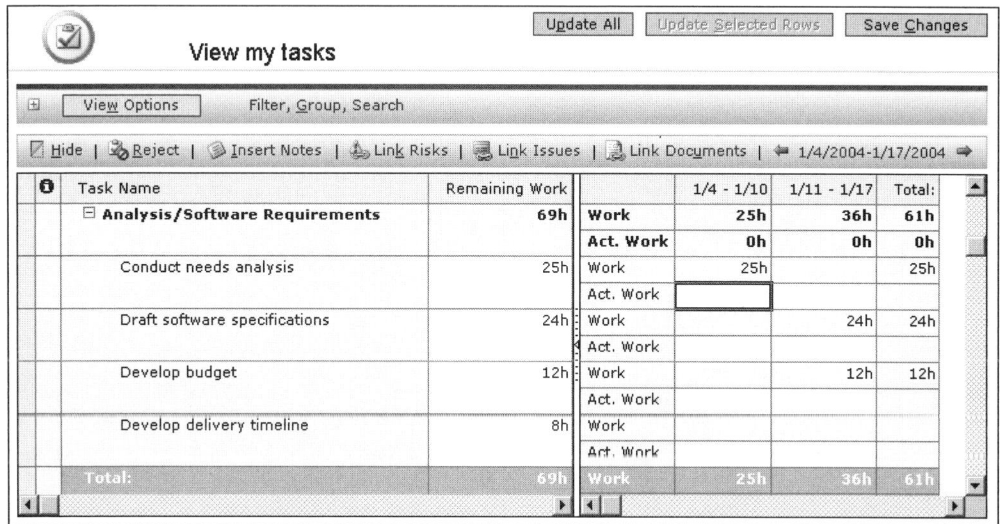

**Figure 1-24: View My Tasks page
with weekly reporting**

Using the *Resources should report their total hours worked during the entire time period set up above* option, the organization causes the input cells to represent the total by time period. This is the setting used to gather totals for nonstandard periods such as semimonthly. Figure 1-25 shows the timesheet with this option selected and configured for semimonthly reporting.

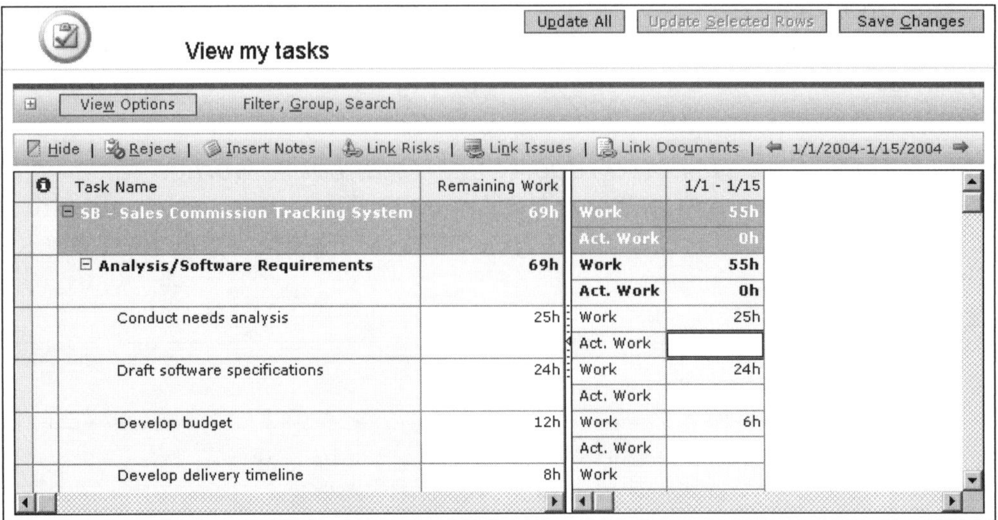

**Figure 1-25: View My Tasks page
with semimonthly reporting**

Warning: Your organization cannot mix daily and weekly reporting methods. If you want your resources to report on a day-to-day basis, select this up front. Once you publish plans using weekly reporting blocks, you cannot easily change this.

In addition to setting the option for how team members report their hours worked each time period, your organization should specify the maximum number of hours a resource may report per day on a task. Doing so limits the daily input to the number specified per task. The system restricts non-daily entries by the aggregate total of the number of working days in the period multiplied by the daily limit. You set this option at the bottom of the Time Period Settings section, shown previously in Figure 1-23.

Define Current Tasks

In Project Server 2003, a "current task" is any task that meets one of the following conditions:

- A task that should have started already but has not started
- A task that has started but is not yet completed
- A task that starts within a specified number of days

In the Define Current Tasks section at the bottom of the Tracking Settings page is the option to set the definition of a "current task". This option is set as a specific number of days and the default value is 10 days, as shown in Figure 1-26. The system uses the number you enter here to determine "current tasks" on each team member's task list in their View My Tasks page.

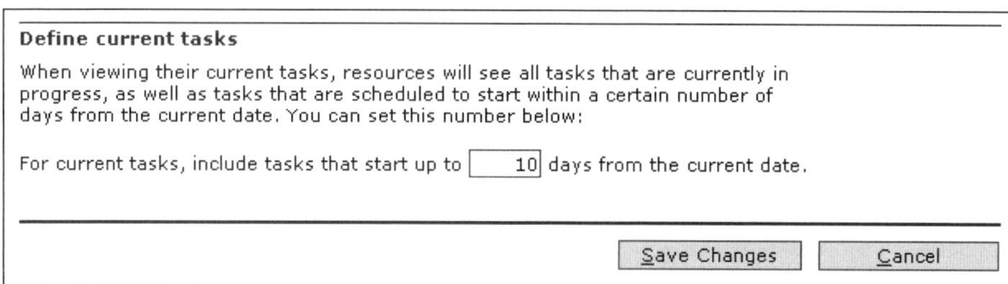

Figure 1-26: Define Current Tasks section

As you can clearly see, the Tracking Settings you select have a major impact on how actuals are entered by team members. Before you publish any projects, you should carefully consider how your organization measures project progress, and then select the appropriate Tracking Settings values.

Module 02

Creating Enterprise Projects

Learning Objectives

After completing this module, you will be able to:

- Create a Project Server login account in Project Professional 2003
- Create a new enterprise project from a blank plan and from an enterprise template
- Save enterprise project information and enterprise project plans
- Apply grouping in the Open from Microsoft Office Project Server dialog
- Work with Offline projects
- Import a project into the enterprise

Logging Into Project Server through Microsoft Project Professional 2003

Before you can access the enterprise features of Project Server 2003 in Project Professional 2003, you must create a Project Server login account on your local machine. To create this Project Server account, launch Project Professional 2003 and then complete the following steps:

1. Click Tools ➢ Enterprise Options ➢ Microsoft Office Project Server Accounts.

The system displays the Project Server Accounts dialog shown in Figure 2-1.

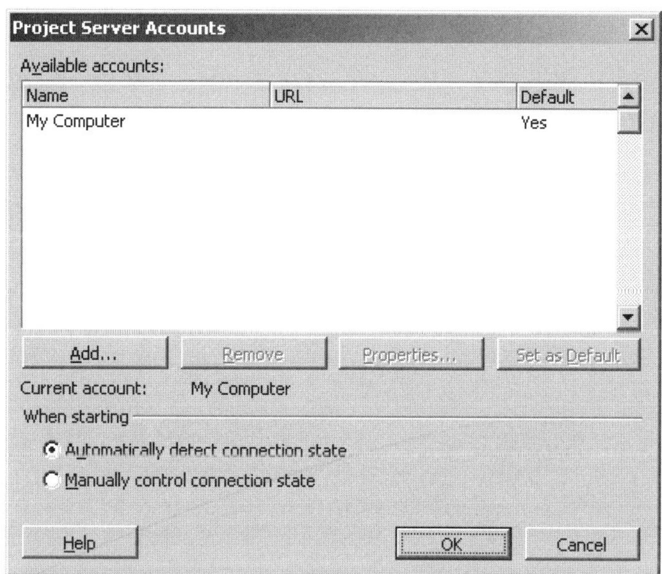

**Figure 2-1: Project Server
Accounts dialog**

You can access the Project Server Accounts dialog directly from the Windows user interface without starting Project Professional 2003 by clicking the Start ➢ Programs ➢ Microsoft Office Tools ➢ Microsoft Office Project Server Accounts.

2. Click the *Add* button.

The system displays the Account Properties dialog shown in Figure 2-2.

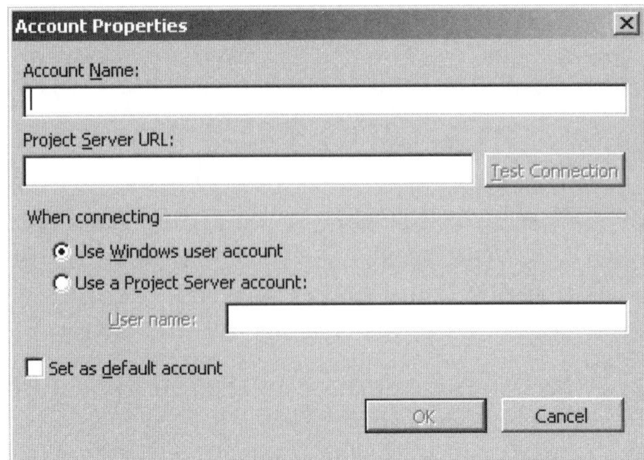

**Figure 2-2: Account Properties
dialog**

3. Enter a friendly descriptive name for your new account, such as My
   Project Server, and enter a valid Project Server URL.

4. Click the *Test Connection* button to verify that you have a working
   connection to the Project Server shown in Figure 2-3.

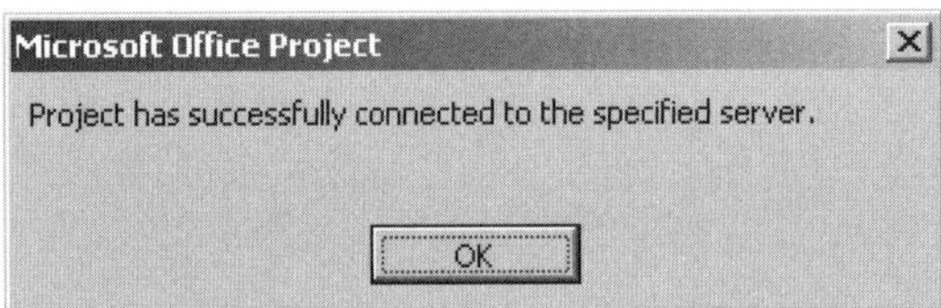

**Figure 2-3: Project Server
confirmation message**

If the system is unable to connect with Project Server 2003 using the
specified URL, it displays the connection error message shown in Figure 2-4.

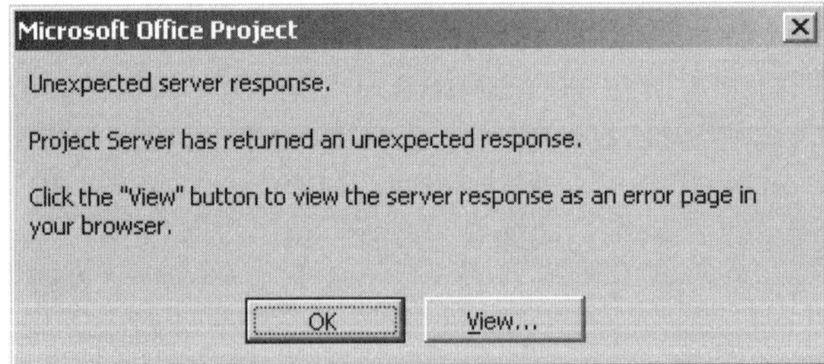

**Figure 2-4: Unexpected server
response warning message**

To learn more about the connection error, click the *View* button. The system
displays more information about the problem in an Internet Explorer window,
as shown in Figure 2-5.

> The server at 'http://edale/projectsever' returned the following error to Project.
>
> ---
>
> **The page cannot be found**
>
> The page you are looking for might have been removed, had its name changed, or is temporarily unavailable.
>
> ---
>
> Please try the following:
>
> - Make sure that the Web site address displayed in the address bar of your browser is spelled and formatted correctly.
> - If you reached this page by clicking a link, contact the Web site administrator to alert them that the link is incorrectly formatted.
> - Click the Back button to try another link.
>
> HTTP Error 404 - File or directory not found.
> Internet Information Services (IIS)

**Figure 2-5: Project Server connection error
in an Internet Explorer window**

Notice in Figure 2-5 that a spelling error in the Project Server URL caused the connection error. You can solve this problem simply by changing the Project Server URL to the correct address, in the example the correct address is http://edale/projectserver.

5. After a successful test connection, select the *Use Windows user account* option or the *Use a Project Server account* option as appropriate for your system. If you choose the latter option, you must enter your account in the User Name field. Most EPM implementations use Windows authentication because the collaboration features provided by Windows SharePoint Services require it.

6. Select the *Set as default account* option if this is your only Project Server account or if it is your primary connection. Some environments may contain more than one Project Server instance including testing and development. This feature allows you to set the default account. Figure 2-6 shows the completed Account Properties dialog for the new account.

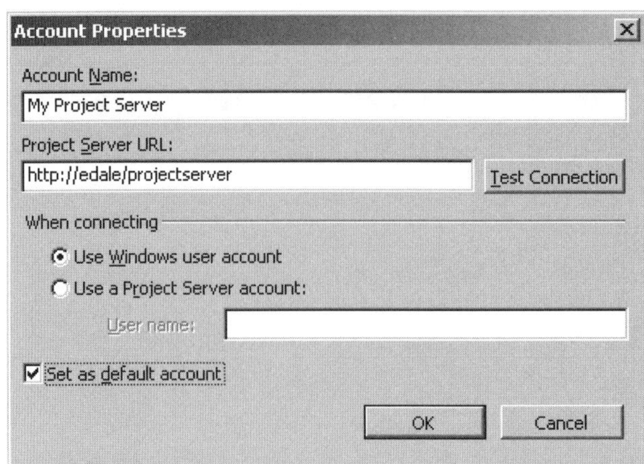

**Figure 2-6: New account information
in the Account Properties dialog**

7. Click the *OK* button and the system redisplays the Project Server Accounts dialog.

8. Select the *Manually control connection state* option, as shown in Figure 2-7.

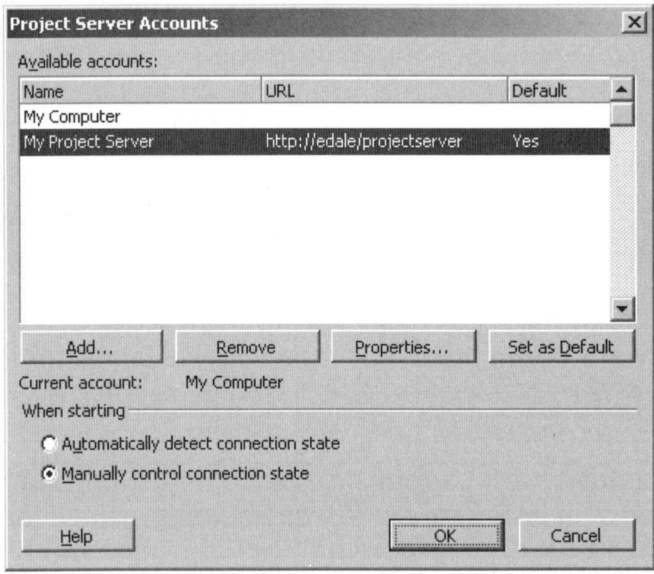

**Figure 2-7: Project Server
Accounts dialog**

Setting the connection state to manual actually gives you more flexibility in using the application, particularly if you regularly connect to more than one Project Server instance, or if you need to work with projects in Offline mode.

9. Click the *OK* button and then close Project Professional 2003.

After you create your first user login account in Project Professional 2003, log into Project Server 2003 by exiting and restarting Project Professional 2003. The system displays the Project Server Accounts dialog shown in Figure 2-8. Select your new login account and click the *Connect* button.

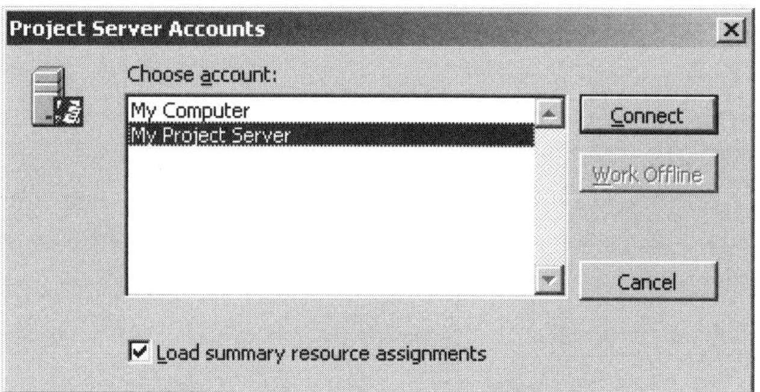

**Figure 2-8: Project Server
Accounts dialog**

In the Project Server Accounts dialog, the system selects the *Load summary resource assignments* option by default, as shown in Figure 2-8. This option determines whether Project Server loads resource assignment information from all projects in the system when you open a project containing resources. If you wish to see resource assignment information for only the active project, deselect this option the next time you launch Microsoft Project Professional.

Creating an Enterprise Project

You create an Enterprise Project using either of the following methods:

- You create the project in the Project Professional 2003 client while connected to Project Server 2003 with enterprise features enabled and you save the project in the Project Server database.

- You import the project into the Project Server database using the Import Projects Wizard in the Project Professional 2003 client while connected to Project Server 2003 with enterprise features enabled.

Warning: Do not open an .mpp project file, click File ➢ Save As, and then save the project in the Project Server database. Saving an .mpp project file directly in the Project Server database avoids all of your organization's standards for setting project, resource, and task information in the project.

To create a project under the first condition, you may begin either with a blank project or with an enterprise template. To create a new project using an enterprise template, click File ➢ New. The New Project side pane displays on the left side of the screen, as shown in Figure 2-9.

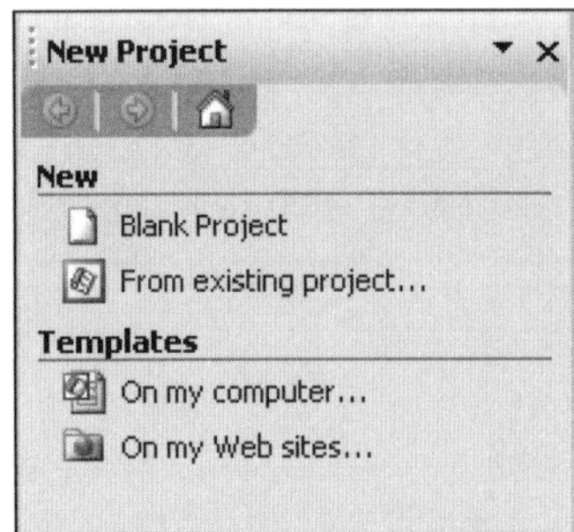

**Figure 2-9: New Project
sidepane**

The New Project side pane provides you with options to create a new project in four ways:

- From a blank project
- From an existing project
- Using local or enterprise templates
- Using templates found on the Web

The *On my Web Sites* link allows you to browse My Network Places. Click the *On my computer* link and the system opens the Templates dialog shown in Figure 2-10. There are three tabs in the dialog. The *General* tab contains your personal templates, while the *Project Templates* tab contains pre-defined templates that ship with the software. Click the *Enterprise Templates* tab to find all of your organization's enterprise templates.

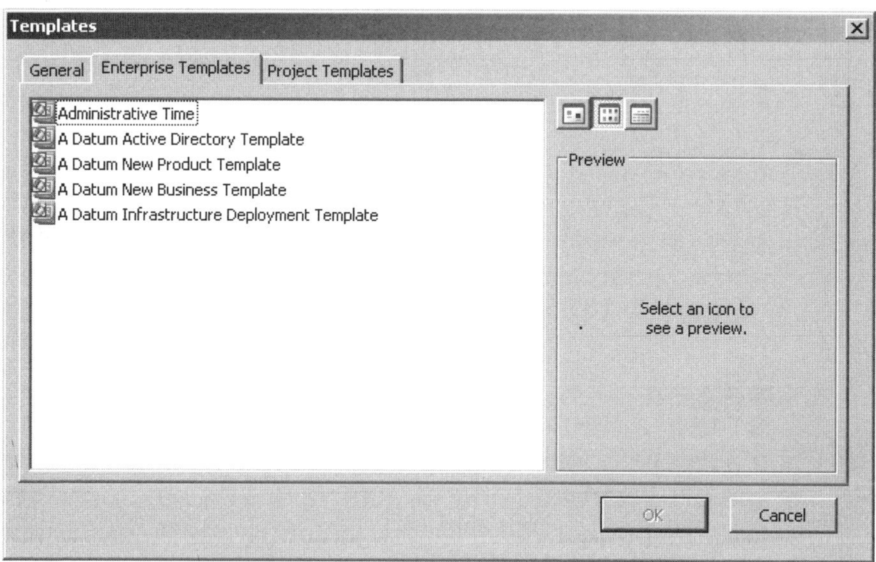

Figure 2-10: Templates dialog with Enterprise Templates tab selected

To apply the list view of the enterprise templates as shown in Figure 2-10, click the *List* button in the upper right corner of the Templates dialog.

Select a template and click the *OK* button. The first thing you should do with your new project is to name and save it in the Project Server database. Click File ➢ Save to open the Save to Project Server dialog shown in Figure 2-11. Name the new project according to the naming convention of your organization and then click the *Save* button.

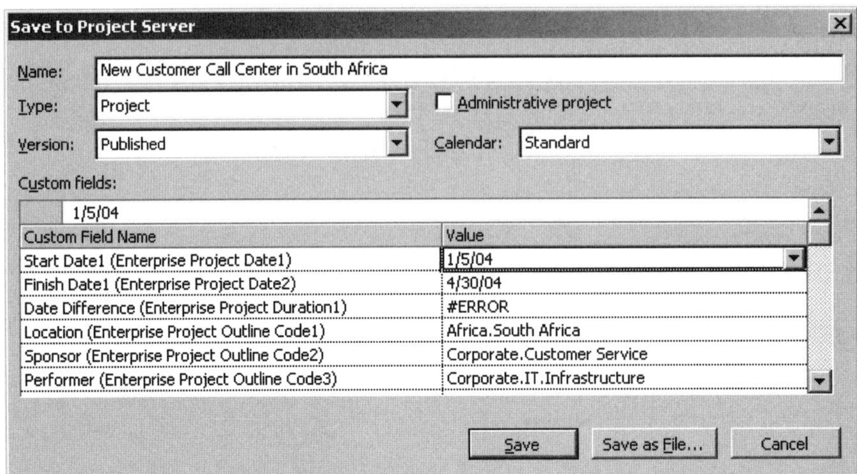

Figure 2-11: Save to Project Server dialog

The Custom Field Name and Value section of the dialog contains custom field information defined for your enterprise. Some of these fields may require values as a precondition to saving the project. You can easily recognize these required fields as the dialog will display an asterisk * after the name of each required field.

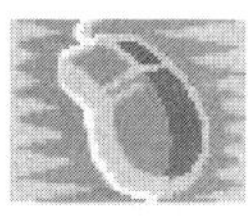 **Hands On Exercise**

Exercise 2-1

Create a new blank project and save it in the Project Server database.

1. Connect to Project Server 2003 if you are not already connected.

2. Create a new project from blank project and save it by selecting File ➢ Save.

3. Name your new plan student#+test1 (eg: 04test1).

4. Fill in the enterprise Project fields and make your own entry decisions.

5. Click the *Save* button in the Save to Project Server dialog.

Exercise 2-2

Create a new project from an enterprise template.

1. Connect to Project Server 2003 if you are not already connected.

2. Click File ➢ New.

3. In the New Project sidepane, select the *On my computer* option.

4. Click the *Enterprise Templates* tab and select an enterprise project template for your organization.

5. Click the *OK* button to open it.

6. Click File ➢ Save.

7. Name your new plan student#+test2 (eg: 04test2).

8. Fill in the Enterprise Project fields and make your own entry decisions.

9. Click the *Save* button.

Opening and Closing Project Plans

When you click File ➢ Open, the Open from Microsoft Office Project Server dialog displays as shown in Figure 2-12. In this dialog, you will see only the projects that you have permission to see. For each project, the dialog displays the project Name and Version, along with indicators that show if someone has the project checked out and by whom, as well as the last modified date. At the bottom of the dialog, notice that you may open projects read-only or read/write. Clicking the *Open from File* button opens a traditional file browser. From the file browser window, it is also possible to select other supported file formats and ODBC sources.

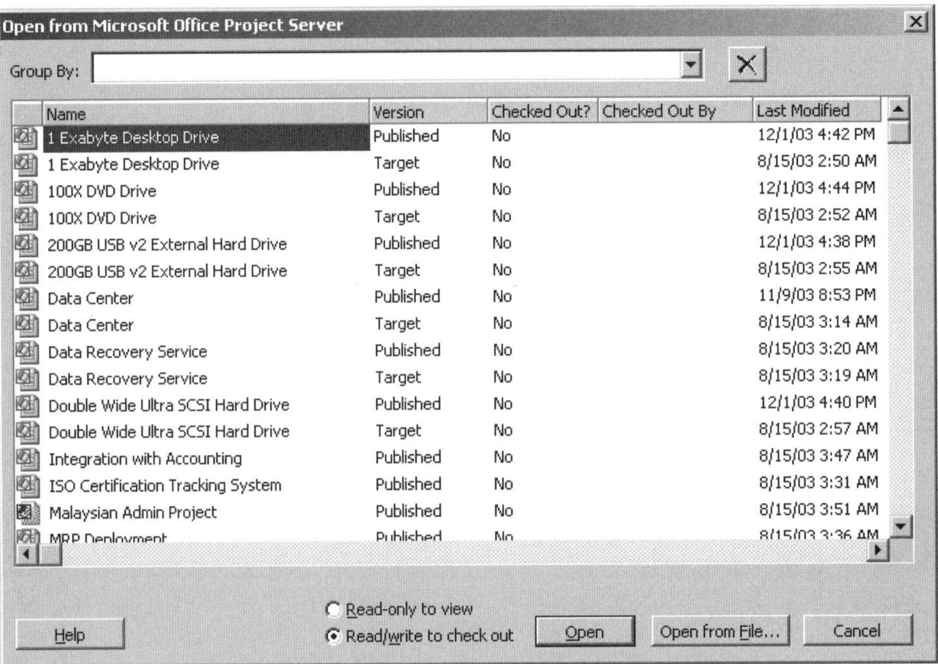

Figure 2-12: Open from Microsoft Office Project Server dialog

 If any projects in this dialog appear to be grayed-out, this indicates that you have permission to view, but not to save these projects. To open these projects, you must select the *Read-only to view* option at the bottom of the dialog and then click the *Open* button.

The Open from Microsoft Office Project Server dialog contains two new features in Project Server 2003; a *Group By* pick list and a *Delete* button. The *Group By* pick list allows you to group the projects according to one of your organization's custom enterprise Project outline codes. To group your projects, click the *Group By* pick list and select a custom field. In Figure 2-13, I am selecting the Location field from the *Group By* pick list.

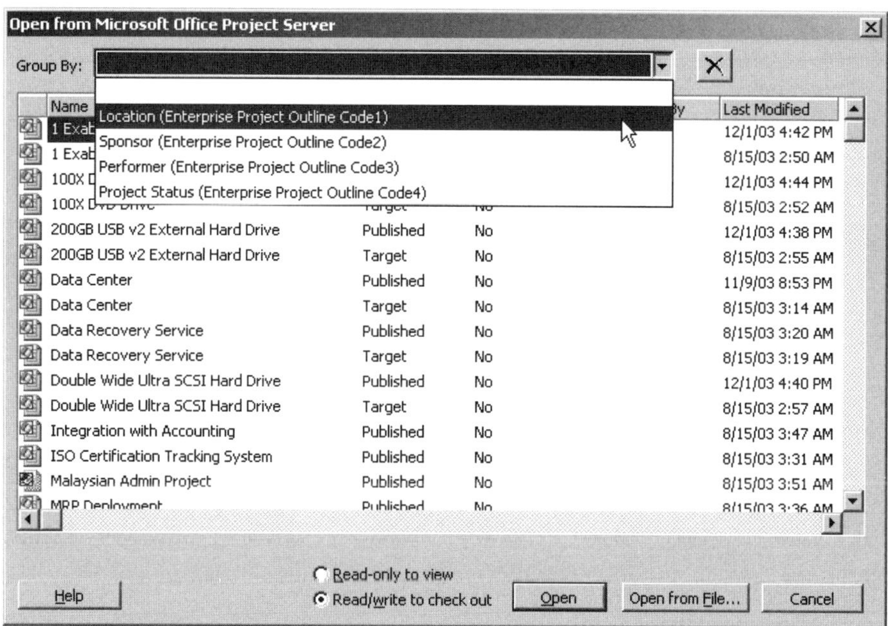

**Figure 2-13: Group By pick list in the Open from
Microsoft Office Project Server dialog**

Once you select an outline code field in the *Group By* pick list, the system applies grouping to the list of projects according to the values in the selected field. Notice that Location is the field used for grouping in Figure 2-14.

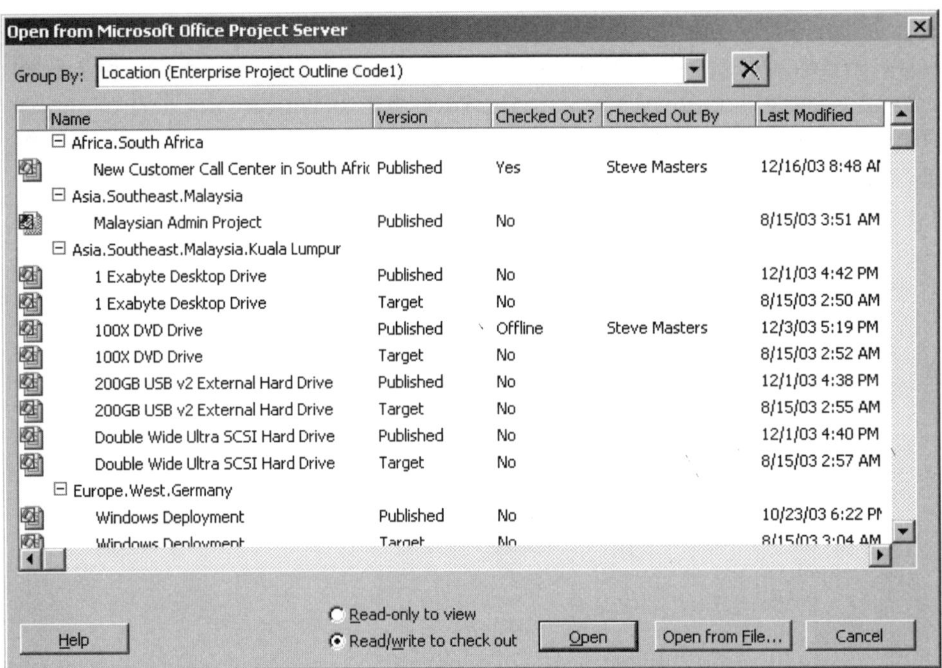

**Figure 2-14: Grouping applied in the Open from
Microsoft Office Project Server dialog**

The *Delete* button appears in the Open from Microsoft
Office Project Server dialog by default. If your Project Server
administrator has denied you permission to delete projects,
and you attempt to delete a project by clicking the *Delete*
button, the system will stop you by displaying a dialog that
indicates you do not have permission to delete the file.

Warning: If you select a project in the in the Open from
Microsoft Office Project Server dialog and then click the
Delete button, you will permanently delete the selected
project from the Project Server database. There is no Undo
command when deleting projects!

Opening a project file marks it as checked out in the system. Referring back
to Figure 2-14, any other user attempting to open the project from the
server will see that you have it checked out in the Open from Microsoft Office
Project Server dialog and the system limits them to the *Read-only* option.

It is wise to cultivate good habits when opening, saving and closing project files from Project Server. Always make it a rule to use File ➢ Close to close your projects. Remember to save your project before closing it, or the system will prompt you to save it.

Warning: Using the **X** (Close) button in the upper right-hand corner of the project window can lead to your project remaining in a checked out state in the database, even though it appears to close successfully. Close your project plan before closing Project Professional 2003.

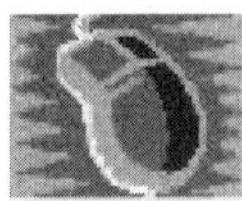

Hands On Exercise

Exercise 2-3

Open a project from the Project Server database and apply grouping to the project list.

1. Connect to Project Server 2003 if you are not already connected.

2. Click File ➢ Open.

3. Look for other plans that are checked out, and note who is working on the plan.

4. Click the *Group By* pick list and select an enterprise Project outline code from the list.

5. Open the project you created in Exercise 2-2 (the file name with your student #+test2).

6. Click File ➢ Close to close the file properly.

Working with Offline Projects

Project Professional 2003 and Project Server 2003 allow you to work on projects in offline mode in situations where you must travel away from your company's network. If you are a traveling project manager and need to take the project offline for updating, you must first open the plan when connected to Project Server 2003. To save it as an offline project so that you can update it while you are traveling, select File ➢ Save Offline. The title bar for your project will change to indicate that your project is in offline mode with the addition of [Offline] at the end of the file name, as shown in Figure 2-15. You can see what this looks like to online users by referring back to Figure 2-14.

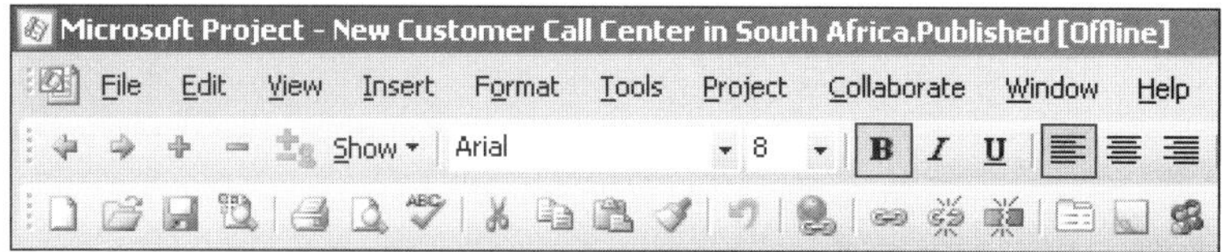

**Figure 2-15: Title bar indicates
an offline file is open**

Saving a project in offline mode is **not** the same as clicking File ➢ Save As, and then saving the file as an .mpp project plan on your hard drive.

While you are traveling, you must log into your local copy of Project Server 2003 which varies slightly from the procedure for logging in when connected to your company's network. You must follow this procedure to work with your offline projects. When you launch Project Professional 2003, select your account in the Project Server Accounts dialog, and click the *Work Offline* button as shown in Figure 2-16. Doing so will log you into Project Server 2003 in offline mode and allow you to work with your offline projects.

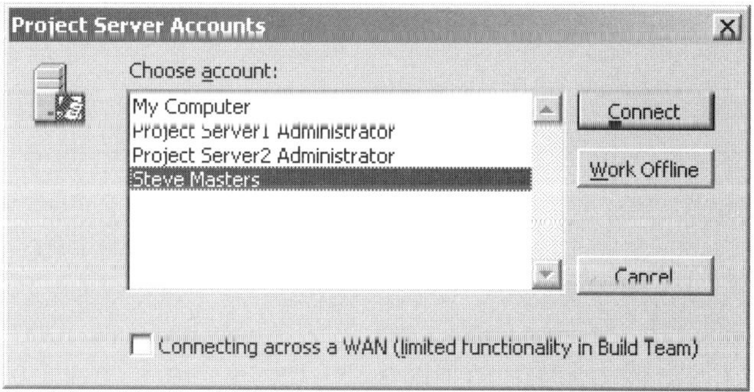

**Figure 2-16: Click the Work Offline button
to work offline with Project Server**

While you are working in offline mode, you can open any offline project by clicking File ➢ Open. The Open from Microsoft Office Project Server dialog displays only offline projects, as shown in Figure 2-17. Select an offline project and click Open.

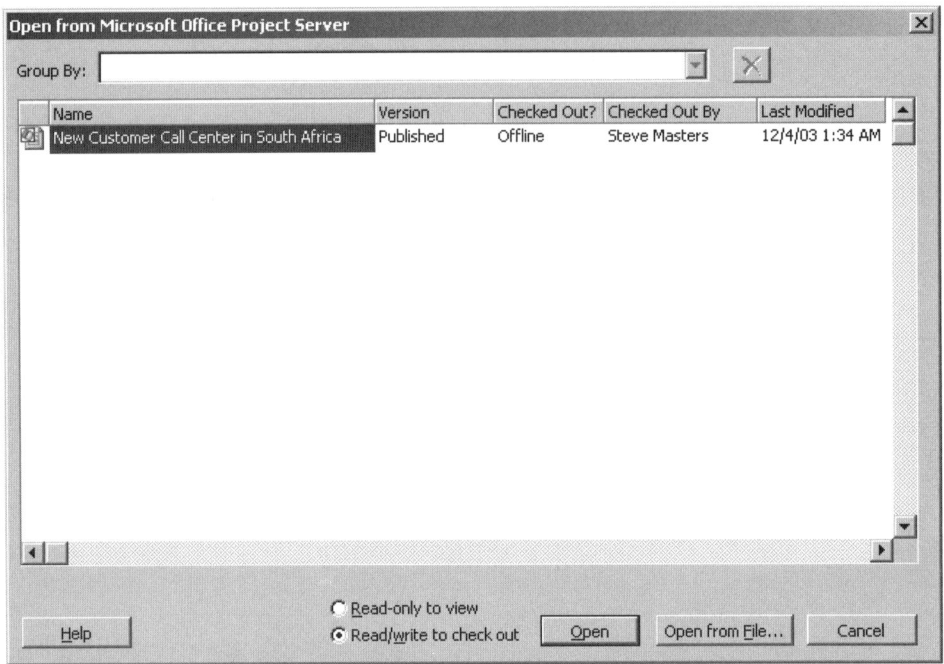

**Figure 2-17: Open from Microsoft Office Project Server
dialog shows only offline projects**

As you update your offline project, you save the project as you normally do by clicking File ➢ Save. While in offline mode, all changes save to a temporary copy of the project on your computer's hard drive.

While working with a project in offline mode, you can perform many activities that you can do while working online, such as adding and editing tasks, setting task dependencies, etc. However, you cannot perform any activity in the project that requires a login connection to the Project Server, such as using the Build Team dialog.

When you return to your office, log into Project Server 2003 normally by selecting your account and clicking the *Connect* button in the Project Server Accounts dialog. To open your offline project, simply click File ➢ Open. The Open from Microsoft Office Project Server dialog lists all projects to which you have access, including your offline projects, as shown in Figure 2-18. Select your offline project and click Open.

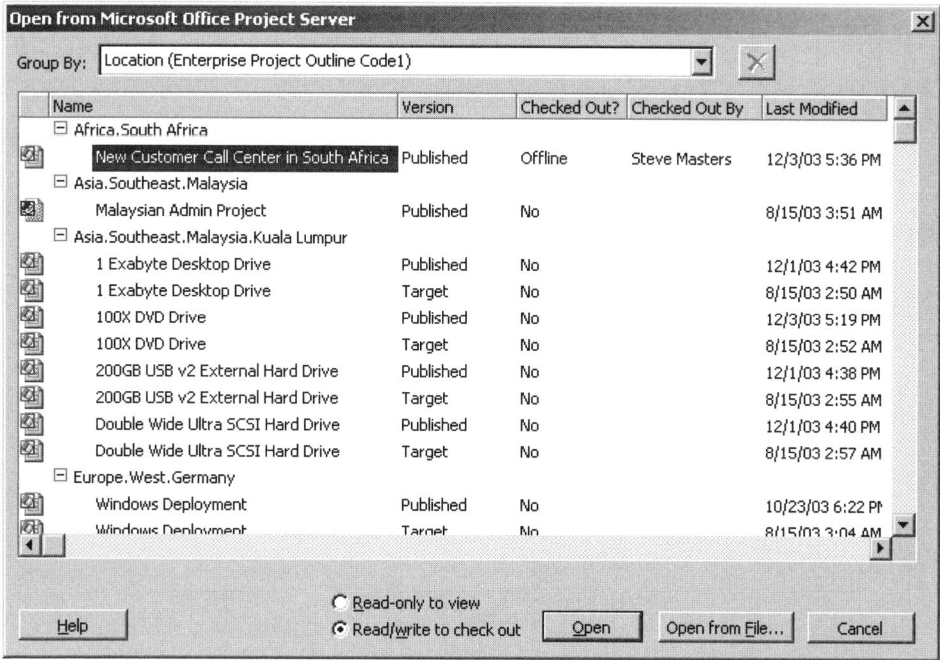

**Figure 2-18: Open from Microsoft Office Project Server
dialog shows all projects including offline projects**

To save the offline project back to the Project Server database as an online
project, click File ➢ Save Online. Project Professional 2003 presents a
confirmation dialog, as shown in Figure 2-19.

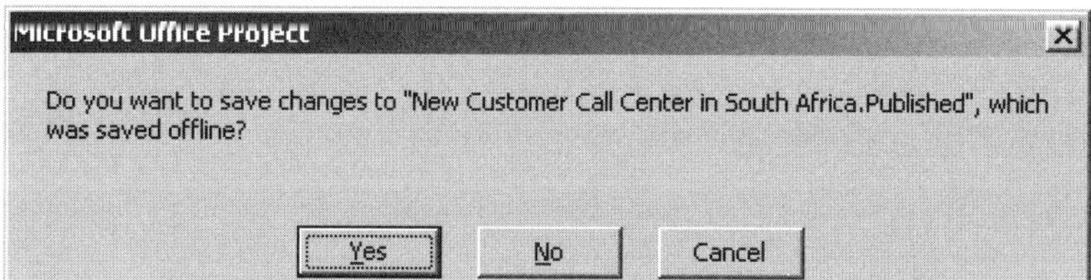

**Figure 2-19: Microsoft Office Project
confirmation dialog**

Click the *Yes* button to save the offline project in the database. When you do
so, Project Server 2003 synchronizes the changes between the offline copy of
the project and the online copy of the project in the database.

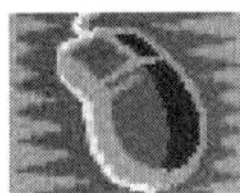

Hands On Exercise

Exercise 2-4

Save a Project offline and then save it Online.

1. Connect to Project Server 2003 if you are not already connected.

2. Click File ➤ Open.

3. Open the project you created in Exercise 2-1 (the file name with your student #+test1).

4. Click File ➤ Save Offline.

5. Click File ➤ Close.

6. Click File ➤ Open and notice that the project displays as an offline project.

7. Open the offline project.

8. Click File ➤ Save Online and save the plan online.

9. When prompted, click the *Yes* button.

Importing Projects

The Import Projects Wizard is a valuable tool that assists you in moving your non-enterprise projects into the enterprise environment. To use this Wizard, you must launch Project Professional 2003 and be connected to Project Server 2003. Click Tools ➢ Enterprise Options ➢ Import Project to Enterprise to access the Import Projects Wizard. The Welcome page of the Import Projects Wizard displays, as shown in Figure 2-20.

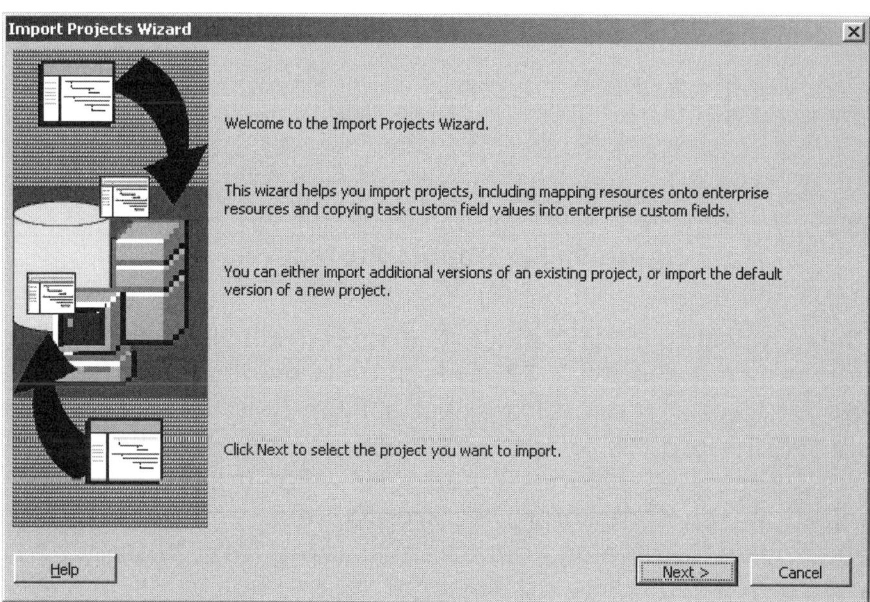

**Figure 2-20: Import Projects Wizard
Welcome Page**

Click the *Next* button to continue. The system displays the Import Project file browser window shown in Figure 2-21. Navigate to the directory containing the project plan to be imported or click the *ODBC* button to select an ODBC connection. You can point at projects stored in databases as easily as you can a file. Locate the plan and click Import to activate the import process.

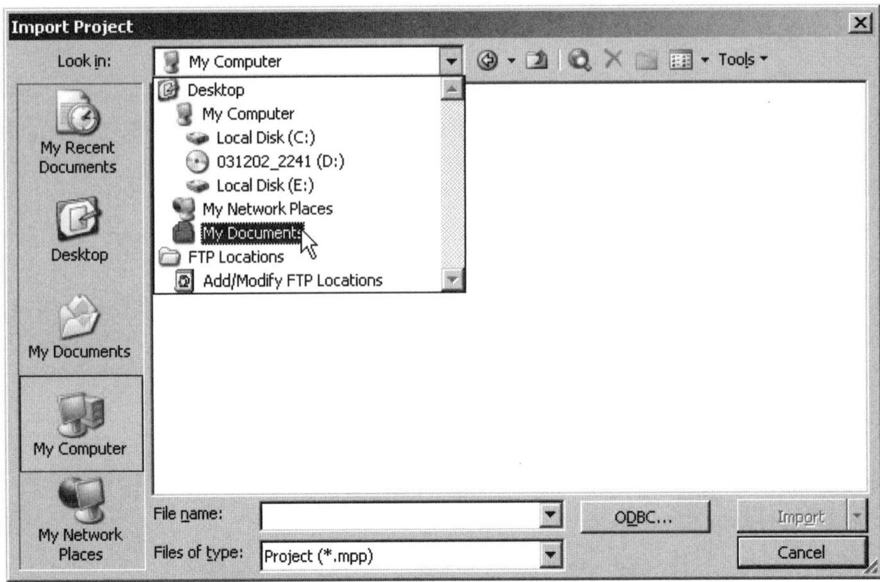

Figure 2-21: Import Project dialog

Once you have selected your project, the system displays the Importing Project page shown in Figure 2-22. This page provides entry fields to name the project, to select a Version, to select a Type (allowing you to import the project as a regular project or as a template), and to select the project Calendar. This page also includes a data grid, allowing you to enter values for your organization's custom enterprise Project fields and outline codes. Enter or select the appropriate values and then click the *Next* button.

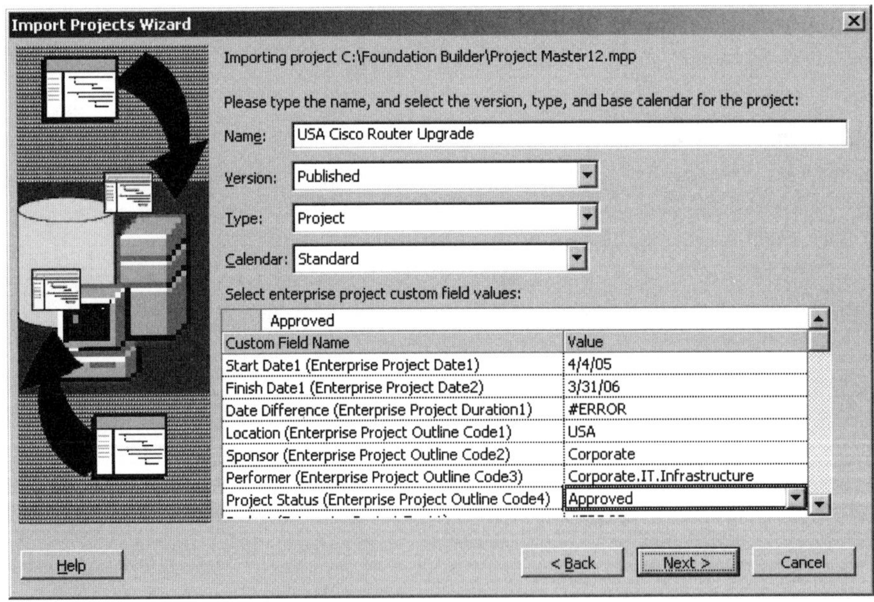

**Figure 2-22: Provide enterprise project information
in the custom enterprise Project fields**

After accepting the project level information, the system displays the Map Project Resources onto Enterprise Resources page, as shown in Figure 2-23. If the system finds local resources in the source plan whose names match enterprise resources exactly, it automatically maps these for you. For resources that the system does not automatically map, you can either keep the resource as a local resource with a local base calendar or manually map the resource to an enterprise resource. Similarly, if you believe the system has mapped a resource in error, you can make a change here. I am mapping a local resource named Adam L. Barr to an enterprise resource named Adam Barr in the example in Figure 2-23. Once you have mapped your project resources, click the *Next* button to continue.

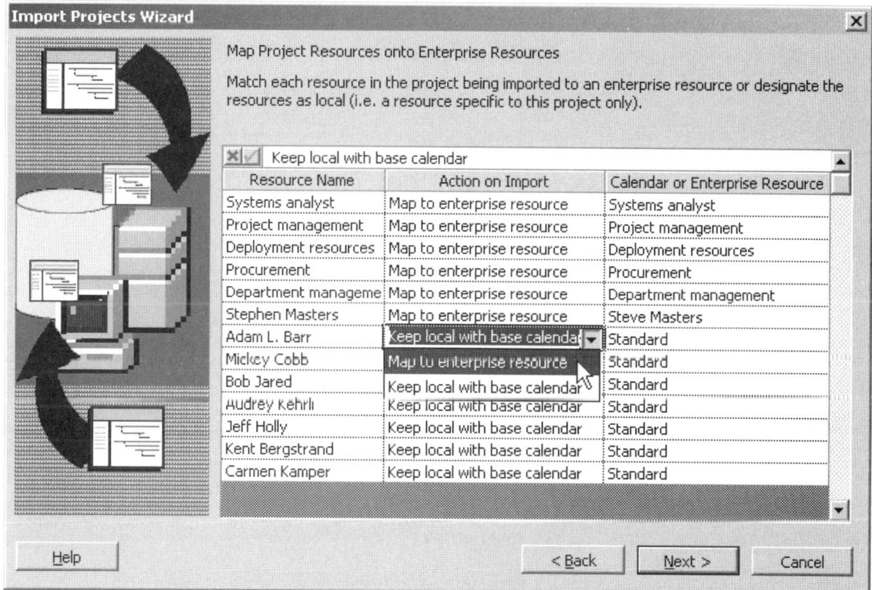

Figure 2-23: Map the resources in the project

If you are a project manager who also serves as a Project Server administrator, you will see a third option that allows you to import a local resource into the Enterprise Resource Pool.

The Map Task Fields page in the Import Projects Wizard allows you to map values contained in local custom Task fields and outline codes in the project to custom enterprise Task fields and outline codes in the Project Server 2003 system, as shown in Figure 2-24. If any of your enterprise Task fields are required fields, they appear here and the system will not let you continue without setting a field mapping to a field that contains a valid value. When mapping outline codes and custom fields, each mapped field must be destined to the same field type. In other words, you must map a local outline code to an Enterprise outline code, text fields to text fields, and so on. Click the *Next* button to continue.

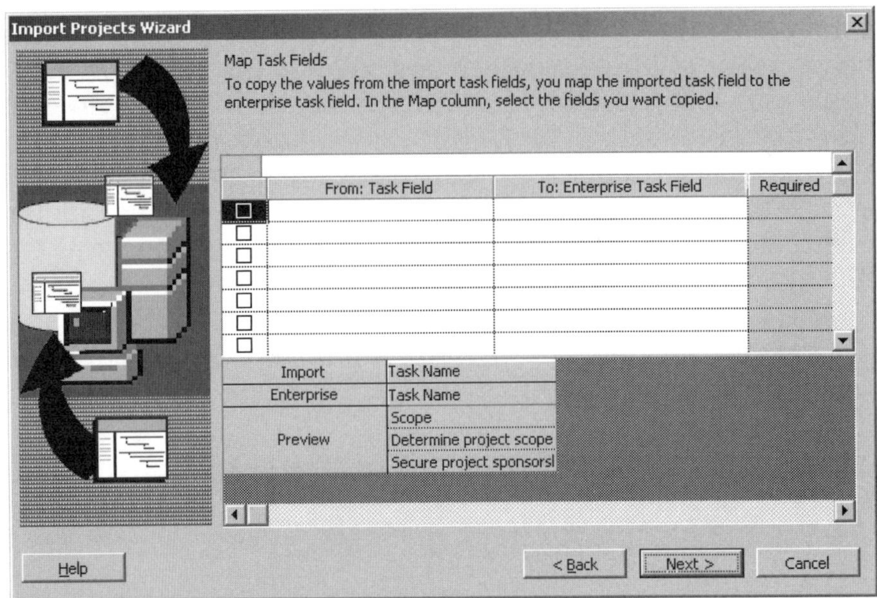

Figure 2-24: Map local Task fields to enterprise Task fields

The system examines the tasks for errors and displays the page shown in Figure 2-25. Any errors found will display with a description of the error in the Error column. In Figure 2-25, notice that I am correcting an Invalid Base Calendar error on three tasks. The system flagged the errors because my enterprise environment does not allow project managers to use local (non-enterprise) base calendars in their projects. Correct all task errors as needed and then click the *Import* button.

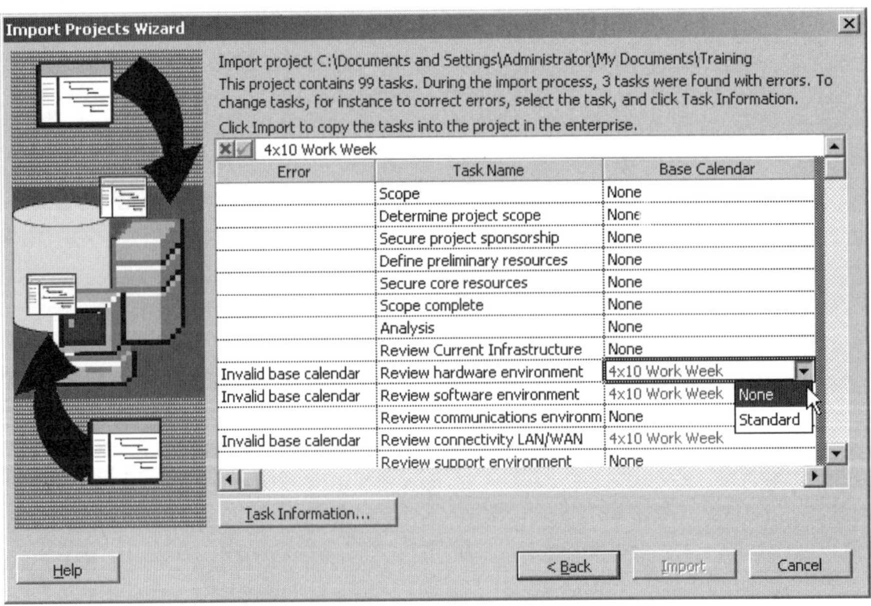

Figure 2-25: Correct task errors before importing the project

To make the process of correcting task errors a little easier, you can also click the *Task Information* button to open the Task Information dialog for the selected task, as shown in Figure 2-26.

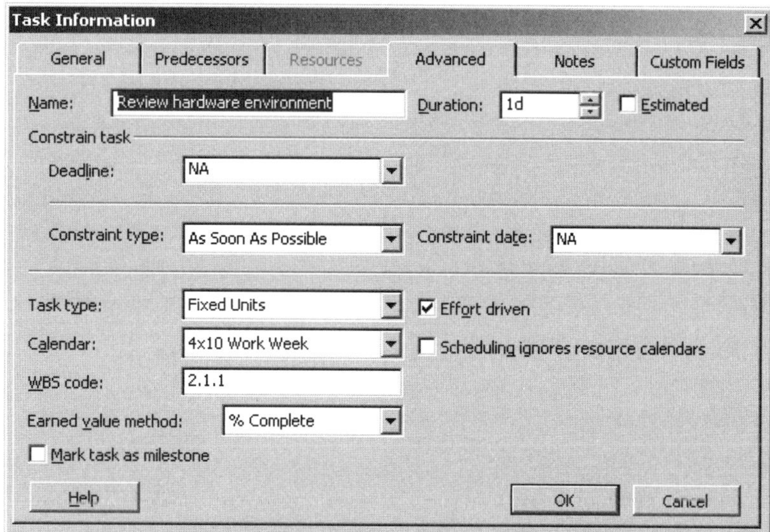

Figure 2-26: Task Information dialog

As the Wizard imports the project, it updates the resources, tasks, and project information as you instructed. When complete, the Import Complete dialog displays as shown in Figure 2-27. The dialog reports the success of the import process and gives you the option to finish or import more projects.

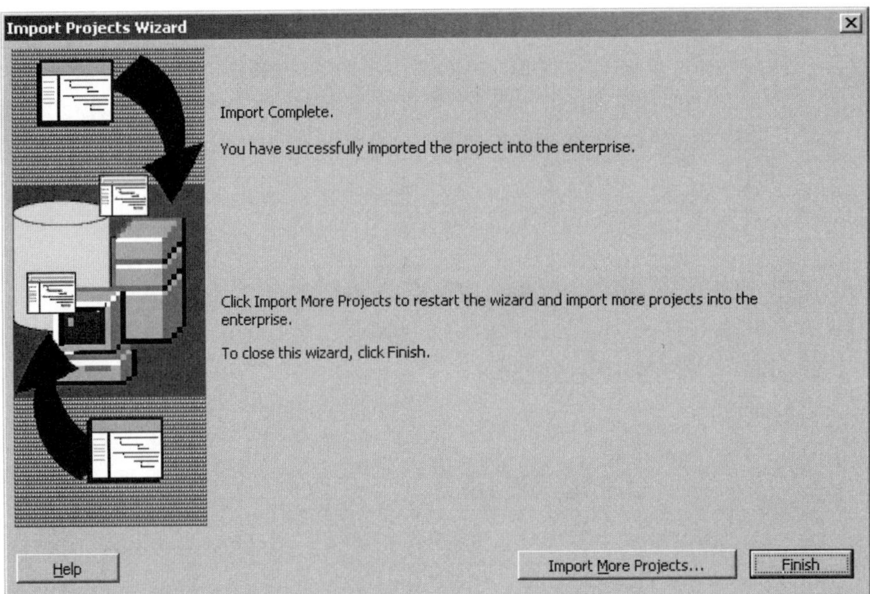

Figure 2-27: Import Complete dialog

Use the Import Projects Wizard to import your non-enterprise projects and templates into your Project Server implementation.

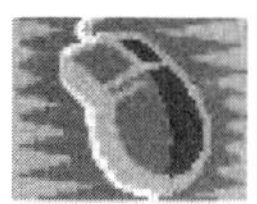

Hands On Exercise

Exercise 2-5

Import a project into the Project Server database using the Import Projects Wizard.

1. Connect to Project Server 2003 if you are not already connected.

2. Click Tools ➢ Enterprise Options ➢ Import Project to Enterprise.

3. Click the *Next* button to continue from the Welcome screen.

4. Navigate to a folder containing .mpp project files, select a project, and then click the *Import* button.

5. Give your project a new name, enter data into the enterprise Project fields at your discretion, then click the *Next* button.

6. Map the local resources to enterprise resources, and map local Task fields to enterprise Task fields, if necessary.

7. Explore the Task Information dialog from the Import Projects Wizard.

8. Review the tasks in the project and make calendar changes as necessary, then click the *Import* button.

9. Click the *Finish* button.

Module 03

Building Project Teams, Assigning Resources and Leveling Assignments

Learning Objectives

After completing this module, you will be able to:

- Use the Build Team dialog to build a project team from the Enterprise Resource Pool

- Indicate whether project team members are Proposed or Committed to a project

- Use local resources as project team members

- Assign resources to tasks using two different methods

- Use the Resource Substitution Wizard

- Level resource overallocations

Building a Project Team

The Build Team dialog in Project Professional 2003 provides you with tools for searching through the enterprise resource pool to find the right resources for your project team. To open the Build Team dialog, click Tools ➢ Build Team from Enterprise. The Build Team dialog displays, as shown in Figure 3-1.

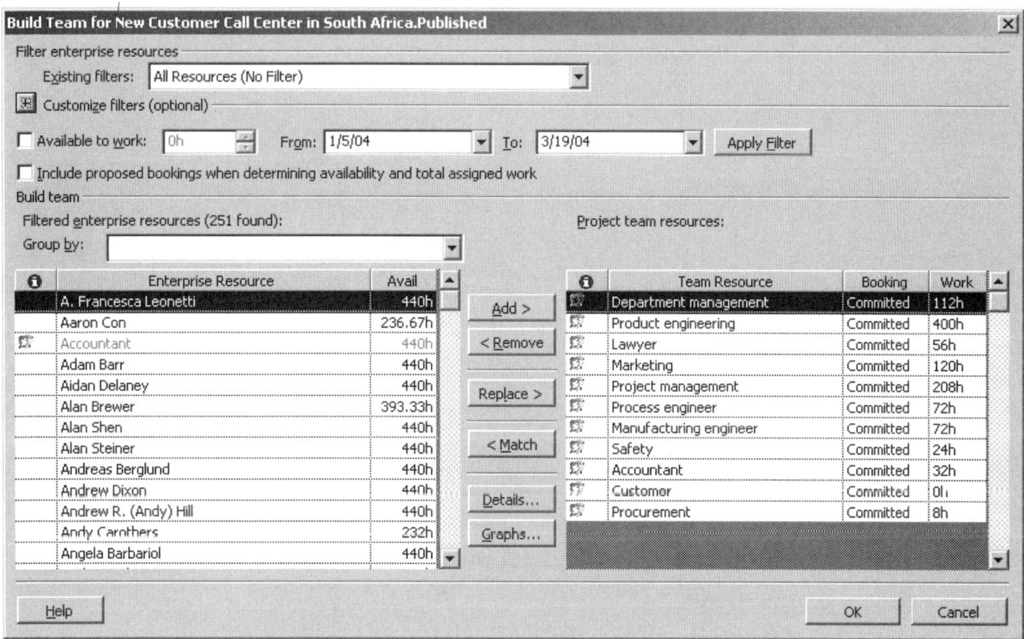

**Figure 3-1: Build Team dialog with
Customize Filters section collapsed**

By default, Project Professional 2003 shows the Customize Filters section collapsed each time you display the dialog. Click the *Expand (+)* button to the left of the Customize Filters section to expand it and show the complete dialog, as displayed in Figure 3-2.

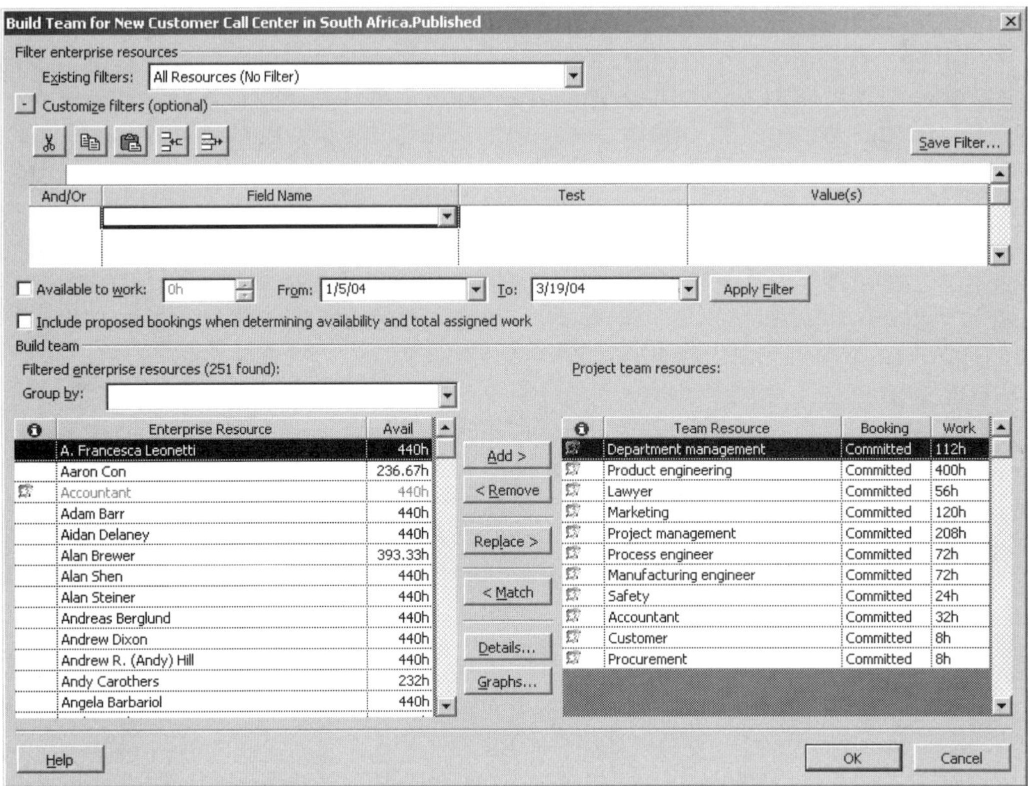

**Figure 3-2: Build Team dialog with
Customize Filters section expanded**

The Build Team dialog searches through your Enterprise Resource Pool, providing you with a quick way to identify resources with the skills, availability, and other criteria needed for the job. The other criteria you can use include anything you have built into resource attribution.

If your Enterprise Resource Pool contains more than 1,000 resources, the system will display a pre-filter dialog to prompt you to filter the enterprise resource list. The system will continue to prompt you to filter the list until the total number of resources displayed is less than 1,000.

The Build Team dialog consists of two sections. The Filter Enterprise Resources section contains filtering tools to restrict the list of enterprise resources to those that meet your filter criteria. The Build Team section consists of two resource lists: the list of resources on the left consists of your current filter list of resources from the Enterprise Resource Pool while the list on the right contains the resources that are members of your project team. Between the two lists are a set of buttons to use for working with the two lists, such as the *Add*, *Remove*, *Replace*, and *Match* buttons.

Using Filters in the Build Team Dialog

The Build Team dialog offers three ways to filter resources:

- Use a pre-existing filter

- Create your own custom filter

- Filter for availability within a date range

To use a pre-existing filter, click the *Existing filters* pick list at the top of the dialog and select a filter. The Existing filters list offers enterprise filters, standard filters, and your personal filters. When you select a filter, the system applies your filter immediately and restricts the enterprise resources list on the left.

Your Project Server administrator can build and save resource filters in the Enterprise Global that are available to all users on the Existing filters list.

To create your own ad hoc custom filter, use the grid in the Customize Filters section. The grid consists of four columns: the And/Or, Field Name, Test, and Value(s) columns. In the Field Name column, you can select any resource field available in the system, including both standard and custom fields. In Figure 3-3, I am selecting the Department (Enterprise Resource Outline Code1) field in the Field Name column.

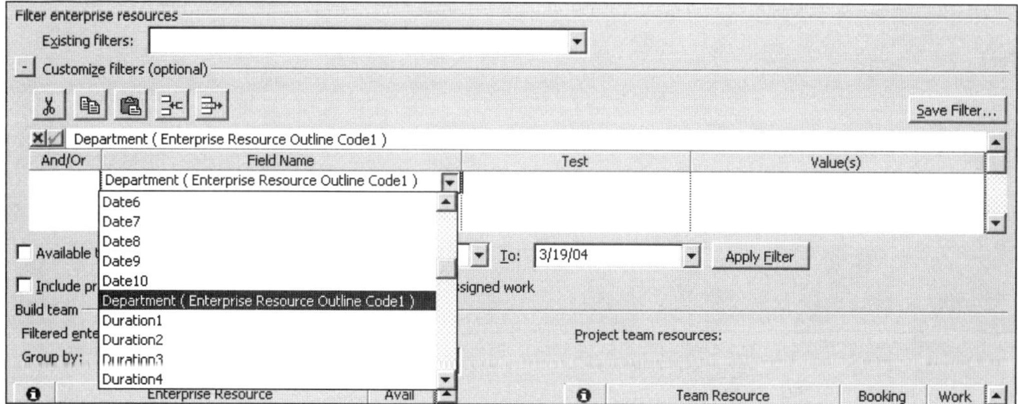

**Figure 3-3: Select any resource field
in the Field Name column**

You must specify the comparison test for your filter criteria in the Test column. The tests available in this column include:

- equals
- does not equal
- is greater than
- is greater than or equal to
- is less than
- is less than or equal to
- is within
- is not within
- contains
- does not contain
- contains exactly

After you specify the Field Name and Test values, you must select or enter a comparison value in the Value(s) column. Unlike its 2002 predecessor, Project Server 2003 displays the list of values found in the resource field selected in the Field Name column. Project Server 2002 expected you to know the possible field values. For example, in Figure 3-4, I am selecting the Accounting value from the list of values found in the Department field.

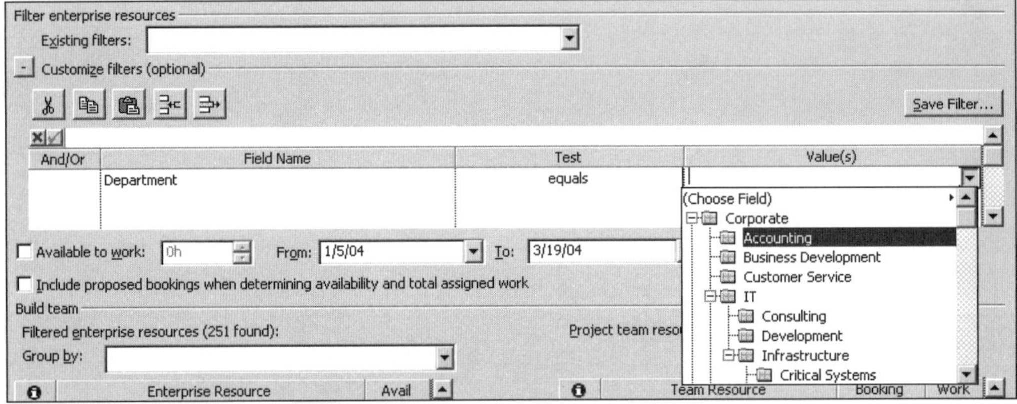

**Figure 3-4: Select an entry
in the Value(s) column**

As you select an item from the list of values in the Value(s) column, you can select an existing field by floating your mouse pointer over the *Choose Field* option at the top of the pick list. When you do so, a list of available fields will display in place of the list of field values.

The Customize filters grid allows you to specify multiple criteria in your filter by using the And/Or column to add conditions to your custom filter. Figure 3-5, shows a custom filter with conditions placed on both the Department and Language fields to search for members of the Accounting department who are also fluent in French.

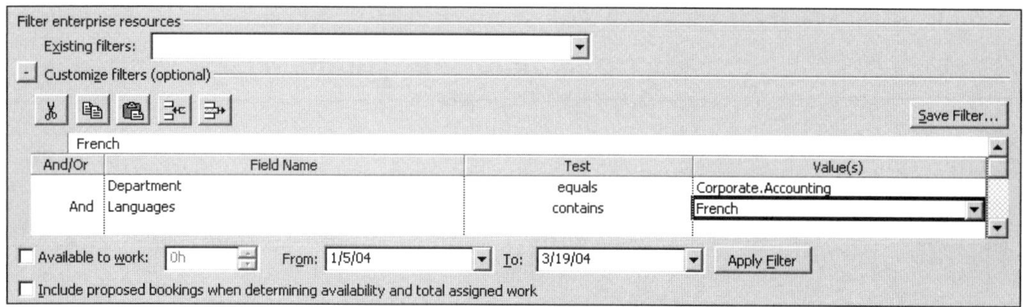

Figure 3-5: Custom filter

When you finish building your custom filter, you must click the *Apply Filter* button to restrict the enterprise resources list with your filter. Figure 3-6 shows the filtered list of enterprise resources that match my filter criteria. Notice that only two members of the Accounting department are also fluent in French.

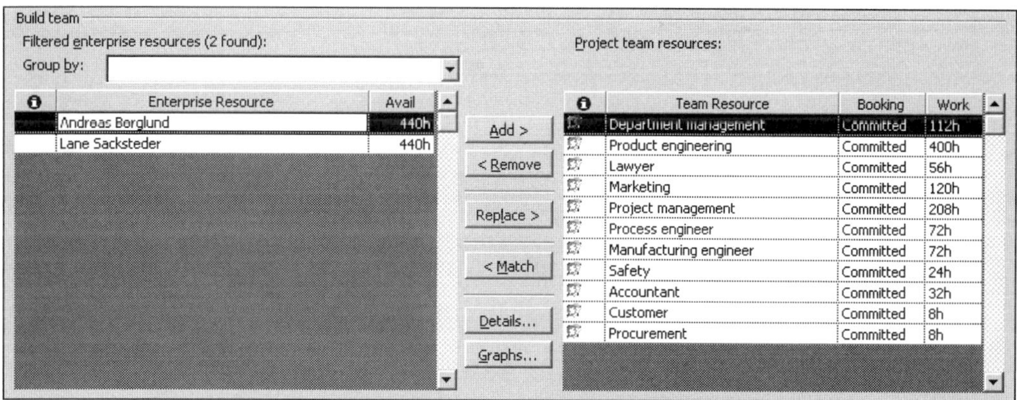

**Figure 3-6: Filtered enterprise resources list
Accountants who are fluent in French**

After you have created and tested your custom filter, you can save it for future use by clicking the *Save Filter* button. The system displays the Save Filter dialog as shown in Figure 3-7. Give your custom filter an original name and click the *OK* button to save it.

**Figure 3-7: Give your Filter
a name and save it**

 MSProjectExperts recommends that you apply a naming convention for your personal custom filters to distinguish them from both the standard filters and the enterprise custom filters. In Figure 3-7, the user has added the initials "SRM" at the beginning of the filter name to indicate that it is a personal custom filter.

 **Warning:** Clicking the *Save Filter* button in the Build Team dialog saves the filter in the active project only. To save your custom filter for use in all of your present and future projects, use the Organizer to copy your filter to your Global.mpt file.

In addition to using Existing filters and creating custom filters, you can also restrict the enterprise resources list by testing for availability during a date range. To use availability filtering, complete the following steps:

1. Select the *Available to work* option to activate availability filtering.

2. Set the availability hours in the *Available to work* field.

3. Specify a date range by setting dates in the *From* and *To* fields.

4. Click the *Apply Filter* button.

In Figure 3-8, I applied an Existing filter to locate members of the Accounting department who speak French, and then applied an Availability filter to find those who have 32 hours of availability from 1/5/04 to 4/30/04.

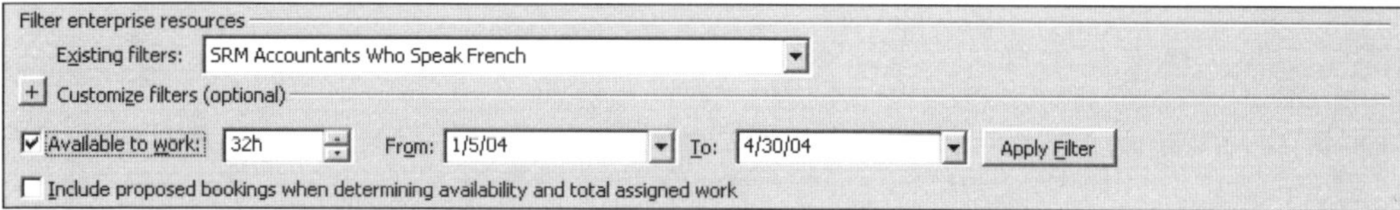

**Figure 3-8: Existing filter and
Availability filter applied**

The system sets the default values in the *From* and *To* fields
to the current Start and Finish dates for the project.

Finally, you have a fourth filtering option in the Build Team dialog that allows
you to determine whether the system considers Proposed bookings in the
filtering process. A Proposed booking indicates a tentative resource
commitment to a project. To include Proposed bookings, select the *Include
proposed bookings when determining availability and total assigned work*
option. To understand how this option works, consider the following example:

> Resource A is booked for 40 hours of work as a Proposed resource in
> another manager's project from October 11-15, 2004. Resource A
> matches the filter criteria for the type of resource that you need in
> your project during the same period. When you build a custom filter
> and deselect this option, the system will display Resource A as an
> available resource. If you select the option, the dialog will not display
> Resource A as an available resource. In Figure 3-9 shown previously,
> notice that I have selected this option in addition to my Existing and
> Availability filters.

Using Grouping

The *Group by* pick list, located just above the Filtered enterprise resources
list, gives you yet another way of refining your resource selections by
applying grouping to the Filtered enterprise resources list. To group by a
value, you can select any resource field available in the system, including
both standard and custom fields. When you select a Group by field, the
system applies grouping immediately to the resource list, with each group
expanded to show all members of the group. As you review your groups of
resources, you can collapse or expand each group as you choose. In Figure
3-9, I selected Skills (Enterprise Resource Outline Code20) as the Group by
field and then collapsed each of the Executive groups.

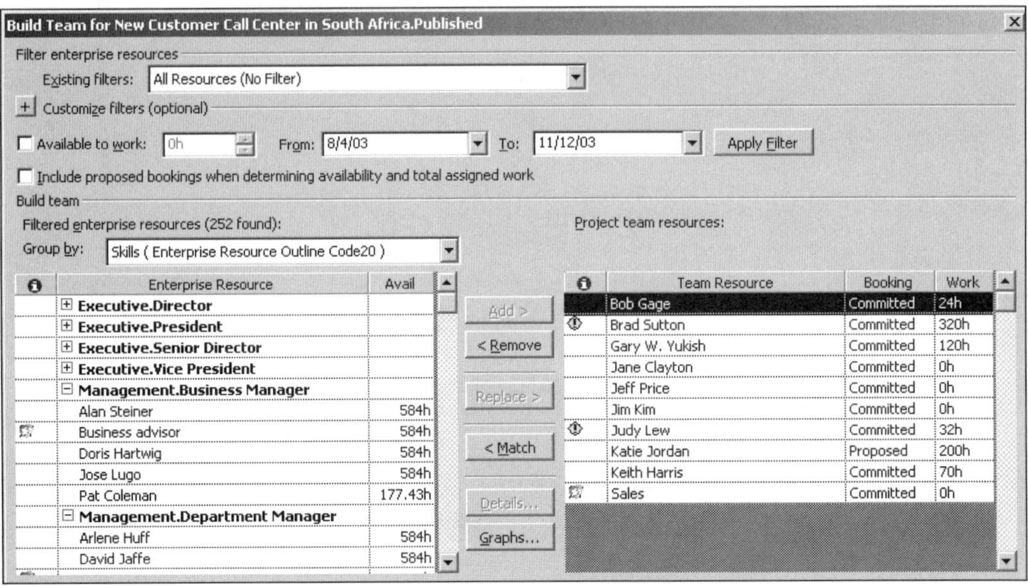

Figure 3-9: Grouping applied to the filtered enterprise resources list

To remove grouping from the Filtered enterprise resources list, select the *Group by* pick list and select the blank field at the top of the pick list.

Viewing Resource Information

Click the *Details* button to display the Resource Information dialog for the selected resource. Figure 3-10 shows the Resource Information dialog for Alan Brewer with the *Custom Fields* tab selected.

You cannot change any of the information found in the Resource Information dialog unless you have Administrator permissions in the enterprise environment. You must also check out the resource before you can change its standard and custom attributes.

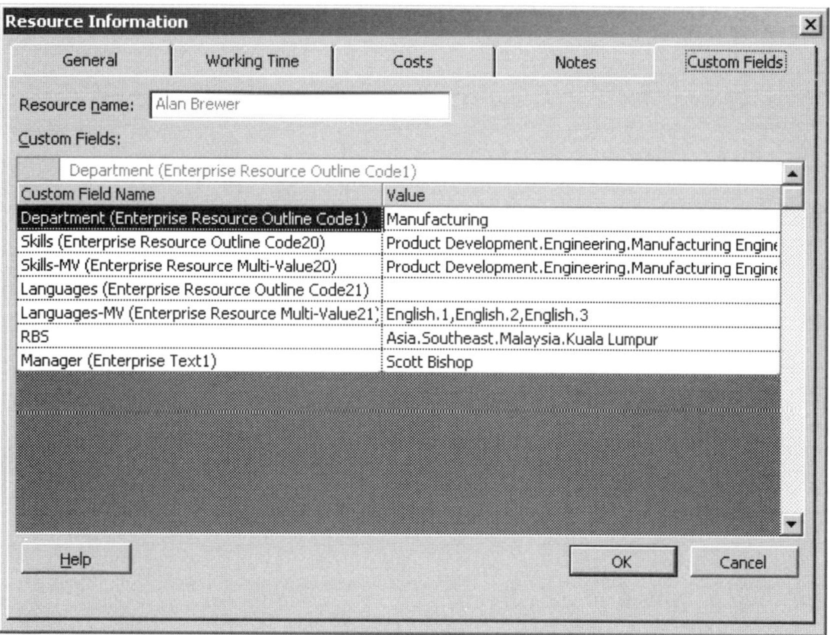

Figure 3-10: Resource Information dialog

The Build Team dialog also gives you direct access to resource availability information using resource graphs. Select one or more resources and click the *Graphs* button to open the Graphs dialog shown in Figure 3-11.

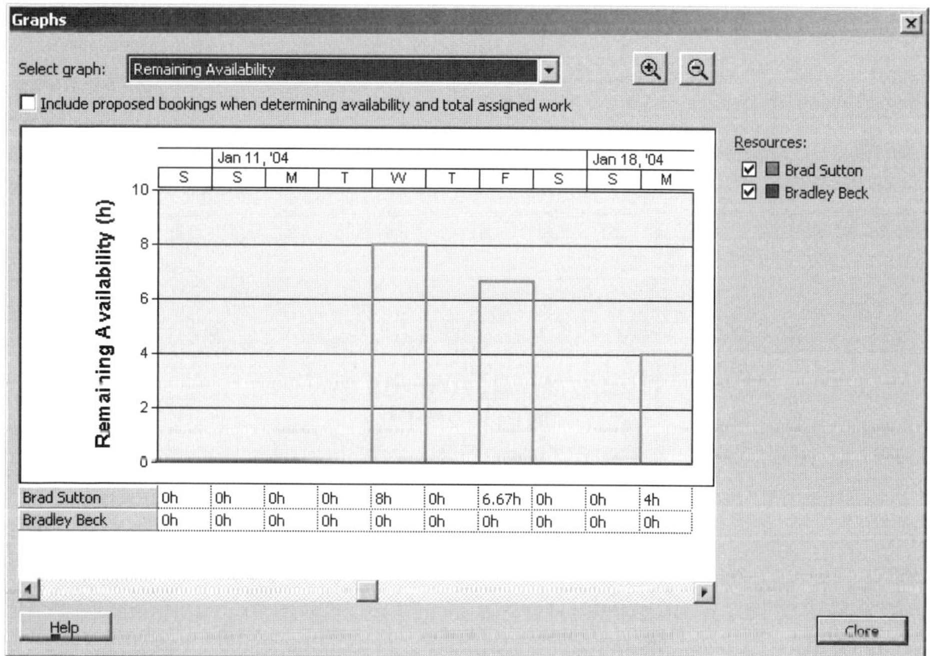

Figure 3-11: Graphs dialog
Remaining Availability graph

Click the *Select graph* pick list at the top of the dialog and select the type of graph you want to display. Your choices include:

- Remaining Availability
- Work
- Assignment Work

The Remaining Availability graph displays a line chart depicting the Remaining Availability for each selected resource across all projects in the portfolio, as shown previously in Figure3-11. Below the graph, the system displays a timescaled data grid showing the Remaining Availability values for each resource.

The Work graph displays a line chart depicting the total amount of assigned Work for each selected resource across all projects in the portfolio, as shown in Figure 3-12. Below the graph is a timescaled data grid showing the Work values for each resource and the totals for all resources.

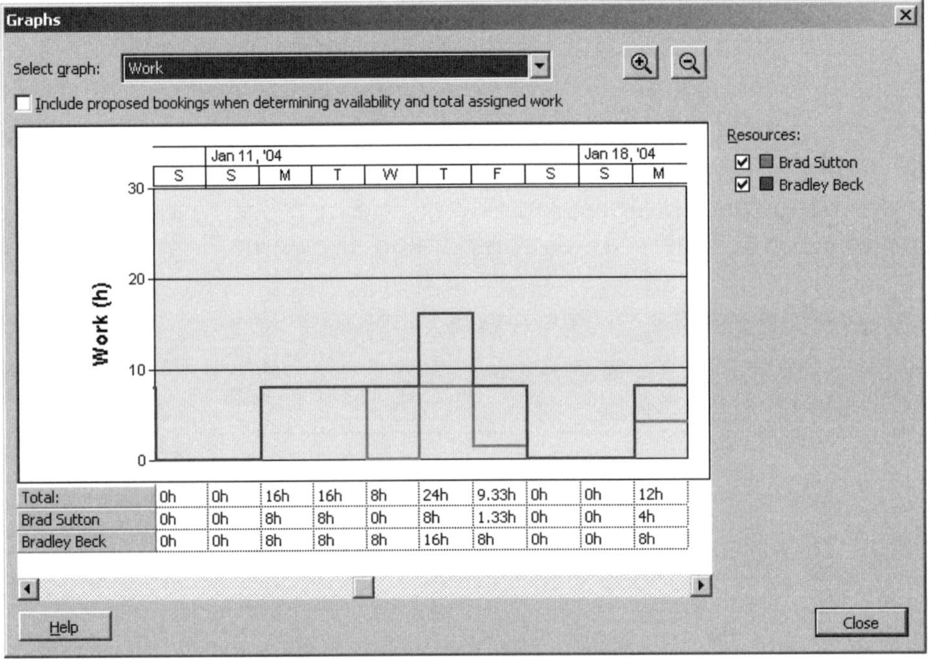

**Figure 3-12: Graphs dialog
Work graph**

The Assignment Work graph displays a combined stacked bar chart and line chart for each selected resource, as shown in Figure 3-13. The stacked bar chart contains one bar segment for the total Work for all selected resources in the Current Project, along with another bar segment for the total Work for all selected resources in all Other Projects. The line chart shows the total Availability for all selected resources. Below the chart appears a time-scaled data grid showing each of the individual values for Current Project, Other Projects, and Availability totaled across all selected resources.

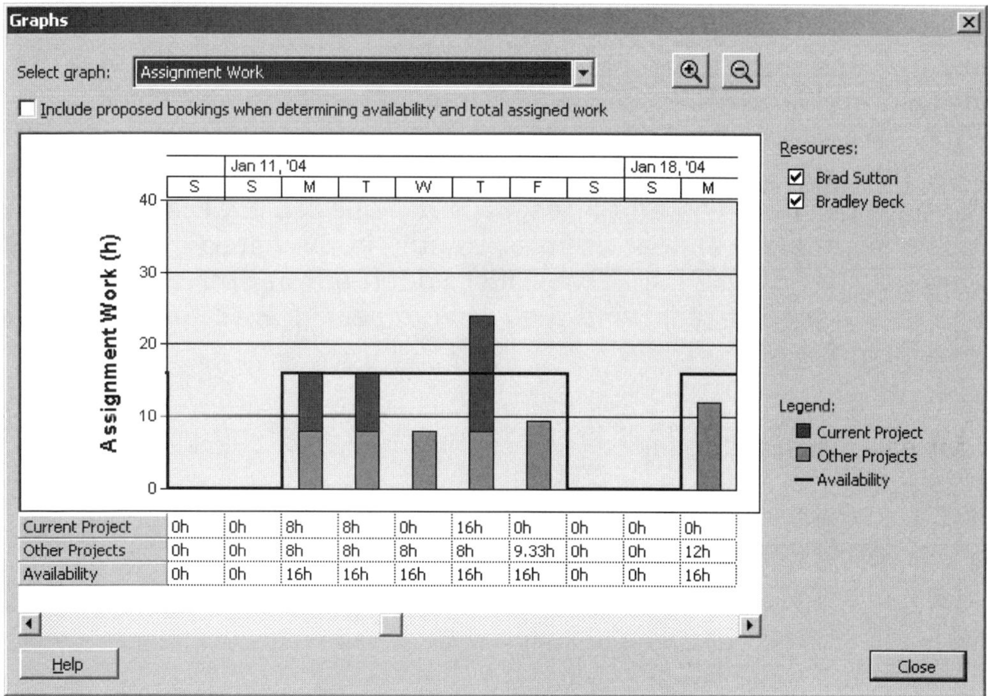

Current Project	0h	0h	8h	8h	0h	16h	0h	0h	0h	0h
Other Projects	0h	0h	8h	8h	8h	8h	9.33h	0h	0h	12h
Availability	0h	0h	16h	16h	16h	16h	16h	0h	0h	16h

Figure 3-13: Graphs dialog
Assignment Work graph

 Notice in Figure 3-13 that the selected resources are overallocated on Thursday, January 15, because assignments total 24 work hours when the resources are only available 16 total 16 hours. As the project manager, I may be concerned about this overallocation.

When you select more than one resource, the Graphs dialog, gives you the option to show or hide the graphs for each resource by selecting or deselecting the checkboxes next to each resource name in the Resources list. To determine whether the system includes proposed bookings in each of the three types of graphs, select or deselect the *Include proposed bookings when determining availability and total assigned work* option. Use the Zoom In (**+**) and Zoom Out (**−**) to change the timescale displayed in each graph.

Adding Resources to Your Team

To add resources to your project ream, select one or more resources from the Filtered enterprise resources list on the left, and then click the *Add* button. To remove resources from your project team, select one or more resources from the Project team resources list on the right, then click the *Remove* button. When you add a resource to your project team, that particular resource will appear as "grayed out" in the Filtered enterprise resources list. In Figure 3-14, I have just added Aaron Con and Angela Barbariol to the project team and they now appear grayed out on the list of Filtered enterprise resources.

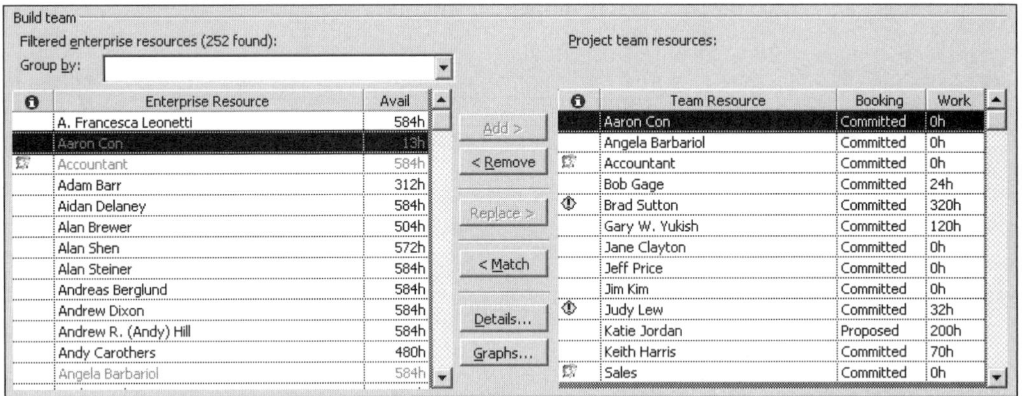

Figure 3-14: Resources appear grayed out on the list of Filtered enterprise resources when they are members of the project team

Notice in Figure 3-14 that the list of Project team resources includes both human resources and a number of Generic resources. The system displays Generic resources with a double-headed icon in the Indicators column of the grid. Notice also that the system displays an overallocation indicator for two resources, Brad Sutton and Judy Lew, who are overallocated either on this project or on one or more projects in the portfolio.

When applicable, the system displays additional indicators in the Build Team dialog, such as overallocation indicators for one or more resources. Float the mouse pointer over the indicator to display more information about the indicator.

To replace resources on the Project team resources list with one from the Filtered enterprise resources list, select a resource in each list, and then click the *Replace* button. The system replaces the former resource with the new resource on every task assignment in the entire project plan. The system also removes the former resource from the list of Project team resources.

The replace feature in the Build Team dialog is available only when the resource you want to replace has zero actual hours posted to the project. Once a resource has reported hours on a project, you must use the Assign Resources dialog to replace that resource.

Use the *Match* button to match the attributes of a selected Project team resource with those found in the Filtered enterprise resources list. How does this button actually work? When you click the *Match* button, the system applies a customized "contains" filter on the resources in the Filtered enterprise resources list using the attributes of the selected Project team resource that your Project Server administrator has designated for skill matching.

For example, in Figure 3-15, I selected the Manufacturing Engineer generic resource from the list of Project team resources and clicked the *Match* button, producing the list of Filtered enterprise resources shown in the figure. Notice in the Customize Filters section that the system built a custom "contains" filter to match the value found in the Skills-MV field.

In most cases, you will probably use the *Match* button to match specific skills between Generic resources and human resources. Since the system shows all matches for a selected resource, including both Generic and human resources, you can use the matching feature to make human-to-human matches as well.

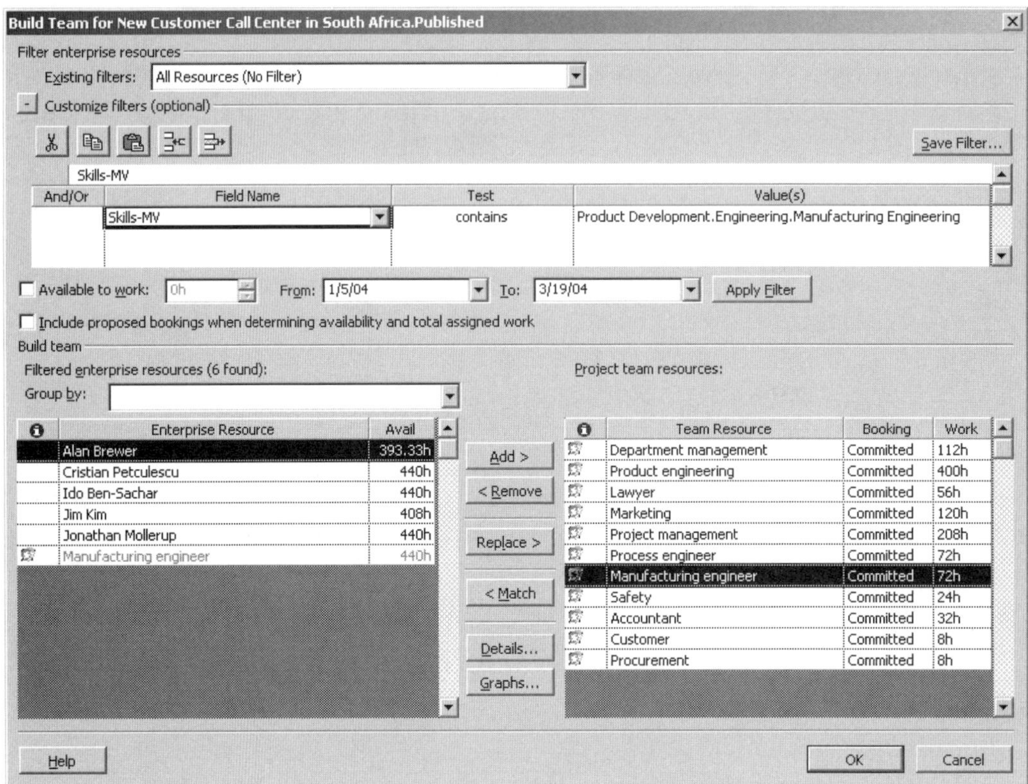

**Figure 3-15: Use the Match button
to match resource attributes**

Using Proposed vs. Committed Booking

A new feature in Project Server 2003, the Booking column in the Project team resources list on the right side of the Build Team dialog, allows you to set a booking type for each team member you add to your team. You can book team members as either Proposed or Committed. A Proposed booking indicates a tentative commitment for the resource, while a Committed booking indicates a firm commitment.

The default Booking type for each project team member is Committed. To change the Booking type for any resource, click the pick list in the Booking column for the selected resource and select the desired booking type. In Figure 3-16, I am changing the booking type for Jeff Price from committed to proposed.

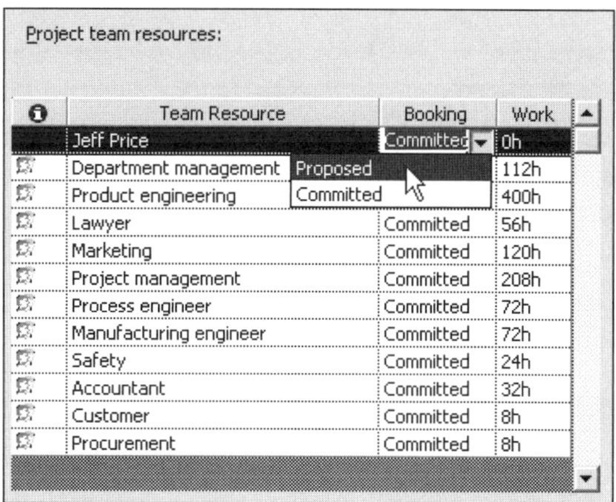

**Figure 3-16: Change Booking type
to Proposed for a resource**

When you book a team member as a proposed resource on a project, the system will handle all task assignments for the proposed resource as proposed assignments. The consequences within Project Server 2003 are as follows:

- Published task assignments do not display for any proposed resources on their View My Tasks page.

- The projects in which a resource is booked as proposed do not display in the View Resource Availability page, nor do the resource's work hours on proposed task assignments.

- Proposed bookings do not affect resource availability. Consequently, these do not appear in the View Resource Availability page.

- The Booking type is a dimension of the OLAP Cube and is available for use in Portfolio Analyzer views.

Even though the system does not display task assignments for a Proposed resource on many pages of Project Web Access, the system does display these task assignments in the View Resource Assignments page of the Resource Center.

 When you receive formal approval to begin the execution of your project, remember to change Proposed bookings to Committed bookings, or substitute Committed resources for Proposed resources. If you forget to do so, Proposed resources in your project will not be able to see their task assignments in the View My Tasks page!

Using Local Resources in an Enterprise Project

A local resource is any project resource not listed in the Enterprise Resource Pool. Use local resources in a project to represent temporary resources, such as consultants or contractors, who may or may not use the Project Web Access timesheet reporting system. Depending on the configuration of your Project Server, the system may allow you to create accounts for your local resources, or the system may prevent you from doing so.

To add a local resource to an enterprise project, complete these steps:

1. Click View ➢ Resource Sheet.

2. Type the name of the local resource.

3. Set the default and custom field information for the local resource, as needed.

4. Double-click the name of a local resource.

5. Click the *Workgroup* pick list and set the value to None, as shown in Figure 3-17.

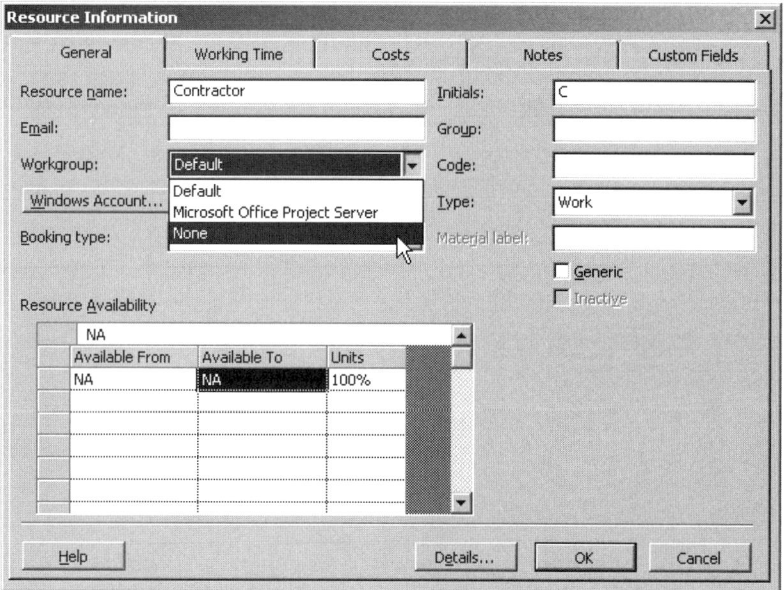

**Figure 3-17: Set the Workgroup value
in the Resource Information dialog**

 Setting the *Workgroup* value to None tells Project Professional 2003 not to try to create a Project Server account for the local resource.

6. Click the *OK* button.

7. Save the project.

The system displays each local resource with a unique indicator in the Indicators column, as shown in Figure 3-18.

	ⓘ	Resource Name	Type	Material Label	Initials	Group	Max. Units	Std. Rate	Ovt. Rate
1		Bob Gage	Work		B		100%	$70.00/h	$105.00/h
2		Brad Sutton	Work		B		100%	$70.00/h	$105.00/h
3		Dale Howard	Work		D		100%	$80.00/h	$120.00/h
4		Gary W Yukish	Work		G		100%	$70.00/h	$105.00/h
5		Judy Lew	Work		J		100%	$70.00/h	$105.00/h
6		Katie Jordan	Work		K		100%	$70.00/h	$105.00/h
7		Keith Harris	Work		K		100%	$70.00/h	$105.00/h
8		Kim Ralls	Work		K		100%	$70.00/h	$105.00/h
9		Reed Koch	Work		R		100%	$70.00/h	$105.00/h
10		Contractor	Work		C		100%	$50.00/h	$75.00/h

Figure 3-18: Local resource indicator

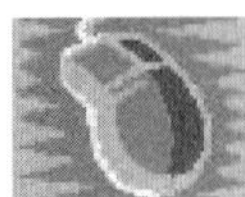 **Hands On Exercise**

Exercise 3-1

Filter and group resources in the Build Team from Enterprise tool.

1. Connect to Project Server 2003 if you are not already connected.

2. From Project Professional 2003, open the project you created in Module 2.

3. Click Tools ➤ Build Team from Enterprise.

4. Expand the Customize Filters section and select an Enterprise Outline code from your business (use a skill code, location code, etc.).

5. Select a Test, then select or type a Value.

6. Click the *Apply Filter* button and note the display changes.

7. Set an *Available to work* filter.

8. Explore the *Group by* options.

Exercise 3-2

View resource information in the Build Team from Enterprise tool.

1. Select a resource in the grid on the left and click the *Details* button to open the Resource Information Dialog.

2. Explore the Resource Information dialog.

3. Click the *OK* button when done.

Exercise 3-3

View resource graphs in the Build Team from Enterprise tool.

1. Select a resource in the grid on the left and click the *Graphs* button.

2. Explore the display for one resource and click the *Close* button when finished.

3. Select multiple resources in the grid, then click the *Graphs* button and explore how the system handles multiple resources in the display.

4. Select and deselect the checkboxes for each resource in the dialog to show and hide the resource graph lines.

Exercise 3-4

Build a project team in the Build Team from Enterprise tool.

1. Use the Build Team dialog to build a team for your project.

2. Add at least one Generic resource to the project team.

Exercise 3-5

Use the Build Team from Enterprise tool to match and replace Generic resources with human resources.

1. Select a Generic resource in the right-hand grid and then click the *Match* button.

2. Select a human resource in the left-hand grid and then click the *Replace* button.

3. Click the *OK* button and review the effect in the plan.

Exercise 3-6

Add a local resource named Outside Contractor to your project and set the set the local resource's Workgroup value to None.

Assigning Resources

After you build your team, you must assign your team members to specific tasks in your project plan. The system provides you with two methods for assigning resources to tasks. Each of these methods has both advantages and disadvantages. These two methods are:

- Assign Resources dialog
- Task Entry view

Assign Resources Dialog

To open the Assign Resources dialog, select one or more tasks then click the *Assign Resources* button on the Standard toolbar shown in Figure 3-19.

**Figure 3-19: Assign
Resources button**

You can also activate the Assign Resources dialog by clicking Tools ➢ Assign Resources. Either choice displays the Assign Resources dialog shown in Figure 3-20.

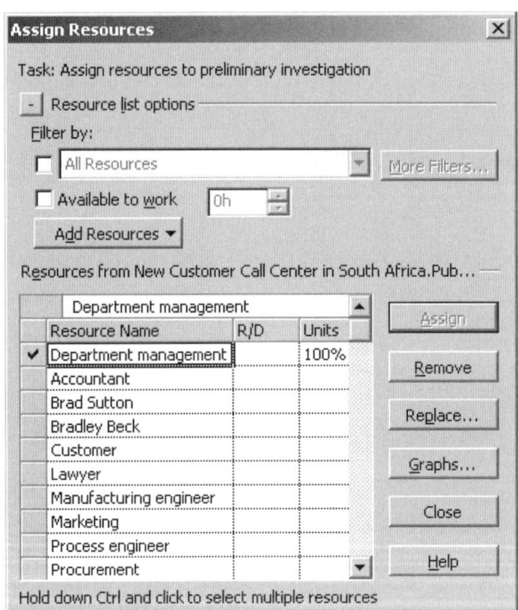

**Figure 3-20: Assign
Resources dialog**

The advantage of the Assign Resources dialog is that it allows you to control one very important value in the assignment process, which is the Request/Demand (R/D) field. The Resource Substitution Wizard uses the Request/Demand value to determine which resource assignments are eligible for substitution process, and does not alter resource assignments attributed as Demand. I will cover the Resource Substitution Wizard in the next section.

You can select as many tasks as you want when using the Assign Resources dialog. You can also change the selected tasks without closing the dialog by simply clicking outside the dialog.

To assign a resource from the Assign Resources dialog, select one or more tasks, select the desired resource, set the Units value, and then click the *Assign* button.

You must select a resource and click the *Assign* button before you can set a Request/Demand value. You cannot select an R/D value for multiple tasks simultaneously, as this value is set for each task individually.

To replace an assigned resource with another resource, select the assigned resource, then click the *Replace* button. The system displays the Replace Resource dialog, as shown in Figure 3-21. Select the new resource and then click the *OK* button.

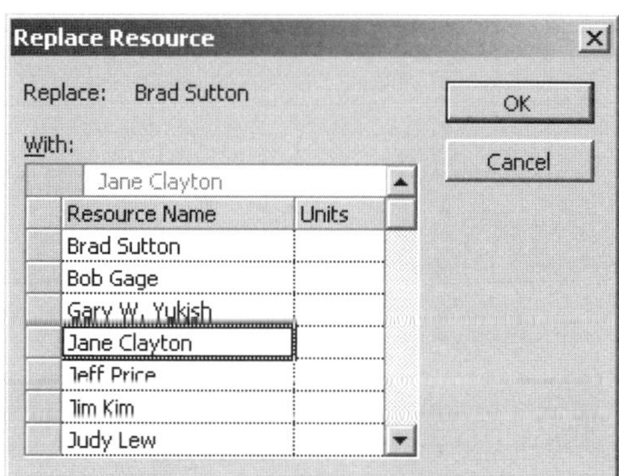

Figure 3-21: Replace Resource dialog

To remove a resource from a task assignment, select the resource and then click the *Remove* button.

Warning: Be careful when you remove a resource from an Effort Driven task. If you do so, the work assigned to the removed resource will be added to the work assigned to the remaining resources, and will increase the Duration of the task proportionately.

To graph the assignment work and availability for resources, select one or more resource and then click the *Graphs* button. The system displays the Graphs dialog, shown previously in Figure 3-14, 3-15, and 3-16.

Task Entry View

Apply the Task Entry view by clicking Window ➤ Split. The Task Entry view is a combination view consisting of the Gantt Chart in the top pane and the Task Form in the bottom pane, as shown in Figure 3-22.

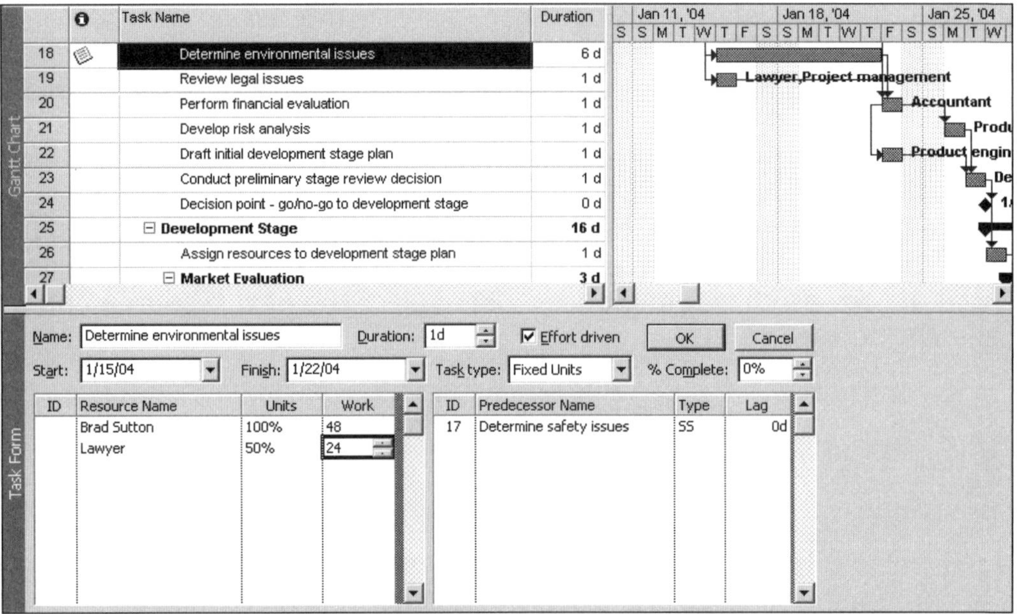

Figure 3-22: Task Entry view

The advantage of the Task Entry view is that it allows you to take complete control over both the task values and the assignment values for each resource. You can easily specify multiple resources along with setting Units, Work, or Duration values. You can also specify whether the resource assignments on the selected task are Effort Driven, and you can even set the Task Type in this view. To assign one or more resources to a task, select the task in the Gantt Chart pane, set the desired values in the Task Form pane, and then click the *OK* button.

To use the Task Entry view for making initial task assignments, use the following techniques:

1. In the upper pane, select the task for which you want to make task assignments.

2. In the lower pane, select one or more resources.

3. In the lower pane, set a Units and/or Work value for each resource.

4. Click the *OK* button.

Be sure to select only one task in the upper pane as the Task Entry view allows you to make assignments for only one task at a time.

To change the Task Type for any task, complete the following steps:

1. In the upper pane, select the task whose Task Type you wish to change.

2. In the lower pane, click the *Task Type* pick list and select Fixed Units, Fixed Work, or Fixed Duration.

3. Click the *OK* button.

The Task Type value you select determines whether the Units, Work, or Duration value is fixed or "locked" in the assignment process.

To set whether a task is effort driven or non-effort driven, select or deselect the *Effort driven* option. You normally use effort driven scheduling to shorten the Duration of a task by adding additional resources to the task. Effort driven scheduling keeps the total Remaining Work constant on the task while you add or remove resources.

To assign additional resources to a task using effort driven scheduling, select one or more additional resources, set a Units value for each resource, and then click the *OK* button. Do not specify a Work value for each additional resource, as the system will calculate the Work value.

MSProjectExperts recommends that your organization establish a standard methodology for assigning resources to tasks in all of your organization's projects. Consistent use of a resource assignment methodology by all project managers will provide consistent resource usage information in the Project Server database.

 **Hands On Exercise**

Exercise 3-7

Assign resources to a task using the Assign Resources tool.

1. Using the same project plan from the previous exercise, click the *Assign Resources* button on the Standard toolbar.

2. Select a task in the Gantt chart and notice that the resource selection changes in the Assign Resources dialog.

3. Click the *Replace* button, select an actual resource in the Replace Resource dialog, and then click the *OK* button.

4. Set the *R/D* value to Demand.

5. Adjust the Units value and note the changes in the plan.

6. Click the *Graphs* button and explore the display for one resource.

7. Explore filtering in the dialog.

Exercise 3-8

Assign resources to a task using the Task Entry view.

1. Select a task and then click Window ➤ Split to apply the Task Entry view.

2. Select a resource, and set the *Units* value to 50% and the *Work* value to 40 hours.

3. Click the *OK* button and note how the Duration value is calculated for the task.

4. Confirm that the *Effort Driven* option is selected for this task.

5. Add a second resource to the task at 50% Units but do not set a Work value for the resource.

6. Click the *OK* button and note how the Duration value is shortened significantly.

7. Change the Task Type for the task and click the *OK* button.

8. Click Window ➤ Remove Split to close the lower pane and return to the Gantt Chart view.

Using the Resource Substitution Wizard

The Resource Substitution Wizard is an automation tool that can substitute resources in one project plan or across many plans. The Wizard makes resource substitutions based on skill code, availability, and other user-defined criteria. Because you can apply the Wizard's output directly to plans or save it as a file, it is equally powerful as a modeling tool and as a staffing tool.

The algorithm used by the Wizard will substitute resources based on the following criteria:

- **Skill Set** – The Wizard's primary purpose is to substitute human resources for Generic resources based on a skill set. In order to work correctly, there must be at least one Enterprise Resource Outline Code defined with the *Use this code for matching generic resources* option selected. In addition, each of your resources must have a value set for this field.

- **Availability** – The Wizard substitutes resources based on availability. To get the best results from the Wizard, you may want to try leveling the plan first before running the Wizard.

- **Request/Demand** – The Wizard substitutes resources based on the R/D value specified for each resource assignment. The Wizard will substitute resources on assignments that are marked as Request, based on the most available matching resource. The Wizard respects all resource assignments marked as Demand and will not substitute resources on these assignments.

- **Priority** – The Wizard weights assignments by the Priority number of each project identified by the user at Wizard run time. The Wizard gives Projects with a higher Priority number first consideration when matching resources.

- **Pool Selection** – The Wizard confines its resource selection to the restriction you set at run time. You may select specific resources, the entire pool, or only resources defined in the selected projects.

- **RBS level** – The Wizard applies the RBS condition you specify at run time to the resource selection, if applicable. This feature relies on the value assigned to each resource in the RBS field (Enterprise Resource Outline Code30).

- **Resource Freeze Horizon** – The Wizard will not make resource substitutions on assignments that occur earlier than a specified Resource Freeze Horizon date.

Running the Wizard

Open the project or projects in which you want to run the Resource Substitution Wizard and then click Tools ➢ Substitute Resources.

If you have the Resource Management toolbar displayed, you can click the *Resource Substitution Wizard* button on the toolbar.

The system displays the Resource Substitution Wizard welcome screen shown in Figure 3-23.

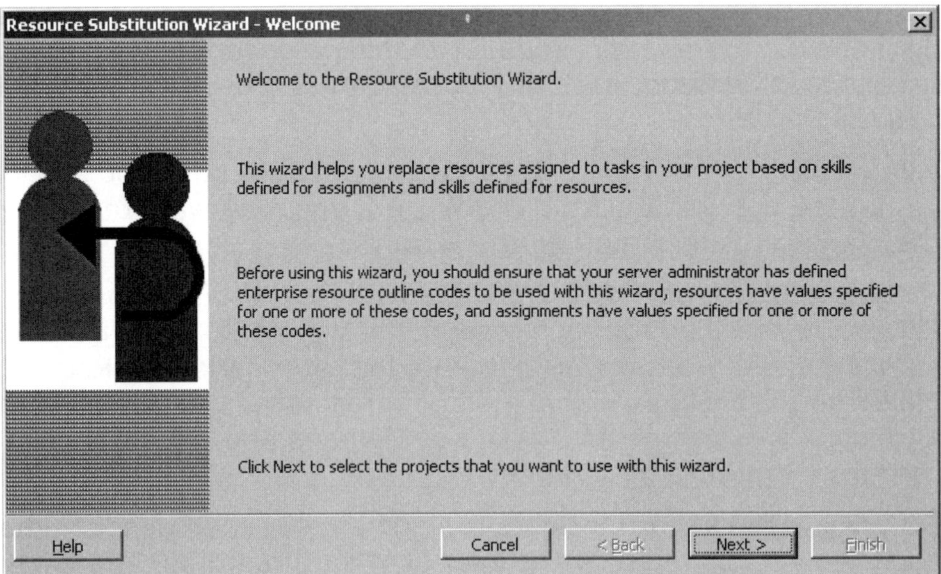

**Figure 3-23: Resource Substitution Wizard
Welcome page**

Click the *Next* button to continue. The system displays Step 1 of the Wizard, the Choose Projects page, as shown in Figure 3-24.

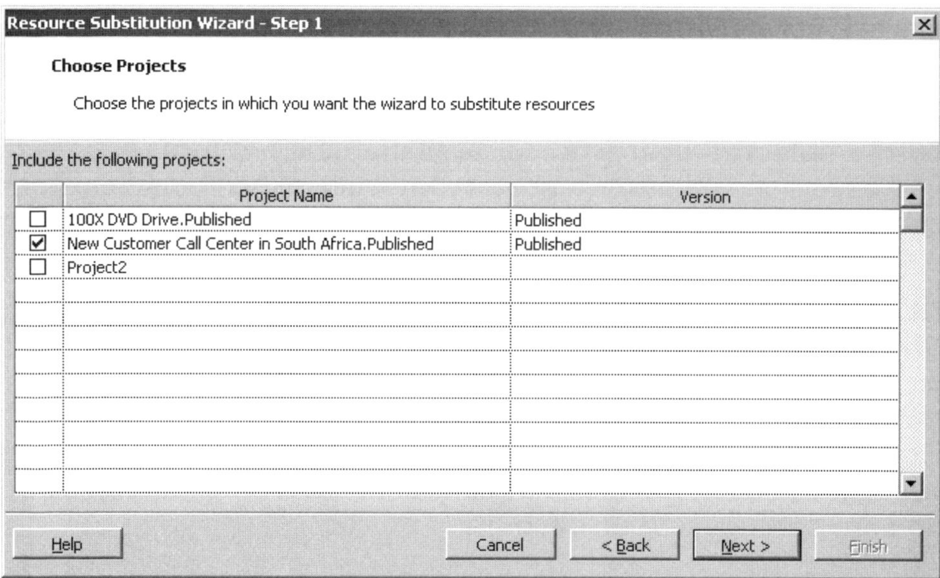

**Figure 3-24: Resource Substitution Wizard
Choose Projects page**

When you run the Resource Substitution Wizard, the system assumes that you want to make resource substitutions on all open projects, including any blank projects you may have open. Deselect any projects in which you do not want resource substitutions performed and then click the *Next* button. The system displays Step 2 of the Wizard, the Choose Resources page, as shown in Figure 3-25.

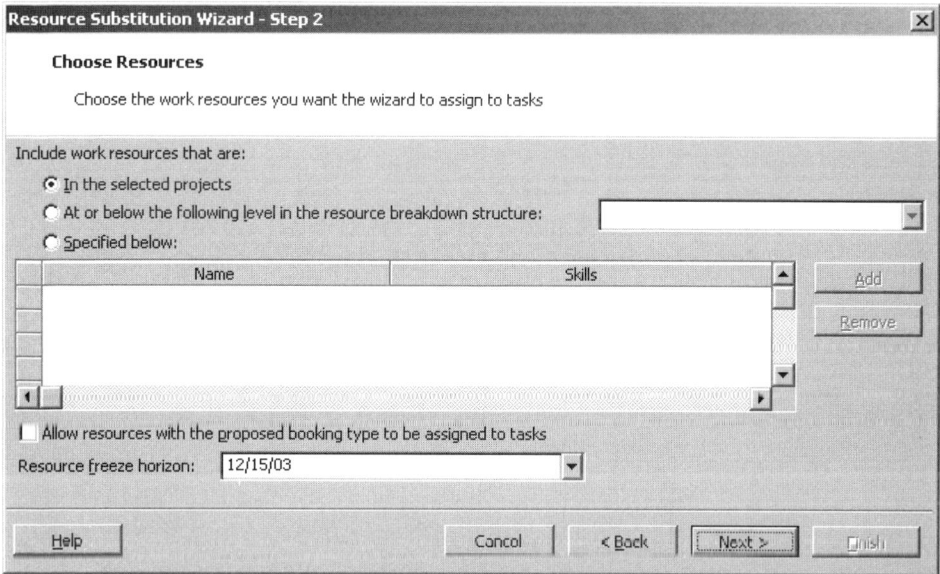

**Figure 3-25: Resource Substitution Wizard
Choose Resources page**

In the Choose Resources page, you must select the resources for the Wizard to consider in the substitution process. There are three resource substitution options:

- **In the selected projects** indicates that one or more of the projects you have selected has a team already built. When you choose this option, the system will use only resources specified in the selected plans.

- **At or below the following level in the Resource Breakdown Structure** allows you to select a branch of your RBS outline code. The pick list contains the value list for your RBS. The Wizard will consider all resources at or below that branch of the RBS. For example, in Figure 3-26, I have selected the Africa branch of my RBS structure, which will cause the Wizard to consider resources from Egypt, Jordan, and South Africa in the substitution process.

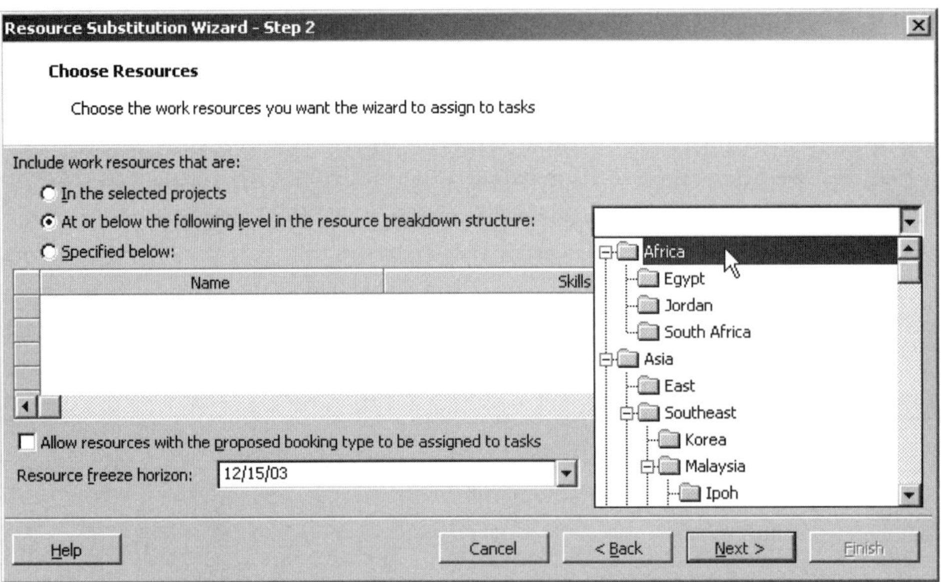

**Figure 3-26: Resource Substitution Wizard
Select a branch of the RBS outline code**

- **Specified below** allows you to select resources from the Enterprise Resource Pool by clicking the *Add* button. The system opens the Build Team dialog with the *Replace* and *Match* buttons disabled.

In addition to the options available at the top of the page, there are two more at the bottom of the page. The first option forces the Wizard to consider resources with the Proposed booking type during the substitution process. The second option allows you to specify a Resource Freeze Horizon date before which the Wizard will not substitute resources. Specify your desired settings and then click the *Next* button to continue. The system displays Step 3 of the Wizard, the Choose Related Projects page, shown in Figure 3-27.

The date of the Resource Freeze Horizon defaults to the current date.

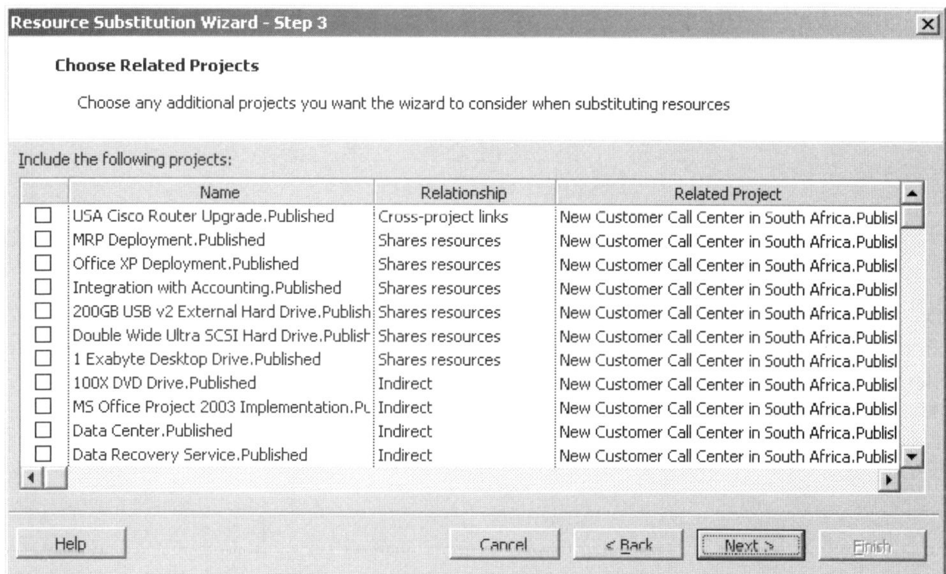

**Figure 3-27: Resource Substitution Wizard
Choose Related Projects page**

Step 3 of the Resource Substitution Wizard displays a list of projects that either have a relationship with one or more of your selected projects. The system determines related projects in two ways: either through cross-project dependencies between the projects, or through by the sharing of common resources between the projects. The system displays the type of relationship between projects in the Relationship column.

When projects share common resources, the system describes this relationship as either a direct or an indirect relationship. A direct relationship exists between two or more projects when they share one or more of the same resources. The system denotes a direct relationship between projects by displaying Shares Resources in the Relationship column, such as several of the projects shown in Figure 3-27. When projects have a direct relationship, resource substitutions made in one project can directly affect all other projects whose relationship is direct.

An Indirect relationship exists between your selected projects and other projects when the other projects share one or more resources with a project that has a Direct relationship with one of your selected projects. In other words, the relationship is "second cousin" in nature. To understand the Indirect relationship between projects, consider the example shown in Table 3-1.

Project A	Project B	Project C
Steve Garcia	Steve Garcia	Debbie Kruse
Marcia Bickel	Marcia Bickel	Evie Pruitt
Vic Merchant	Sue Burnett	Sue Burnett
George Stewart	David Erickson	David Erickson

**Table 3-1: Project C has an Indirect
relationship to Project A**

In Table 3-1, Project A has a direct (Shares Resources) relationship to Project
B through the two common resources, Steve Garcia and Marcia Bickel.
Project B has a direct (Shares Resources) relationship to Project C through
two other shared resources, Sue Burnett and David Erickson. Since Project A
is directly related to Project B, and Project B is directly related to Project C,
then Project C is Indirectly related to Project A. You can visualize this
relationship in Figure 3-28.

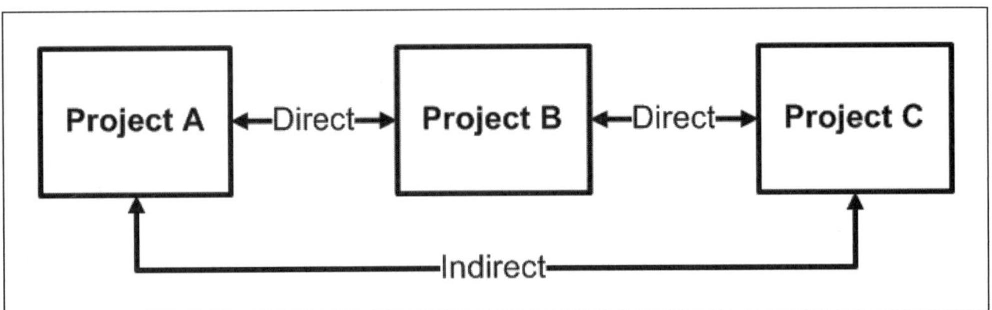

**Figure 3-28: Project A has an Indirect
relationship with Project C**

You may be wondering why is it necessary for the Resource Substitution
Wizard to determine whether a project has any kind of relationship with your
selected projects. This is done to alert you that your resource substitutions
could have a "ripple affect" on the related projects.

With this information in mind, select any related projects in which you want
the Wizard to perform resource substitutions and then click the *Next* button
to continue. The system displays Step 4 of the Wizard, the Choose
Scheduling Options page, as shown in Figure 3-29.

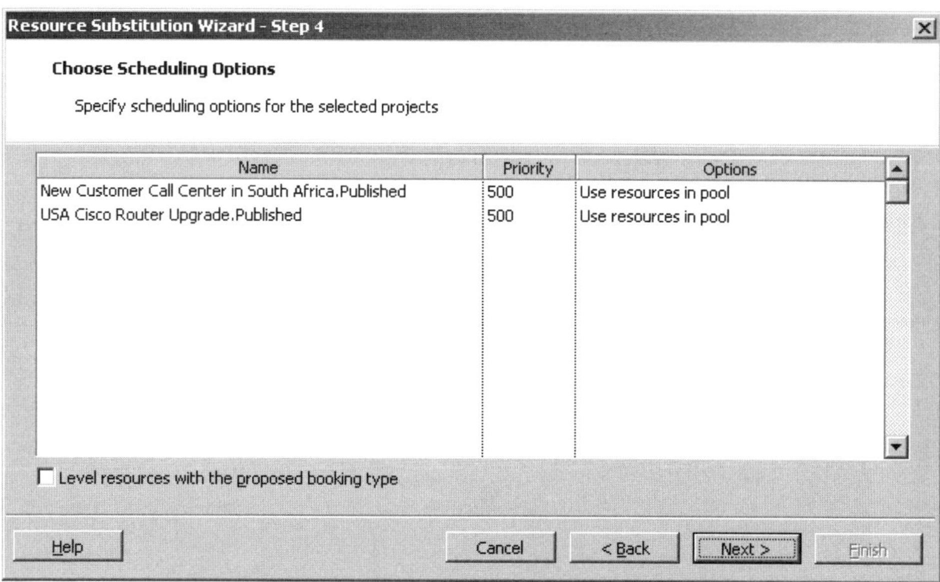

**Figure 3-29: Resource Substitution Wizard
Choose Scheduling Options page**

Step 4 of the Resource Substitution Wizard allows you to set the relative priority for each selected project by increasing or decreasing the Priority number of each project in relationship to the others. You can set the Priority number of each selected project from 0 (lowest priority) to 1000 (highest priority). The Wizard uses the priority value for each project to determine which project has first rights to an available resource with the highest priority projects taking precedence.

You may set an Options value for each project to determine whether to substitute resources from the Enterprise Resource Pool or from the selected project only. In addition, you may also choose to level Proposed resources that may become overallocated during the substitution process. To do so, select the *Level resources with the proposed booking type* option and click the *Next* button to continue. The system displays Step 5 of the Wizard, the Substitute Resources page, as shown in Figure 3-30.

Select the *Use resources in project* option if you want to optimize the use of resources in your project team for one or more projects. Select the *Use resources in pool* option if you want to staff your project with the most available resources for one or more projects.

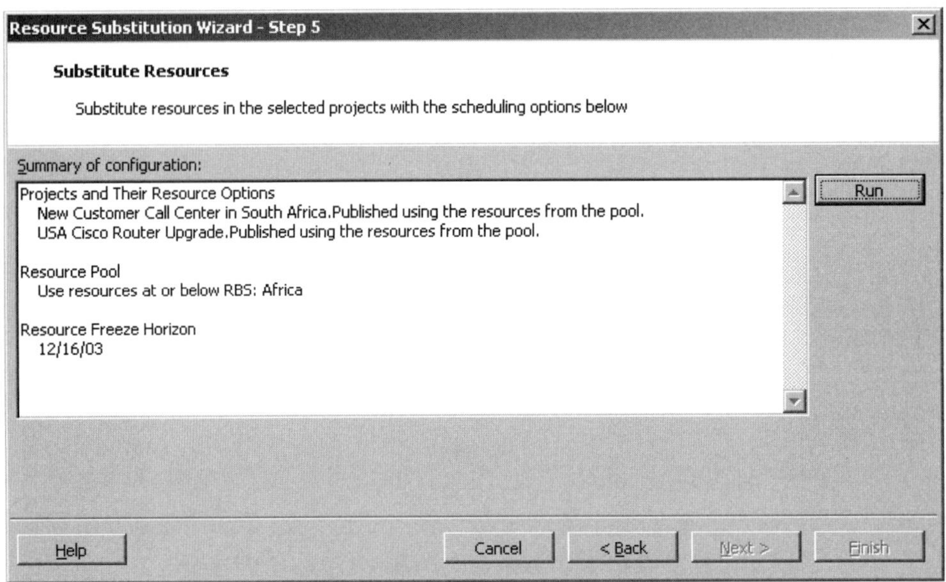

**Figure 3-30: Resource Substitution Wizard
Substitute Resources page**

The page displays a textual summary of the substitution options you have chosen during the previous four steps. If you notice a mistake here, you can either cancel the run or step back through the dialogs to make changes. When you are satisfied with your selections click the *Run* button to activate the Wizard and make the resource substitutions. After you click the *Run* button, click the *Next* button. The system displays Step 6 of the Wizard, the Review Results page, shown in Figure 3-31.

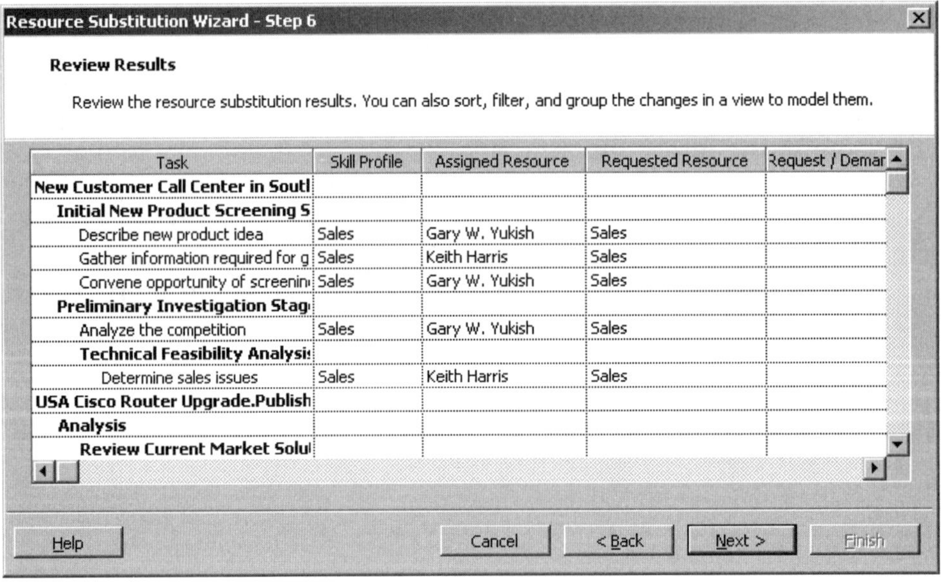

**Figure 3-31: Resource Substitution Wizard
Review Results page**

The system displays the results of the resource substitution process for each task. The display contains the task name, the skill set acted upon, the name of the new resource assigned by the Wizard, the original resource, and the Request/Demand status of the original assignment. Review the results of the resource substitution process and click the *Next* button when you are satisfied with the results.

MSProjectExperts recommends that you thoroughly review the results of the substitution process. Before moving on to the Step 7 page, confirm that the resource substitutions are acceptable to your resource planning needs. If the results of the resource substitution process are not acceptable, click the *Cancel* button and then make modifications to your projects and/or to the resource assignments in the projects.

The system displays Step 7 of the Wizard, the Choose Update Options page, shown in Figure 3-32.

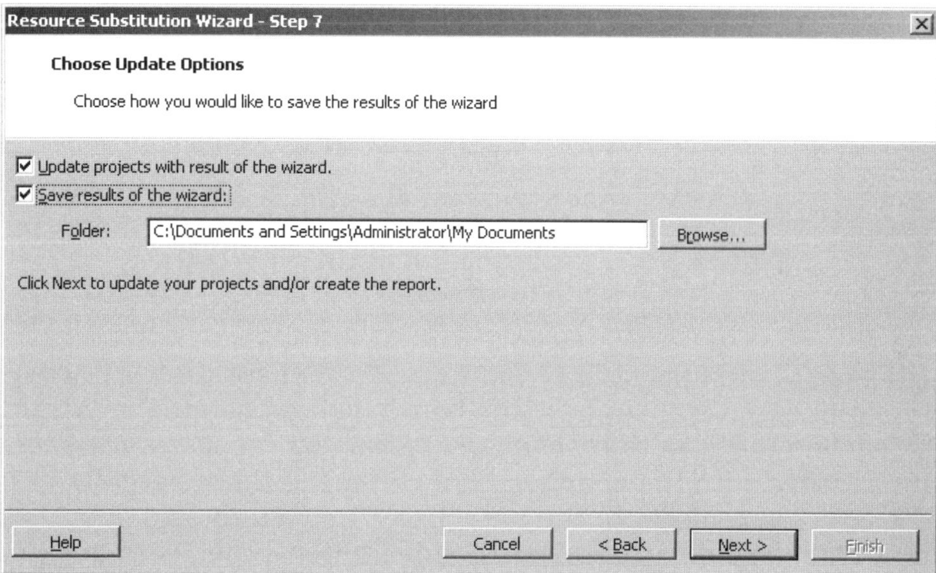

**Figure 3-32: Resource Substitution Wizard
Choose Update Options page**

The Step 7 page allows you to select the destination of the substitution results. To cancel the process and abandon the substitutions, click the *Cancel* button. To update the selected projects with the chosen resources, select the *Update projects with result of the wizard* option. To save the results of the substitution process for later review, select the *Save results of the wizard* option allowing you to save the results as a standard project file to your hard drive or a network version in a network share. Click the *Next* button to continue. The system displays Step 8 of the Wizard, the Finish page, as shown in Figure 3-33.

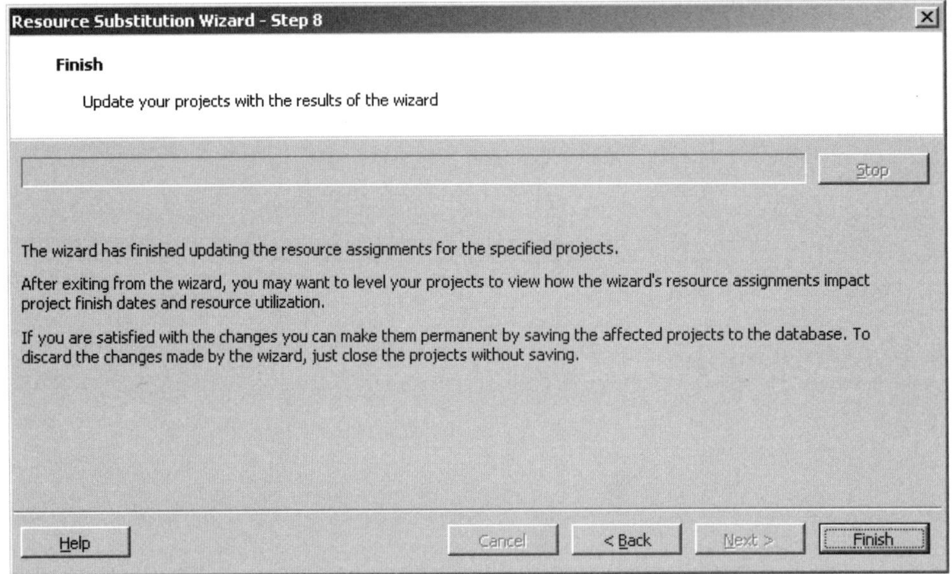

Figure 3-33: Resource Substitution Wizard
Finish page

The Finish page is the final step of the Resource Substitution Wizard, where the system makes several suggestions before you proceed. The Wizard suggests leveling the plan to resolve any remaining resource overallocations. If you are satisfied with the changes, you can make them permanent by saving the affected projects to the database. The Wizard also informs you that you can still abandon the resource substitution changes to any project simply by not saving the project plan to the database. Click the *Finish* button to complete the process.

MSProjectExperts recommends that you use extreme caution when using the Resource Substitution Wizard. This tool is not a "magic pill" that can solve all of your resource allocation issues, nor will it prevent resource overallocations from occurring in your projects.

MSProjectExperts recommends that you use the Resource Substitution Wizard as a means to do "trial resource loading" on a group of future planned projects for analysis of resource allocation issues. For the most part, you should use the two manual methods for making resource assignments to tasks, which are the Task Entry view and the Assign Resources dialog.

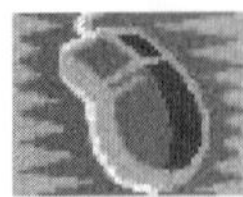 **Hands On Exercise**

Exercise 3-9

Run the Resource Substitution Wizard.

1. Using the same plan you used in Exercise 3-8, make sure that you have selected at least one actual resource for each generic resource in your plan. You may add up to two actual resources matching the generic resource specified in the plan.

2. Click Tools ➤ Substitute Resources, and then click the *Next* button in the Welcome screen.

3. On the Choose Projects page, select only the project on which you are working.

4. Include resources from the selected projects and do not select any related projects.

5. Continue clicking the *Next* button, and then click the *Run* button to run the Wizard.

6. View your results.

7. Select the *Update projects with result of the wizard* option and then click the *Finish* button.

Leveling Overallocated Resources

During the process of assigning resources to tasks, resources may become overallocated. Methodologies for leveling overallocated resources are integral for the effective use of the resource functionality in Project Professional 2003.

Overallocation Defined

A resource overallocation occurs when you assign a resource to perform more work than the resource can accomplish in the working time available. For example, if you assign a resource to perform 32 hours of work in a single 8-hour working day, then that resource is overallocated. Project Professional 2003 determines which resources are overallocated based on the work values for assigned tasks, the maximum number of units available for the resource, and the calendar used by the resource.

Resource Leveling Defined

Resource leveling is the process of resolving resource overallocations. You have two choices for leveling overallocated resources:

- Manual leveling

- Automatic leveling

Manual leveling includes any approach that you, the project manager, use to resolve the overallocation. Manual methods include approaches such as adding resources to an effort-driven task to shorten the duration of the task, increasing the availability of overallocated resources, or substituting an available resource for the overallocated resource. The number of manual leveling methods available to you is limited only by your own imagination and creativity.

Automatic leveling refers to the use of the built-in leveling routines in Project Professional 2003. When Project Professional 2003 levels a resource overallocation, the software delays tasks or splits tasks according to single or multiple leveling factors. Keep in mind that automatic leveling cannot and will not change the resources assigned to a task or the assignment Units for each resource on the task.

Basic Leveling Techniques

If you want to tackle automatic leveling using Project Professional 2003's built-in leveling capabilities, you should first display the Resource Management toolbar by clicking View ➤ Toolbars ➤ Resource Management. This toolbar contains buttons to apply the Resource Allocation view and the Task Entry view, as well as offering you the ability to launch the Resource Substitution Wizard, find overallocations, and add users from the pool.

While you are engaged in resource leveling, a couple of Views will be useful to you. The Leveling Gantt view displays the pre-leveling and post-leveling view of each task in your project. To apply this view, click View ➢ More Views ➢ Leveling Gantt. The Resource Allocation view also allows you to level one overallocated resource at a time. To apply this view, click View ➢ More Views ➢ Resource Overallocation.

Project Professional 2003 supports two types of leveling scenarios. You can level a plan only within its available slack or you can completely level the plan. If you choose to level a plan within its available slack, the system will level all overallocations to the best of its ability, but will not change the finish date of your project. You can use this approach to determine the head count your project will require in order to meet the date. If you level the project completely, the system will attempt to level every resource overallocation, which often results in a finish date later than originally scheduled.

If you want to know the earliest realistic date that your project can finish, then level the project completely. If you absolutely must finish the project by a certain date, then you should level only within available slack, and then use other methods of manual leveling to finish the leveling process.

To use the automatic leveling capabilities of Project Professional 2003, click Tools ➢ Level Resources. The Resource Leveling dialog displays as shown in Figure 3-34.

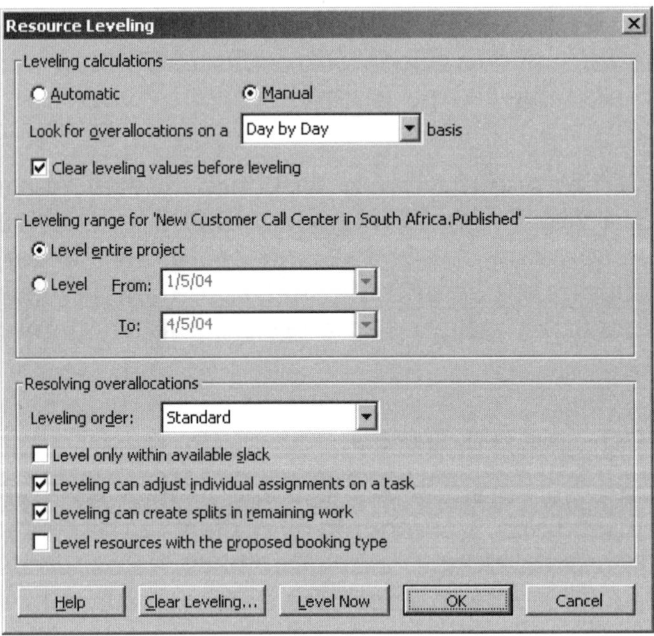

Figure 3-34: Resource Leveling dialog

The Resource Leveling dialog offers you three sets of leveling options:

- Leveling calculations
- Leveling range
- Resolving Overallocations

The **Leveling Calculations** section allows you to select how the system levels overallocated resources. The first part of this section allows you set the leveling process to either Automatic or Manual. To maintain as much control of the leveling process as possible, you should set this option to *Manual* so that the system will level only when you click the *Level Now* button. If you select the *Clear leveling values before leveling* option, the system will remove any leveling previously applied before leveling your project. If you deselect this option, the system will level on top of previous values. You can also specify the time sensitivity used in leveling by setting the *Look for overallocations on a ____ basis* option of minutes, hours, days, weeks, or months.

MSProjectExperts recommends that you never select Automatic leveling in the Resource Leveling dialog. When applied, Automatic Leveling will not only level the active project, but will also level all other open projects in need of leveling, and do so without asking your permission!

The options in the **Leveling Range** section allow you to select tasks for leveling based on a date range or you may simply select the entire project.

The **Resolving Overallocations** section offers several important options. The *Leveling Order* option affects how the system determines which tasks to delay or split when resolving resource allocations. You should select either the Standard leveling order or the Priority, Standard leveling order for the leveling process. Select the *Level only within available slack* option to force the system to honor the finish date set of your project. Select the *Leveling can adjust individual assignments on a task* option to allow the system to make changes to one resource assigned to a task independently from another resource assigned to the same task. Select the *Leveling can create splits in remaining work* option to allow the system to split tasks to resolve overallocations. Select the *Level resources with the proposed booking type* option to include Proposed resources in the leveling process.

The Standard leveling order uses five factors to determine which tasks to delay or split. These factors are predecessors, amount of total slack, start date, priority number, and constraints. The Priority, Standard leveling order uses the same five factors, but it gives precedence to the task Priority number.

By default, Project Professional 2003 **does not** level overallocated resources with the Proposed booking type. Because all resource overallocations are a risk to your project finish date, MSProjectExperts recommends that you include resources with the Proposed booking type in the leveling process.

After selecting your leveling options, click the *Level Now* button. If you have a resource View currently applied, the system displays the Level Now dialog, as is shown in Figure 3-35. You may select the *Entire Pool* option to level all overallocated resources or you can choose the *Selected resources* option to level only those resources that you have selected. Click the *OK* button when you are ready and the system performs the leveling according to your specifications.

Figure 3-35: Level Now dialog

For best results with resource leveling, use the following methodology when leveling overallocated resources:

1. Level in any resource view, such as the Resource Usage view

2. Level only one overallocated resource at a time

3. Clear the results of resource leveling in any task view, such as the Leveling Gantt view

After applying Service Pack 1, Project Professional 2003 levels resource overallocations in a project based on each resource's overallocations across **all projects** in the Project Server database, even if you do not have any other projects open at the time you level. To level resource overallocations only in the current project, exit and relaunch Project Professional 2003, deselect the *Load summary resource assignments* option in the Project Server Accounts dialog, and then click the *Connect* button. When you open a project, you will see the resource assignments in that project only.

Assigning Leveling Priorities to Tasks

You can set the task priority used by the leveling system by opening the Task Information dialog, shown in Figure 3-36. The Priority field is accessible from the *General* tab, as shown in the figure. You can set priorities to any value between 0 and 1000, where 1000 indicates to the system not to level and all other priorities are relative to one another. To work with priorities across many tasks, consider inserting the column into a task view such as the Gantt Chart view.

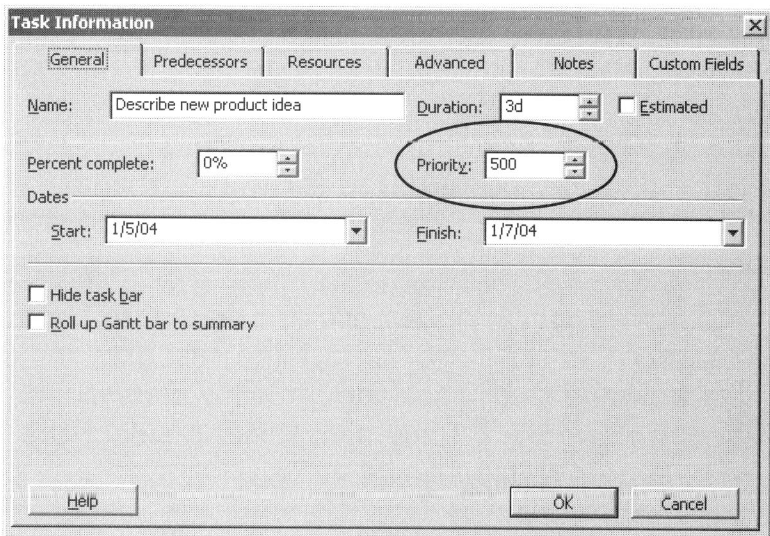

**Figure 3-36: Task Information
dialog – Set task priority**

For simplicity's sake, this course offers only a brief presentation on resource leveling. msProjectExperts presents a complete treatment of the subject in the Advanced Project Professional 2003 course.

Avoid Creating Resource Overallocations
When Assigning Resources to Tasks

Given that leveling resource overallocations is a complex and potentially cumbersome process, it is much better to avoid creating resource overallocations at the time you make resource assignments. Project Server 2003 offers you several methods to accomplish this, including the following:

- In the Assign Resources dialog of Project Professional 2003, select the desired resource and click the *Graphs* button. Click the *Select Graph* pick list and select the *Remaining Availability* graph. This graph shows you the resource's Remaining Availability across all projects in the portfolio. Scroll to the time period required for the task and determine the resource's availability during that time period.

- In Project Professional 2003, click View ➤ Resource Usage. Right-click in the timephased grid (yellow/white timesheet) and select the *Remaining Availability* details from the shortcut menu. Examine the resource's assigned Work and Remaining Availability across all projects in the portfolio. Scroll to the time period required for the task and determine the resource's availability during that time period.

- Log into Project Web Access and navigate to the Resource Center page. Select the resource in question and then click the *View Availability* button. Click the *Choose a View* pick list and select the *Remaining Availability* view. Scroll to the time period required for the task and examine the resource's Remaining Availability during that time period. If necessary, expand the Details section at the bottom of the page and study the project work assigned to the resource during that time period.

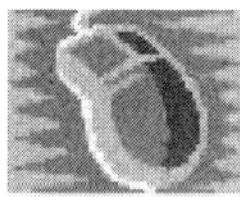

Hands On Exercise

Exercise 3-10

Level overallocated resources.

1. Set leveling priorities for tasks.
2. Select Tools ➢ Level Resources.
3. Set your leveling options.
4. Click the *Level Now* button.
5. Select Tools ➢ Level Resources and deselect the *Clear leveling values before leveling* option.
6. Select the *Entire project* option when prompted and then click the *OK* button.
7. Save and close your project plan.

Module 04

Publishing and Republishing Work Assignments

Learning Objectives

After completing this module, you will be able to:

- Control default publishing behavior
- Publish work assignments to resources
- Take over assignments for another Project Manager
- Republish assignment information
- Understand the Project Server Spooler
- Request progress
- Add a published field to each user's timesheet on the View My Tasks page

Understanding Project Server Publishing

When you publish both the project and the task assignments, you will encounter the following default behaviors using Project Server 2003:

- The project is visible in both Project Center views and detailed Project views in Project Web Access.

- Information in both custom Project and Task fields populates the Project Center views and detailed Project views.

- The system processes information about the project into the OLAP cube, which makes the information available for viewing in Portfolio Analyzer views.

- Resource availability information shown in the Resource Center view includes resource information from the new project.

- The new project displays on the list of available projects in the Risks, Issues, and Documents pages.

- Resources can see their task assignments for the project on their timesheet in the View My Tasks page.

- Resource assignments for the project are visible in the View Resource Assignments page.

The act of publishing assignments controls who will receive task updates from resources working on the project. Project Server 2003 designates the project manager who initially publishes the assignments as the Manager of those assignments. The assignment manager receives task updates from team members assigned to the selected tasks.

Although only one project manager may open and revise a project plan at one time, more than one manager can be involved in managing and updating the plan. In some organizations, for instance, multiple resource managers are responsible for assigning work and updating progress in a single plan. To accommodate this, each manager must open the project and publish the assignments for resources they manage. Remember that when you publish an assignment, the updates for that task will flow back to you.

Controlling Default Publishing Behavior

You can control Project Professional 2003's default publishing behavior on a project-by-project basis by making changes in the Options dialog. Click Tools ➤ Options, and then select the *Collaborate* tab in the Options dialog, as shown in Figure 4-1. The *Collaborate* tab of the Options dialog contains the default values for the following Collaboration options:

- The system uses information from the Project Server Accounts dialog to set the values for the Collaborate using, Project Server URL, and Identification for Project Server fields. The information displayed here is set by the session; therefore, the only value you can change is the E-mail address field.

To display the Project Server Accounts dialog, click Tools ➤ Enterprise Options ➤ Microsoft Office Project Server Accounts.

- When you select the *Allow resources to delegate tasks using Project Server* option, you give permission to your project team members to delegate their tasks to other resources if your Project Server administrator has enabled task delegation in your environment. If your administrator has disabled task delegation, then this setting will have no effect on the local plan.

- The *Publish New and Changed Assignments updates resources' assignments when* option allows you to determine what the system recognizes as a change to an assignment when you click Collaborate ➤ Publish ➤ New and Changed Assignments. Selecting the *Start, Finish, % Complete or outline changes* option causes the system to mark the task for an update only when one of these factors change. Selecting the *Any task information* option causes the system to mark a task for updating when any information on the task changes.

This is an important setting, and being aware of it can spare you much grief when trying to understand system behavior. For example, if you select the first of the two options, the system will not update a task simply because you changed the name of the task in the project plan.

- The *On every save, publish the following information to Microsoft Project Server* option allows you to automate publishing with a project save. You have the choice to select one or both New and Changed assignment and/or Project Summary with or without full project plan information.

MsProjectExperts recommends that you do not select any of the automatic publish on save options so that you can retain control of publishing manually and avoid unintended consequences. Imagine that you have decided to spend a day or two making significant changes to your plan and on the first day you decide to save your plan before breaking for lunch. If you forget to turn this option off, the system will push out your half-baked changes to the team.

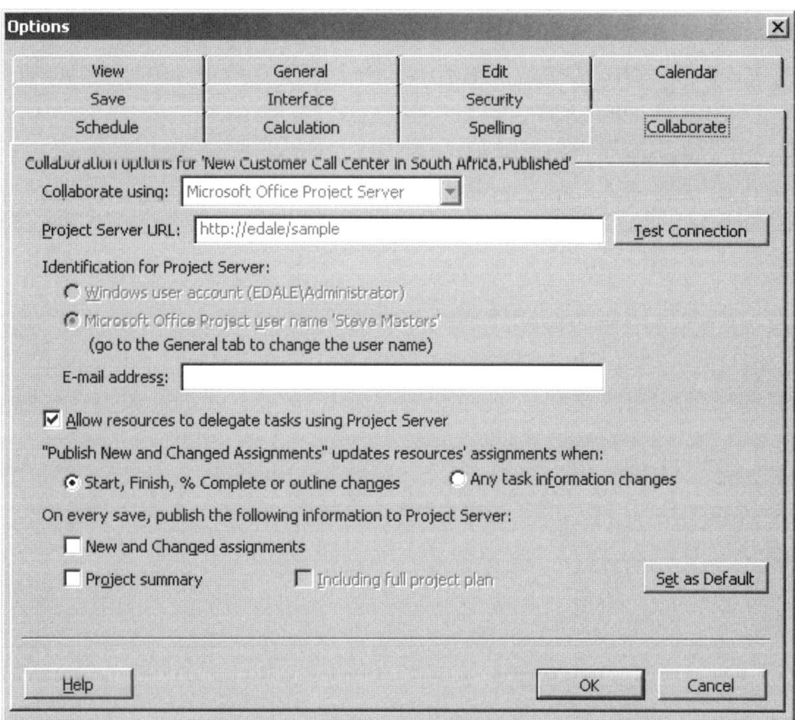

**Figure 4-1: Options dialog
Collaborate page**

Publishing: Best Practices

As with opening and saving project plans, it is important to develop good publishing habits with Project Professional 2003. Some of these good habits include:

- Do not publish resource assignments until you are ready to inform project team members of their task work in the plan.

- When you are ready to publish, it is best to have only one project open.

- When you have been updating a plan, do not publish the plan until after you have saved your changes to the server.

- Do not open a project from the server, save it as an .mpp file, and then attempt to publish the .mpp plan. The system will prevent you from publishing the .mpp project, since it is a non-enterprise project.

Saving a project plan to Project Server 2003 takes longer than saving an mpp file. Saving and Publishing take much longer than saving alone. Therefore, you should never activate both auto-save and automatic publishing, as the interruptions to your workflow will quickly become unbearable.

Publishing Project and Assignment Information

You access publishing functions by clicking Collaborate ➢ Publish, as shown in Figure 4-2. You have three publishing choices plus the option to republish assignments. The differences between these publishing options are as follows:

- **All Information** automatically selects all information eligible to be published, including new and changed assignments, as well as the plan and plan details.

- **New and Changed Assignments** selects all new and not previously published assignments, as well as assignments that have changed according to the criteria you selected on the Collaborate page of the Options dialog.

- **Project Plan** publishes only project information and not assignments to Project Server.

- **Republish Assignments** allows the manager to republish task assignments whether or not they have changed according to the system criteria.

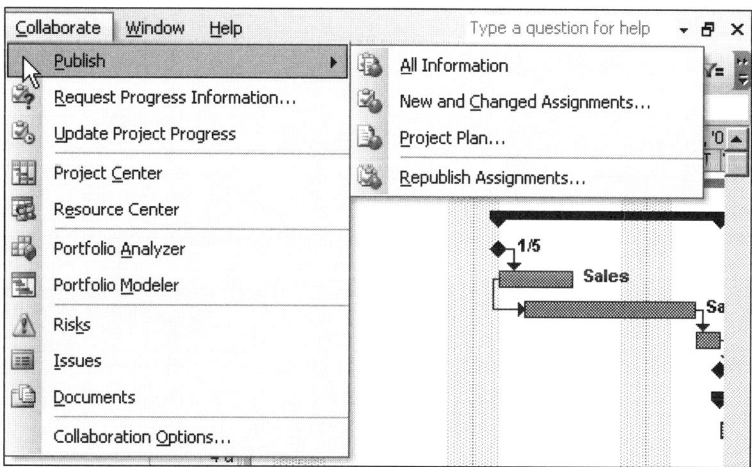

Figure 4-2: Publish menu choices

Publishing All Information

When you click Collaborate ➢ Publish ➢ All Information, Project Professional 2003 publishes all available project information and assignments. Before publishing, the system will present the alert shown in Figure 4-3. You may click the *OK* button to continue or the *Cancel* button to stop the action. If you click the *OK* button, the publishing operation will continue without further user interface activity.

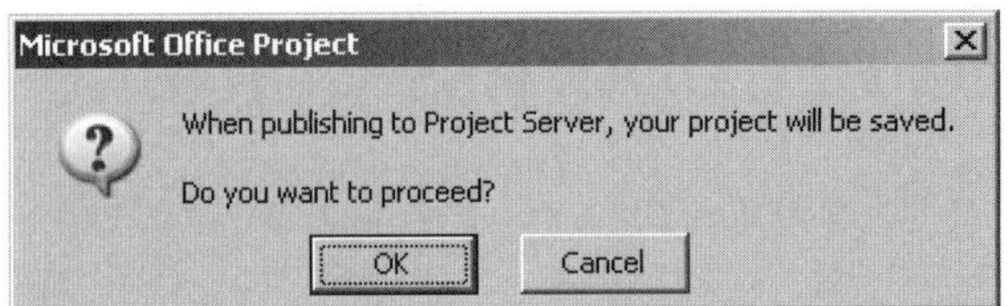

**Figure 4-3: Microsoft Office
Project alert**

Publishing New and Changed Assignments

When you click Collaborate ➢ Publish ➢ New and Changed Assignments, the system first displays the same alert box shown in Figure 4-3. When you click the *OK* button, the system opens the Publish New and Changed Assignments dialog shown in Figure 4-4. The system first selects all eligible task assignments and lists them in the dialog. You may refine the selection by clicking the *Publish new and changed assignments for* pick list at the top of the dialog and then selecting Entire project, Current view, or Selected items from the list. Selecting the *Current view* option limits the selection to only what is currently visible in the project view, including any filters you may have applied to the view. Choosing the *Selected items* option assumes that you have selected one or more tasks in the plan for which to publish assignments. The system groups the assignments by resource. You can change this by selecting the *Task* option below the task list display.

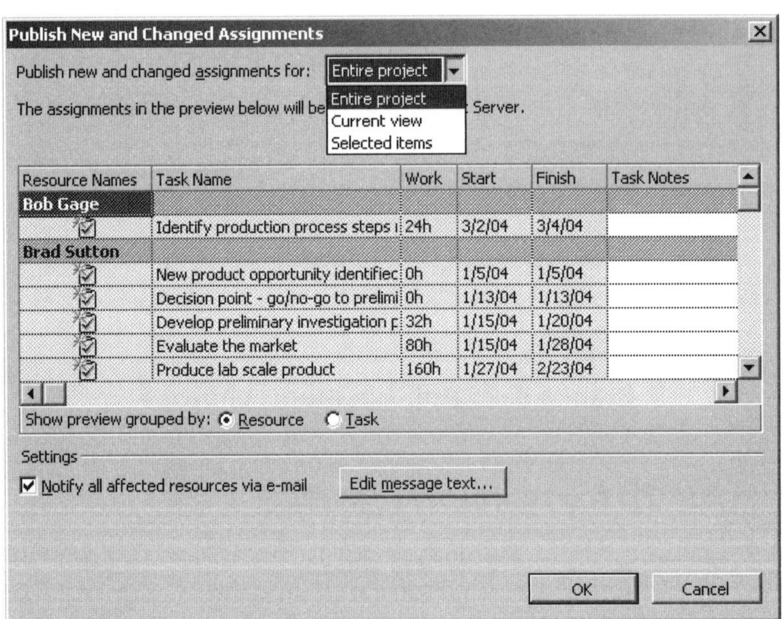

**Figure 4-4: Publish New and Changed
Assignments dialog**

When you publish assignments, the system sends e-mail notifications automatically to the resources who are receiving the assignments if your system has the notification engine enabled. These notification e-mails contain a link back to Project Web Access. You can personalize the message sent by clicking the *Edit message text* button to open the Edit Message Text dialog shown in Figure 4-5. Replace the existing message or add a personalization to it, and then click the *OK* button.

To stop an e-mail notification from generating, deselect the *Notify all affected resources via e-mail* option in the Settings section of the dialog.

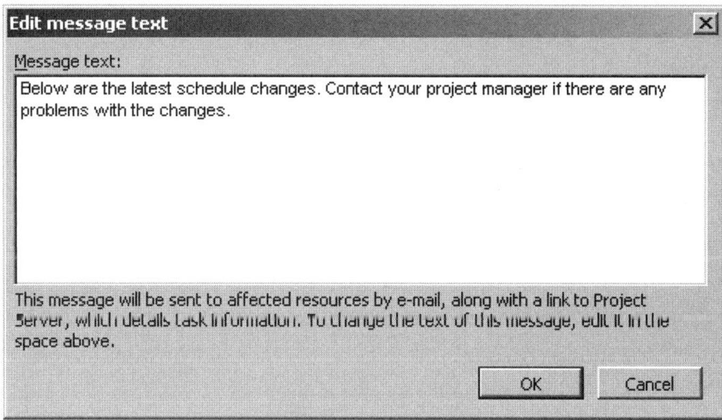

**Figure 4-5: Personalize your
e-mail message**

Publishing the Project Plan

When you click Collaborate ➤ Publish ➤ Project Plan, the system opens the Publish Project Plan dialog shown in Figure 4-6. Here you can choose to publish either the Summary (Project Summary Task) or the entire plan along with the Summary.

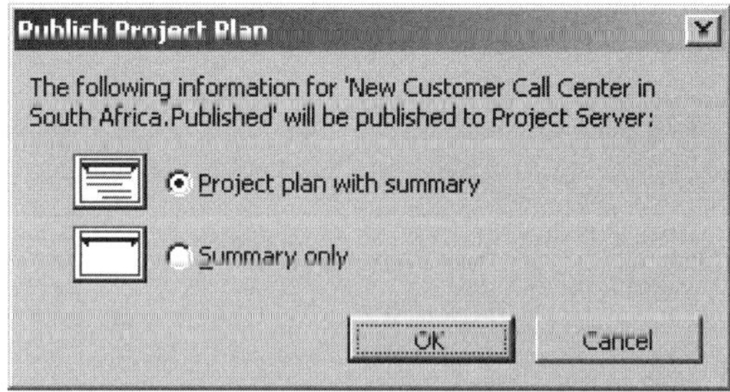

**Figure 4-6: Publish Project
Plan dialog**

After applying Project Server 2003 SP1 the system automatically publishes projects when you save and close an enterprise project. The system publishes the project plan information automatically, even if you do not click Collaborate ➢ Publish ➢ Project Plan while the plan was open. This automatic publishing behavior guarantees that the project data is always "in synch" between the Microsoft Project plan and Project Web Access. If you explicitly click Collaborate ➢ Publish ➢ Project Plan, the system publishes your project information immediately.

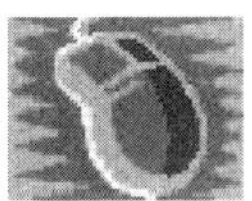

Hands On Exercise

Exercise 4-1

Publish your plan to the Microsoft Project Server.

1. Connect to Project Server 2003 if you are not already connected.

2. Open your plan student#+test2 (eg: 04test2).

3. Before publishing, make sure that you assign some tasks to some of your special classroom resources.

4. Select Collaborate ➢ Publish ➢ All Information.

5. Click the *OK* button when prompted.

6. Save and close your plan.

Republishing Assignments

You must use the Collaborate ➢ Publish ➢ Republish Assignments option for the following situations:

- To take over as the manager of another manager's project, either temporarily or permanently.

- To "push" actuals to a team member's timesheet in Project Web Access after you enter actual work or update task progress manually in the Microsoft Project plan.

- To "push" the new method of tracking to each team member's timesheet in Project Web Access after the Project Server administrator changes your organization's default method of tracking progress.

- To "unhide" a task assignment when a team member hides an assignment accidentally on his/her timesheet in Project Web Access.

When you click Collaborate ➢ Publish ➢ Republish Assignments, the system opens essentially the same dialog you see when you Publish Assignments. Shown in Figure 4-7, there are several important differences in this dialog besides the title change to Republish Assignments. Notice in Figure 4-7 that there are two additional options in the Settings section at the bottom of the dialog.

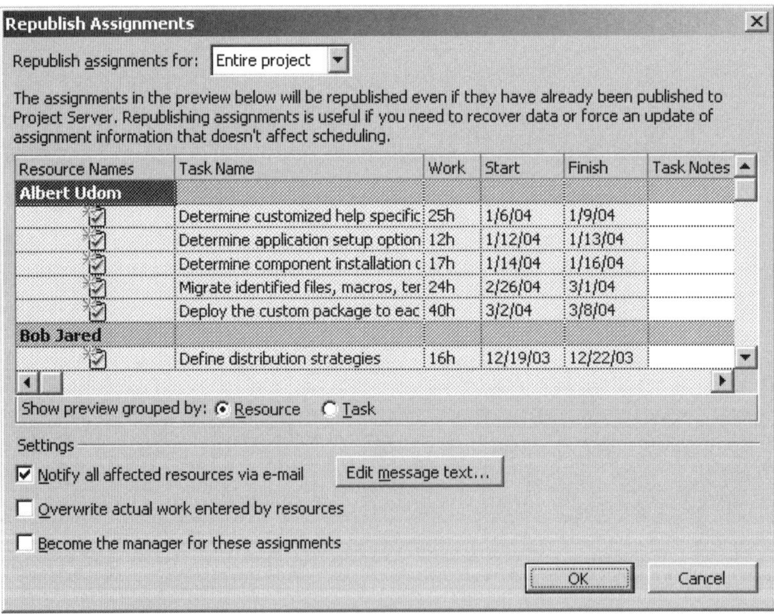

**Figure 4-7: Republish Assignments
dialog**

Republishing to Take Over as the Manager of a Project

You may need to take over as the manager of a project temporarily while the original manager is away on vacation, or you may need to take over permanently if the original manager leaves the company. You can take over as the manager of another manager's project in two ways: take over the entire project or take over only selected tasks.

To take over as the manager of the entire project, complete the following steps:

1. Open the other manager's project.

2. Click Collaborate ➤ Publish ➤ Republish Assignments.

3. Select the *Become the manager for these assignments* option.

4. Click the *OK* button.

To take over as the manager of only selected tasks in the project, you must first select only the tasks you will manage, or you must filter the project to display only the tasks you will manage. After either selecting or filtering the tasks, then complete the following steps:

1. Open the other manager's project.

2. Click Collaborate ➤ Publish ➤ Republish Assignments.

3. If you selected only certain tasks in the project, click the *Republish Assignments for* pick list at the top of the dialog and choose the *Selected items* option.

4. If you filtered the task list, click the *Republish Assignments for* pick list at the top of the dialog and choose the *Current view* option.

5. Select the *Become the manager for these assignments* option.

6. Click the *OK* button.

Completing either of the preceding sets of steps causes Project Server 2003 to redirect all current and future task updates from project team members to you instead of the original manager. If this is a temporary takeover, when the original project manager returns to work, he/she must complete the exact same steps to return the flow of task updates back to them.

If you de-select the e-mail notification option, the updates for the tasks will flow to you without the resource being aware of the change.

Republishing After Entering Actuals Manually in the Microsoft Project Plan

You may need to enter actuals manually in the Microsoft Project plan when a team member reports task progress to you using a method other than the Project Web Access timesheet. When you manually enter task progress in the Microsoft Project plan, you can "push" task progress to the resource's timesheet in Project Web Access by completing the following steps:

1. Click Collaborate ➤ Publish ➤ Republish Assignments.

2. Select the *Overwrite actual work entered by resources* option.

3. Click the *OK* button.

After entering actual progress in the Microsoft Project plan, the Republish Assignments feature will "synch up" the new Actual Work values with the user's timesheet.

Republishing to Push a New Method of Tracking Progress to Each Team Member's Timesheet

If your Project Server administrator changes your organization's default method of tracking progress after you have already published one or more enterprise projects, you must "push" the new method of tracking to each team member's timesheet in Project Web Access by completing the following steps:

1. Open an enterprise project for which you are the manager.

2. Click Collaborate ➤ Publish ➤ Republish Assignments.

3. Click the *OK* button.

4. Save and close the project.

5. Repeat steps #1-4 for every project in which you are the manager.

Warning: Only unstarted tasks will use the new method of tracking progress on each user's View My Tasks page. In-progress tasks will continue to use the former method of tracking progress until the tasks are completed.

Republishing to Unhide a Hidden Task on a Team Member's Timesheet

To "unhide" a task that a team member has hidden on his/her timesheet in Project Web Access, complete these steps:

1. Determine exactly which project task the team member hid.

2. Open the project in question.

3. Click View ➤ Resource Usage.

4. Locate the resource and then select the task assignment that the team member hid.

5. Click Collaborate ➤ Publish ➤ Republish Assignments.

6. Click the *Republish assignments for* pick list at the top of the dialog and choose the *Selected items* option.

7. Click the *OK* button.

After performing the preceding set of steps to "unhide" a hidden task, you might also want to remind the team member not to hide unstarted or in-progress tasks. Teach your team members to hide **only** completed tasks and cancelled tasks on their timesheets in Project Web Access.

Hands On Exercise

Exercise 4-2

Take ownership of another manager's tasks by republishing the assignments.

1. Connect to Project Server 2003 if you are not already connected.

2. Open the project plan belonging to the student next to you.

3. Select a couple current tasks.

4. Select Collaborate ➢ Publish ➢ Republish Assignments.

5. Select the *Become the manager for these assignments* option.

6. Click the *OK* button.

7. Save and close the plan.

Understanding the Project Server Spooler

The Project Server Spooler works with you behind the scenes as a silent and barely visible partner until something goes wrong. The Spooler application starts when you launch Project Professional 2003 and stays active but idle until it is required. The Spooler icon appears in the tray area on the right end of your Windows Taskbar. In Figure 4-8, the Spooler icon is the one on the left.

**Figure 4-8: Spooler icon
at left end of system tray**

The Spooler functions much like the print spooler on your computer. It queues publishing jobs in the background so you can continue to work uninterrupted when the server cannot immediately respond to your publishing action.

If an error occurs during publishing, the Spooler icon displays a flashing red exclamation point next to the computer graphic, shown in Figure 4-9, and the system displays an alert dialog shown in Figure 4-10.

**Figure 4-9: Spooler icon
shows an error**

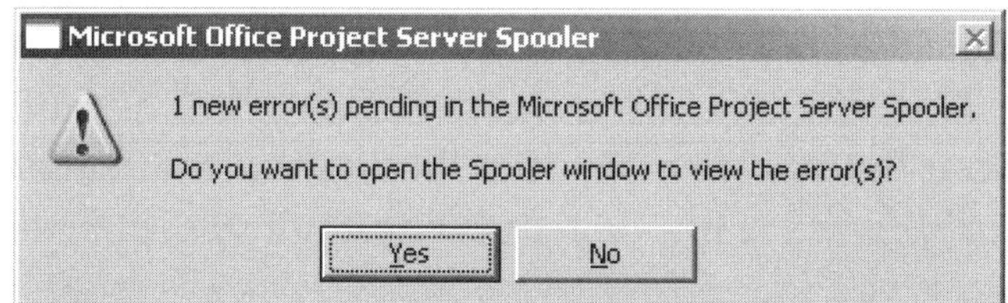

**Figure 4-10: Microsoft Office Project Server
Spooler dialog**

If you click the *Yes* button in the Spooler dialog or double-click the Spooler icon in the system tray, the system displays the Spooler window shown in Figure 4-11. You can investigate the specific error once the Spooler window is open. Only two actions are available for solving the Spooler error from the *Actions* menu: Retry or Undo. Clicking Actions ➢ Retry will repeat the publishing action, while clicking Actions ➢ Undo will "roll back" the publishing action.

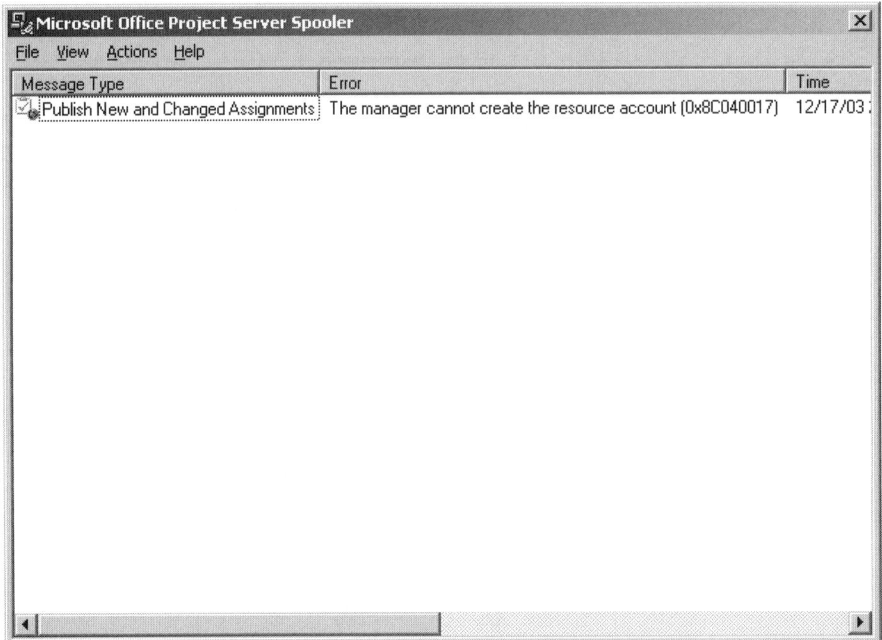

**Figure 4-11: View the error detail
in the Spooler window**

The improper use of local resources in an enterprise project causes of the Spooler error shown in Figure 4-11. Refer to the Using Local Resources in an Enterprise Project topic in Module 03 for the required steps to manage local resources properly in an enterprise project.

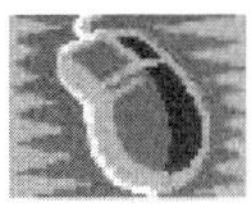

Hands On Exercise

Exercise 4-3

Examine the Microsoft Project Server Spooler for publishing errors.

1. Connect to Project Server 2003 if you are not already connected.

2. Locate the Spooler icon on the task bar.

3. Double click the Spooler icon to open the Spooler window.

Requesting Task Progress Outside the Normal Flow

In the normal flow of project communication, Resources report progress against tasks through their timesheet based on the periodic reporting requirements established by the business. Occasionally you may want to remind a resource that progress is due or to send you a progress report that is out of the ordinary reporting cycle. To accomplish this, click Collaborate ➤ Request Progress Information to open the Request Progress Information dialog shown in Figure 4-12. You will typically do this for specific tasks, so select the tasks first, and the dialog will automatically choose the *Selected items* option in the *Request progress information for* pick list.

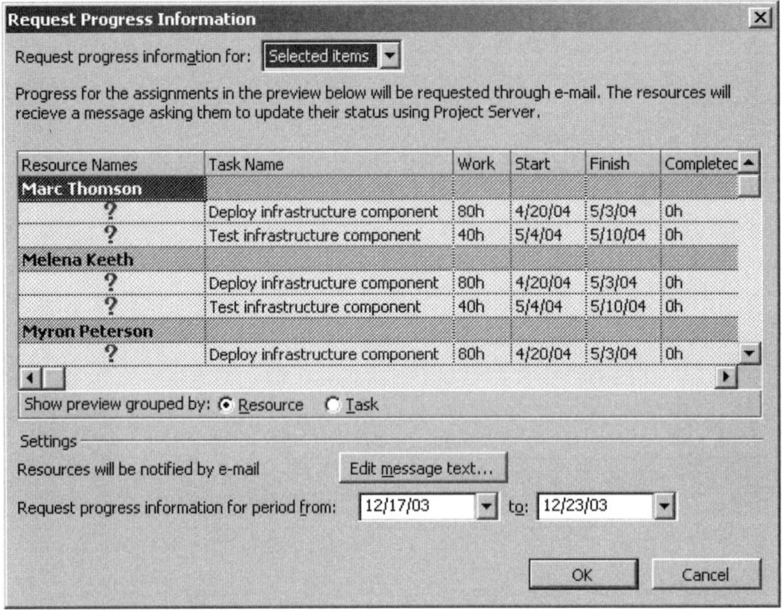

Figure 4-12: Request Progress Information dialog

The system notifies the affected resources of this request through e-mail. It also marks the task in your plan with the icon shown in Figure 4-13. This icon appears in the Indicators field in your project plan. The icon also appears in the users' timesheet indicating that a progress request is pending for the task.

Figure 4-13: Request Progress Information task indicator

 MSProjectExperts recommends that you do not use the Request Progress Information feature because it **does not require** that the resource submit progress to you immediately. Instead, use good project communication techniques, such as a phone call, an e-mail message, or a personal visit to the resource to request the status information.

Hands On Exercise

Exercise 4-4

Request progress information from your team members.

1. Connect to Project Server 2003 if you are not already connected.
2. Open the test2 project plan.
3. Select two tasks that have one of the special classroom resources assigned.
4. Click Collaborate ➤ Request Progress Information.
5. Click the *OK* button to send the request.
6. Save the project plan.

Determining Timesheet (Published) Fields

The default fields displayed in the task list portion of each user's timesheet in Project Web Access are the same for each tracking method; however, the fields available for data entry vary. The default fields are:

- Indicator
- Task Name
- Work
- % Work Complete
- Actual Work
- Remaining Work
- Start
- Finish
- Update Sent
- Project
- Assigned to
- Lead Name

You can supplement the default columns by adding additional fields to the list of published fields. Additional fields can include standard fields, custom fields, and enterprise custom fields. You can add these simply to provide additional information to your team member or as additional reporting fields.

To supplement the list of fields available for a project in each team member's timesheet, complete the following steps:

1. Open the project in which you want the additional fields to appear.

2. Click Tools ➢ Customize ➢ Published Fields to open the Customize Published Fields dialog shown in Figure 4-14.

3. From the Available fields list on the left, select one or more additional fields, and then click the *Copy* button (**>**).

4. Select each field in the Fields in the Tasks View list. If you want to allow the user to report information through the field, select the *Let resource change field* option.

5. Click the *OK* button.

You must republish any previously published assignments in your project to "push" the change to your team members' sheets by clicking Collaborate ➢ Publish ➢ Republish Assignments.

In Figure 4-14, notice that I added the Actual Start and Actual Finish fields to the list of Published fields, and that I checked the *Let resource change field* option so that the resources can edit the data in this field.

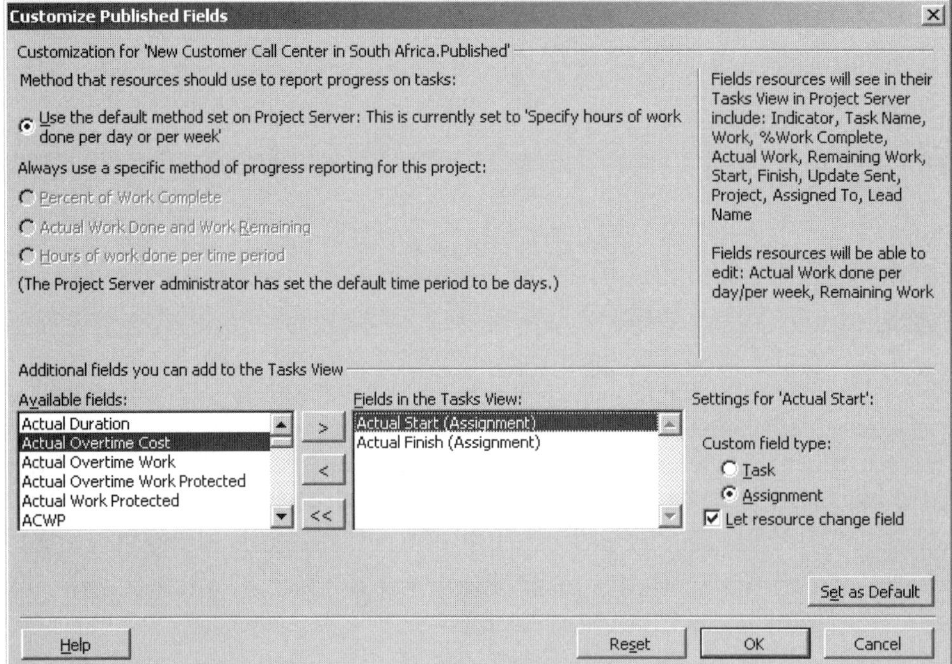

Figure 4-14: Customize Published Fields dialog

You can add additional published fields on a project-by-project basis. If your organization wishes to add a standardized list of custom fields for every project, your Project Server administrator should add the additional fields to each of your organization's enterprise project templates.

 Once you add additional published fields to your team members' timesheets for a given project, your Project Server administrator must also add these fields to the Timesheet view for all users. The Project Server administrator can determine the order of each field in the Timesheet view.

The system displays the additional published fields in the task list portion of each team member's View My Tasks page, as shown in Figure 4-15. Notice in the figure that I am entering an Actual Start date for a task.

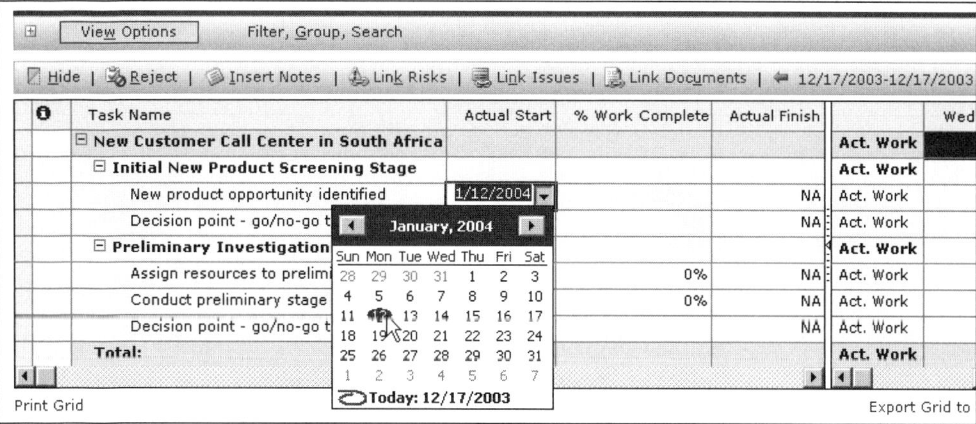

**Figure 4-15: Additional Published fields
added to the View My Tasks page**

When determining the fields that you want pushed to the timesheet, keep in mind that enterprise Task fields do not carry discreet values at the assignment level. These are not suitable for capturing values entered by resources unless you always have only one resource assigned to each task.

Module 05

Project Web Access Overview

Learning Objectives

After completing this module, you will be able to:

- Understand the basic features of the Microsoft Project Web Access user interface

- Select additional options in the Actions pane of a Project Web Access page

- Use Customization Tabs and the Action Bar on a Project Web Access page

- Use the Action Bar on a Project

- Manipulate the data grid on a Project Web Access page

- Print or export the data grid on a Project Web Access page

Using the Project Web Access User Interface

You access information in Project Server 2003 through the Project Web Access pages in Internet Explorer. When you enter a valid URL for your company's Project Web Access site in the address bar of Internet Explorer, the system automatically logs you into the site when using Windows Authentication. The Project Web Access Home page displays by default each time you access the site. Figure 5-1 shows a typical project manager's Home page.

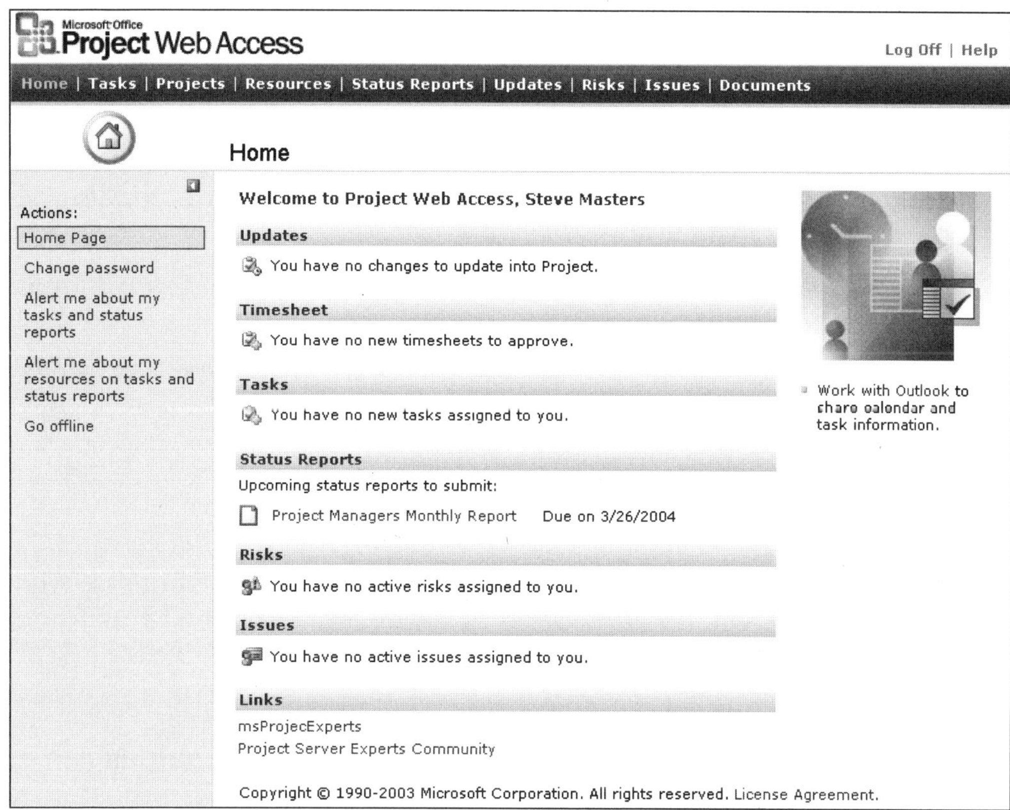

**Figure 5-1: Project Web Access
Home page for a project manager**

The central area of the Home page contains links for the relevant sections of Project Web Access, based on your security permissions. In Figure 5-1, there are sections for Updates, Timesheet, Tasks, Status Reports, Risks, Issues, and Links. The Home page for every user contains the Tasks, Status Reports, Issues, and Risks sections. The Updates section appears only on the Home page of project managers. The Timesheet section appears only on the Home page for those users who have timesheet approval authority. The Links section contains hyperlinks for two Internet sites that contain helpful information for project managers.

133

Menu Bar

The Project Web Access user interface offers a blue and white menu bar at the top of each page. This menu bar lists your viewable selections, based on your role in the project management environment. Figure 5-2 shows the Project Web Access menu bar for a project manager.

**Figure 5-2: Project Web Access menu bar
for a project manager**

The options available on the Project Web Access menu bar include:

- **Home** – The default page which is displayed each time you log into Project Web Access.

- **Tasks** – Displays the View My Tasks page used by all team members to enter and submit actual work values.

- **Projects** – Displays the Project Center page where you can access project views and project analysis features.

- **Resources** – Displays the Resource Center page where you can view resource information and resource analysis features.

- **Status Reports** – Displays the Status Reports Overview page. Managers can use this page to create Status Report requests, while team members will use this page to enter and submit Status Reports.

- **Updates** – Displays the Updates page. Project Managers use the Updates page to receive, review, and update actual progress.

- **Risks** – Displays the Risks page where all interested parties can create risks, track risks, and develop contingency plans in case those risks occur.

- **Issues** – Displays the Issues page where all interested parties can create and track issues relating to a specific project.

- **Documents** – Displays the Documents page where all interested parties can upload documents either to a specific project or to a public document library.

- **Admin** – Displays the Administration Overview page. Administrators use this menu to control and manage the Project Server environment.

- **Log Off** – Logs off the current user and displays the Project Server logon page.

- **Help** – Displays a context-sensitive Help window in a sidepane on the right side of Project Web Access pages.

Actions Pane

Most of the pages in Project Web Access include an actions pane or "sidepane" on the left side of the page. The links in each respective actions pane offer additional actions that you can take. Figure 5-3 shows the actions pane for the Home page, while Figure 5-4 shows the actions pane for View My Tasks page. Figures 5-5 and 5-6 show the actions pane for the Project Center and Resource Center pages respectively.

Keep in mind while viewing the figures that these are samples and that you may see the same menus in your system with slight variations. The selections may vary according to the way your Project Server administrator configures your system and change over time as you use the application. For instance, a link selection appears on some of these as soon as you use the custom link feature for the first time.

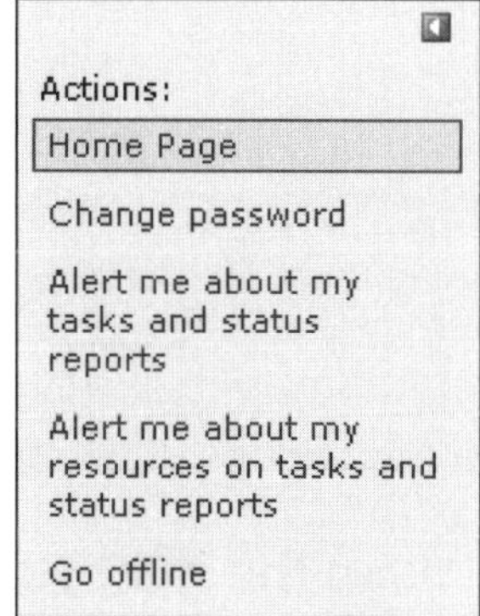

**Figure 5-3: Home page
actions pane**

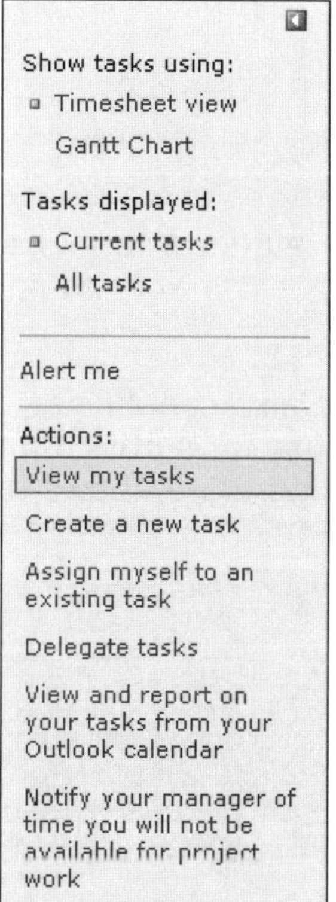

**Figure 5-4: View My Tasks
actions pane**

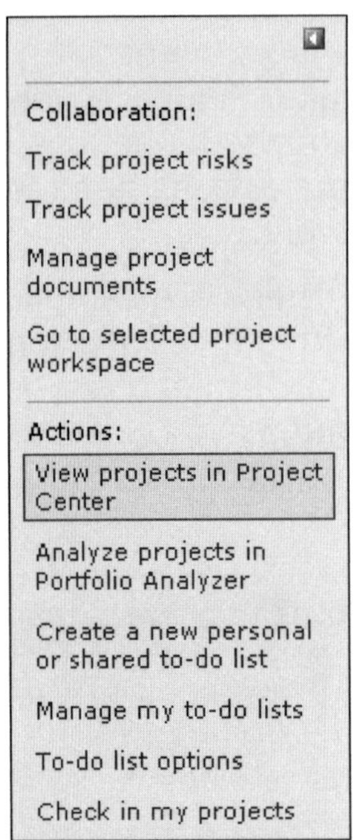

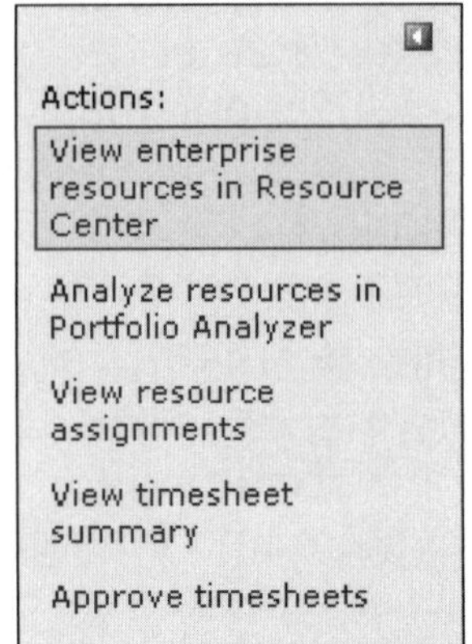

**Figure 5-6: Resource
Center actions pane**

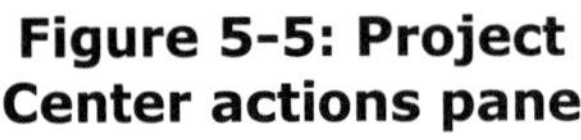

**Figure 5-5: Project
Center actions pane**

The Home page also contains an additional link on the right side of the page which you can use for setting up Project Web Access to work in conjunction with Outlook. Figure 5-7 shows the *Work with Outlook* link on the right side of the Home page

**Figure 5-7: Home page
option for using Outlook**

You can collapse the actions pane by clicking the blue and white arrow button in the upper right corner of the pane. Click this button again to expand the actions pane.

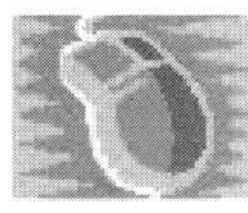

Hands On Exercise

Exercise 5-1

Explore the features of the Project Web Access user interface.

1. Launch your Internet Explorer.

2. Enter the URL of your organization's Project Web Access page.

3. Notice that the system logs you into Project Web Access automatically.

4. Notice the main content area of the Home page, along with the menu bar and the choices in the actions pane on the left.

5. Click the *Projects* item on the menu bar to display the Project Center page.

6. Notice the choices available in the actions pane for the Project Center page.

7. Collapse the actions pane on the Project Center page, and then expand the actions pane again.

Customization Tabs

Many pages in Project Web Access contain customization tabs at the top of the page, similar to the worksheet tabs found at the bottom of Excel workbooks. When you select each tab, it displays additional options for customizing the information presentation on the current page in Project Web Access.

For example, the View My Tasks page offers the *View Options* tab, the *Filter, Group, Search* tab, and the *Delegation* tab, as shown in Figure 5-8. Notice that all three tabs are collapsed.

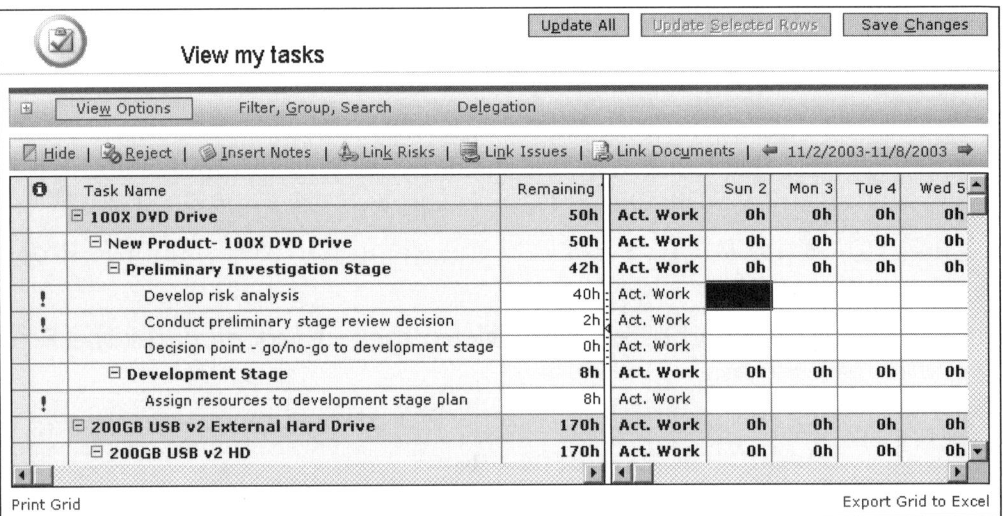

**Figure 5-8: View My Tasks page
with customization tabs collapsed**

You can expand any customization tab to reveal all of its options simply by clicking on it. Once expanded you collapse it by clicking the customization tab a second time. Figure 5-9 shows the expanded *View Options* tab for the View My Tasks page.

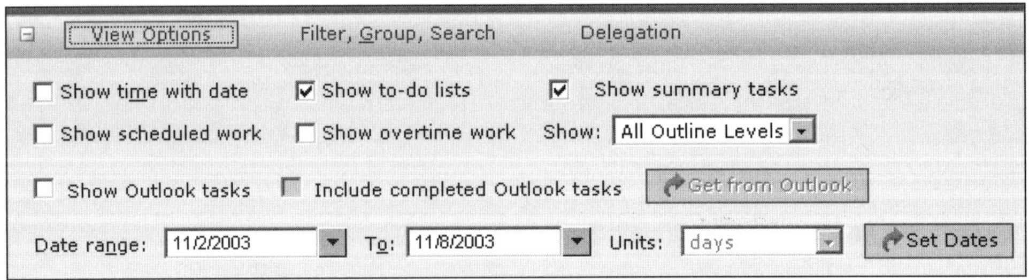

Figure 5-9: View Options tab expanded

The *View Options* tab offers you the option of viewing additional information on the current page. Two important viewing options on the View My Tasks page are the *Show scheduled work* and the *Show overtime work* options. These options allow you to view scheduled work, actual work, and overtime work in your timesheet.

Figure 5-10 shows the expanded *Filter, Group, Search* tab. As its name implies, this tab offers you the option of filtering, grouping, or searching the data shown on the current page.

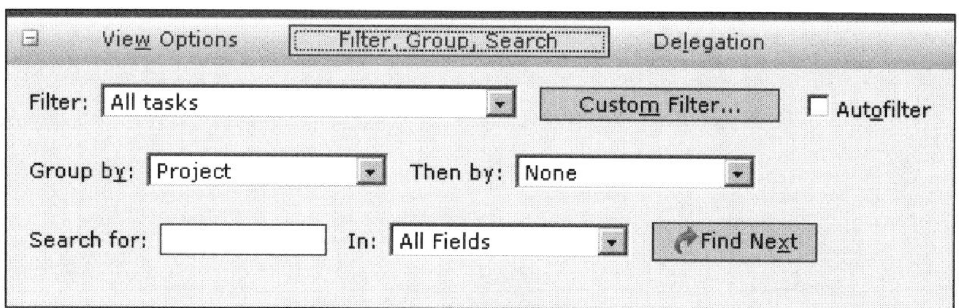

Figure 5-10: Filter, Group, Search tab expanded

The *Filter, Group, Search* tab allows you to use an existing filter or to create your own custom filter by clicking the *Custom Filter* button. In addition, you can apply autofiltering to the columns in the page, much the way the autofilter works in Excel. You can also apply grouping to the data on the page, using two levels of grouping. In Figure 5-10, notice that you can apply two levels of grouping by selecting values in the *Group by* and *Then by* pick lists. Finally, you can search through the information on the current page by entering the search text in the *Search For* field and then selecting the search fields.

Team members use the *Delegation* tab for the formal delegation of a task to a colleague. Figure 5-11 shows the *Delegation* tab on the View My Tasks page.

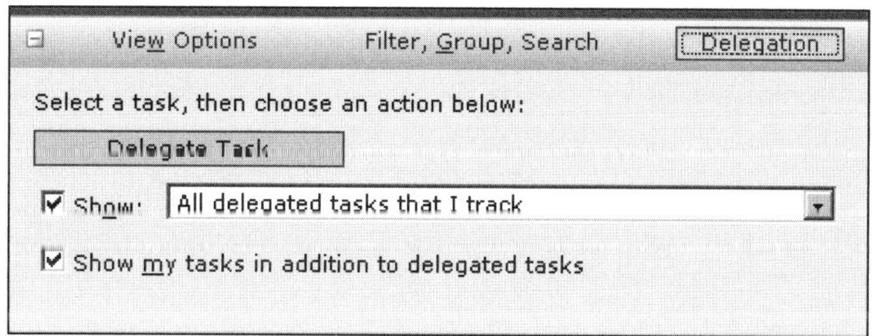

Figure 5-11: Delegation tab expanded

In addition to the *Delegate Task* button, which allows you to delegate a task to another team member, options are included to show delegated tasks and regular tasks.

Action Bar

Several pages in Project Web Access contain a data grid or "spreadsheet" in the center of the page, including the View My Tasks page, the Project Center and Resource Center pages, and the Updates page. There is a toolbar known as an action bar at the top of the grid on each of these pages. Each action bar offers you additional actions which are available to the currently-displayed grid. Figures 5-12 through 5-15 show the action bars for each of these pages.

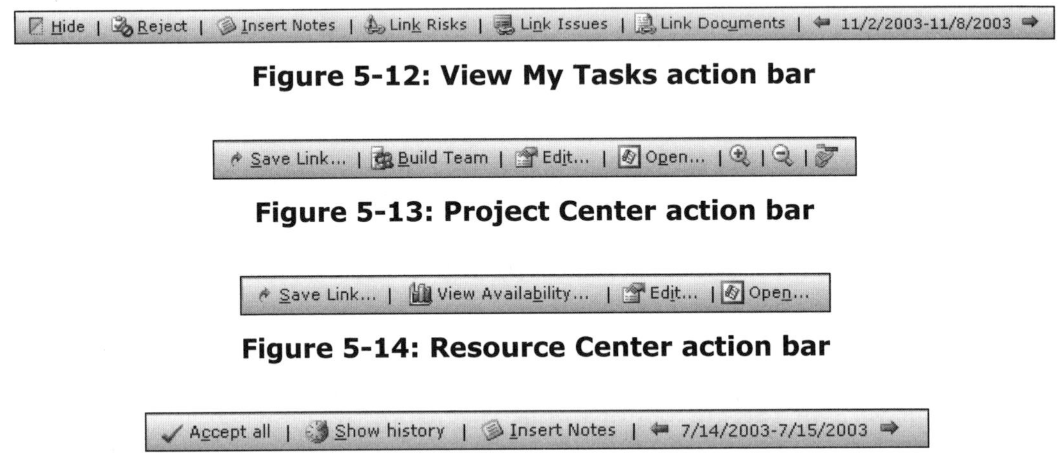

Figure 5-12: View My Tasks action bar

Figure 5-13: Project Center action bar

Figure 5-14: Resource Center action bar

Figure 5-15: Updates action bar

To use the action bar on any of these pages, simply select an item in the data grid and click the desired action button. For example, to link a document to a task on the View My Tasks page, select the desired task in the data grid and then click the *Link Documents* button on the action bar.

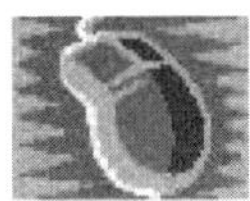

Hands On Exercise

Exercise 5-2

Explore the use of customization tabs and the action bar for the Project Center data grid.

1. Click the *Projects* item on the menu bar to display the Project Center page, if the page is not already displayed.

2. Click the *View Options* tab to expand the options and then study the available options.

3. Click the *Filter, Group, Search* tab to expand the options and then study the available options.

4. Click the *Group by pick* list and select the Owner item.

5. Notice how the system groups the projects by the Owner of each project.

6. Click the *Group by* pick list and select the *None* option.

7. Click the *Filter, Group, Search* tab again to collapse the options on that tab.

8. Notice the buttons on the action bar at the top of the data grid.

Manipulating the Data Grid

As was mentioned previously, a number of pages in Project Web Access contain a data grid or "spreadsheet" in which to display task, resource, and assignment data. For example, refer to the task grid on the View My Tasks page, as previously shown in Figure 5-8.

Some grids have a vertical split bar separating the grid into two sections, while other pages contain a single grid only. For example, in Figure 5-8, notice that the system divides the grid on the View My Tasks page into two sections: the task sheet to the left of the split bar, and the timesheet on the right. To work the data in the grid most effectively, it is important to know how to do the following actions:

- **Move the Split Bar:** You move the split bar in the grid, by floating your mouse pointer anywhere over the split bar itself. When the mouse pointer changes from a single arrow to a double-headed arrow, drag and drop the split bar to the new position on the screen. In Figure 5-16, I am dragging the split bar to the left of the Work Status column.

❶	Task Name	Work Status			Sun 23	Mon 24	Tue 25	Wed 26	Thu 27
	⊟ **100X DVD Drive**			**Work**	**0h**	**0h**	**0h**	**0h**	**0h**
				Act. Work	**0h**	**0h**	**0h**	**0h**	**0h**
	⊟ **Preliminary Investigation Stage**			**Work**	**0h**	**0h**	**0h**	**0h**	**0h**
				Act. Work	**0h**	**0h**	**0h**	**0h**	**0h**
	Perform financial evaluation			Work					
				Act. Work					
	⊟ **200GB USB v2 External Hard Drive**			**Work**	**0h**	**0h**	**0h**	**0h**	**0h**
				Act. Work	**0h**	**0h**	**0h**	**0h**	**0h**
	⊟ **200GB USB v2 HD**			**Work**	**0h**	**0h**	**0h**	**0h**	**0h**
				Act. Work	**0h**	**0h**	**0h**	**0h**	**0h**

**Figure 5-16: Dragging the split bar
to the left of the Work Status column**

- **Sort the Grid Data:** To sort the data in the grid, click the light blue column header at the top of the column. The first time you click the column header, the system automatically sorts data in the grid in ascending order based on the values in the selected column. To sort a column in descending order, click the column header a second time. I have applied a descending sort to the Work column in Figure 5-17.

ⓘ	Task Name	▽ Work	Work Status
	⊟ **100X DVD Drive**	**50h**	
	⊟ **Preliminary Investigation Stage**	**37h**	
✓	Develop risk analysis	35h	
✓	Conduct preliminary stage review decision	2h	
	Decision point - go/no-go to development stage	0h	

**Figure 5-17: Descending sort
applied to the Work column**

- **Change Column Widths**: To change the width of any column in the grid, position the mouse pointer over the right edge of the column header of the column whose width you wish to change. The mouse pointer will change from a single arrow to a double-headed arrow. Then click and hold the right edge of the column header, and drag the edge of the column to the proper width. Figure 5-18 shows that I am changing the column width of the Work column.

ⓘ	Task Name	▲ Work	Work Status
	⊟ **200GB USB v2 External Hard Drive**	**80h**	
	⊟ **200GB USB v2 HD**	**80h**	
	⊟ **Preliminary Investigation Stage**	**80h**	
!	Perform financial evaluation	80h	
	⊟ **Double Wide Ultra SCSI Hard Drive**	**80h**	

Figure 5-18: Widen the Work column

 To widen any column in the grid to "best fit" the data in the column, double-click the gridline on the right edge of the column.

- **Move Columns**: To move any column in the grid, click and hold the light blue column header of the column you wish to move, then drag the column and drop it in its new position in the grid. The system displays a thick black vertical line in the grid at each point where you can place the column. For example, I am dragging the Remaining Work column to a new position between the Task Name and Work columns in Figure 5-19.

ⓘ	Task Name	↔ Work	Work Status	Remaining Work
	⊟ 200GB USB v2 External Hard Drive	80h		80h
	⊟ 200GB USB v2 HD	80h		80h
	⊟ Preliminary Investigation Stage	80h		80h
!	Perform financial evaluation	80h		80h
	⊟ Double Wide Ultra SCSI Hard Drive	80h		80h

Figure 5-19: Remaining Work column dragged between the Task Name and Work columns

The system automatically saves any changes you make to the layout of a grid (such as column order, column width, etc.). These will reappear the next time you visit the page. The changes that you make will not impact the layout of the grid on anyone else's local computer.

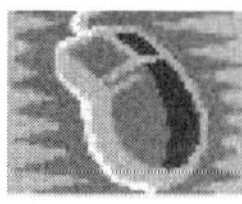

Hands On Exercise

Exercise 5-3

Manipulate the Project Center data grid.

1. Click the *Projects* item on the menu bar to display the Project Center page, if the page is not already displayed.

2. Pull the split bar to the far right side of the data grid so that you can see the Project Name, Duration, Start, and Finish fields.

3. Click the Project Name column head to apply ascending sorting on the data in the column.

4. Click the Project Name column header again to apply descending sorting on the data in the column.

5. Click the Start column header to apply ascending sorting on the column.

6. Narrow the column width of the Start column.

7. Move the Start column to the left of the Duration column.

8. Move the Start column back to its original position to the right of the Duration column.

Printing the Data Grid

Click the *Print Grid* link in the lower left corner of the grid page to print the data contained in the respective data grid. The Print Grid page opens in its own window, shown in Figure 5-20, allowing you to make the following selections before printing:

- Select the specific grid columns that you want to print
- Exclude any grid columns you do not wish to print
- Arrange the grid columns in the order you wish them to be printed
- Format the data in each of the grid columns

Each time you click the *Print Grid* link, the system displays the Arrange Columns pane by default, with all of the columns in the page pre-selected for printing. The Print Grid page contains three sections: a top pane for print settings, a toolbar, and a bottom pane for print preview.

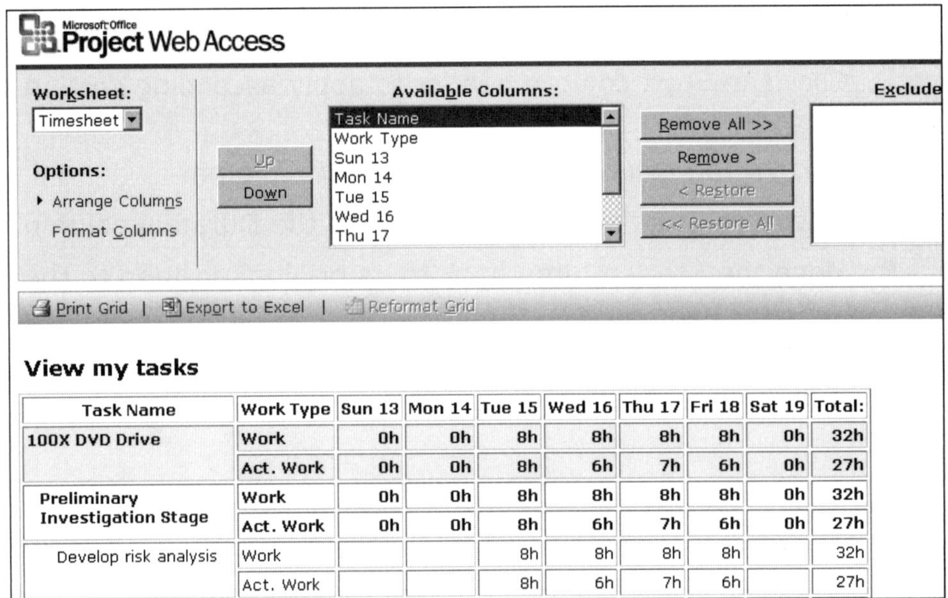

Task Name	Work Type	Sun 13	Mon 14	Tue 15	Wed 16	Thu 17	Fri 18	Sat 19	Total:
100X DVD Drive	Work	0h	0h	8h	8h	8h	8h	0h	32h
	Act. Work	0h	0h	8h	6h	7h	6h	0h	27h
Preliminary Investigation Stage	Work	0h	0h	8h	8h	8h	8h	0h	32h
	Act. Work	0h	0h	8h	6h	7h	6h	0h	27h
Develop risk analysis	Work			8h	8h	8h	8h		32h
	Act. Work			8h	6h	7h	6h		27h

**Figure 5-20: Print Grid page
for View My Tasks page**

The top pane in the Print Grid page contains the options for arranging and formatting the columns. On the left side of the top pane is an actions pane, offering links to display either the Arrange Columns or Format Columns panes.

In addition, the actions pane may also contain additional controls, such as the *Worksheet* pick list shown in Figure 5-21. In the Print Grid page for the View My Tasks page, the *Worksheet* pick list offers the option of printing either the Timesheet or the Task Sheet (Grid Data) portion of the grid.

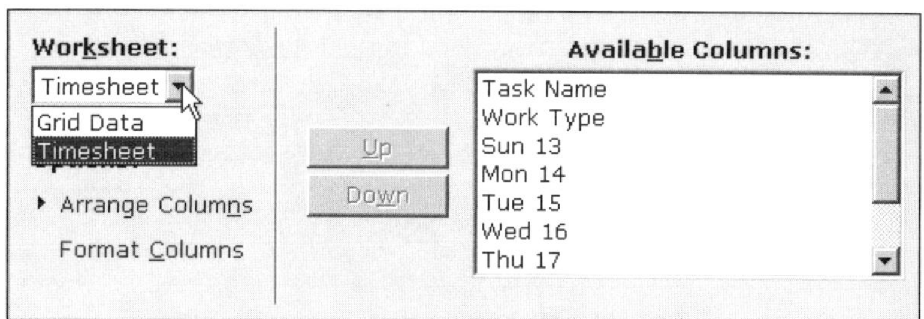

**Figure 5-21: Worksheet
printing options**

Because the system includes all columns for printing by default on the Print Grid page, you need only exclude those columns which you do not wish to print. To exclude a column, select any column in the Available Columns list, then click the *Remove* button. Figure 5-22 shows the columns for Sun 13 and Sat 19 excluded from printing. To change the order of columns to be printed, select the column(s) whose order you wish to change and click either the *Up* or *Down* button.

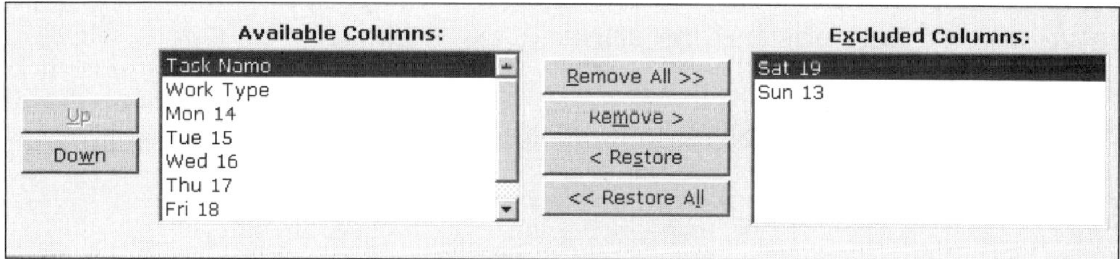

**Figure 5-22: Two columns
excluded from printing**

When you exclude columns from printing, or change the order of columns, you must also click the *Reformat Grid* button on the Print Grid toolbar to display the latest changes in the print preview pane. What you see in the print preview pane is what will print when you click the *Print Grid* button.

To format your print columns in the data grid, click the *Format Columns* link in the actions pane of the Print Grid page. The Format Columns options display in the top pane of the Print Grid page, as is shown in Figure 5-23. Options for formatting the columns in the data grid include setting column widths, data alignment, and text wrapping.

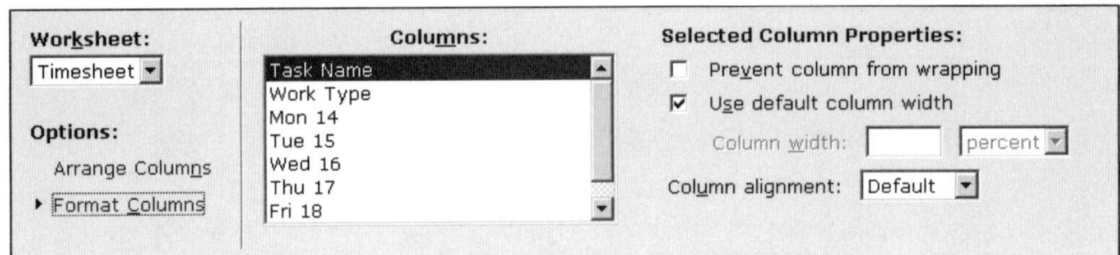

**Figure 5-23: Format Columns section
of the Print Grid page**

When you change the formatting of any columns in the grid, you must also click the *Reformat Grid* button on the Print Grid toolbar to display the latest formatting changes in the print preview pane.

Once you specify your exclusions and set the formatting of the columns in the data grid, you can print the grid by clicking the *Print Grid* button on the toolbar. This displays the Print dialog, shown in Figure 5-24, allowing you to finalize your print settings before printing.

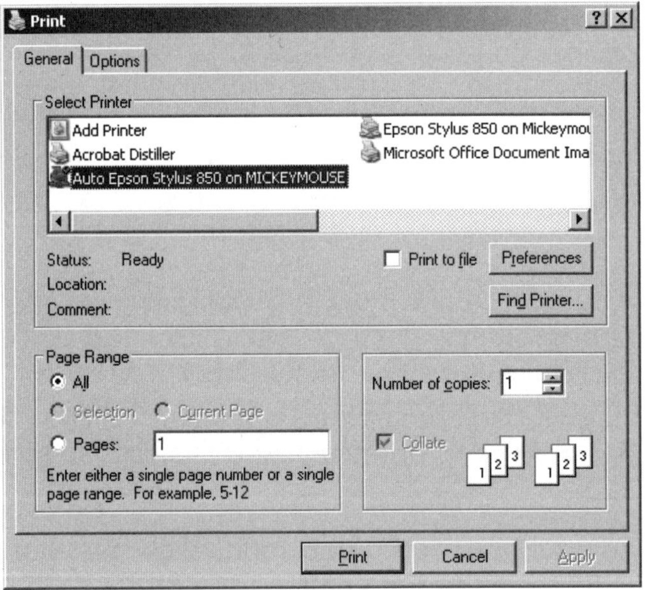

**Figure 5-24: Print dialog
on Print Grid page**

Exporting the Data Grid to Excel

In addition to printing the data grid, you can also export the data grid to an Excel workbook. You can accomplish this in two ways:

- Click the *Export to Excel* button on the toolbar while in the Print Grid page.

- Click the *Export to Excel* link in the lower right corner of the actual data grid.

Whichever method of exporting to Excel used will elicit a warning dialog about interacting with an ActiveX control shown in Figure 5-25. Click the *Yes* button to allow the interaction with the ActiveX control.

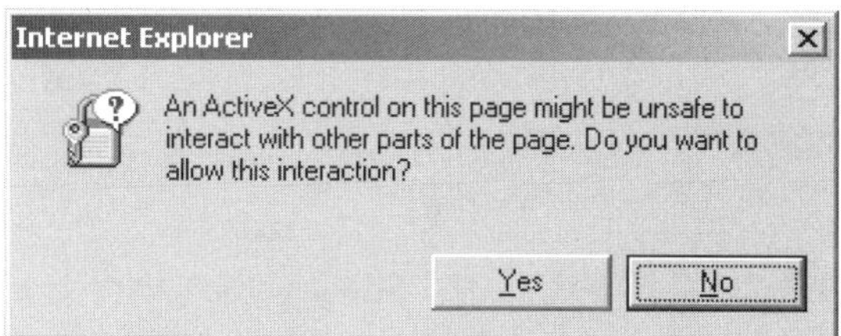

**Figure 5-25: ActiveX Control
warning dialog**

If you click the *No* button in the ActiveX warning dialog, you can choose to export your data to the clipboard instead. From the clipboard, you can save the data as an XML file, which you can open as an XML spreadsheet in Excel.

When you export the grid data to Excel, it is transferred as an XML workbook file containing one or more worksheets as appropriate to the selected data grid. The workbook in Figure 5-26 consists of two worksheets containing information exported from the View My Tasks page. These worksheets contain Timesheet information and the Task Sheet (Grid Data) respectively. The system automatically groups and outlines data in each worksheet for ease of use.

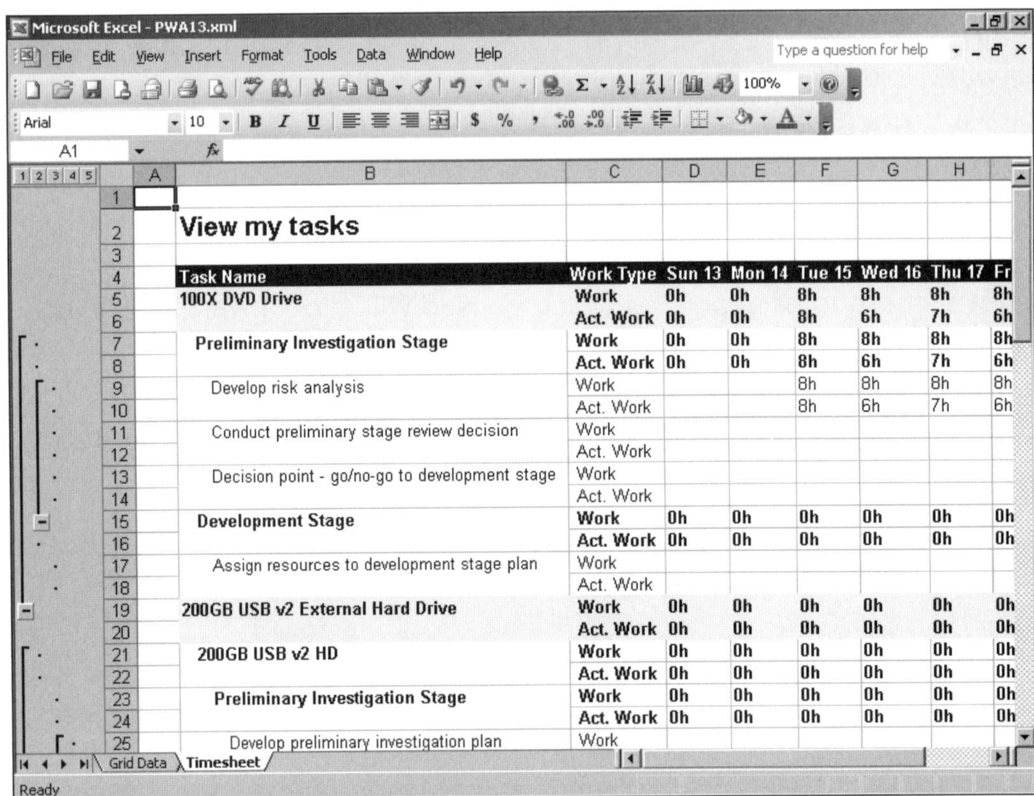

**Figure 5-26: Data grid exported to
Excel as an XML spreadsheet file**

Warning: When you export data in the grid to Excel from the Print Grid page, the exporting process ignores any column exclusions you have set for printing.

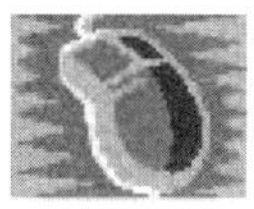

Hands On Exercise

Exercise 5-4

Print and export data in the Project Center data grid.

1. Click the *Projects* item on the menu bar to display the Project Center page, if the page is not already displayed.

2. Click the *Print Grid* link in the lower left corner of the data grid.

3. Maximize the Print Grid window.

4. Select the Owner field in the Available Columns list and then click the *Remove* button.

5. Click the *Reformat Grid* button.

6. If you are connected to a printer, click the *Print Grid* button and print the data grid information.

7. Click the *Export to Excel* button.

8. Examine the data grid information in the Excel workbook.

9. Close the Excel workbook, exit Excel, and then close the Print Grid window.

Module 06

Tracking Progress through Project Web Access

Learning Objectives

After completing this module, you will be able to:

- Report progress on tasks
- Understand timesheet indicators
- Manipulate View options
- Filter, group, and search in the timesheet
- Change displays between the Timesheet and Gantt Chart views
- Insert a Note on a task
- Propose a new task to your manager
- Reject a task
- Hide a task
- Delegate a task and take a lead role in managing a task
- Link risks, issues, and documents to tasks
- Notify your manager of nonworking time

Working with Tasks in Project Web Access

When you log on to Project Web Access, your personal Home page alerts you to any new task assignments you've received. In figure 6-1, you can see that Keith Harris has four new tasks assigned to him. These four new tasks are the result of a project manager, or managers, publishing New and Changed Assignments in a project.

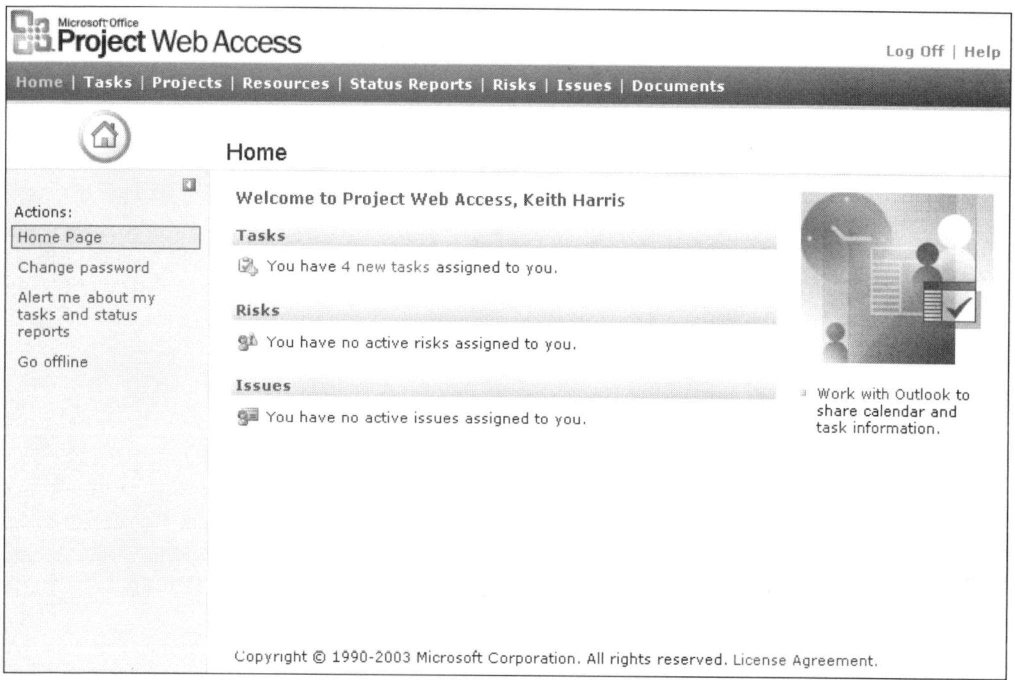

**Figure 6-1: Project Web Access
Home page**

To view your task assignments in the View My Tasks page, use one of the following methods:

- Click the *Tasks* menu at the top of the page.

- Click the *Tasks* link in the information center of the page.

- Click the ___ *new tasks* link in the Tasks section of the page.

When you select any of these, the system displays the View My Tasks page, as shown in Figure 6-2. In the figure, notice the actions pane on the left side of the page. The links in the top half allow you to choose between a Timesheet view and a Gantt Chart view. The lower section lists all of the task activities available to you in the View My Tasks page. As a resource on a project, here is where you access most of the functions that comprise the core daily work management routine. The functions in the toolbar and the options in the customization tabs augment the activities in the actions pane. At the heart of this display is the time entry grid itself, which is where resources enter their time and periodically send updates to managers.

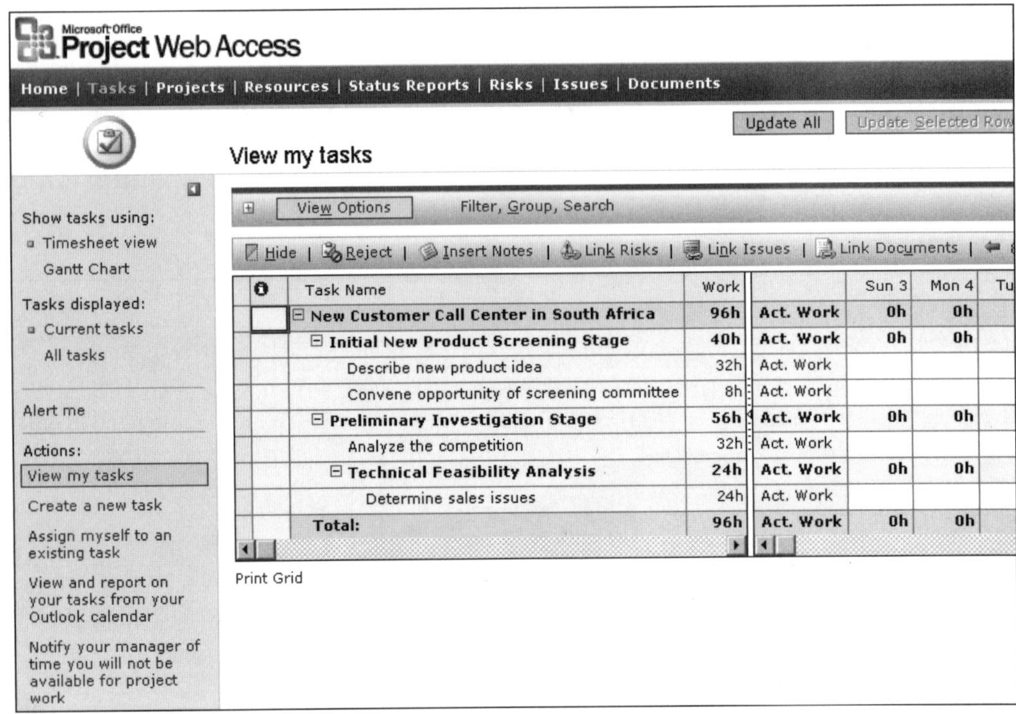

❶	Task Name	Work			Sun 3	Mon 4	Tu
	⊟ **New Customer Call Center in South Africa**	96h	Act. Work		0h	0h	
	⊟ **Initial New Product Screening Stage**	40h	Act. Work		0h	0h	
	Describe new product idea	32h	Act. Work				
	Convene opportunity of screening committee	8h	Act. Work				
	⊟ **Preliminary Investigation Stage**	56h	Act. Work		0h	0h	
	Analyze the competition	32h	Act. Work				
	⊟ **Technical Feasibility Analysis**	24h	Act. Work		0h	0h	
	Determine sales issues	24h	Act. Work				
	Total:	96h	Act. Work		0h	0h	

Figure 6-2: View My Tasks page
Timesheet view

You access all of the task tracking functions from the View My Tasks page, which includes the following:

- Report progress on project tasks according to the tracking method selected for the organization or for the individual project.

- Reject tasks assigned to you by a manager.

- Delegate tasks to other resources.

- Create new tasks for approval by a manager.

- Assign existing tasks to yourself.

- Insert Notes on tasks to communicate additional information to the project manager.

- Link documents, issues, and risks to tasks.

- Manage project task assignments in Outlook.

- Send work day changes to managers who need to react to scheduling changes.

- View and interact with assignment information, and receive updates and progress information requests from managers.

All of these functional areas support the sharing of project information. Progress reporting, task rejections, and task delegations generate immediate communication events between a resource and the manager of the affected task or tasks. Project Server 2003 directs all of these change events to the project manager(s) who act as a gatekeeper for all plan-changing transactions. Inserting Notes, documents, and issues adds a more passive informational flow to the collaborative process.

Understanding the Timesheet

All users of Project Web Access within your organization should be well versed in using the Timesheet view, because everyone in your organization could potentially become a project team member with task assignments. At the very least, make sure that anyone who will have assignment work in the system knows how to use the timesheet.

Timesheet indicators

The Indicators that appear in the column on the left side of the task list alert you to task status, and show you which tasks have associated notes, risks, issues, and documents. Table 6-1 shows the task status indicators that you will commonly see in this column.

To understand the meaning of any indicator, simply float your mouse pointer over the indicator to display a tool tip with an explanation of the indicator.

Indicator	Description
	Task is new from manager or newly delegated task
	Task is overdue
	Task has update pending
	Task was updated by the manager
	Task was rejected by the manager
	Task is complete
	Progress information is requested by the manager
	Task delegation requested
	Task delegation approved
	Task delegation approved with actuals to be submitted to the delegator
	Task has Notes
	Task has linked Risks
	Task has linked Issues
	Task has linked Documents
	Task is new but not sent to manager
	Task is new but not yet approved
	Task is new and self-assigned by resource
	Task is a new self-assignment by a resource, but not yet approved
	Task has been cancelled by the manager

Table 6-1: Indicator descriptions

Understanding the Timesheet Toolbar

The toolbar shown in Figure 6-3 provides access to a number of functions, including the following:

- **Hide** removes tasks from your timesheet.

- **Reject** sends a task rejection for a selected task.

- **Insert Notes** allows you to add notes to tasks.

- **Link Risks** allows you to create and link risks to tasks.

- **Link Issues** allows you to create and link issues to tasks.

- **Link Documents** allows you to link documents to tasks.

- **Date Range** selector allows you to set the date range for the display.

Figure 6-3: Timesheet toolbar

Activities Available from the Actions Pane

The activities available in the actions pane on the View My Tasks page are as follows:

- **View My Tasks** refreshes the current view selected, whether it is the Timesheet or Gantt Chart view.

- **Create a New Task** opens the Create New Task wizard.

- **Assign myself to an existing Task** opens the Assign Myself to an Existing Task wizard.

- **View and report on your tasks from your Outlook Calendar** allows you to transfer nonworking time from your Outlook calendar.

- **Notify Your Manager of time you will not be available for project work** allows you to submit nonworking time such as vacation and sick leave to your manager.

View Options

Click the *View Options* tab at the top of the timesheet display to control the data set displayed in the grid based on standard criteria, by date range, and by type. Expanding the tab reveals the options shown in Figure 6-4. The options that you control on this tab are as follows:

- **Show time with date** determines whether to display both dates and times, or dates only, in the grid.

- **Show to-do lists** determines whether to display to-do list tasks in the timesheet.

- **Show summary tasks** determines whether to display summary tasks for each task assignment.

- **Show scheduled work** determines whether to display scheduled work values in the timesheet portion of the data grid.

- **Show overtime work** determines whether to display the Actual Overtime Work field in the timesheet portion of the data grid.

- **Show** allows you to expand or collapse the Outline Level of the tasks displayed in the grid.

- **Show Outlook Tasks** and **Include completed Outlook Tasks** allows you to display your Outlook tasks in your Project Web Access timesheet and to selectively include completed tasks.

- **Date Range** fields allow you to change the date range of the display.

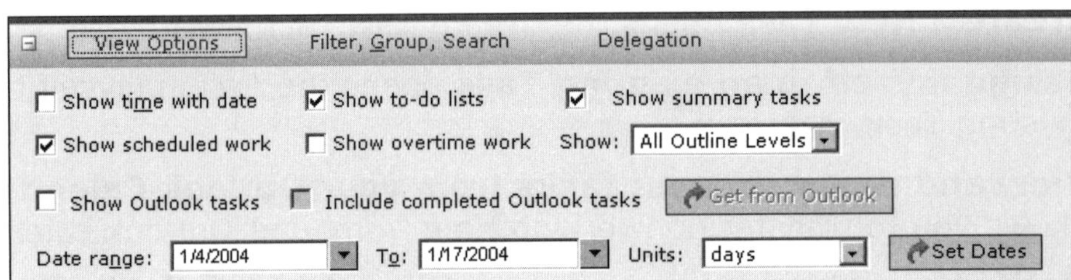

Figure 6-4: Expanded View Options tab

Selecting both the *Show scheduled work* and *Show overtime work* options causes the display to change as shown in Figure 6-5.

❶	Task Name		3/14	3/15	3/16	3/17	3/18	3/19
	⊟ **Analysis**	**Work**	**0h**	**6h**	**8h**	**4h**	**6h**	**7h**
		Act. Work	**0h**	**6h**	**8h**	**4h**	**6h**	**7h**
		Act. Ovt. Work	**0h**	**0h**	**0h**	**0h**	**0h**	**0h**
✓	Review network environment	Work		6h	8h	4h	6h	7h
		Act. Work		6h	8h	4h	6h	7h
		Act. Ovt. Work						
	Identify improvements to network environment	Work						
		Act. Work						
		Act. Ovt. Work						
	⊟ **Design**	**Work**	**0h**	**0h**	**0h**	**0h**	**0h**	**0h**
		Act. Work	**0h**	**0h**	**0h**	**0h**	**0h**	**0h**
		Act. Ovt. Work	**0h**	**0h**	**0h**	**0h**	**0h**	**0h**

**Figure 6-5: View includes both Scheduled
Work and Actual Overtime Work**

You should only use the *Show overtime work* option if your organization tracks overtime work.

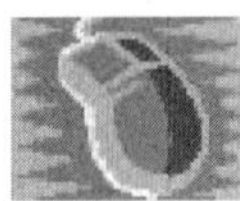

Hands On Exercise

Exercise 6-1

Explore the *View Options* tab on the View My Tasks page of Project Web Access.

1. Log into Project Web Access using the credentials provided by your instructor.

2. Display the View My Tasks page.

3. Click the *View Options* tab.

4. Experiment with each of the available options.

Filtering, Grouping and Searching the Timesheet View

Besides all the view options you can control, you can apply filtering and grouping to your timesheet tasks and you can search through your timesheet tasks to quickly locate specific assignments. Click the *Filter, Group, Search* tab to reveal the options shown in Figure 6-6.

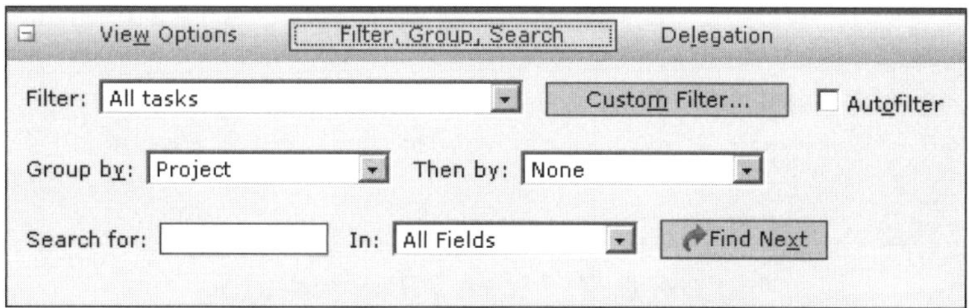

**Figure 6-6: Timesheet view with
Filter, Group, Search tab expanded**

Project Web Access offers you a number of predefined filters on the *Filter* pick list, including:

- All tasks (the default filter)
- Overdue tasks
- Newly assigned tasks
- Completed tasks
- Incomplete tasks
- New tasks added by me
- New assignments added by me
- Tasks deleted by manager
- Tasks changed by a manager
- Tasks pending manager's approval

Click the *Custom Filter* button to filter the task list temporarily. Using the More Filters dialog, you can combine up to three filter tests on fields in the data grid to restrict the data shown in the view. In Figure 6-7, I am selecting the Project Manager field for a filter that will display tasks from only a certain project manager.

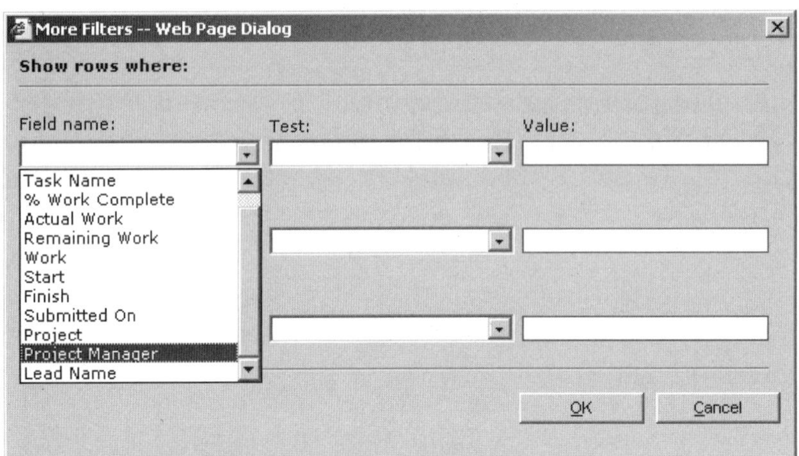

Figure 6-7: More Filters dialog

The default display grouping in the timesheet is by Project and the system presents all tasks first by project and then by summary task. You can specify your own grouping requirements. The system allows you to select two levels of grouping using the following fields in the *Group by* and *Then by* pick lists:

- Task Name
- % Work Complete
- Actual work
- Remaining Work
- Work
- Start
- Finish
- Submitted On
- Project
- Project Manager
- Lead Name

If you publish additional fields using Tools ➤ Customize ➤ Published Fields, and your Project Server administrator includes these fields in the Timesheet view, then these additional fields will also appear on the *Group by* and *Then by* pick lists.

The system provides you with a textual search feature in the timesheet. You can enter a sequence of characters consisting of partial words or whole words and search for the characters in the timesheet. Click the *Find Next* button to activate the search. The system highlights each matching task one instance at a time. You must continue to click the *Find Next* button to locate each additional match.

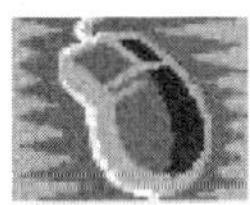 **Hands On Exercise**

Exercise 6-2

Explore the *Filter, Group, Search* tab on the View My Tasks page of Project Web Access.

1. Make sure you have displayed the View My Tasks page.

2. Click the *Filter, Group, Search* tab.

3. Select several different filters from the list and apply them, then observe the results.

4. Click the *Custom Filter* button and use the More Filters dialog to build a custom filter.

5. Experiment with the Group By selections.

6. Use the Search feature to find a task.

Displaying the Gantt Chart View

The Gantt Chart selection in the View My Tasks page allows you to select a traditional Gantt style presentation of your tasks. As shown in Figure 6-8, most of the toolbar and option tabs available in the Timesheet view are also available in the Gantt Chart view. The main difference is that you cannot track progress with the Gantt Chart view when you are tracking hours by period.

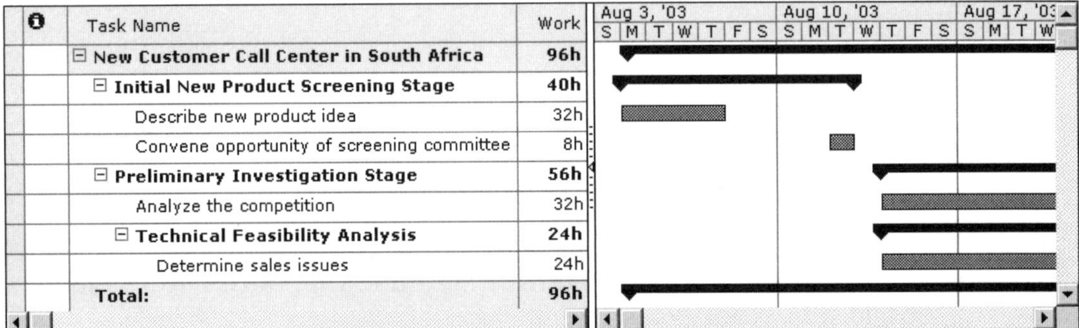

Figure 6-8: Gantt Chart view
View My Tasks page

If your organization uses either the Percent of Work Complete or the Actual Work Done and Work Remaining method of reporting progress, you can use the Gantt Chart view to update your managers. If your organization uses the Hours of Work Done Per Day or Per Week method of tracking progress, then you will not be able to use the Gantt Chart view to track progress and must use the Timesheet view instead.

Current Tasks vs. All Tasks

Another feature of the View My Tasks page is the option to display Current Tasks or All Tasks in your timesheet. This option is sometimes a source of frustration for users who do not understand how Project Web Access defines a "current" task. A "current" task is any task that:

- Should have started before today

- Has started already but is not yet completed

- Starts within the next 10 days (or within the time period specified by your Project Server administrator as a current task)

If you select the *Current Tasks* option, but **do not** see a particular task that you know should be on your timesheet, it may not be a "current" task. Click the *All Tasks* option to see every task on your timesheet.

Reporting Progress in the Timesheet

Your organization uses progress reporting to capture the current state of your assignment work on each task. Your project manager uses the task progress you report to determine the current state of the project. For every organization, accurately tracking project progress is vital to the success of any project.

You report task progress in the View My Tasks page of Project Web Access. Depending on your organization's default method of tracking progress, you enter progress in one of three ways:

- If your organization uses the Percent of Work Complete method, enter progress in the % Work Complete and Remaining Work columns.

- If your organization uses the Actual Work Done and Work Remaining method, enter progress in the Actual Work and Remaining Work columns.

- If your organization uses the Hours of Work Done per Day or per Week method, enter progress in the Actual Work cells in the timesheet for the day or week during which you performed the work, and enter your remaining work in the Remaining Work column.

Setting Up the Timesheet to Enter Actuals

To use the Hours of Work Done per Day or per Week method for tracking progress most effectively, I suggest that you first customize the setup of the View My Tasks page. To do this, complete the following steps:

1. Click the *View Options* tab to expand the list of options.

2. Select the *Show scheduled work* option.

3. Select the *Show summary tasks* option, if it is not already displayed.

Displaying summary tasks in the timesheet can help you to distinguish between two tasks that have the same name in the same project.

4. Click the *View Options* tab again to collapse the tab options.

5. Drag and drop the Remaining Work field (column) from its present location to a new location to the right of the Task Name column.

6. Adjust the column widths of any column, if necessary.

7. Scroll the timesheet to the first day of the reporting period.

In Figure 6-9, I have set up my View My Tasks page according to the steps detailed above.

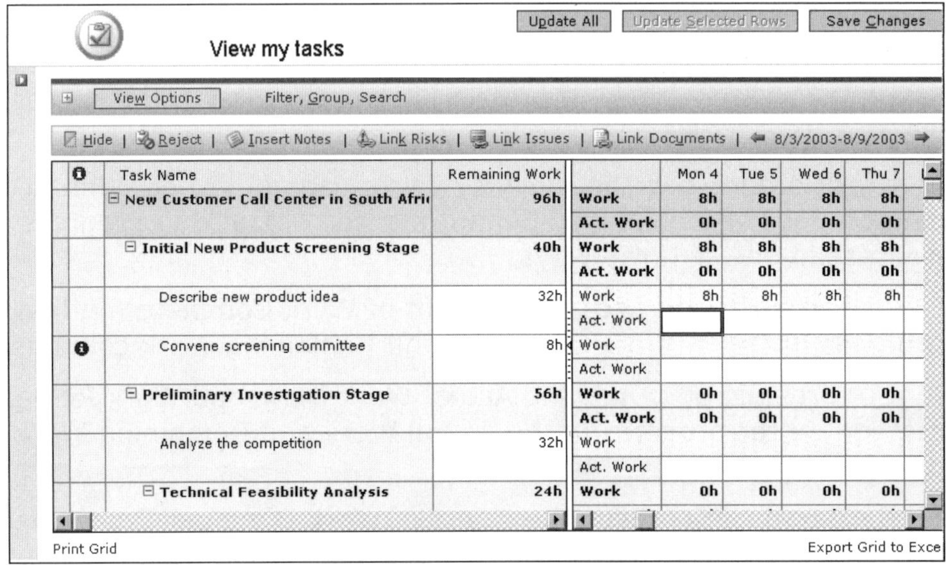

**6-9: View My Tasks page
prepared for progress reporting**

Entering and Submitting Progress

After you have set up the View My Tasks page for easy entry, you can begin the formal process of entering and submitting progress. Suggested best practices include:

- Enter Actual Work values in the Timesheet on a **daily basis** for each task on which you have worked.

- Save your changes at the end of each day by clicking the *Save Changes* button (doing so will save the actuals without sending them to the project manager).

- Adjust the Remaining Work value at the end of the week if you believe you have more work or less work than the Timesheet has calculated for the task.

- If you change the Remaining Work value for any task, document the reason for making the change by clicking the *Insert Notes* button and adding a note.

- If you need to add any type of project documentation, such as a Word or Excel file, click the *Link Documents* button and upload the document to the Documents library for the project.

- If you need to add any type of formal Issue documentation to the task, click the *Link Issues* button and add the issue to the Issue list for the project.

- If you have discovered any previously unknown risks to either the task or to the project as a whole, click the *Link Risks* button and document the risk.

- Submit your progress to the manager at the end of the week or as otherwise required by your organization by clicking either the *Update Selected Rows* or the *Update All* buttons at the top of the View My Tasks page.

As a best practice, MSProjectExperts recommends that you enter actuals on a **daily** basis and update them to your manager on a **weekly** basis.

When you enter progress in the timesheet, the system formats the numbers in red as you enter them. The numbers will remain formatted in red until the manager has updated your progress into the project plan, saved the project plan, and then republished the project plan. You also see indicators in the Indicators column to remind you of the status of your progress.

In Figure 6-10, I entered progress on the task Describe new product idea. I entered 8 hours of work each day from Monday through Wednesday, and entered 6 hours of work on Thursday.

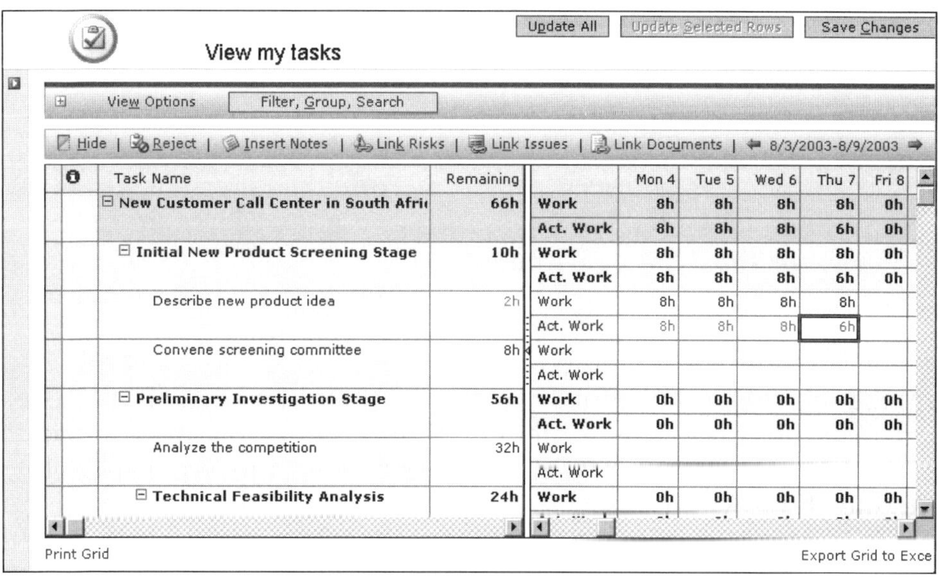

	Task Name	Remaining			Mon 4	Tue 5	Wed 6	Thu 7	Fri 8
	New Customer Call Center in South Afric	66h	Work		8h	8h	8h	8h	0h
			Act. Work		8h	8h	8h	6h	0h
	Initial New Product Screening Stage	10h	Work		8h	8h	8h	8h	0h
			Act. Work		8h	8h	8h	6h	0h
	Describe new product idea	2h	Work		8h	8h	8h	8h	
			Act. Work		8h	8h	8h	6h	
	Convene screening committee	8h	Work						
			Act. Work						
	Preliminary Investigation Stage	56h	Work		0h	0h	0h	0h	0h
			Act. Work		0h	0h	0h	0h	0h
	Analyze the competition	32h	Work						
			Act. Work						
	Technical Feasibility Analysis	24h	Work		0h	0h	0h	0h	0h

**Figure 6-10: Task progress
entered in the timesheet**

In the previous figure, the system calculates that I have 2 hours of Remaining Work on this task. However, I finished early so I no longer need the two hours of Remaining Work. To show that I finished early, I enter a zero (0) in the Remaining Work column, as shown in Figure 6-11. Notice that the Indicators column shows a blue check mark representing a completed task.

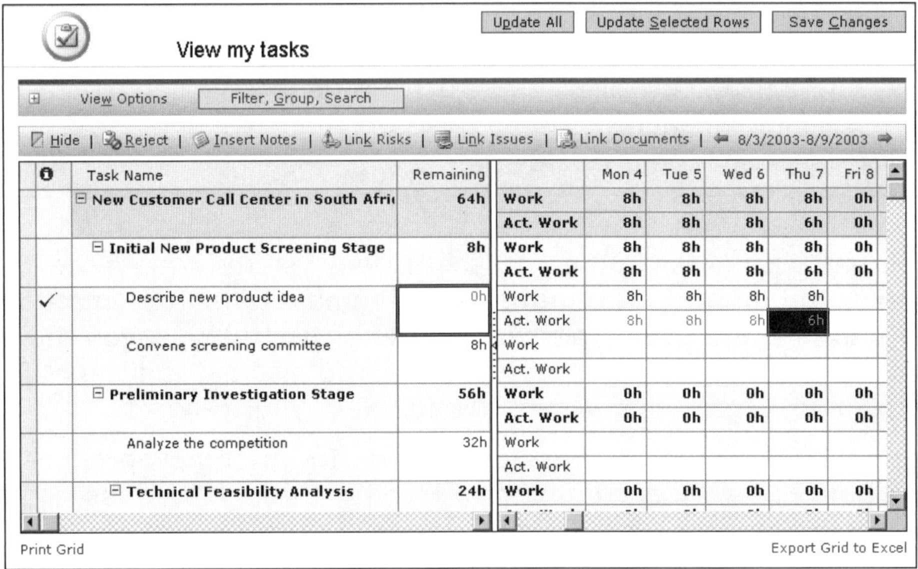

ⓘ	Task Name	Remaining		Mon 4	Tue 5	Wed 6	Thu 7	Fri 8
	⊟ New Customer Call Center in South Afric	64h	Work	8h	8h	8h	8h	0h
			Act. Work	8h	8h	8h	6h	0h
	⊟ Initial New Product Screening Stage	8h	Work	8h	8h	8h	8h	0h
			Act. Work	8h	8h	8h	6h	0h
✓	Describe new product idea	0h	Work	8h	8h	8h	8h	
			Act. Work	8h	8h	8h	6h	
	Convene screening committee	8h	Work					
			Act. Work					
	⊟ Preliminary Investigation Stage	56h	Work	0h	0h	0h	0h	0h
			Act. Work	0h	0h	0h	0h	0h
	Analyze the competition	32h	Work					
			Act. Work					
	⊟ Technical Feasibility Analysis	24h	Work	0h	0h	0h	0h	0h

**Figure 6-11: Adjust Remaining Work
to 0 hours to shown an early finish**

The Remaining Work field displays in the timesheet regardless of tracking method. Remaining work is an important input for any task that finishes with more or less work than originally predicted.

Because I adjusted the Remaining Work value, I also need to add a task Note to document the reason for adjusting the number. To add a task Note, click the *Insert Note* button on the toolbar. I have entered my note in the Project Web Access Assignment Notes dialog, as shown in Figure 6-12. Click the *OK* button to add the Note to the task.

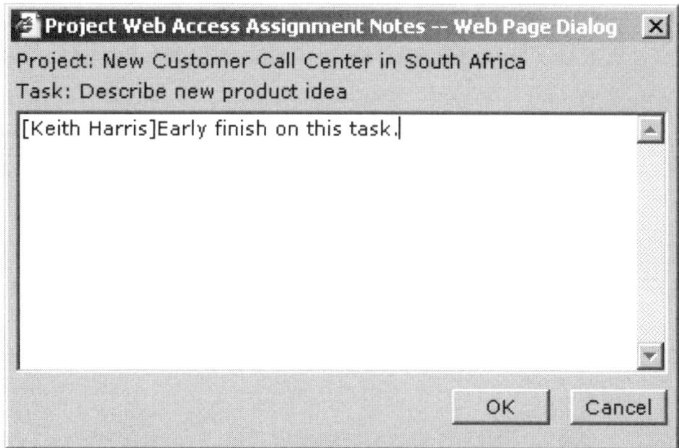

Figure 6-12: Enter a task Note

To submit task progress to your manager, click the *Update All* button. You can also perform this action selectively by first selecting one or more task rows in the grid for which you have entered progress and then click the *Update Selected Rows* button. When you use either method, the system submits the task progress to your manager and a Project Web Access dialog notifies you that your update succeeded, as displayed in Figure 6-13.

**Figure 6-13: Updates sent
to the manager**

If you are not ready to update progress to your manager, click the *Save Changes* button to save your entries. The system will store your entries until you are ready to send them. The system confirms your save as shown in Figure 6-14.

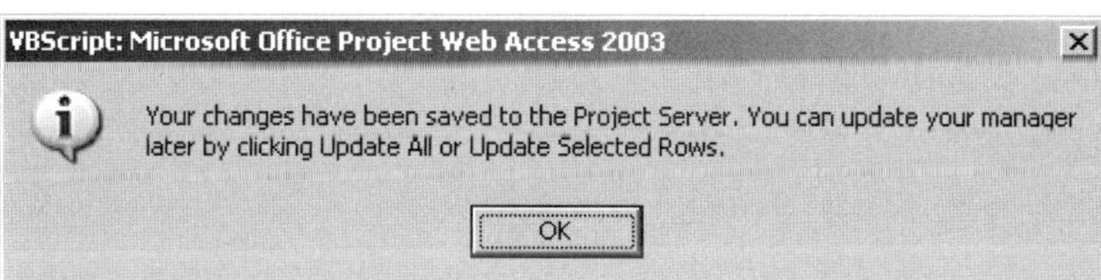

Figure 6-14: Time entries saved

Hands On Exercise

Exercise 6-3

Enter progress in the Timesheet and update the manager.

1. Make sure you have displayed the View My Tasks page.
2. Select the Timesheet display, if not currently displayed.
3. Make time entries into your current tasks.
4. Click the *Save Changes* button to save the hourly entries without updating the manager.
5. Click the *Update All* button to send the updates to the manager.
6. Click the *OK* button when prompted.

Using Other Task Activities

Along with reporting progress, other important task-related activities in the View My Tasks page include:

- Rejecting tasks
- Delegating tasks
- Creating new tasks
- Assigning yourself to tasks

Rejecting a Task

Rejecting a task or tasks through the timesheet is very simple. Highlight the task rows that you want to reject and click the *Reject* button in the toolbar. The system first displays a warning and confirmation alert as shown in Figure 6-15.

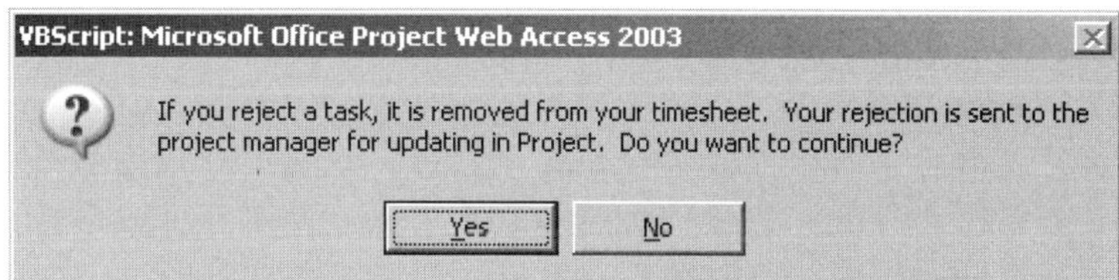

Figure 6-15: Task rejection warning

If you click the *Yes* button, the system then removes any rejected tasks from your timesheet and sends a notification to the project managers for the affected tasks as shown in Figure 6-16.

Figure 6-16: Task rejections notification

Once you click the *Yes* button, you have "passed the point of no return" and the system removes the task from your timesheet. Your manager may choose to reject your task rejection, thereby republishing the task and making it reappear on your timesheet. If your manager approves your task rejection and removes you from the task, it will no longer appear on your timesheet.

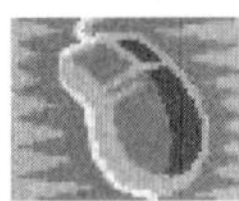 **Hands On Exercise**

Exercise 6-4

Reject a task assignment from the project manager.

1. Make sure you have displayed the View My Tasks page.
2. Select the Timesheet display, if not currently displayed.
3. Select a task without actual reported hours in the timesheet.
4. Click the *Reject* button in the toolbar.
5. Click Yes when the warning dialog displays.
6. Click the *OK* button when prompted.

Delegating a Task

Before you can delegate a task, you must expand the *Delegation* tab by clicking it, or by clicking the *Delegate tasks* link from the actions pane. The *Delegation* tab contains the necessary functions to delegate tasks, along with the view options relating to delegated tasks, as shown in Figure 6-17.

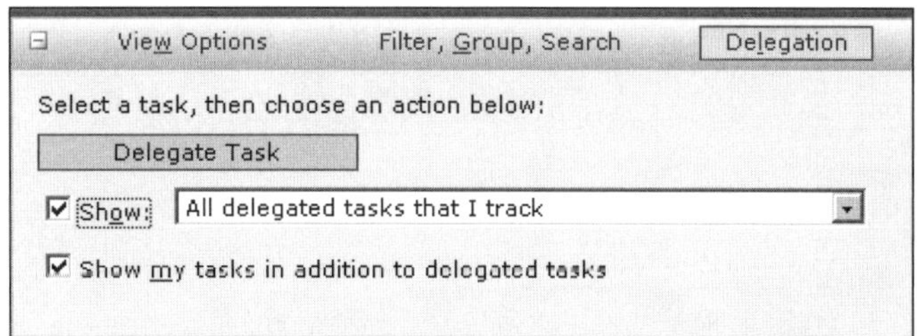

Figure 6-17: Delegation tab expanded

The Show delegated tasks selector on the *Delegation* tab gives you three choices:

- All delegated tasks that I track

- All delegated tasks that I am the Lead for

- All delegated tasks that I track but am not the Lead for

Additionally, you may choose to show or not show your regular tasks along with the tasks that you have delegated. You may selectively display delegated tasks only. To delegate a task, select the task that you want to delegate, and then click the *Delegate Task* button. The system opens the Task Delegation page shown in Figure 6-18.

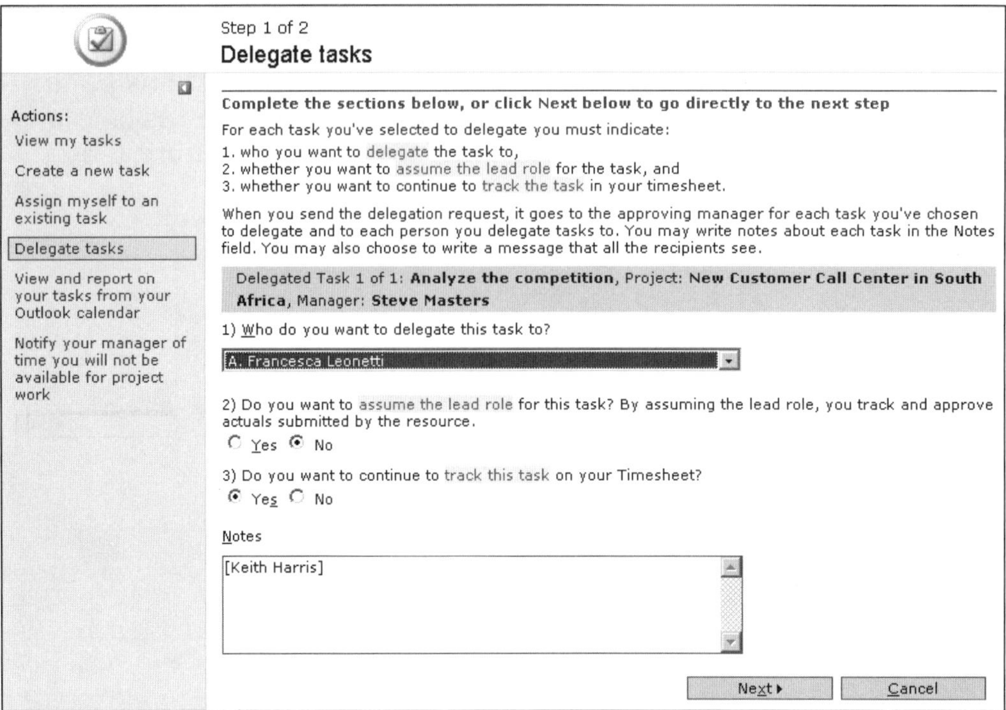

Figure 6-18: Task delegation - Step 1

On the Step 1 page, you must select the person to whom to delegate the task, choose whether to assume the lead role for the delegation, and select whether to track the task in your timesheet. You should also enter a task Note to document the reason for the delegation.

If you assume the Lead Role for the task delegation, the person to whom you delegate the task will update task progress to you. You must review and approve their task progress, and update it to your manager. In a sense, you become an intermediary in the process of updating and approving task progress. You must have security permission in the Project Server system to assume a lead role.

Once you have made your selections, click the *Next* button at the bottom of the page to continue to the Step 2 page shown in Figure 6-19. You may also click the *Cancel* button to abandon the delegation process. On the Step 2 page, the system displays a summary of the actions you are about to process. This page is your last opportunity to make changes to your task delegation or cancel the action entirely. Click the *Send* button to send the delegation proposal to the other resource and to the manager responsible.

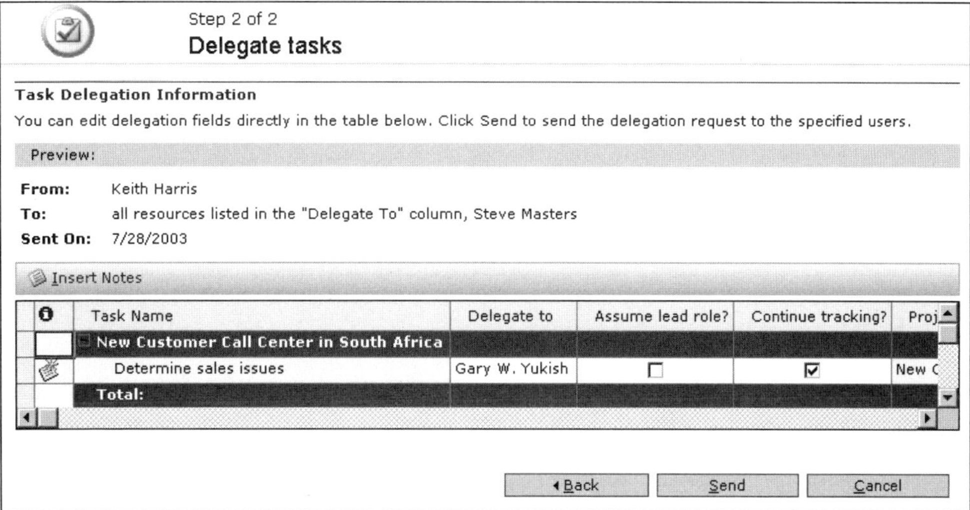

Figure 6-19: Task delegation step 2

After you click Send, the system confirms your successful delegation request as shown in Figure 6-20.

Figure 6-20: Delegation confirmation

Hands On Exercise

Exercise 6-5

Delegate a task assignment to another team member.

1. Make sure you have displayed the View My Tasks page.
2. Select the Timesheet display, if not currently displayed.
3. Click the *Delegation* tab.
4. Select a task in the timesheet and click the *Delegate Task* button.
5. Select a person to whom to delegate the task.
6. Leave the next two options at their defaults.
7. Add a note to the delegated task.
8. Click the *Send* button when the preview screen displays.
9. Click the *OK* button when prompted.

Creating a New Task

Team members can create and propose new tasks to their project managers through Project Web Access. Whereas the system sends task delegation requests to the project manager the moment you create them, creating new tasks is an explicit two-step process:

1. Create the new task.

2. Update the new task to the project manager for approval.

To create the new task, click the *Create a new task* link in the actions pane. The system opens the Create a New Task page as shown in Figure 6-21.

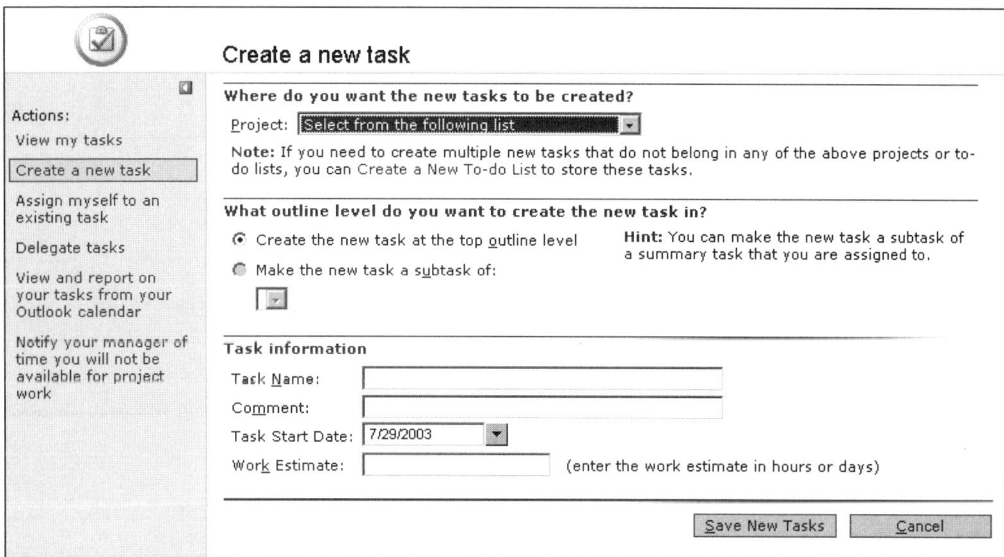

Figure 6-21: Create a New Task page

The *Project* pick list at the top of the page allows you to select an existing project or To-Do list. In the second section of the page, select the outline level for the new task in the selected project. By default, create the task at the top outline level is selected.

> If you select a To-Do list from the *Project* pick list, the system will display the entry page for the selected To-Do list.

In the Task Information section of the page, provide a task name and make sure that you add a comment unless you are certain the project manager will know what you are doing. Select a proposed start date and enter a work estimate in hours or days. Indicate which value you are using by typing an "h" or a "d" character after the number you enter. Click the *Save New Tasks* button to save your new tasks requests to your timesheet.

Once you have created and saved the new task, Project Web Access redisplays your View My Tasks page. The new task is now visible in the timesheet and contains indictors that let you know its status. In Figure 6-22, you can see the new task I created, along with the screentip that indicates that I need to send the new task to the project manager for approval and updating into the project plan.

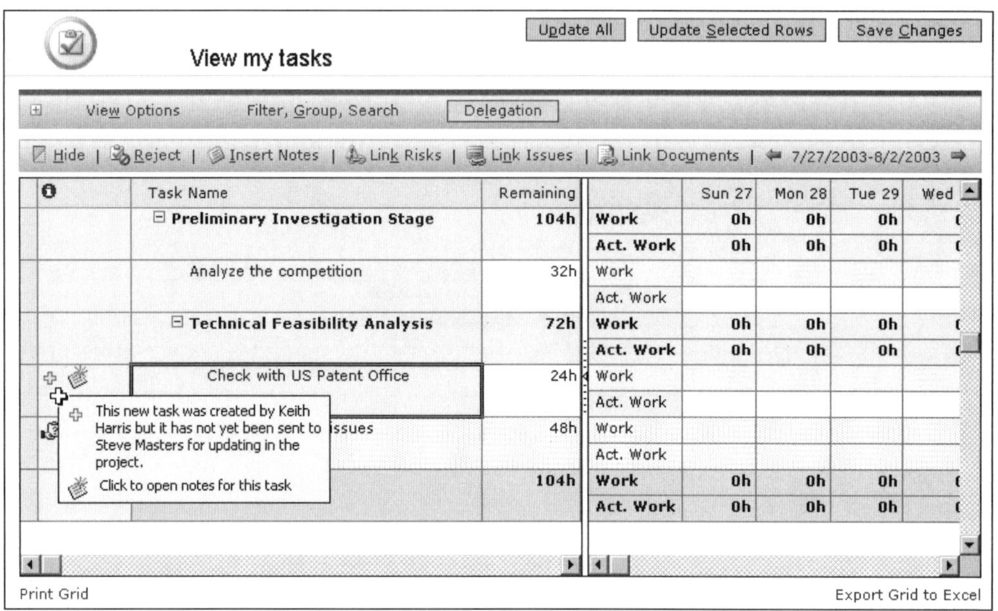

**Figure 6-22: New task created
on the View My Tasks page**

Once you create your new task, your second step is to update the new task to the project manager for approval. To send the new task to the project manager, select the task in the task list, and then click the *Update Selected Rows* button. Alternately, you can simply click the *Update All* button to send your new task and any other pending updates to your project manager(s).

The system allows you to enter actual progress on the new task before you submit it to your project manager. If you do so, the system will submit the new task request to your project manager along with your actual progress.

Using Task Creation for Collaborative Planning

You can leverage the New Task creation feature during the planning phase of your projects to allow team leaders and team members to create some of the tasks in the work plan. In order to allow these users to create tasks that fall below summary tasks in the plan, you must assign the user responsible for creating the tasks to the summary task to begin with. This means that you must at least dummy up this structure in your plan.

In other words, you'll need to create the summary task by both creating it as a task with an appropriate name and by adding at least one subtask to it in order to apply the indentation that, in itself, defines a task as being a summary task. Then you must assign the resource responsible for detailing the tasks below the summary task to the summary task itself.

Assigning resources to summary tasks is generally not a good idea as it causes work demand to be overstated. The system will add the work rollup from the summary task to the resource, as well as the work from each of the individual subtasks. This is not a problem before entering the phase of a project when tracking commences, nor is it a problem as long as you can live with overstatement of work for the resources doing the planning. Remove the resources from the summary tasks as soon as possible.

Assigning Yourself to an Existing Task

A new feature of Project Server 2003 allows you to assign yourself to an existing task through the View My Tasks Page. To do so, click the *Assign myself to an existing task* link in the actions pane. The system displays the Assign Myself to an Existing Task page, shown in Figure 6-23. The *Project* pick list at the top of the page lists all of the projects in which you are assigned project work. The center section of the page lists all of the tasks to which you can assign yourself.

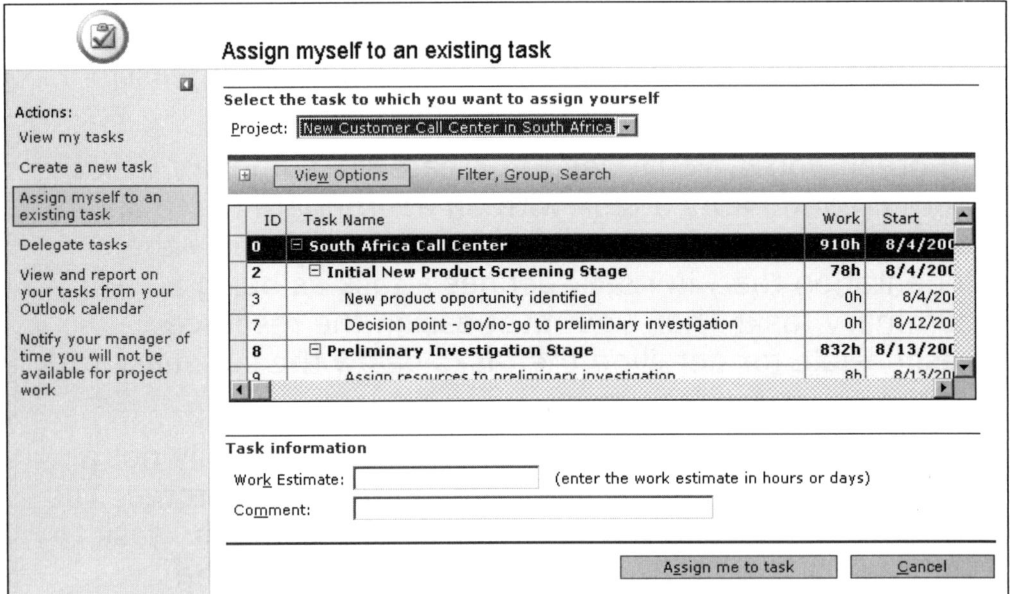

**Figure 6-23: Assign Myself
to an Existing Task page**

To assign yourself to an existing task, select a project from the *Project* pick list and then select a task from the list of tasks displayed. Enter a Work Estimate of your work on the selected task and an optional Comment, then click the *Assign me to task* button. The system displays the confirmation message shown in Figure 6-24. Click the *OK* button to continue. The system redisplays your timesheet, including the new task assignment. You must click either the *Update All* or *Update Selected Rows* button to send the updated task assignment to your manager.

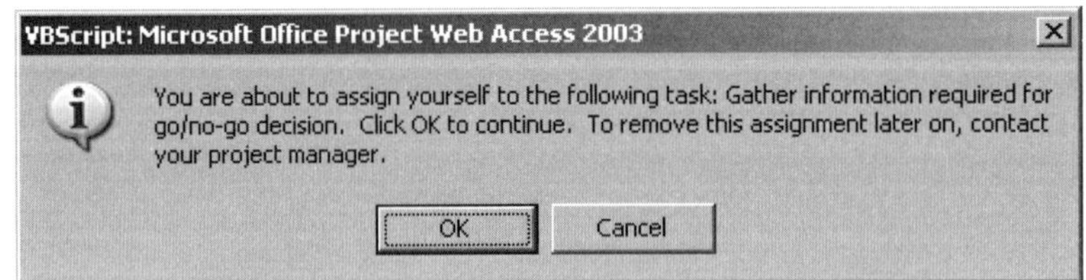

**Figure 6-24: Assign myself to an
existing task confirmation message**

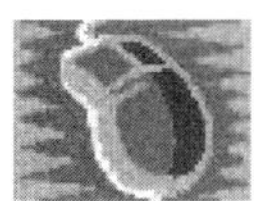 **Hands On Exercise**

Exercise 6-6

Create and submit a new task to your project manager.

1. Make sure you have displayed the View My Tasks page.
2. Select the Timesheet display, if not currently displayed.
3. Click Create a new task in the actions pane.
4. Select a project.
5. Enter the task information.
6. Click the *Save New Tasks* button when complete.
7. Float the mouse pointer over Indicator icon for the new task.
8. Click the *Update All* button.

Exercise 6-7

Assign yourself to an existing task.

1. Make sure you have displayed the View My Tasks page.
2. Select the Timesheet display, if not currently displayed.
3. Click the *Assign myself to an existing task* link in the actions pane.
4. Select a project and then select a task.
5. Enter a Work Estimate value and a Comment.
6. Click the *Assign me to task* button.
7. Click the *OK* button to confirm the action.

Hiding Tasks

Use the *Hide* button to remove completed and cancelled tasks from your timesheet. Completed and cancelled tasks will display on your timesheet indefinitely unless you manually hide them from view. Once hidden, tasks do not redisplay unless your manager republishes them. To hide a task, select it in the task list and then click the *Hide* button. The warning dialog, shown in Figure 6-25, allows you to confirm your action or cancel it. Click the *Yes* button to continue.

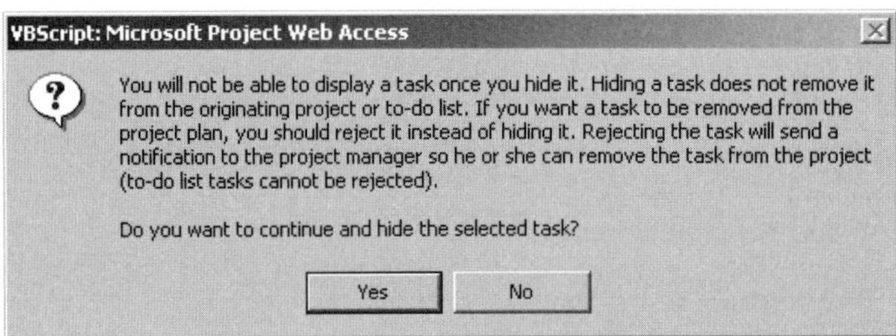

Figure 6-25: Warning dialog

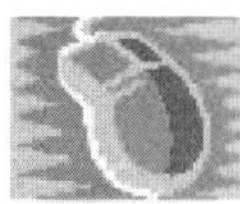

Hands On Exercise

Exercise 6-8

Hide a task on your timesheet.

1. Make sure you have displayed the View My Tasks page.
2. Select the Timesheet display, if not currently displayed.
3. Select a task in the timesheet.
4. Click the *Hide* button on the toolbar.
5. Click the *Yes* button to continue.

Inserting Task Notes

To insert a Note for a task, select the task on the View My Tasks page and then click on the *Insert Notes* button on the toolbar. The system opens the Project Web Access Assignment Notes dialog shown in Figure 6-26.

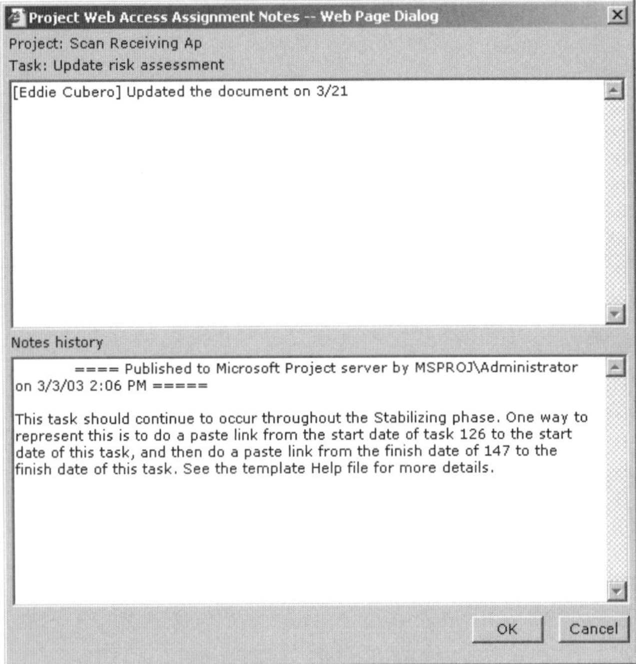

**Figure 6-26: Project Web Access
Assignment Notes dialog**

The dialog contains a current note area at the top and a history of notes previously added to the task in the bottom half. You may make changes in either text area; however, you should make your new entry in the upper text box. The system annotates the note in the upper text area with your name to indicate that you are the one adding the note. Saving the new note automatically adds a timestamp to the record as well. Click the *OK* button to add the note. Your new note now appears when you reopen the notes dialog for the task.

Notes entered through the timesheet are visible to you and the corresponding manager for only the selected task. These notes are not visible to other team members, and cannot be seen in other views in the system other than the View My Tasks and Updates views.

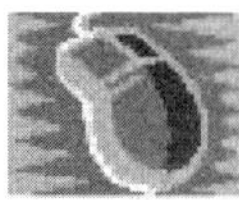

Hands On Exercise

Exercise 6-9

Add a Note to a task.

1. Make sure you have displayed the View My Tasks page.
2. Select the Timesheet display, if not currently displayed.
3. Select a task and click the *Insert Notes* button.
4. Add appropriate text for the Note and click the *OK* button when finished.

Linking Documents to Tasks

Link project-related documents to tasks by selecting a task and then clicking the *Link Documents* button on the toolbar. The system displays the document list for the selected task, as shown in Figure 6-27. The document list shows all of the documents linked to the task, if any exist. To add an existing document to the document list, click the *Upload Document* button on the toolbar.

Figure 6-27: Document list for a task

In addition to adding documents at the task level, you can also add documents at the project level by clicking the *Documents* menu at the top of the Project Web Access page.

Linking Issues to Tasks

An issue is any type of problem or concern which you might have during the life of the project, and which you want to communicate to those who have an interest in the project. Examples of project issues could include a shortage of resources needed to complete the project on time, or an unanticipated hardware upgrade that you need in order to move forward with project work.

Similar to handling document linking, you link issues to tasks by selecting a task and then clicking the *Link Issues* button on the toolbar. The system displays the Issues list for the selected task, as shown in Figure 6-28. The Issues list shows all of the issues linked to the task, if any exist. To add a new issue to the Issues list, click the *New Issue* button on the toolbar. To link the task to existing issues, click the *Link Project Issues* button.

Figure 6-28: Issues list for tasks

In addition to adding issues at the task level, you can also add issues at the project level by clicking the *Issues* menu at the top of the Project Web Access page.

Linking Risks to Tasks

The Project Management Institute defines a risk as "an uncertain event or condition that, if it occurs, has a positive or negative effect on a project objective." Risks have both causes and consequences. If a risk occurs, the consequence can be either negative or positive. As a part of your organization's risk management methodologies, you may need to log and document known risks to your project work.

As with documents and issues, you can also link risks to tasks by selecting a task and then clicking the *Link Risks* button on the toolbar. The system displays the Risks list for the selected task, as shown in Figure 6-29. The Risks list shows all of the risks linked to the task, if any exist. To add a new risk to the Risks list, click the *New Risk* button on the toolbar. To link the task to existing risks, click the *Link Project Risks* button.

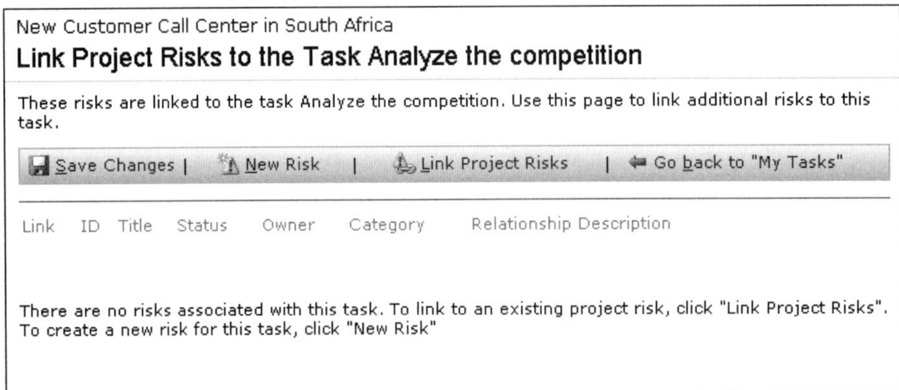

Figure 6-29: Risks list for tasks

In addition to adding risks at the task level, you can also add risks at the project level by clicking the *Risks* menu at the top of the Project Web Access page.

Managing Project Tasks in Outlook

The *View and report on your tasks from your Outlook calendar* link in the View My Tasks page allows you to import and manage project tasks in Outlook. I will discuss this topic in Module 7, along with other features of using Project Web Access in Outlook.

Notifying Managers of Working Day Changes

Within Project Web Access, you can notify your manager of changes in your working schedule using the *Notify your manager of time you will not be available for project work* link. Before you can use this option, however, your manager must assign you to at least one task in an Administrative project. Organizations use Administrative projects to track non-project time for employees in the organization.

To notify your manager of a change in work schedule, click the *Notify your manager of time you will not be available for project work* link in the actions pane. If a manager has not already assigned you to at least one task in an Administrative project, the system displays the warning page shown in Figure 6-30.

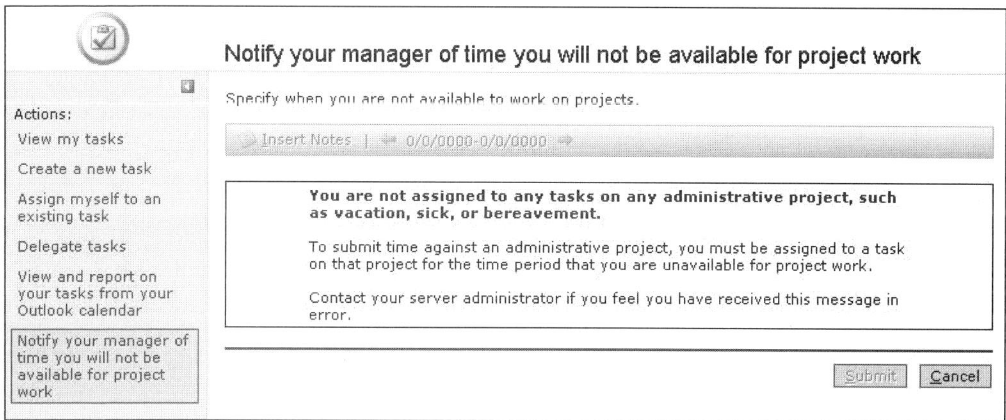

Figure 6-30: Warning page

If a manager has already assigned you to one or more tasks In an Administrative project, the system displays the Notify Your Manager of Time You Will Not Be Available for Project Work page shown in Figure 6-31.

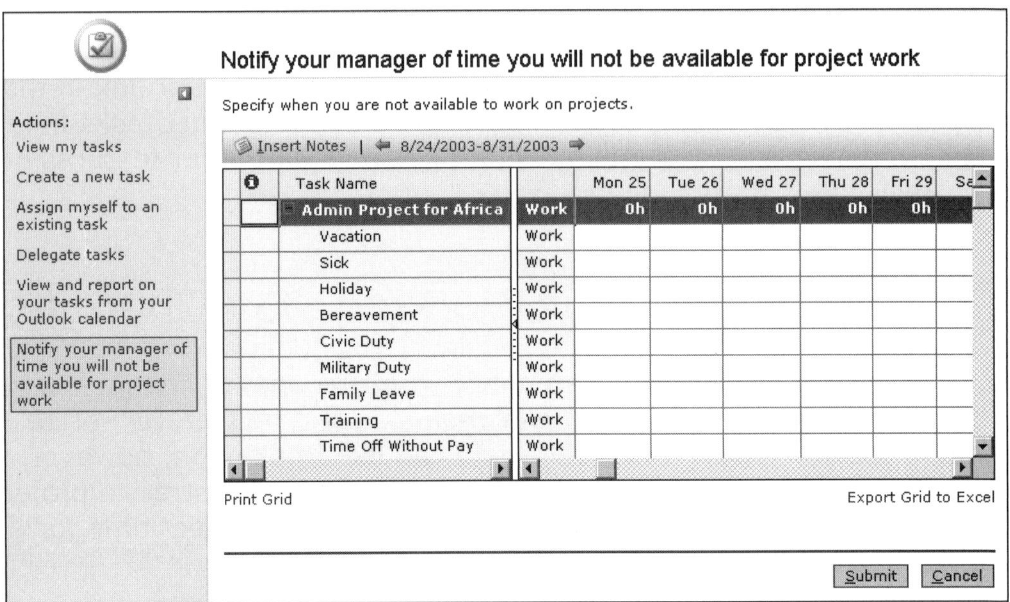

**Figure 6-31: Notify Your Manager of Time You
Will Not Be Available for Project Work page**

Scroll to the desired date in the date grid and select the type of time that causes you to be unavailable for project work. Enter your nonworking time in the date grid and add an optional note by clicking the *Insert Note* button. When you have finished, click the *Submit* button. The system displays a confirmation message indicating a successful update of your nonworking time, as shown in Figure 6-32.

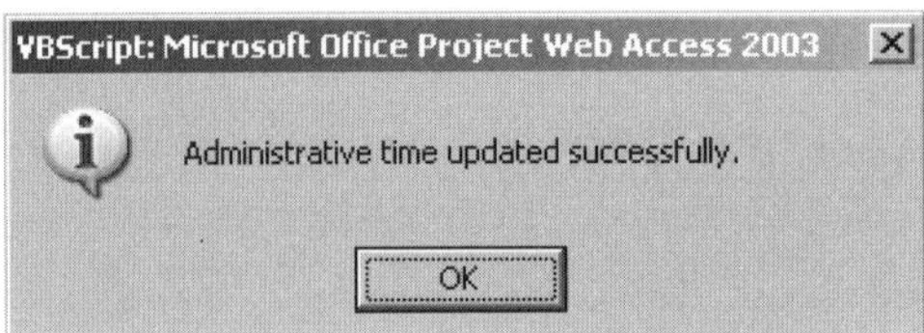

**Figure 6-32: Confirmation
message**

Click the *OK* button to continue. Your manager will receive your nonworking time update in the same manner as that person would receive your normal task progress updates.

Module 07

Working with Outlook

Learning Objectives

After completing this module, you will be able to:

- Manage your Project Web Access tasks in your Outlook Calendar
- Display Project Web Access pages in Outlook

Managing Project Tasks in Outlook

Shown in Figure 7-1, the *Work with Outlook* link on the Home page offers you the option to work with Project Web Access in Outlook.

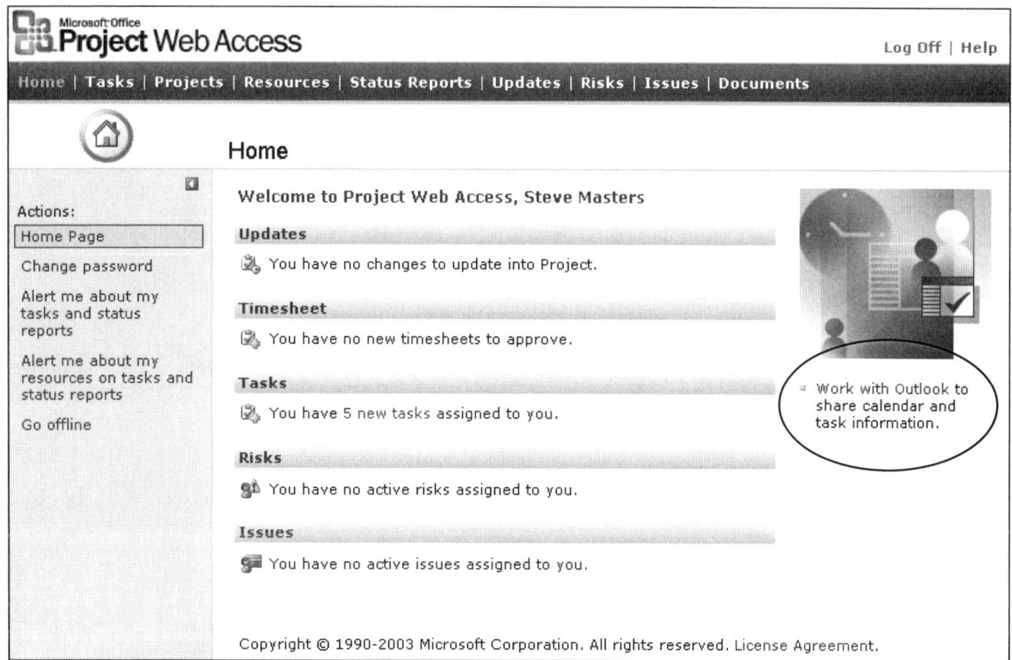

**Figure 7-1: Home page for a project manager
in Project Web Access**

Shown in Figure 7-2, the *View and report on your tasks from your Outlook calendar* link also offers you the same option of working with Project Web Access in Outlook.

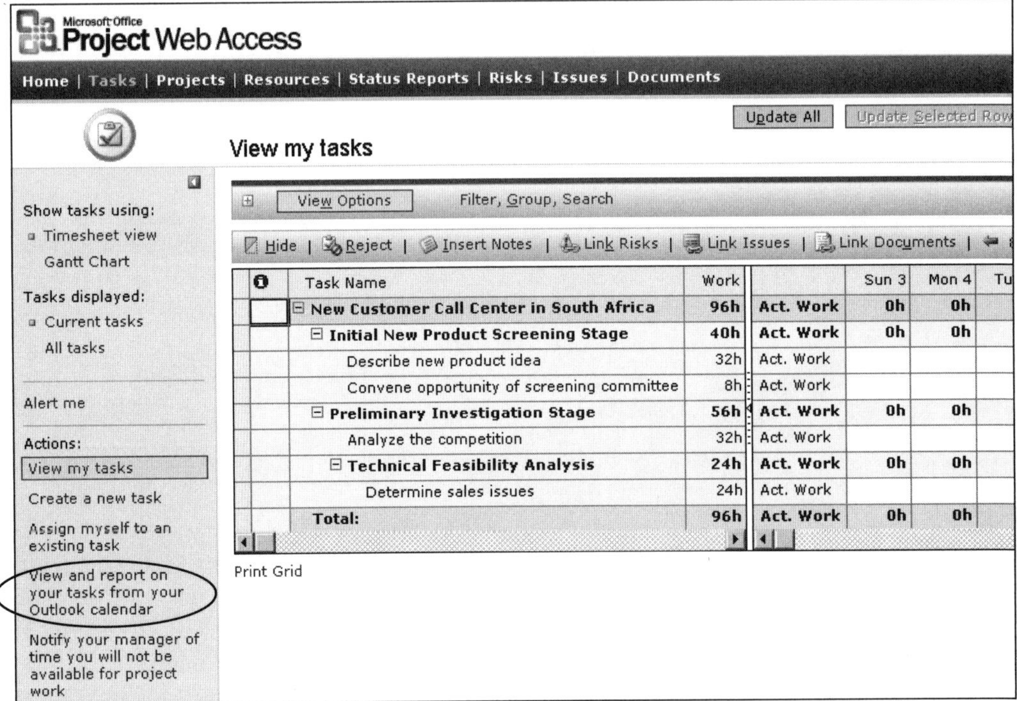

ⓘ	Task Name	Work		Sun 3	Mon 4	Tu
	⊟ **New Customer Call Center in South Africa**	**96h**	**Act. Work**	**0h**	**0h**	
	⊟ **Initial New Product Screening Stage**	**40h**	**Act. Work**	**0h**	**0h**	
	Describe new product idea	32h	Act. Work			
	Convene opportunity of screening committee	8h	Act. Work			
	⊟ **Preliminary Investigation Stage**	**56h**	**Act. Work**	**0h**	**0h**	
	Analyze the competition	32h	Act. Work			
	⊟ **Technical Feasibility Analysis**	**24h**	**Act. Work**	**0h**	**0h**	
	Determine sales issues	24h	Act. Work			
	Total:	**96h**	**Act. Work**	**0h**	**0h**	

Figure 7-2: View My Tasks page
Timesheet view

When you click the links shown in either Figure 7-1 or 7-2, the system displays the Work with Outlook page shown in Figure 7-3. This page prompts you to download and install the Outlook add-in.

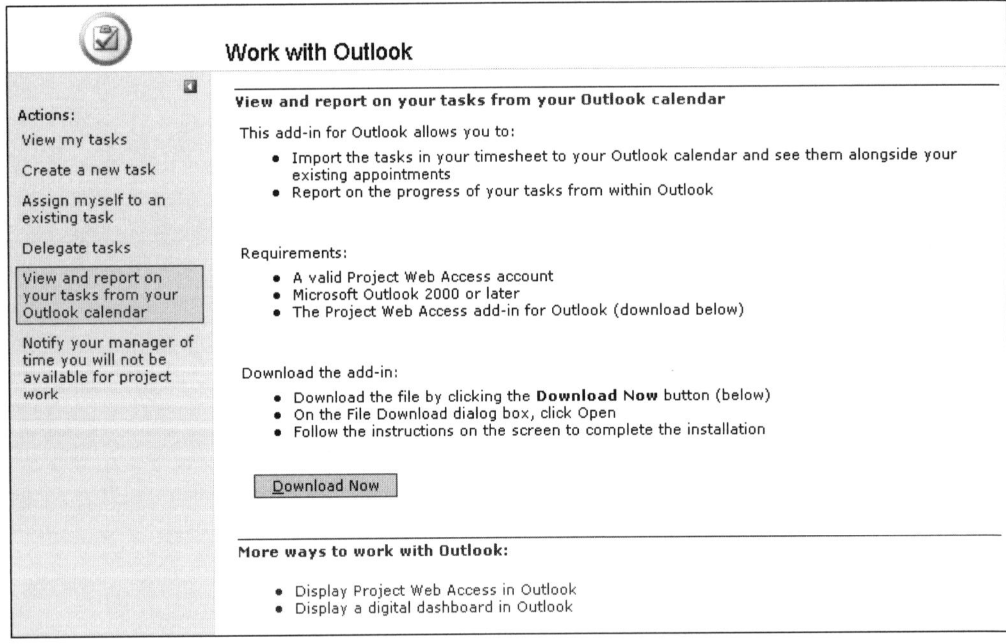

Figure 7-3: Work with Outlook page

Click the *Download Now* button to begin the process of downloading and installing the add-in. The system displays the dialog shown in Figure 7-4 warning you about a potentially unsafe ActiveX control.

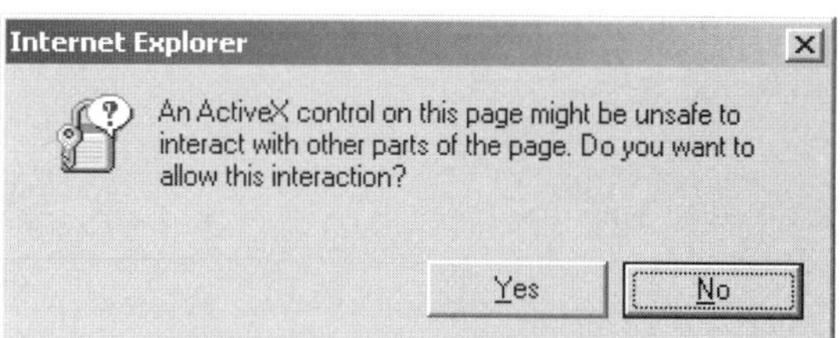

**Figure 7-4: ActiveX
warning dialog**

 The appearance of the ActiveX warning dialog is dependent on the security settings in your Internet Explorer browser

Click the *Yes* button to continue. The system displays the File Download dialog shown in Figure 7-5, and asks whether to save or to open the downloaded ActiveX control.

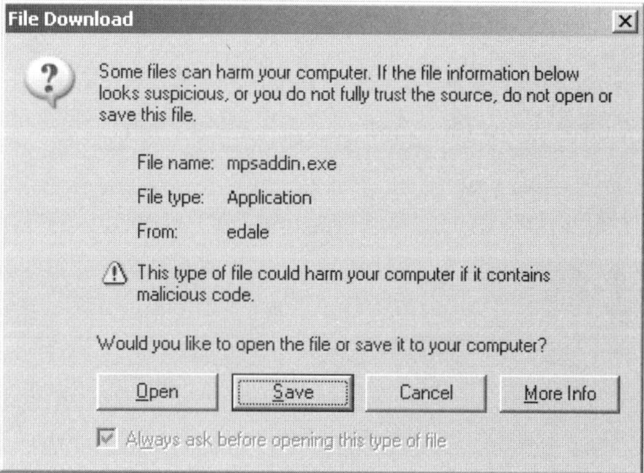

**Figure 7-5: File Download
dialog**

Click the *Open* button to download and install the ActiveX control. The system displays the Microsoft Office Project Add-In for Outlook Setup dialog shown in Figure 7-6.

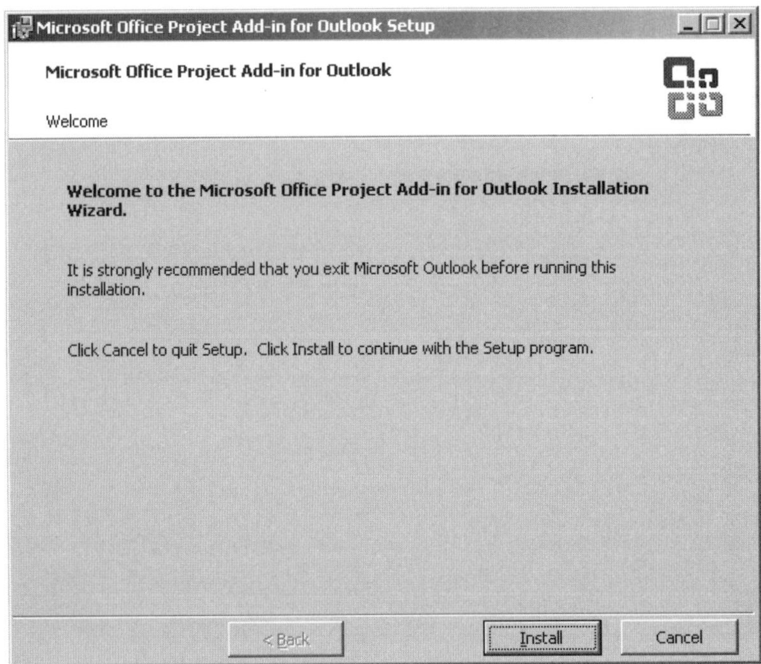

**Figure 7-6: Microsoft Office Project
Add-In for Outlook Setup dialog**

Click the *Install* button to complete the installation of the add-in. The system displays the confirmation message shown in Figure 7-7. Click the *OK* button to continue.

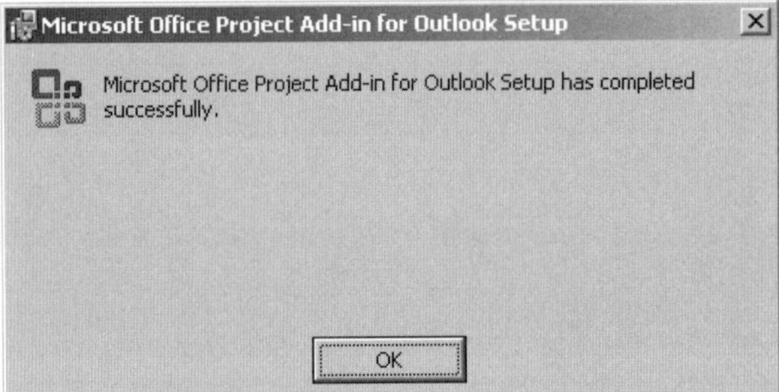

**Figure 7-7: Outlook add-in
successfully installed**

When you have completed the previous steps, you can launch your Outlook program. The first time you launch Outlook after installing the Outlook add-in in Project Web Access, the system automatically opens a Help window in Outlook with more information about how to work with project tasks in Outlook, as shown in Figure 7-8.

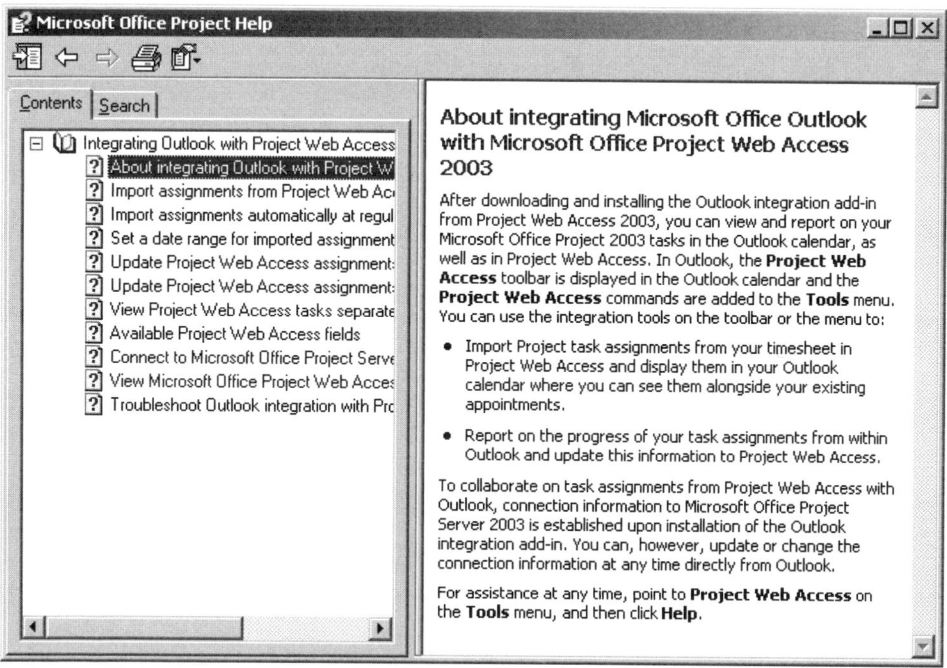

**Figure 7-8: Microsoft Office Project
Help window in Outlook**

When you close the Help window, your Outlook interface will offer two new features: a Project Web Access toolbar and a *Project Web Access* menu item on the Tools menu. The system displays these two new features in Figure 7-9 and Figure 7-10.

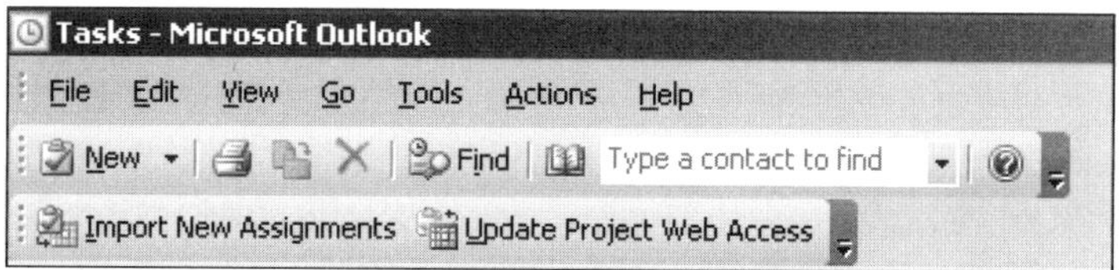

**Figure 7-9: Project Web Access toolbar
below the Tasks toolbar**

If the Project Web Access toolbar is not visible in Outlook, click View ➢ Toolbars and select Project Web Access.

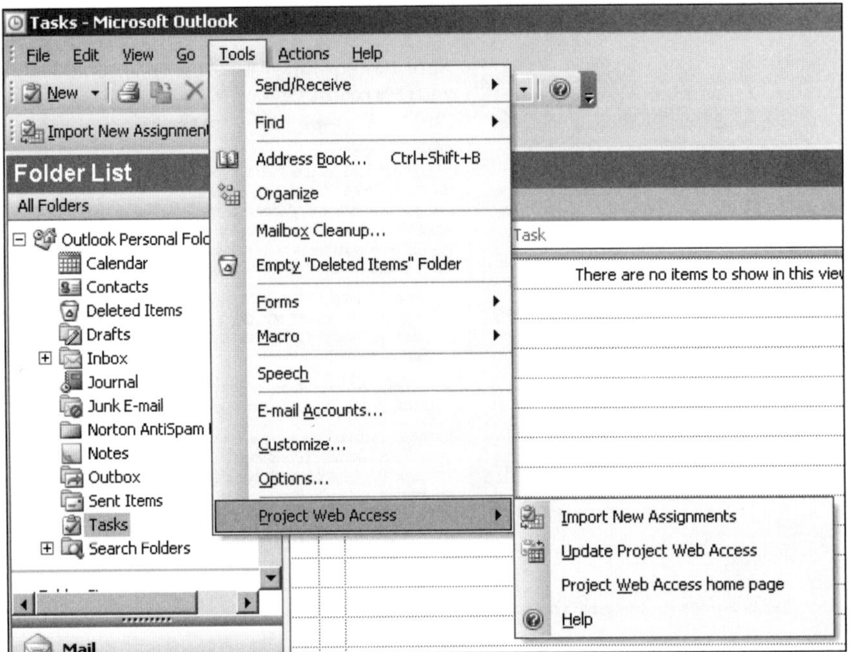

**Figure 7-10: Project Web Access menu
item on the Tools menu in Outlook**

To work with project tasks in Outlook, you must click the *Import New Assignments* button. The system displays the Import Assignments from Project Web Access dialog, as shown in Figure 7-11.

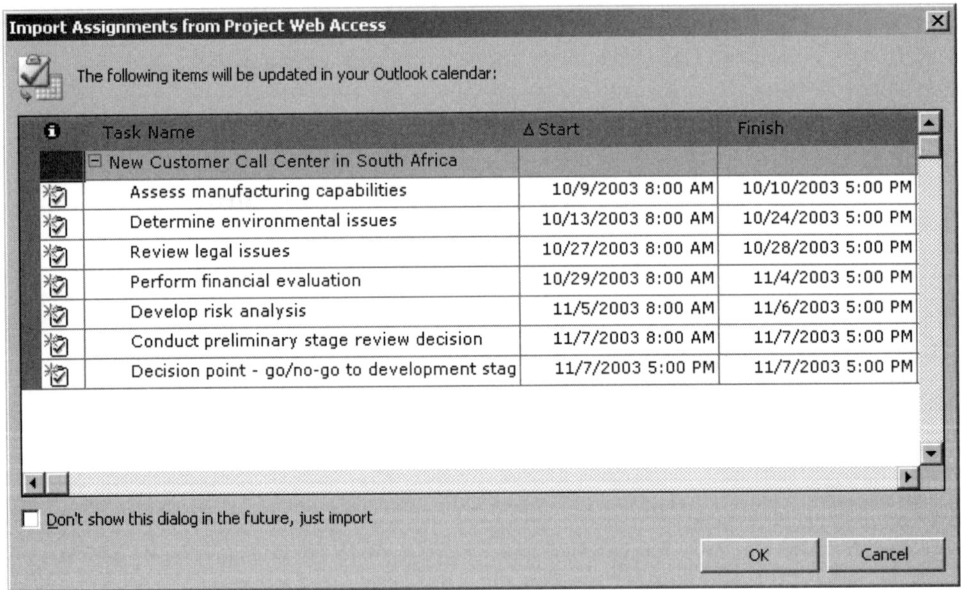

**Figure 7-11: Import Assignments from
Project Web Access dialog**

The dialog is for informational purposes only, and requires no decision on your part except that you click the *OK* button to confirm the import of assignments into Outlook. If you wish, you may select the *Don't show this dialog in the future, just import* option to automatically import tasks into Outlook.

The system displays tasks from Project Web Access as appointments on your Outlook calendar. For example, in Figure 7-12 you can see my Project Web Access tasks during the month of October.

Contrary to what you might assume, Outlook does not display Project Web Access tasks on the Tasks page. Project tasks display only as appointments on the Calendar page of Outlook.

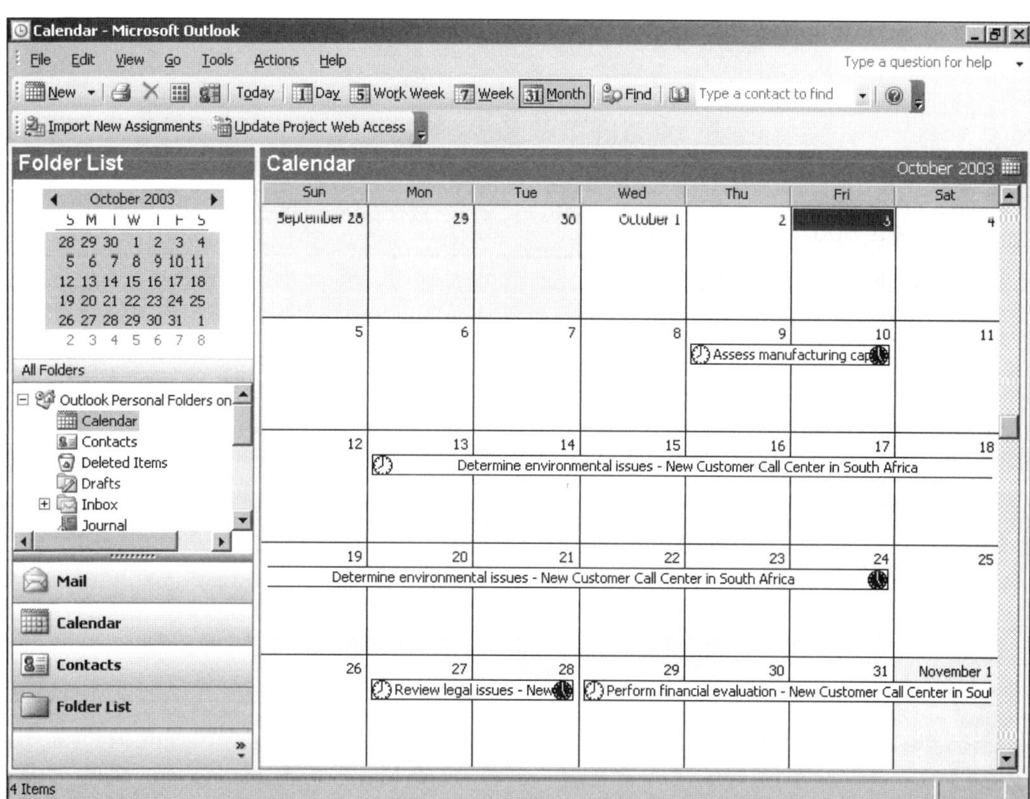

**Figure 7-12: Project Web Access tasks
as Outlook appointments**

To enter progress on any of your project tasks in Outlook, apply the Calendar view and then double-click the project task. Outlook presents the detailed appointment window for the project task. In this window, select the *Project Web Access* tab to access your timesheet, as shown in Figure 7-13.

To enter progress on a project task in Outlook, use the same method that you would use in Project Web Access:

- Enter Actual Work on the date during which you performed the work.

- Adjust the Remaining Work estimate, if necessary.

- Insert a task Note if you adjusted the Remaining Work estimate.

- To save your changes and not update your project manager, click the *Save Changes* button.

- To update your progress to the project manager, click the *Update Project Manager* button.

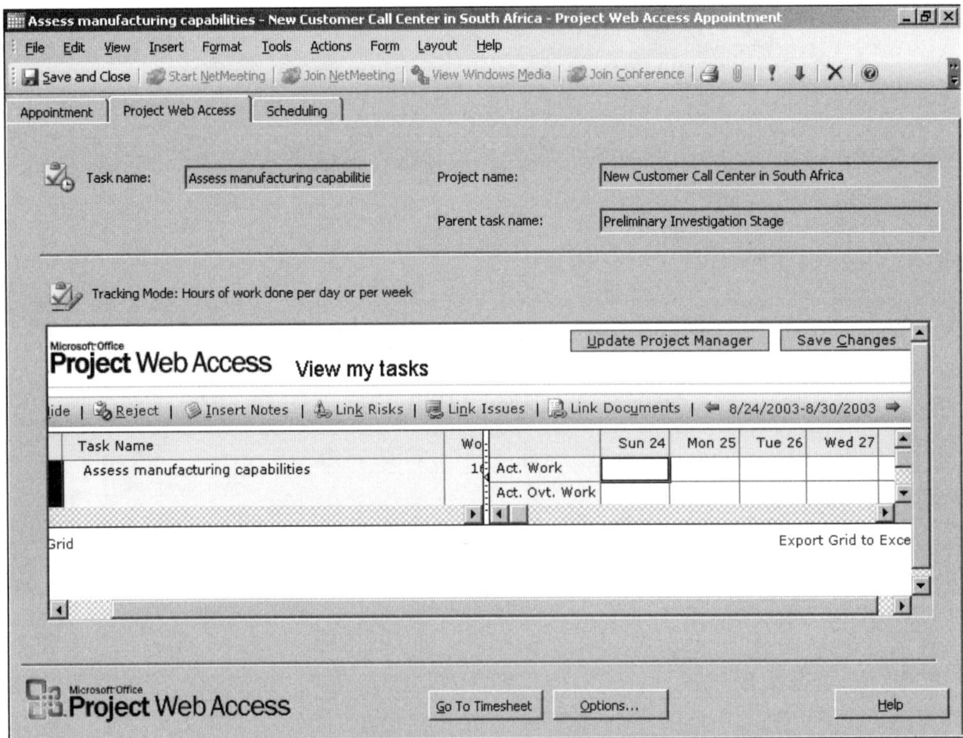

**Figure 7-13: Detailed appointment window
in Outlook for a project task**

Click the *Go To Timesheet* button to launch your Internet Explorer and navigate to your View My Tasks page in Project Web Access.

When you have finished entering progress for your project task in Outlook, click the *Save and Close* button in the detailed appointment window. If you have saved your project task progress on your timesheet in Outlook, but have not yet updated your project manager, you can update the progress to your manager by clicking the *Update Project Web Access* button on the Project Web Access toolbar.

Automatically Import Project Tasks into Outlook

If you want to import Project Web Access tasks automatically into your Outlook calendar, you must be using Windows User Account authentication in Project Server 2003. If this is the case, you can set up the process to occur automatically in Outlook by clicking Tools ➤ Options and then selecting the *Project Web Access* tab, as shown in Figure 7-14. Specify the automatic options that you wish to use in the Options dialog and then click the *OK* button when you are finished.

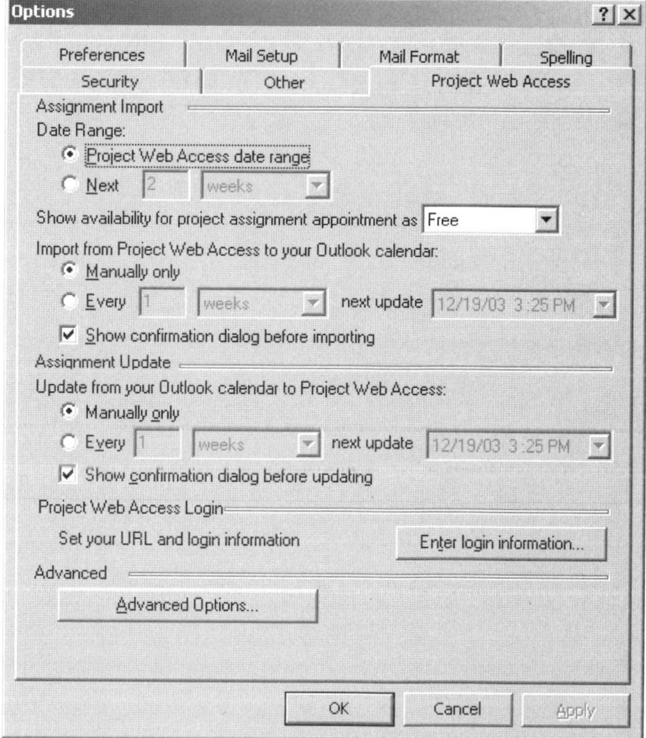

**Figure 7-14: Project Web Access
options in Outlook Options dialog**

Click the *Advanced* button to select whether Outlook automatically sends your task updates to your project manager or accepts them only on your timesheet for manual updating to your project manager. You may also choose whether Outlook creates reminders for your Project Web Access tasks in Outlook.

Displaying Project Web Access in Outlook

At the bottom of the Work with Outlook page, there are two additional links in the More Ways to Work with Outlook section, as shown in Figure 7-15. These links offer you the following options:

- **Display Project Web Access in Outlook** allows you to place a shortcut to a Project Web Access page in Outlook or to display a Project Web Access page as the Home page of a new or existing Outlook folder.

- **Display a digital dashboard in Outlook** allows you to select a link for an existing digital dashboard link and create a shortcut to it in Outlook or display it as the Home page of a new or existing Outlook folder.

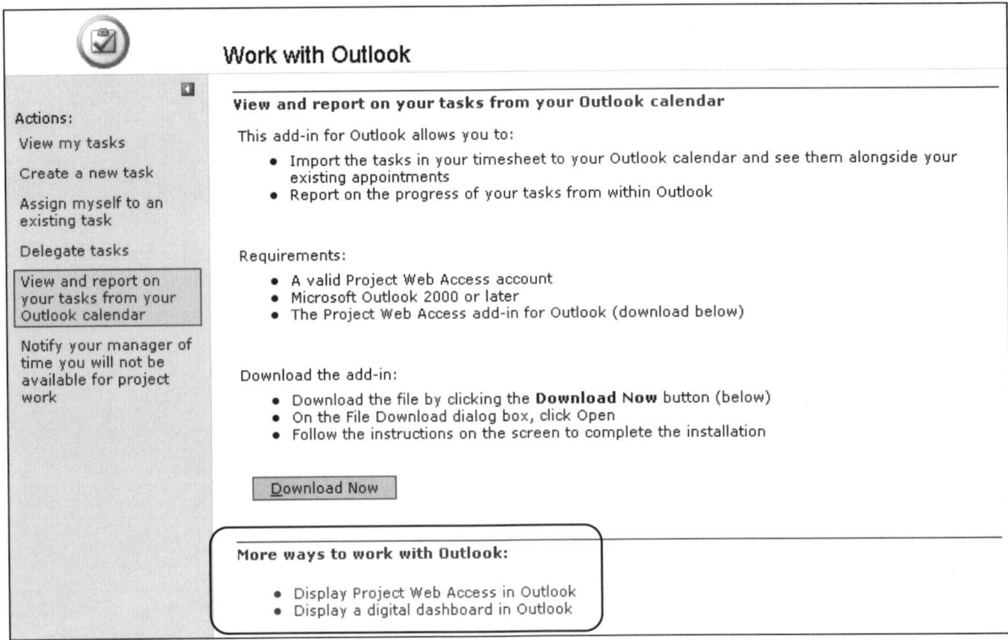

Figure 7-15: Work with Outlook page

When you click the *Display Project Web Access in Outlook* link, the system displays the familiar ActiveX warning dialog shown previously in Figure 7-4. Click the *Yes* button to continue. The system presents the Display Project Web Access Page in Outlook dialog shown in Figure 7-16. This dialog allows you to determine which specific Project Web Access pages the system will display in Outlook and to determine how Outlook displays the pages.

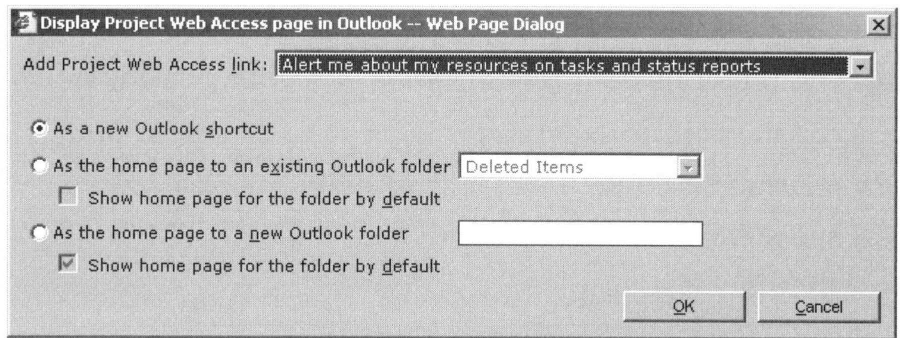

**Figure 7-16: Display Project Web Access
page in Outlook dialog**

Click the *Add Project Web Access link* pick list and select the page you want
to display in Outlook. The pick list contains a user-sensitive list of options
based on your permissions within Project Server. For example, the system
lists the following pages for a user with Project Manager permissions:

- Alert me about my resources on tasks and status reports
- Alert me about my tasks and status reports
- Analyze projects in Portfolio Analyzer
- Analyze resources in Portfolio Analyzer
- Approve timesheets
- Assign myself to an existing task
- Change password
- Check in my projects
- Create a new personal or shared to-do list
- Create a new task
- Delegate Tasks
- Go offline
- Home Page
- Manage my to-do lists
- Miscellaneous reports
- Notify your manager of time you will not be available for project work
- Request a status report
- Set rules for automatically accepting changes
- Status Reports archive
- Status Reports overview
- Submit a status report

- To-Do list options
- View and report on your tasks from your Outlook calendar
- View and submit issues on all projects
- View and submit issues
- View and submit risks on all projects
- View and submit risks
- View and upload documents on all projects
- View and upload documents
- View and upload public documents
- View enterprise resources in Resource Center
- View history of past task changes
- View issue summary for all projects
- View issue summary for my projects
- View my tasks
- View projects in Project Center
- View resource assignments
- View risk summary for all projects
- View risk summary for my projects
- View status report responses from your team members
- View task changes submitted by resources
- View timesheet summary

> As you might surmise, a user with Administrator permissions will see more options on the *Add Project Web Access link* pick list, while users with Resource Manager, Executive, or Team Member permissions will see fewer options.

In Figure 7-17, notice that I want to display the View My Tasks page in Outlook.

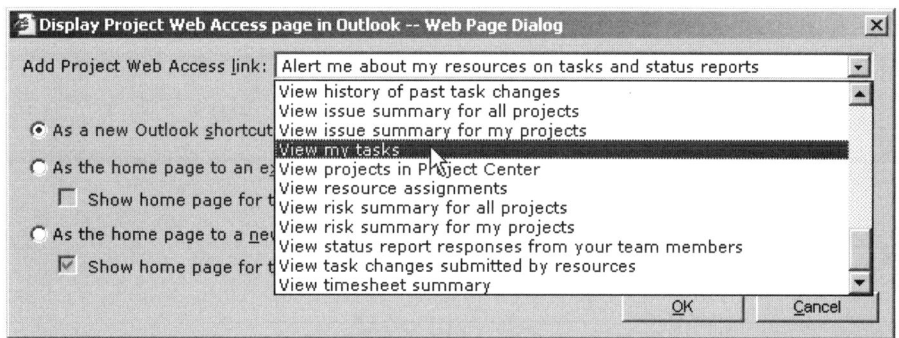

**Figure 7-17: Select the View My Tasks page
to display in Outlook**

Once you have selected the Project Web Access page to display in Outlook, you must also select the option for how you want the page displayed in Outlook and then click the *OK* button. Select the *As the home page of a new Outlook folder* option to create a new folder in Outlook. Choose the *As the home page of an existing folder* option if you have already created a folder. If you select either of these two options, Outlook displays your selected Project Web Access page as shown in Figure 7-18.

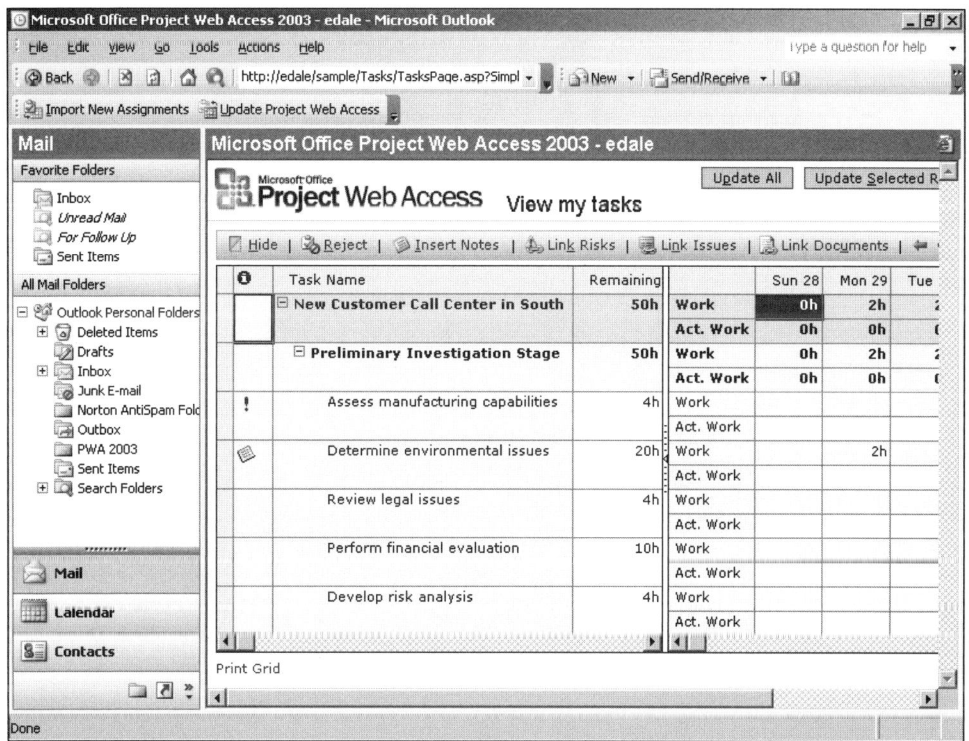

Figure 7-18: Project Web Access page in Outlook

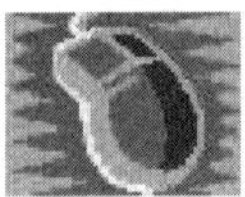

Hands On Exercise

Exercise 7-1

Display Project Web Access in Outlook.

1. Navigate to the Home page in Project Web Access.

2. Click the *Work with Outlook* link on the right side of your Home page.

3. In the Display Project Web Access in Outlook dialog, click the *Add Project Web Access link* pick list and select the *View My Tasks* page.

4. Select how you want the system to display the information in Outlook.

5. Click the *OK* button when finished.

6. Open Outlook and display the results.

Updating Progress through Project Web Access

Learning Objectives

After completing this module, you will be able to:

- Set view options on the View Task Changes Submitted by Resources page in Project Web Access

- Filter, group and search on the View Task Changes Submitted by Resources page in Project Web Access

- Accept or reject an update from a resource

- Reschedule uncompleted work from the past into the current reporting period

- Set and run rules for automatically accepting updates from resources

- Approve or reject a timesheet for a resource

- View unsubmitted timesheets for resources

Applying Updates in Project Web Access

The reporting cycle completes through the Updates page in Project Web Access where you accept or reject the updates project team members send to you. Notice that when you log on to Project Web Access, the Home page displays the number of new updates you have pending in the Updates section of the page. In Figure 8-1, Steve Masters has six task changes indicated in the Updates section of his Home page.

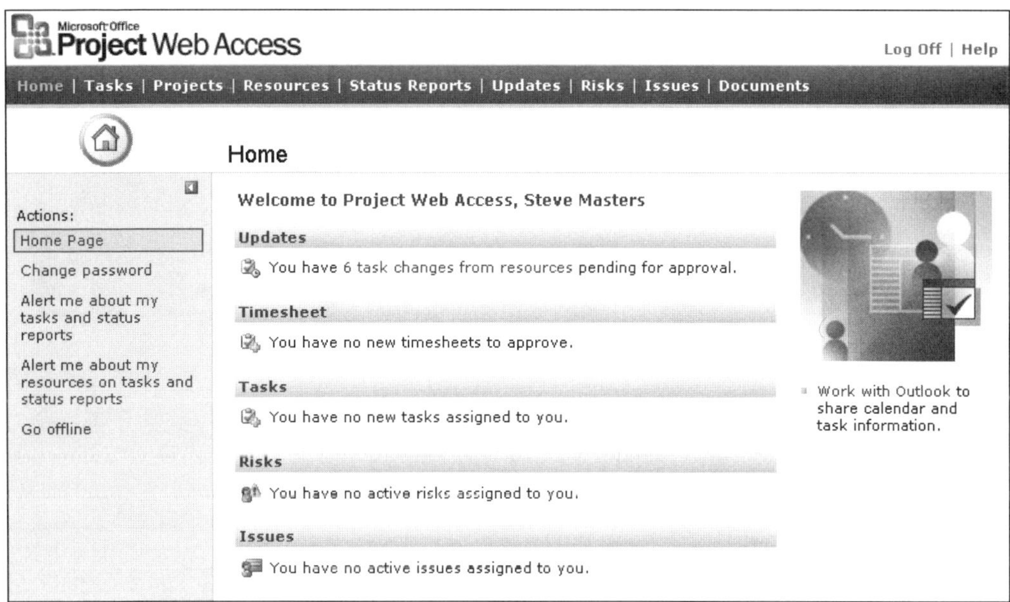

**Figure 8-1: Home page with 6 task changes
in Updates section of page**

Click the *Updates* link or the *Updates* menu option on the main navigation menu to display the View Task Changes Submitted by Resources page shown in Figure 8-2. This page is very similar to the layout of the View My Tasks page. For example, both pages allow you to apply either a Timesheet or Gantt Chart format to the view. In addition, the View Options tab and the Filter, Group, Search tab are nearly identical in both pages. In the case of the View Task Changes Submitted by Resources page, however, an *Apply Rules* tab replaces the *Delegation* tab seen in the View My Tasks page. The similarity is not surprising in that both pages deal with precisely the same information. Of course, the View Task Changes Submitted by Resources page presents the information from the project manager's point of view.

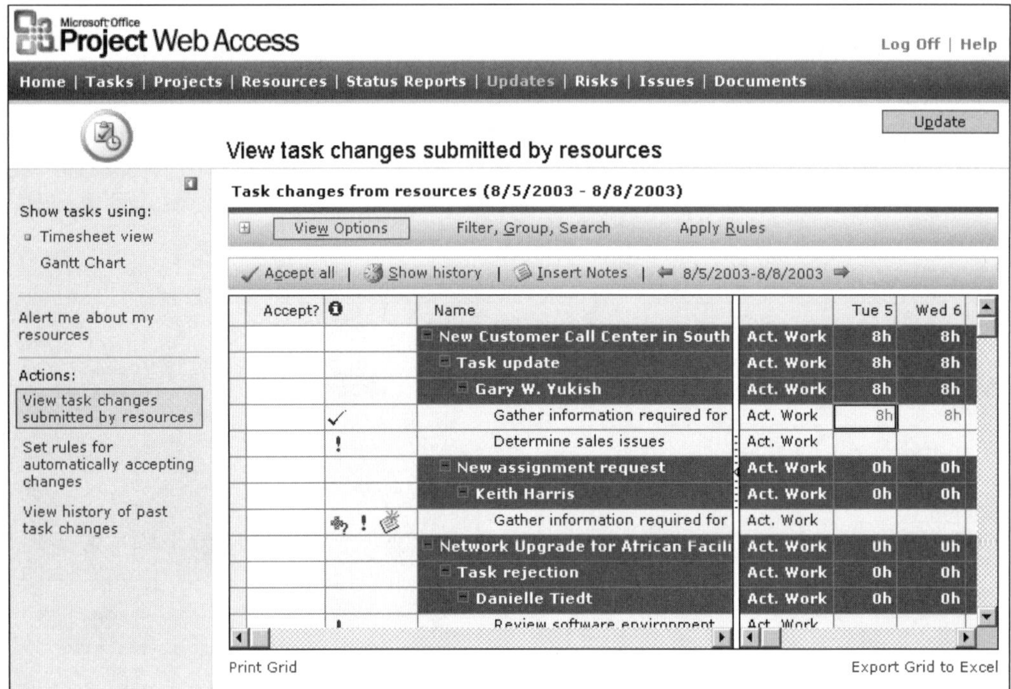

**Figure 8-2: View Task Changes
Submitted by Resources page**

The actions pane on the left side of the View Task Changes Submitted by Resources page allows you to apply either a Timesheet view or a Gantt Chart view to personalize your page. Click the *Alert me about my resources* link to set up e-mail alerts about the assignment work of your resources. This displays the Alert Me about My Resources on Task Updates page, which I will discuss further in Module 9.

The *Set rules for automatically accepting changes* option complements the *Apply Rules* tab. Click the link in the actions pane to create rules, and then click the *Apply Rules* tab to apply your rules to the updates received. Finally, the actions pane also contains the *View history of past task changes* link.

Setting View Options

Click the *View Options* tab to see the view options for the View Task Changes Submitted by Resources page. As in the View My Tasks page, you can display time with dates, show scheduled and overtime work, select the outline level of task updates shown in the view, and navigate to a specific date range. A new feature in Project Server 2003 is the *Show timesheet status* option. Select this option to determine which team members' timesheets are approved by their resource manager. When this option is selected, the system will place an asterisk symbol next to unapproved work in the Actual Work field. When you float the mouse pointer over an Actual Work value, the system will display a tooltip, as shown in Figure 8-3.

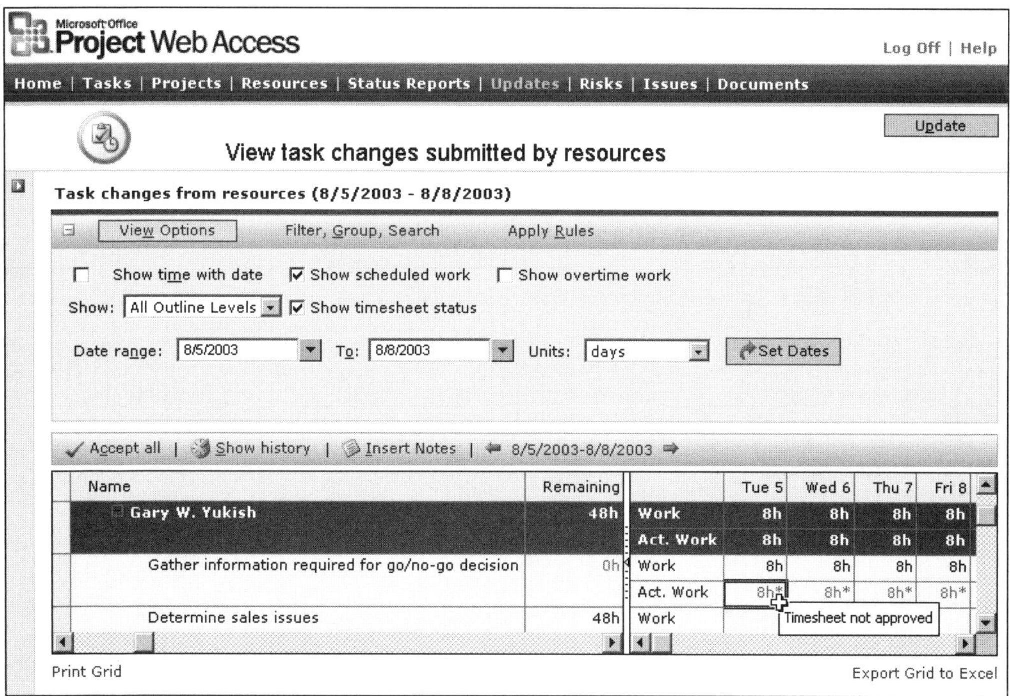

**Figure 8-3: View Task Changes Submitted by Resources
page with Show timesheet status option selected**

Setting Filter, Group, Search Options

Expanding the *Filter, Group, Search* tab reveals the options shown in Figure
8-4. Default filters include:

- All task changes
- All task updates
- All new tasks
- All task delegation requests
- All resource declined tasks
- All new assignment requests
- All declined task delegation requests
- All completed tasks
- All incomplete tasks
- All overdue tasks
- All tasks pending approval
- All tasks updated into Project

213

Because you can create your own custom filters the same way as in the View My Tasks page, we will not cover the process again in this module. In addition to filtering, you can also apply up to three levels of grouping using the following criteria:

- Accept?
- From
- Project
- Task change type
- Sent date
- Work
- Remaining work
- Start
- Finish
- % Complete

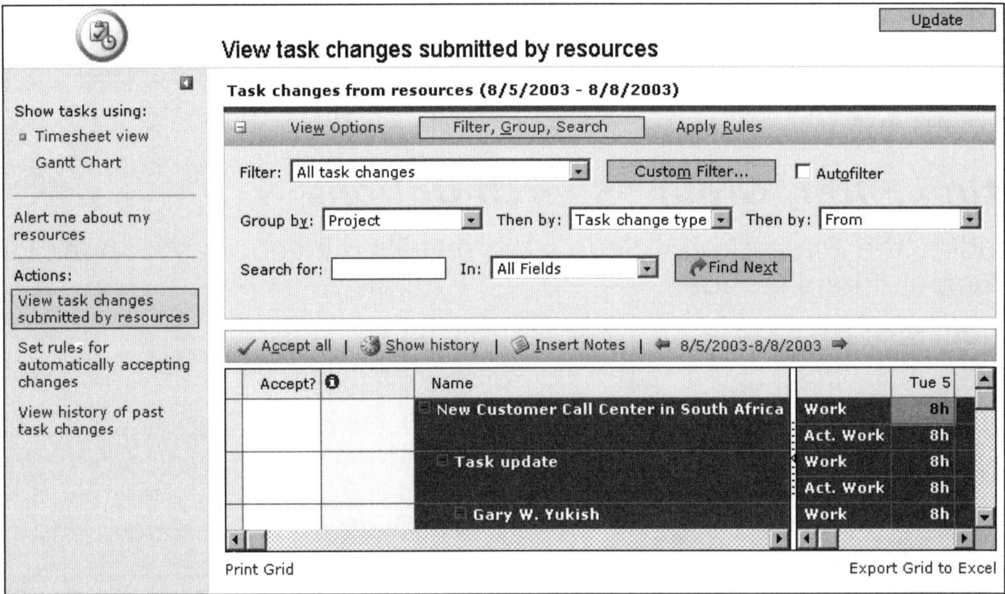

Figure 8-4: Filter, Group, Search options

The default Grouping format applied to the View Task Changes Submitted by Resources page is by Project, then by Task Change Type, and then by the resource's name (found in the From field).

Accepting and Rejecting Updates

What type of updates will you receive from your team members in the View Task Changes Submitted by Resources page? Updates can include any of the following:

- Task updates about the current status of task work

- Rejected tasks

- New assignment requests in which a member has assigned himself/herself to an existing task

- New task requests

- Task delegation requests

It is your responsibility as the project manager to either accept or reject any updates submitted by your team members. Accepting a task update automatically transfers the updated task information into the appropriate project plan. If you reject any updates from your team members, the team member will need to take the appropriate action in response to your rejection. This process guarantees that you as the project manager will always serve as the "gatekeeper" between your project team members and the actual project plan.

Before you can process any updates from your project team, you must set an Accept or Reject value in the Accept column. In Figure 8-5, I have accepted the first task update and am accepting the second update as well. You can also use the *Accept all* button on the toolbar to set all updates in the view to Accept.

When you reject an update, the system will notify the affected resource with an e-mail message. You might reject a task update when a resource accidentally types an incorrect Actual Work value, forgets to update Remaining Work, or fails to annotate a new task request. When you reject a task update, the system **does not** allow you to edit the text of the e-mail message.

Before you process updates, pay special attention to any task update that includes a Note icon in the Indicators column. A note attached to a task update usually means that your team members are trying to give you additional information about their task updates.

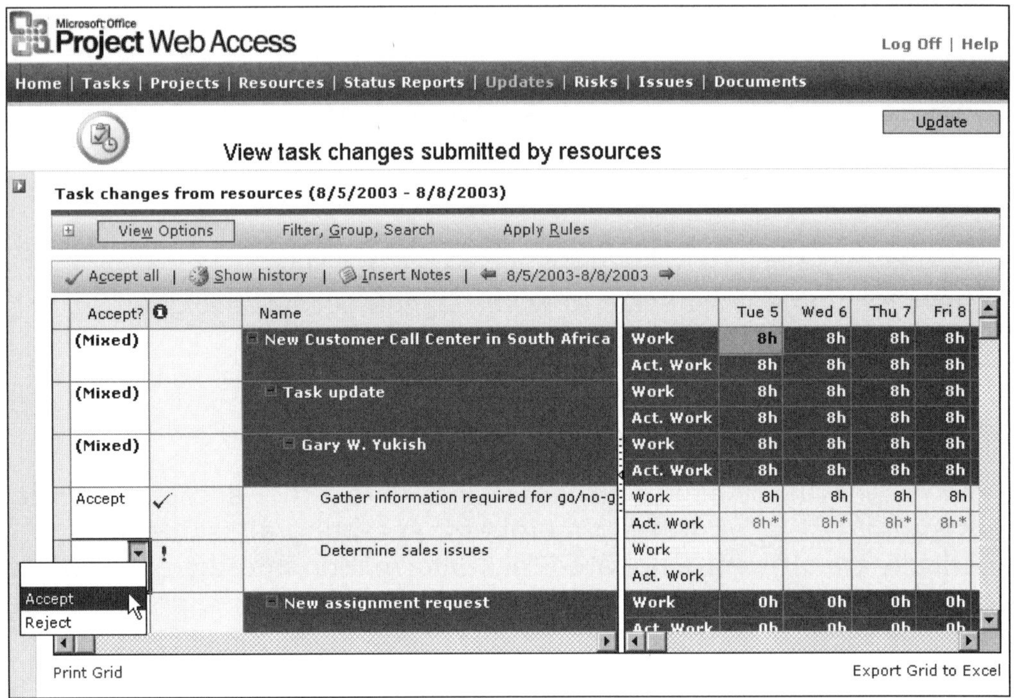

**Figure 8-5: View Task Changes Submitted by Resources page
Accept and reject updates**

Click the *Update* button to accept and reject according to your selections.
You may see a logon screen flash briefly as the system goes to work. In
processing the updates, the system launches Project Professional 2003 if it is
not already open, and opens any project plans affected by the updates. The
system also makes changes to each of the open project plans according to
the type of update. Once the system has processed all updates in each
project, it displays the confirmation dialog shown in Figure 8-6.

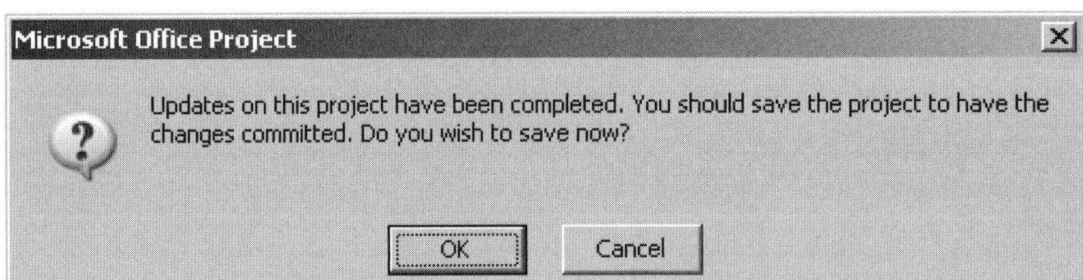

Figure 8-6: Update confirmation dialog

If you want to save the changes to your projects, click the OK button to
continue. If you want to review the task changes before saving the project,
click the Cancel button.

MSProjectExperts recommends that you routinely click the *Cancel* button after processing the updates. Doing so will allow you to determine which tasks have been updated, which tasks have been affected by the task updates, and how the task updates impact the current state of your project plan. After you have reviewed the results of the update process, remember to save and publish your project using the Collaborate ➢ Publish ➢ All Information command.

When the system completes the updates, it displays the confirmation dialog shown in Figure 8-7. Click the *OK* button to continue.

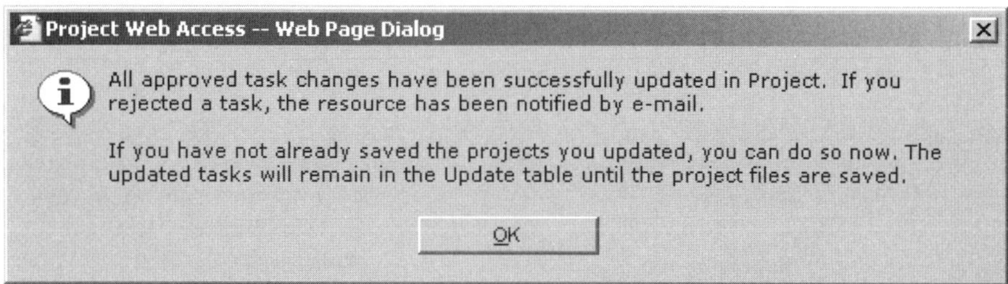

Figure 8-7: Task changes updated

Click the *OK* button in confirmation dialog and the system redisplays the View Task Changes Submitted by Resources page. Shown in Figure 8-8, the system indicates that it no longer has information to display. As soon as the next resource sends an update, the view populates.

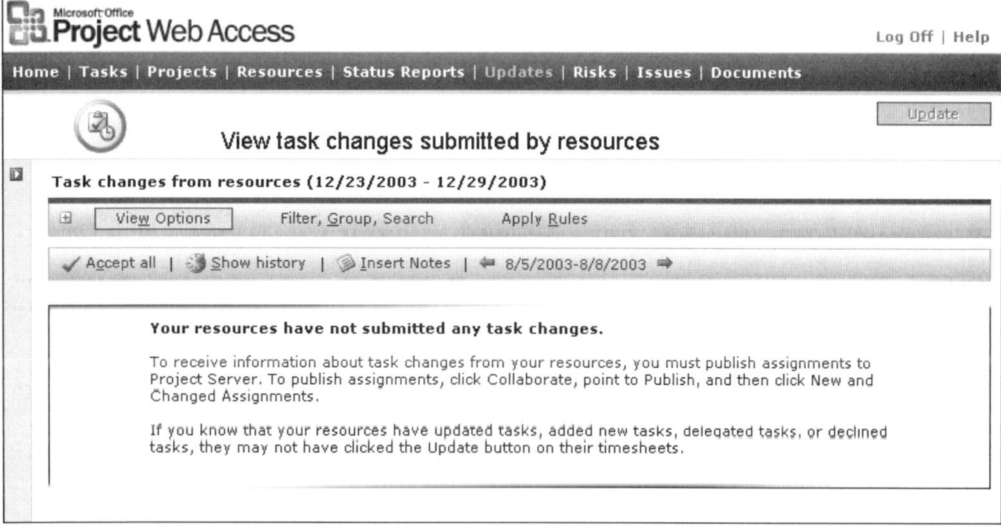

Figure 8-8: No task changes in the queue

Rescheduling Uncompleted Work

After updating task status information into your enterprise project, you must locate and update incomplete tasks that remain in the past reporting period. These tasks mostly comprise un-started and started tasks for which the assigned resource performed no work at all during the last reporting period. When a resource reports progress on a task, and you subsequently update the progress into the plan, the system automatically reschedules the incomplete work to begin after the update status date. The system **does not** automatically reschedule work on current tasks that were not updated by resources.

Figure 8-9 shows a project that contains both completed and uncompleted work during the first reporting period of the project. Notice that in Phase I, Sarah Baker completed her work on the Design P1 Deliverable during the January 2 reporting period. Notice also that Dave Harbaugh completed no work on either the Design P2 Deliverable or Build P2 Deliverable tasks during the same time period.

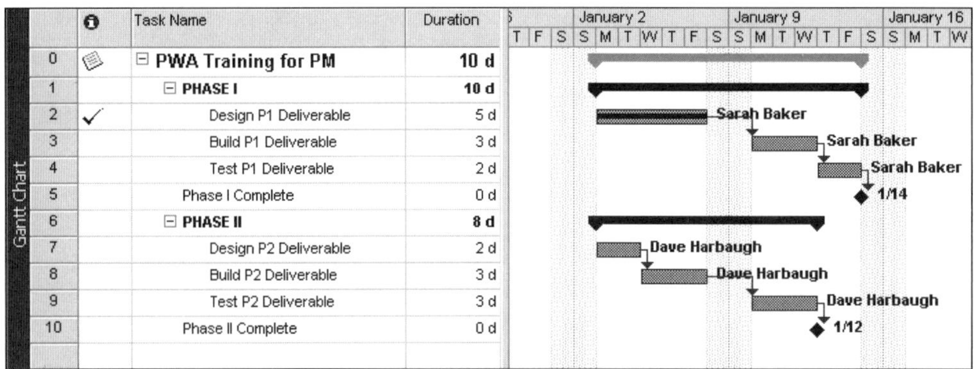

**Figure 8-9: Uncompleted work in
a past reporting period**

Because Dave Harbaugh did not complete his task work in the past reporting period, the current project schedule is no longer accurate. To address situations such as the one shown in Figure 8-9, you must reschedule uncompleted work from the past reporting period into the current reporting period by completing the following steps:

1. Click Tools ➤ Tracking ➤ Update Project.

2. Select the *Reschedule uncompleted work to start after* option.

3. Click the *Reschedule uncompleted work to start after* pick list and select a date one day **before** which work will resume on the uncompleted tasks.

4. Select the *Entire project* option, as shown in Figure 8-10.

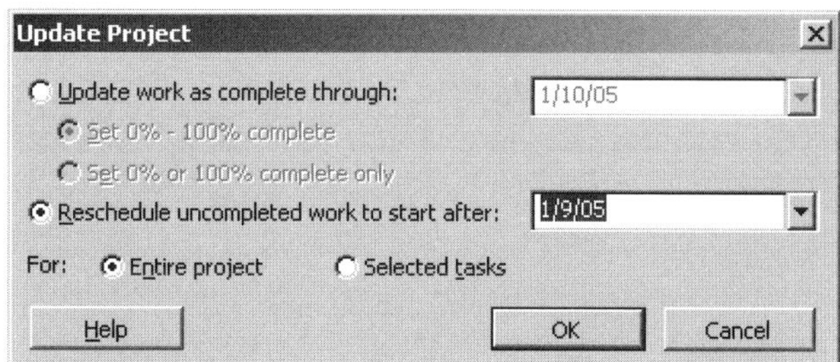

Figure 8-10: Update Project dialog

5. Click the *OK* button.

Project Professional 2003 reschedules tasks with unstarted and uncompleted work from past reporting periods into the current reporting period by setting a Start No Earlier Than (SNET) constraint on the relevant tasks. Figure 8-11 shows the new project schedule after rescheduling uncompleted work. Notice the constraint indicator on the Design P2 Deliverable task in Figure 8-11.

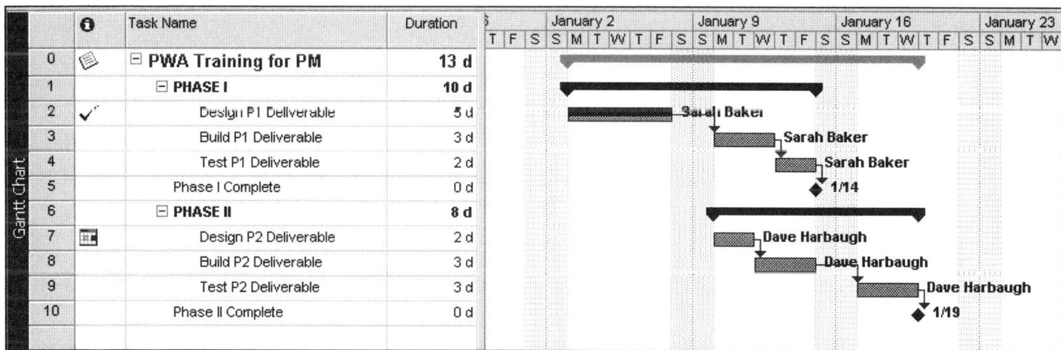

**Figure 8-11: Uncompleted work rescheduled
into the current reporting period**

Hands On Exercise

Exercise 8-1

Accept and reject task updates from resources.

1. Click the *Updates* menu item from the main menu in Project Web Access.
2. Set *Accept* on a task line in the left-most column.
3. Set *Reject* on a task line in the left-most column.
4. Notice but do not click the *Accept all* button on the toolbar.
5. Click the *Update* button.
6. Click the *Cancel* button to review your task updates.
7. Save your project.
8. Click the *OK* button when prompted.

Exercise 8-2

Reschedule uncompleted work from the past reporting period into the current reporting period.

1. Study your project to determine if it contains any tasks with uncompleted work in the past reporting period.
2. Reschedule the past uncompleted work, if necessary.

View History of Past Task Changes

Click the *View history of past task changes* link in the actions pane or click the *Show history* button on the toolbar to open the View History of Past Task Changes page shown in Figure 8-12. Use the View Options and Filter, Group, Search functions as you have learned elsewhere in this chapter to refine the data selection shown in the view as well as the presentation.

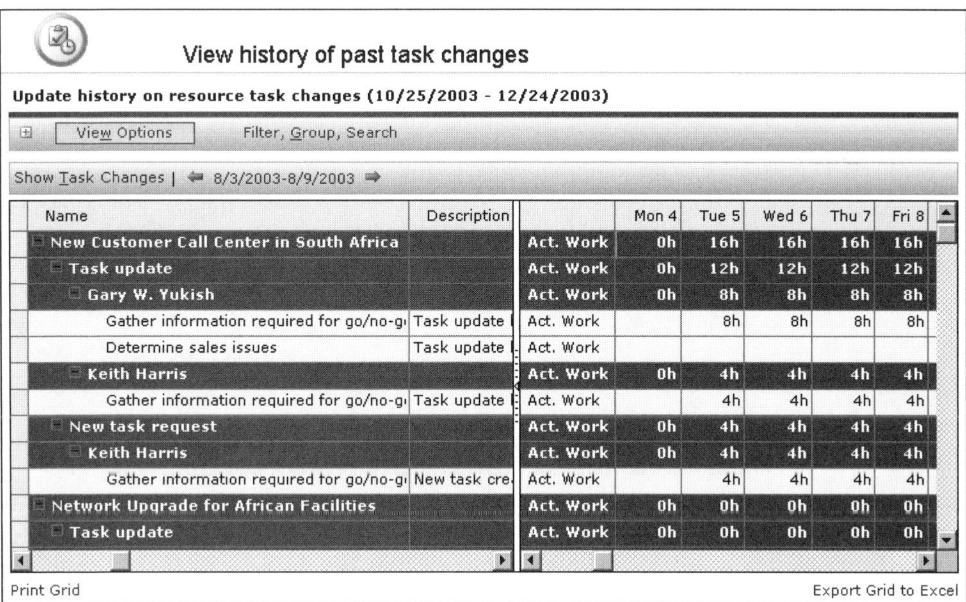

Figure 8-12: View History of Past Task Changes page

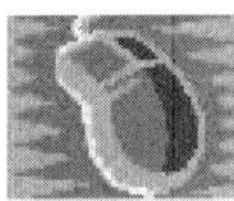

Hands On Exercise

Exercise 8-3

View the history of past task changes in Project Web Access.

1. From the View Task Changes Submitted by Resources page, click the *Show history* button on the toolbar.

2. Examine the history of past task changes.

Setting Rules for Accepting Task Updates

The Set Rules feature allows you to create logical rules for quickly updating tasks in your projects. When you apply a rule, the system processes only those task changes that meet the criteria defined in the rule. To create a new rule, click the *Set rules for automatically accepting changes* link in the actions pane. The system applies the Set rules for automatically accepting changes page, as shown in Figure 8-13.

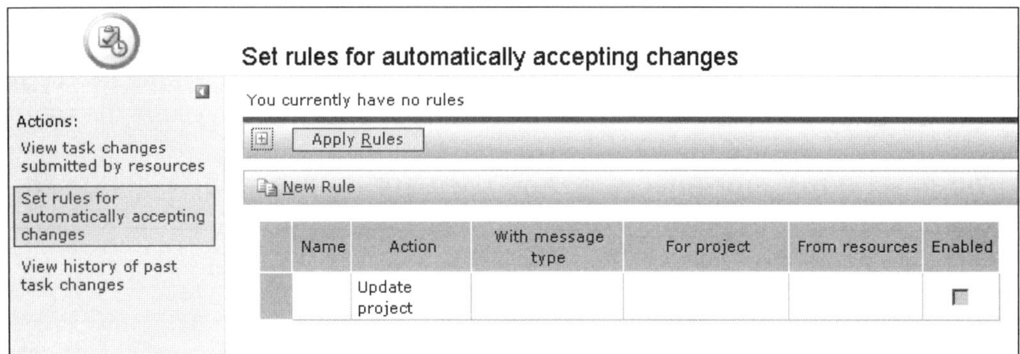

**Figure 8-13: Set rules for
automatically accepting changes page**

Click the *New Rule* button to open the Step 1 page as shown in Figure 8-14.

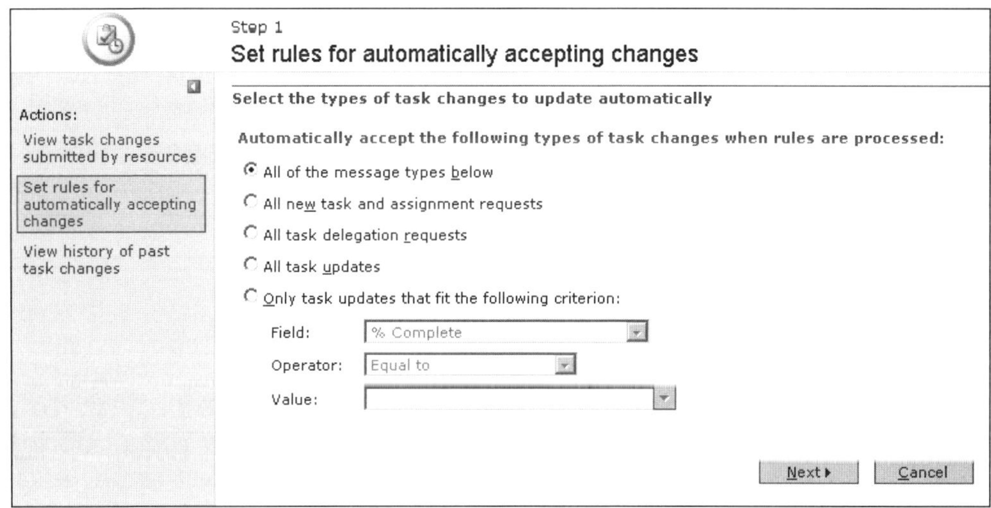

Figure 8-14: Set rules - Step 1

The first step is to select the types of task changes to update automatically. Select one of the following options:

- All of the message types below

- All new task and assignment requests

- All task delegation requests

- All task updates

- Only task updates that fit the following criterion

Select the first option to update all message types, including new task requests, new assignment requests, task delegation requests, and task updates. Select one of the next three options to pinpoint the specific type of message to update automatically. You can create a rule for each message type separately if you wish. Select the last option to create the most specific selection criteria for your new rule, and then set field-based selection tests. In Figure 8-15, notice that I am creating a rule to only update task updates for tasks that are less than 100% complete.

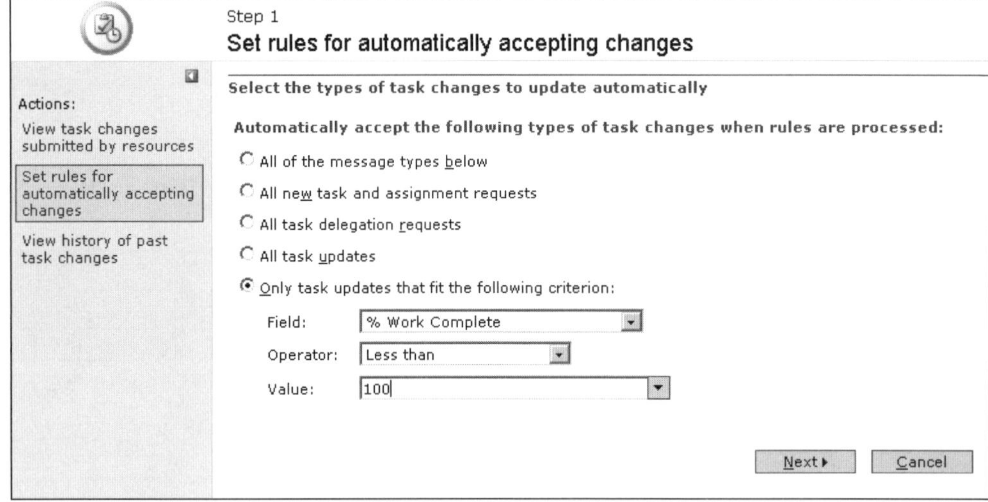

Figure 8-15: Step 1 page
Update tasks less than 100% complete

Click the *Next* button to display the Step 2 page. Select the projects to which the new rule will apply. Choose the *All current and future projects* option to update any of your projects automatically. Choose the *Only the projects specified below* option to select specific projects for updating. Select the projects you wish to update from the Available projects list, and then click the *Add* button. You can also include any future projects you will create by selecting the *Including all future projects* option as well. Notice in Figure 8-16 that I have selected two specific projects for automatic updating.

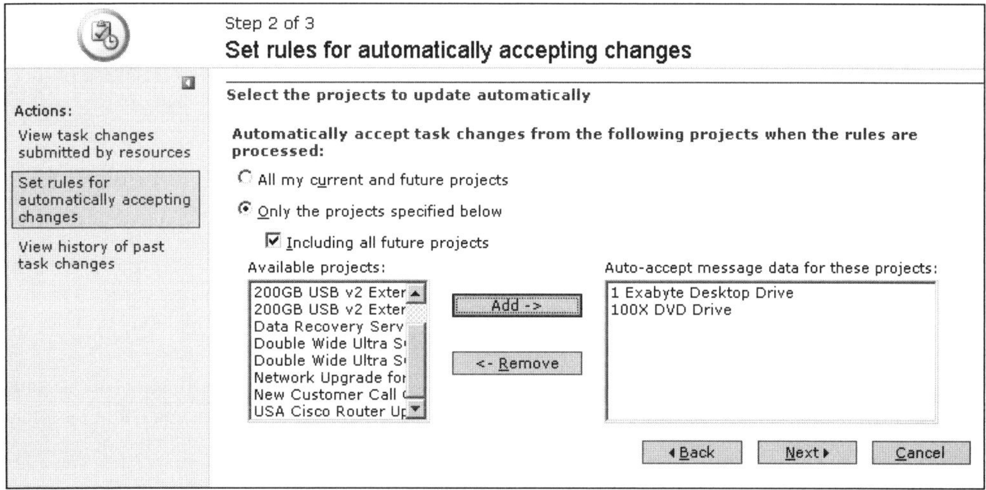

Figure 8-16: Set rules - Step 2
Select projects to which the new rule applies

Click the Next to continue to the Step 3 page, as shown in Figure 8-17.

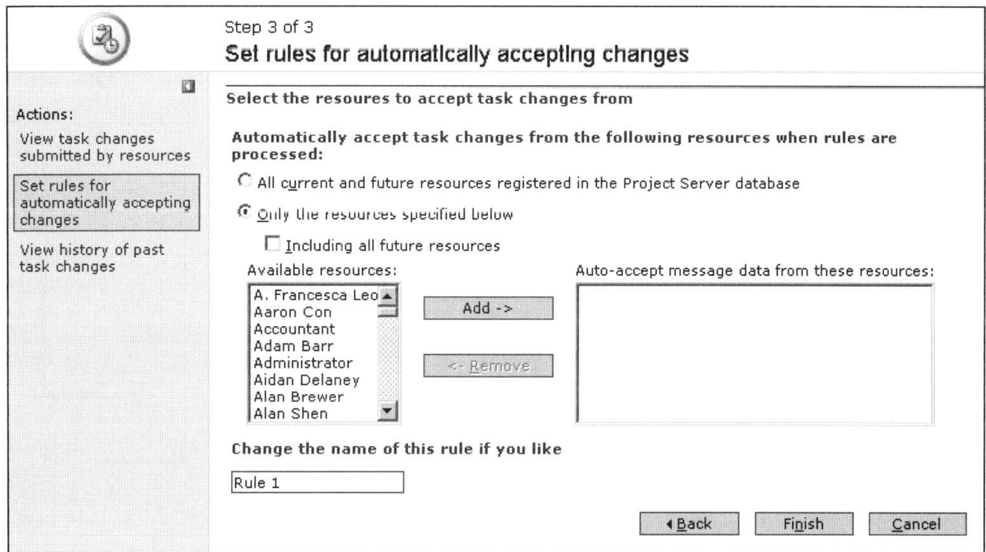

Figure 8-17: Set rules - Step 3
Select resources to which the new rule applies

The last step in the new rule creation process is to select the resources to which the rule applies. As you can see, a rule can be very specific or very broad in its application. You can even create a rule to update a task based on meeting specific criteria that applies to only one resource in only one project. Give your new rule a name and select the desired resources. Click the *Finish* button to complete the rule creation process.

When you click the *Finish* button, the Set Rules page redisplays showing your new rule indicating an enabled state as shown in Figure 8-18. Note at the top of the Set rules page that once you have created your first rule, the system reports how many rules you have created. The toolbar offers options to modify, copy, or delete a rule, providing that you have selected a rule in the grid. Use the Copy Rule feature to create new rules based on rules you have previously created. Deselect the *Enabled* option for a rule to disable the rule without removing it from the system, which allows you to re-enable it later.

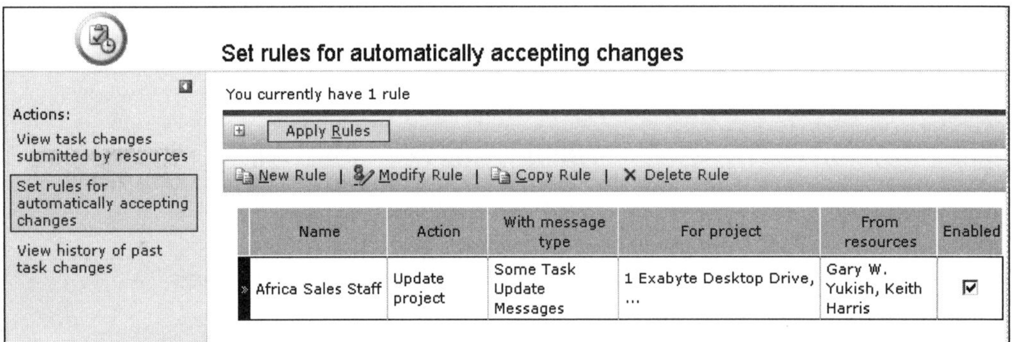

**Figure 8-18: Set rules page
displays a new rule**

The next time you have task updates, run your automated rules first to accept all automatic updates. To run rules, click the *Apply Rules* tab at the top of the View Task Changes Submitted by Resources page. The system displays the Apply Rules page, shown in Figure 8-19. If you click the *Apply resource change rules to* pick list, you can choose to apply the rule to all projects specified in each rule or to a specific project. After making this decision, click the *Run Rules Now* button to run the rules.

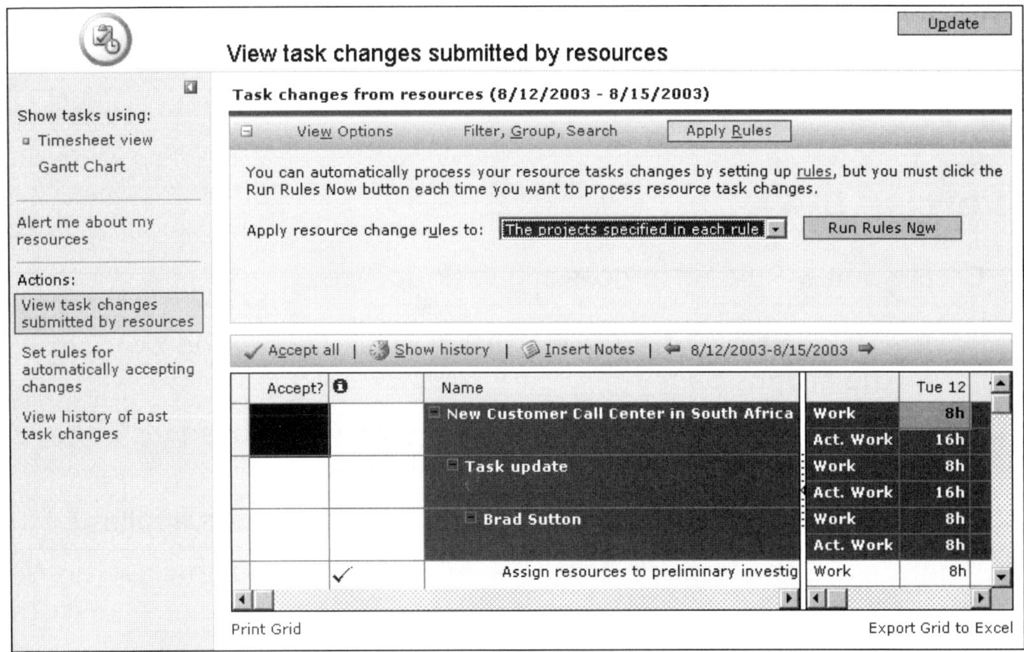

Figure 8-19: Apply Rules tab

When you click the *Run Rules Now* button, the system opens each project specified in your rules and updates messages for only those resources specified in your rules. When the updates are completed, the system displays the confirmation message shown in Figure 8-20.

**Figure 8-20: Successful update
using rules**

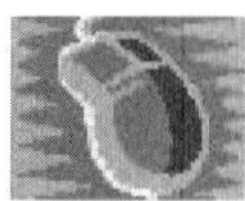

Hands On Exercise

Exercise 8-4

Create a new Rule for processing task updates.

1. Click on the *Set rules for automatically accepting changes* link in the actions pane.

2. In the Set rules for automatically accepting changes page, click the *New Rule* button on the toolbar.

3. Select a type of task changes to which the Rule applies.

4. Select the projects that the Rule will update and click the *Next* button.

5. Select the resources that the Rule will update and enter a name for the new rule.

6. Click the *Finish* button to create the new Rule.

Exercise 8-5

Apply your new Rule to one or more task updates.

1. Click the *View task changes submitted by resources* link in the actions pane.

2. Click the *Apply Rules* tab.

3. Click the *Apply resource changes rules to* pick list and explore your options.

4. Click the *Run Rules Now* button.

5. Click the *OK* button to save changes to the active project.

6. Click the *OK* button in the confirmation message in Project Web Access.

Timesheet Approval

A new feature of Project Server 2003 is the timesheet approval process. This process allows people like resource managers, line managers, or team leaders to approve the timesheets of resources before the project manager processes the actuals contained in each resource's timesheet.

Before you can use the timesheet approval process, your Project Server administrator must enable timesheet approval within Project Server.

If you are a manager who was been granted timesheet approval authority within Project Server, the system displays a Timesheet section on your Home page in Project Web Access, as shown in Figure 8-21.

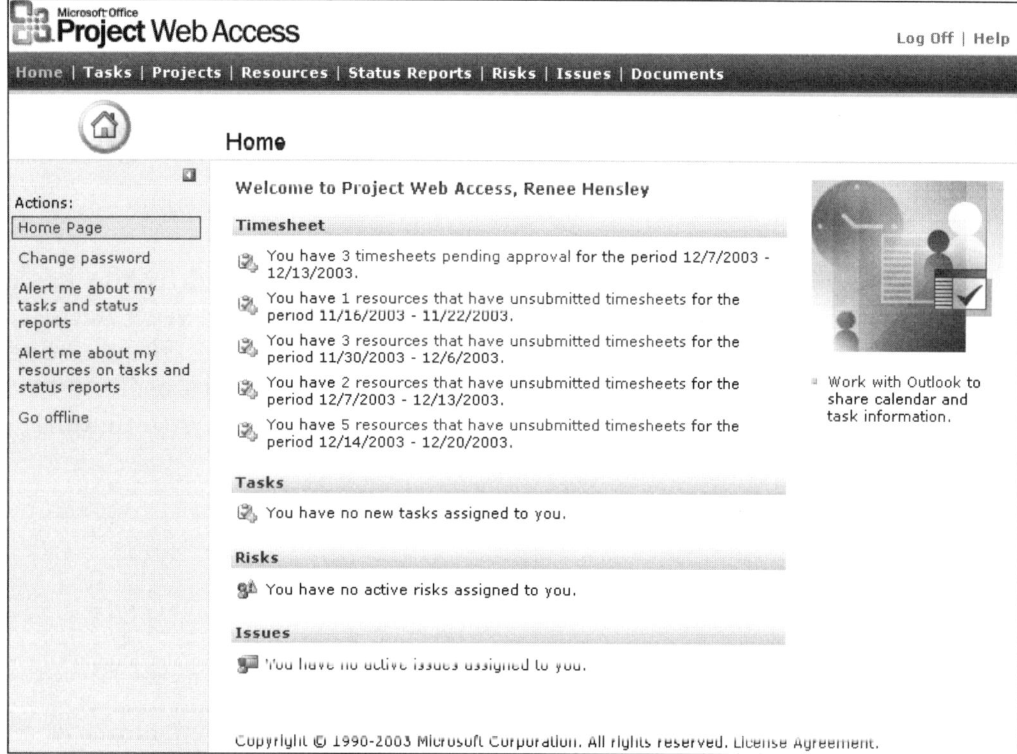

Figure 8-21: Timesheet section of Home page

The Timesheet section of the Home page contains information about the number of timesheets pending approval and the number of resources that have unsubmitted timesheets for specific reporting periods. To begin the timesheet approval process, click the *Timesheet* link at the beginning of the section or click the ____ *timesheets pending approval* link. The system displays the Approve Timesheets page shown in Figure 8-22.

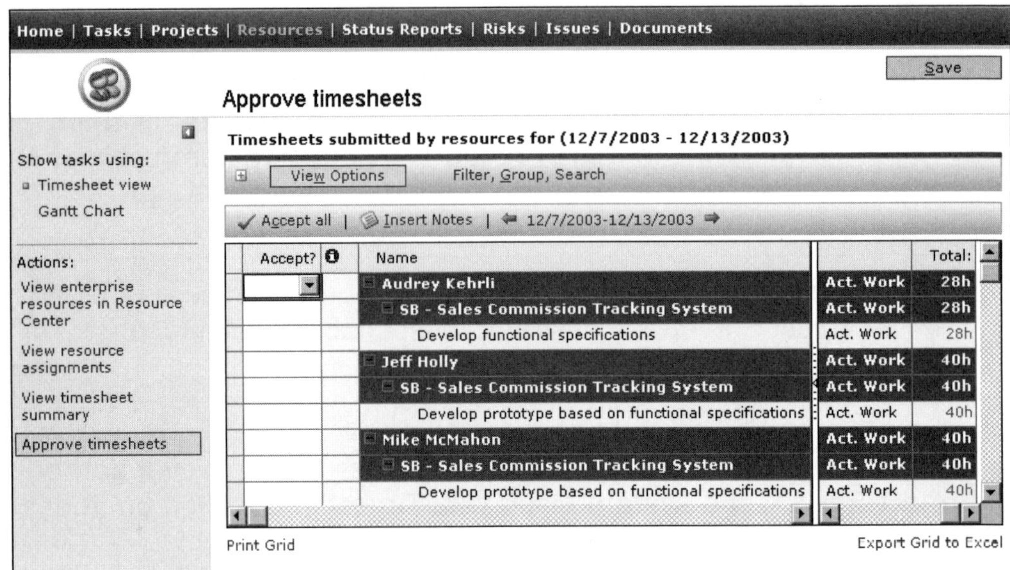

Figure 8-22: Approve Timesheets page

You can also access the Approve Timesheets page by clicking the *Approve timesheets* link in the Resource Center actions pane.

The page displays each task submitted for approval, grouped by the assigned resource and then by project. As with other pages in Project Web Access, the Approve Timesheets page contains a *View Options* tab and a *Filter, Group, Search* tab at the top of the grid. The *View Options* tab offers options to display Overtime Work and to select an outline level, as shown in Figure 8-23.

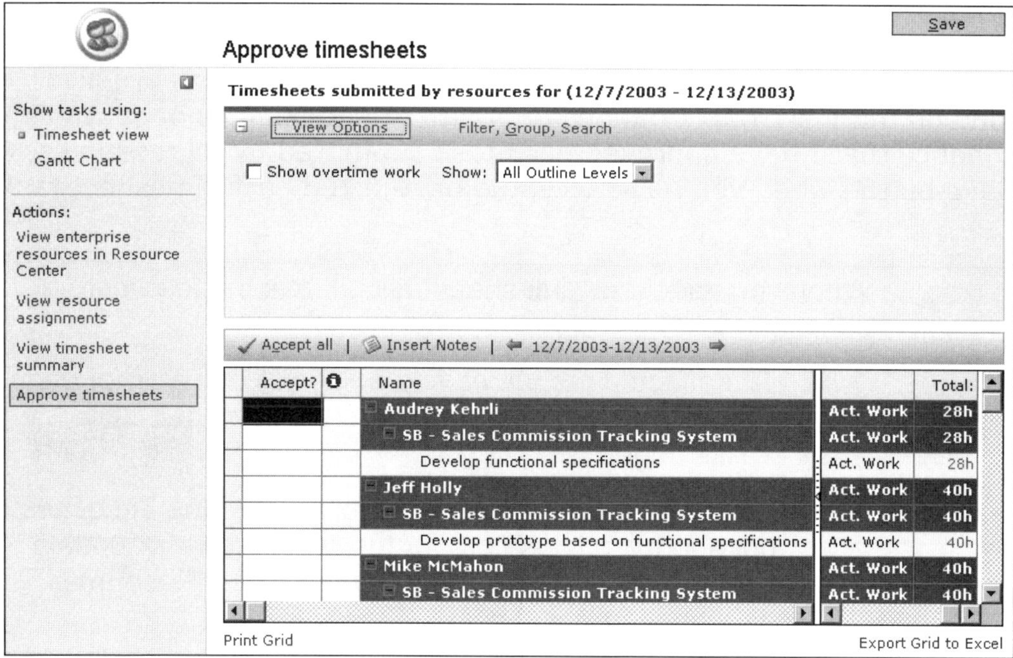

**Figure 8-23: Approve Timesheets page
View Options tab**

The *Filter, Group, Search* tab, shown in Figure 8-24, offers filtering by all assignments or by a custom filter, along with grouping and searching capabilities covered in previous modules.

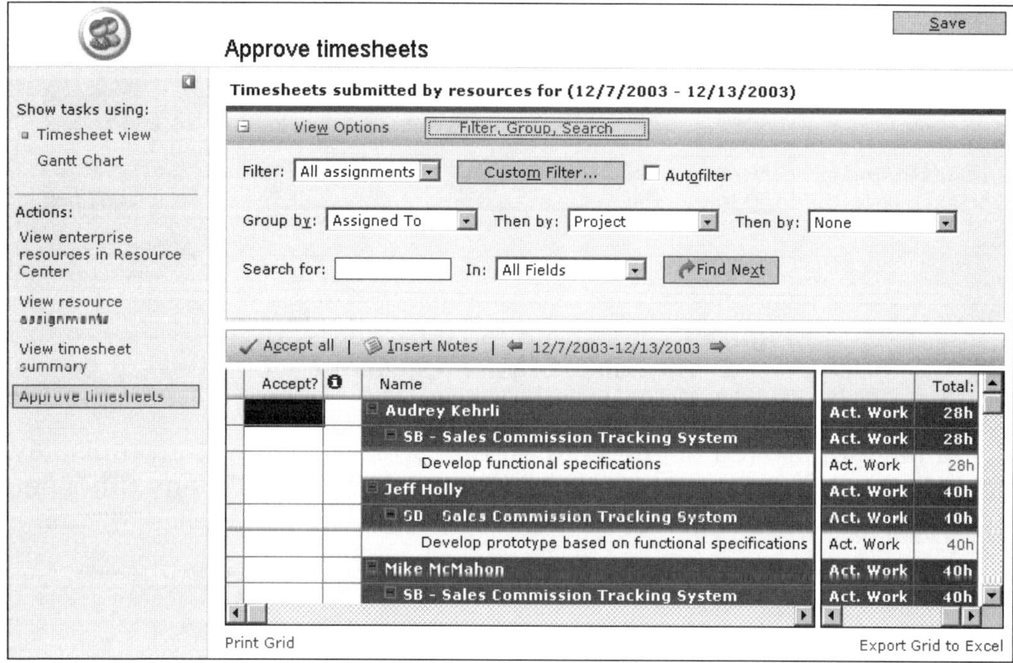

**Figure 8-24: Approve Timesheets page
Filter, Group, Search tab**

As with the approval of task updates on the View Task Changes Submitted by Resources page, you can select an Accept or Reject value for each timesheet task on the Approve Timesheets page. The page includes an *Accept All* button, an *Insert Notes* button, and a *date selector* button, as are also included on the View Task Changes Submitted by Resources page. In Figure 8-25, notice that I have approved each task submitted by all resources. Click the *Save* button when you have accepted or rejected each timesheet task.

When you reject any timesheet tasks, it has the following consequences:

- The affected resources see a special indicator for each rejected task in the Indicators column of their View My Tasks page.

- The resource's project manager will see the Timesheet not approved indicators for the resources task update on the View Task Changes Submitted by Resources page, previously shown in Figure 8-3.

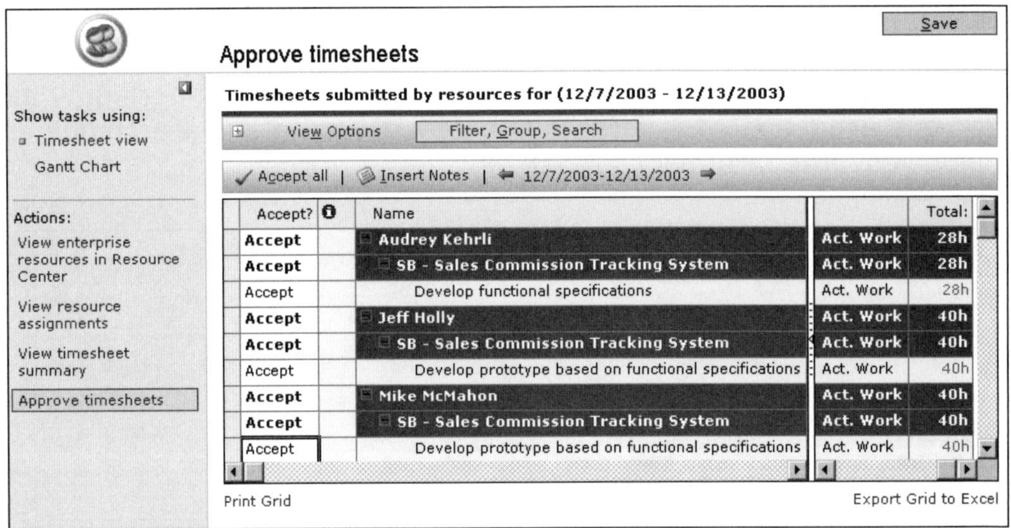

Figure 8-25: Approve Timesheets page
Timesheet tasks approved

Once you have approved or rejected all timesheets, the system redisplays the page indicating that your resources have not submitted any timesheet changes for the current period, as shown in Figure 8-26.

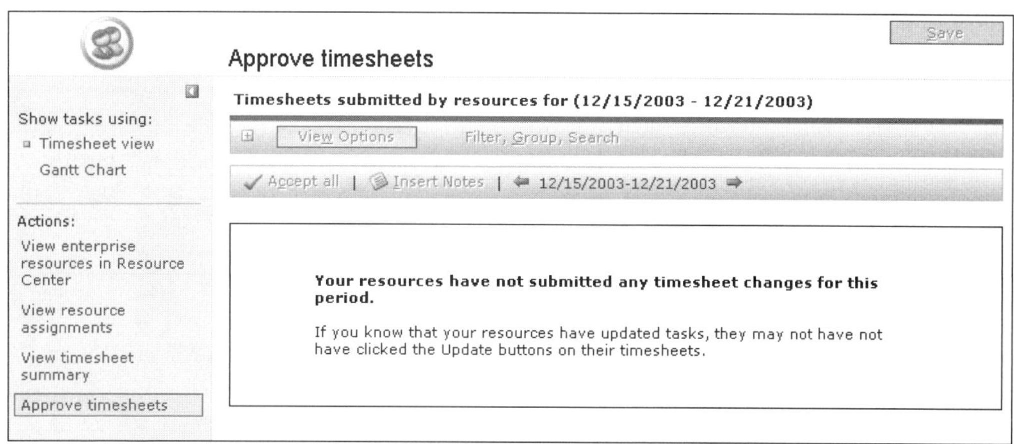

**Figure 8-26: Approve Timesheets page
No timesheets to approve**

By default, a project manager can update a task even when you have **rejected** the timesheet containing the task, thus allowing the project manager to overrule your rejection of a timesheet. If your organization is using a timesheet approval process, then MSProjectExperts recommends that you establish standard procedures for handling timesheets that are either unapproved or rejected.

Viewing Unsubmitted Timesheets

The Timesheet section of the Home page shows you both timesheets pending approval and unsubmitted timesheets. If you click the ____ *resources that have unsubmitted timesheets* link for a specific period, the system displays the View Timesheet Summary page shown in Figure 8-27. The display includes each task that is scheduled during the selected period, grouped by the assigned resource and then by project.

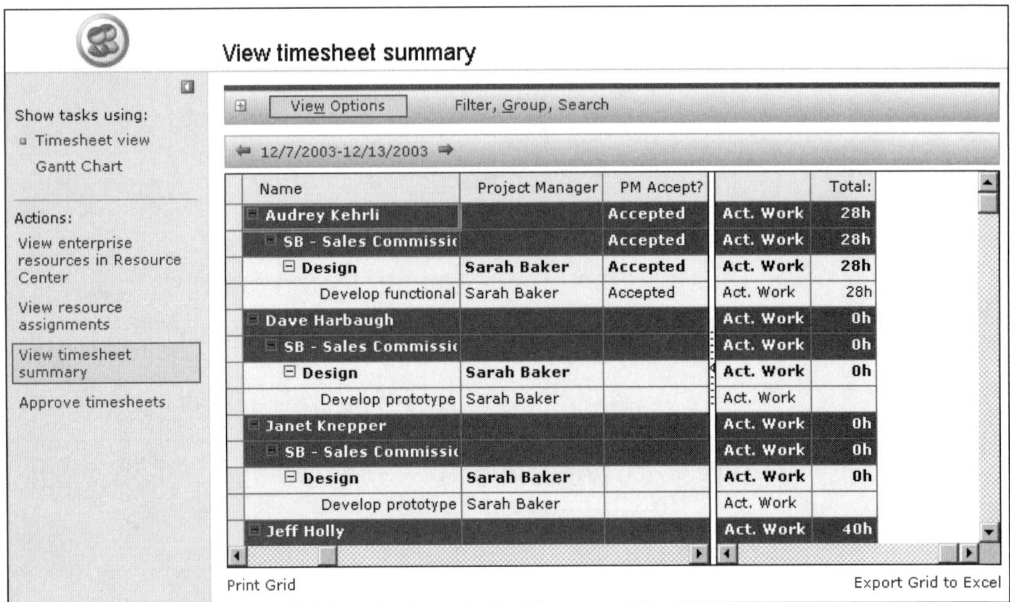

Figure 8-27: View Timesheet Summary page

As with the Approve timesheets page, the View Timesheet Summary page contains a *View Options* tab and a *Filter, Group, Search* tab. The *View Options* tab is identical on both pages. The *Filter, Group, Search* tab shown in Figure 8-28 contains the following filters:

- All timesheets
- All approved timesheets
- All rejected timesheets
- All submitted timesheets not yet approved
- All unsubmitted timesheets
- Custom filter

The *Filter, Group, Search* tab offers the same grouping and searching capabilities covered in previous modules.

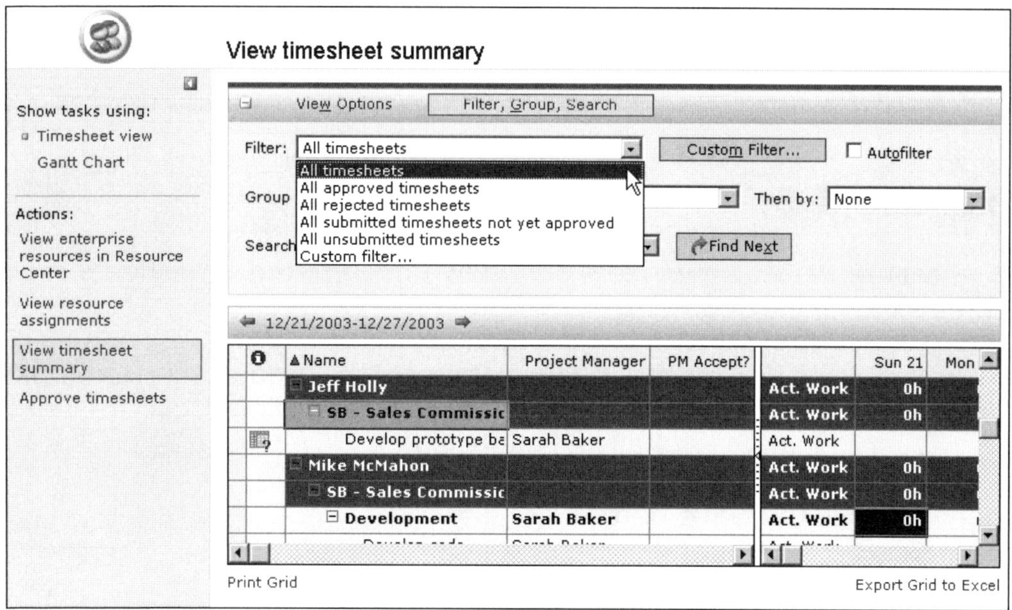

**Figure 8-28: View Timesheet Summary page
Filter, Group, Search tab**

The View Timesheet Summary page does not allow you to take any action on any user's timesheet, and is for informational purposes only. The left portion of the grid contains a number of columns that you can use for determining the update and approval status of each task. These columns include the following:

- Indicators
- Name
- Project Manager
- PM Accept?
- Assigned To
- Project
- Timesheet Status

You can use the PM Accept? column to determine whether the project manager has approved or rejected a task update, regardless of whether you have approved or rejected the user's timesheet. You can use the Timesheet Status column to determine whether the resource has submitted the timesheet to you for approval.

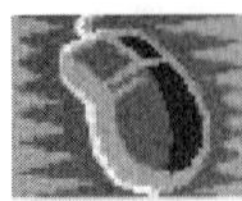

Hands On Exercise

Exercise 8-6

Accept or reject timesheets and view unsubmitted timesheets for your resources.

1. Click the *Timesheet* link in the content area of the Home page in Project Web Access.

2. Accept or reject a timesheet.

3. Click the *Save* button.

4. Click the *Home* menu.

5. Click a link in the Timesheet section for an unsubmitted timesheet during a specific time period.

6. Examine the information shown in the View Timesheet Summary page.

Axioms for Success with Tracking

To be successful in tracking project progress using Project Server 2003, your organization should keep the following in mind:

- Everyone in your organization who is responsible for reporting progress should enter their time and send their updates on a standard day each week.

- Managers should deal appropriately with anyone who is responsible for reporting progress, but who fails to cooperate or participate fully in the process. You must take all necessary steps to ensure the full participation of everyone in your organization in order to validate the project data in the system.

- Your organization should track and manage the absence of resources during each update cycle. If necessary, you can implement surrogate processes for absent resources.

- Project managers should enter time for absent resources directly in the project plan and then push the changes back to the resources by republishing the updated assignments.

- Your organization should also track and manage the absence of managers during each update cycle. For updating purposes, other managers can take over tasks owned by absent managers and process the updates.

- Stay current with progress reporting and updates to make sure that you are managing your projects with current data.

Module 09

Using the Home Page

Learning Objectives

After completing this module, you will be able to:

- Change your password for Project Server authentication
- Set alerts and reminders for yourself
- Set alerts and reminders for resources that you manage
- Go offline with Project Web Access
- Go online with an offline copy of Project Web Access

Using Features from the Home Page

When a project manager logs into Project Web Access, the system displays a Home page similar to the one shown in Figure 9-1. Because the navigation system is adaptive in Project Web Access, the system displays menu selections according to your group membership. The main menu bar displayed across the top of the Home page for Steve Masters shows only those menus that a project manager has permission to view. If Steve had an administrator's account, the system would also display an *Admin* menu selection in addition to the menus displayed for a project manager. By default, Team Members do not see the menu choices for Resources, Updates, or Admin.

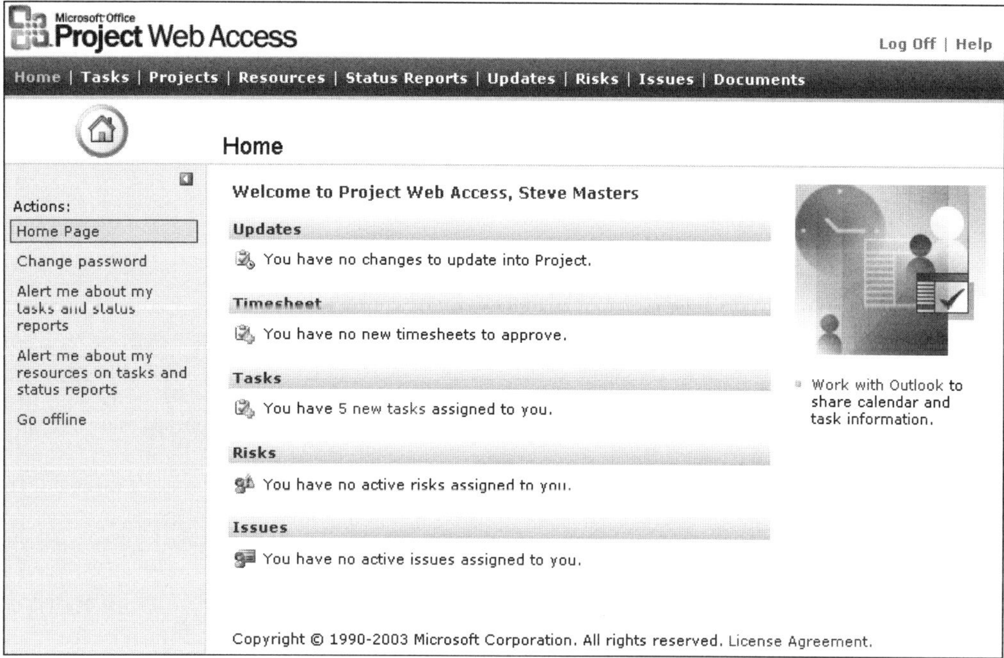

**Figure 9-1: Home page in Project Web
Access for a project manager**

In the actions pane on the left, the system displays the available actions according to group membership. The available actions for a project manager are as follows:

- Home Page
- Change password
- Alert me about my tasks and status reports
- Alert me about my resources on tasks and status reports
- Go offline

Changing Your Password

Click the *Change password* link in the actions pane to change your password. Only users defined with Project Server authentication can change their passwords in Project Server 2003. Windows users change passwords according to domain policy. If you log on with a Project Server account, clicking Change password from the actions pane displays the Change Password page shown in Figure 9-2.

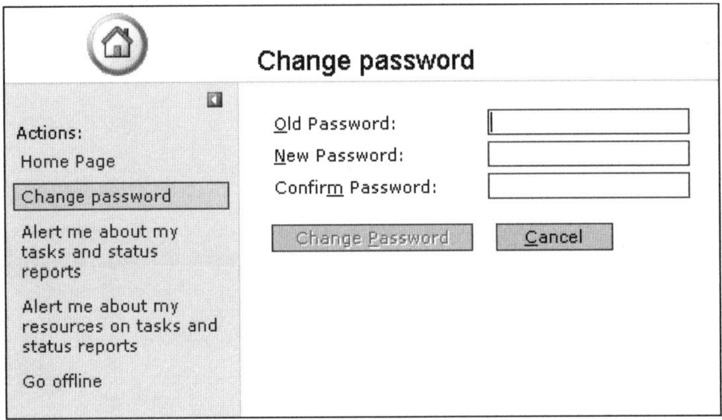

Figure 9-2: Change Password page

 The system displays an error message on the Change Password page if you attempt to change your password while logged on as a Windows authenticated user.

To change your password, enter your old password, type a new password and confirm it, and then click the *Change Password* button. The system reports success displaying the confirmation dialog shown in Figure 9-3.

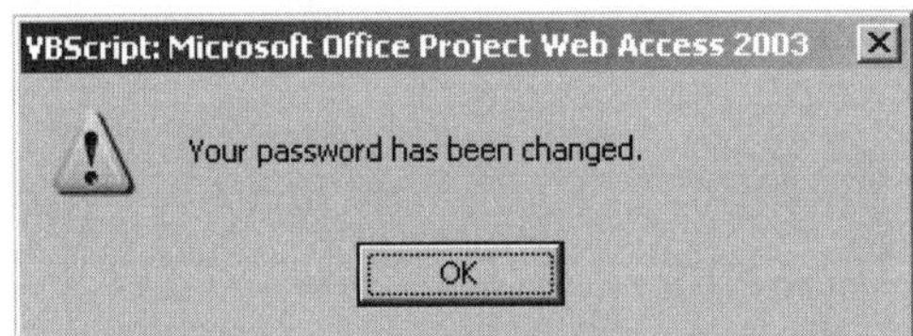

**Figure 9-3: Password change
is successful**

Setting Alerts and Reminders for Yourself

Project Web Access allows you to receive alerts and reminders via e-mail messages using its alerts and reminders engine. You can determine whether the system sends you immediate notification of certain events and you can create personalized criteria-based reminders for yourself. Click the *Alert me about my tasks and status reports* link in the actions pane to display the Alert Me about My Tasks and Status Reports page shown in Figure 9-4.

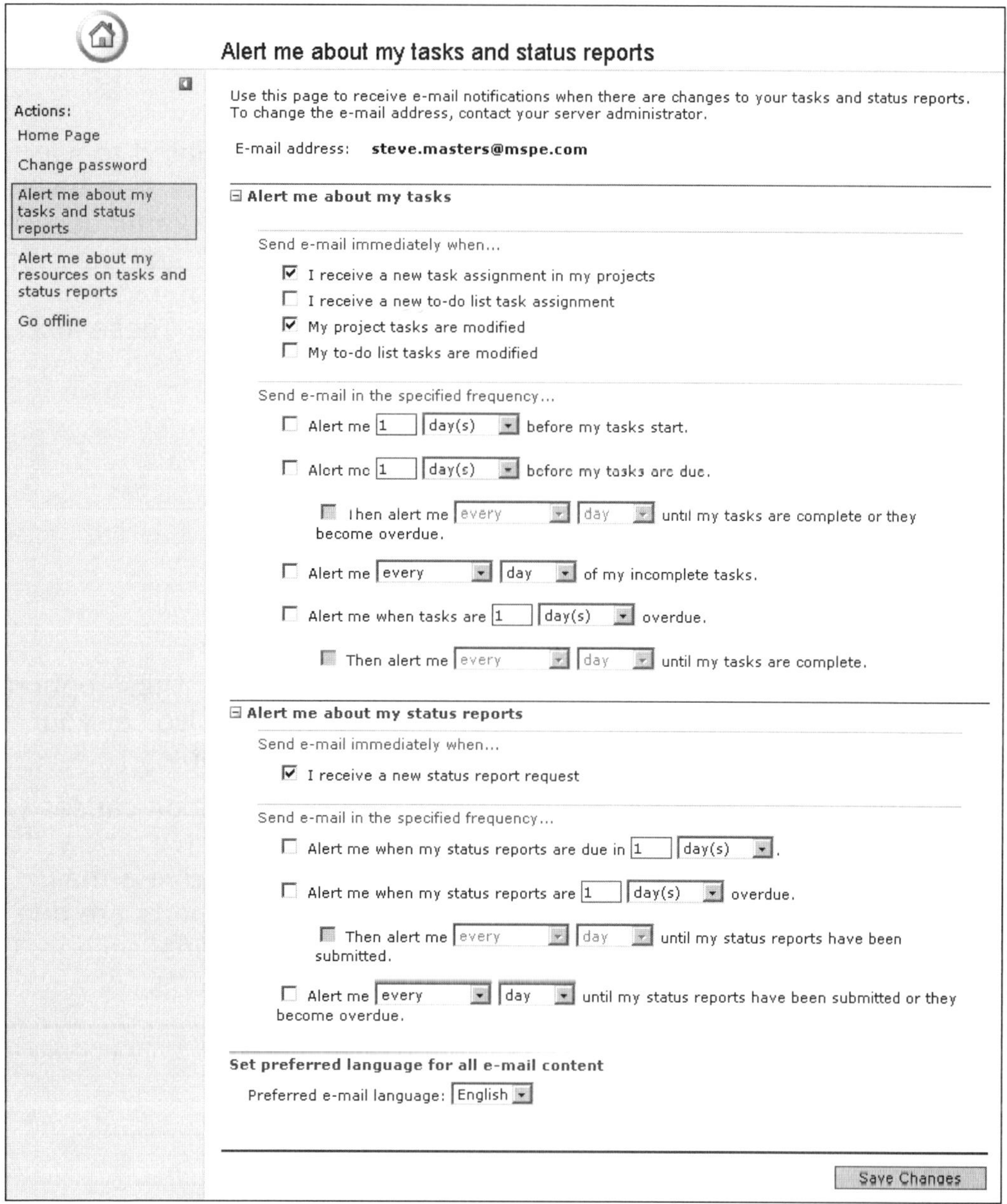

Figure 9-4: Alert Me about My Tasks and
Status Reports page

The first set of options in the Alert Me about My Tasks section allows you to subscribe to e-mail messages that the system sends immediately when certain events occur. These events are:

- When you receive a new task assignment in a project
- When you receive a new task assignment in a to-do list
- When one of your task assignments is modified in a project
- When one of your task assignments is modified in a to-do list

Notice in Figure 9-4 that the default settings cause the system to alert you only when you receive new task assignments in a project or when your resources modify their project task assignments.

The second set of options allows you to create reminders related to specific task criteria for project work and to-do lists. Each night the system tests your criteria and generates an email message containing the task reminders you've set. You receive an email only if you have set criteria and the system finds an appropriate match between your tasks in the system and your criteria. You can think of the criteria as triggering conditions. These include:

- Before a task starts
- Before a task is due
- Until a task is complete or becomes overdue
- When you have an incomplete task
- When you have an overdue task
- Until an overdue task is complete

Notice in Figure 9-4 that the default settings include none of these options. When you select one or more of these options, you should also set your desired frequency, as you do not have to receive these nightly.

The first option in the Alert Me about My Status Reports section causes you to receive an immediate e-mail message whenever you receive a new status report request. The second set of options causes you to receive e-mail messages at a specified frequency whenever your status reports are due or overdue. You can also set your language preference in the final section. Click the *Save Changes* button when you have made your selections.

Setting Reminders for your Resources

Select the *Alert me about my resources on tasks and status reports* link in the actions pane to display the pages shown in Figure 9-5. The Alert Me about My Resources on Tasks and Status Reports page offers you alerts that the system sends immediately when they occur. You can set an alert to trigger when a resource submits a new task, submits a new task assignment, delegates a task, or updates a task. All of these options are selected by default. Select and deselect these options as you wish.

This page also allows you to set up reminders for your resources about their project work. When you set reminders for your resources, you may choose to have the reminder go to your resource only, to yourself only, or to both you and your resource.

Keep in mind that "my resources" means that each resource is attributed with an RBS value in a subordinate leaf to your own value, or that the resource is managed by you on a project.

Select the reminders you want for your resources. You can also set your language preference in the final section. Click the *Save Changes* button when your selections are complete.

If a resource deselects a reminder option, and the resource's manager selects the same reminder option for the resource, the manager's selection will trump the user's selection.

Alert me about my resources on tasks and status reports

Actions:

Home Page

Change password

Alert me about my tasks and status reports

Alert me about my resources on tasks and status reports

Go offline

Use this page to receive e-mail notifications when there are changes to your resources' tasks and status reports. To change the e-mail address, contact your server administrator.

E-mail address: **steve.masters@mspe.com**

⊟ Alert me about my resources' tasks

Send e-mail immediately when my resources...

☑ Submit new tasks and assignments
☑ Delegate tasks
☑ Update tasks

Send e-mail in the specified frequency for upcoming tasks...

☐ Alert resources [1] [day(s) ▼] before their tasks are due.

⦿ e-mail me only
○ e-mail my resources
○ e-mail me and my resources

Send e-mail in the specified frequency for overdue tasks...

☐ Alert resources when their tasks are [1] [day(s) ▼] overdue.

☐ Then alert resources [every ▼] [day ▼] until their tasks are complete.

⦿ e-mail me only
○ e-mail my resources
○ e-mail me and my resources

Send e-mail in the specified frequency for tasks requiring updates...

☐ Alert resources when their tasks have started for [1] [day(s) ▼] but have no actual work.

⦿ e-mail me only
○ e-mail my resources
○ e-mail me and my resources

⊟ Alert me about my resources' status reports

Send e-mail immediately when my resources...

☑ Submit a status report

Send e-mail in the specified frequency for upcoming status reports...

☐ Alert resources when their status reports are due in [1] [day(s) ▼].

⦿ e-mail me only
○ e-mail my resources
○ e-mail me and my resources

Send e-mail in the specified frequency for overdue status reports...

☐ Alert resources when their status reports are [1] [day(s) ▼] overdue.

☐ Then alert resources [every ▼] [day ▼] the status reports are submitted.

⦿ e-mail me only
○ e-mail my resources
○ e-mail me and my resources

Set preferred language for all e-mail content

Preferred e-mail language: [English ▼]

[Save Changes]

Figure 9-5: Alert me about my resources on tasks and status reports

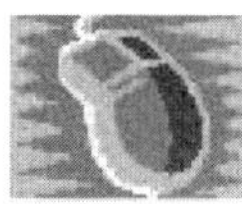 **Hands On Exercise**

Exercise 9-1

Explore the setting of alerts and reminders to yourself, and reminders to your resources.

1. Click the *Alert me about my tasks and status reports* link in the actions pane.

2. Explore the selections.

3. Click the Alert me about my resources on tasks and status reports in the actions pane.

4. Explore the selections.

Taking Project Web Access Offline

Project Web Access leverages the offline capabilities of Internet Explorer and the Windows operating system to provide timesheet and status report functionality offline. Offline functionality is limited to the date range you select and allows you to perform only the following actions:

- Enter timesheet information for later posting to the server.

- Create and/or edit Status Reports that you can later upload to the server.

When you click the *Go offline* link in the actions pane, your system may first display the ActiveX warning dialog shown in Figure 9-6.

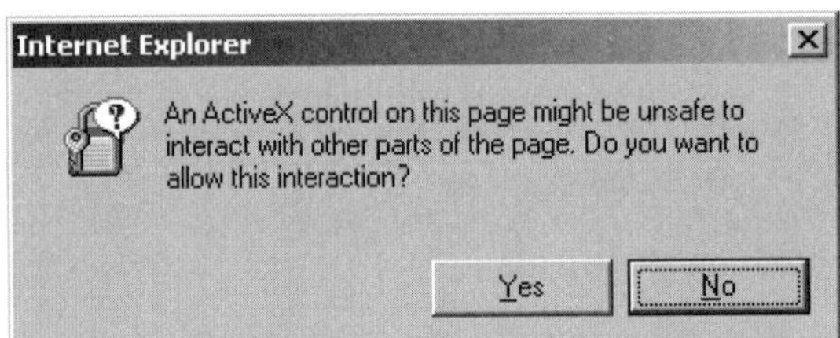

Figure 9-6: ActiveX warning dialog

The appearance of the ActiveX warning dialog is dependent on the security settings in your Internet Explorer browser

Click the *Yes* button in the warning dialog to display the Go Offline page shown in Figure 9-7.

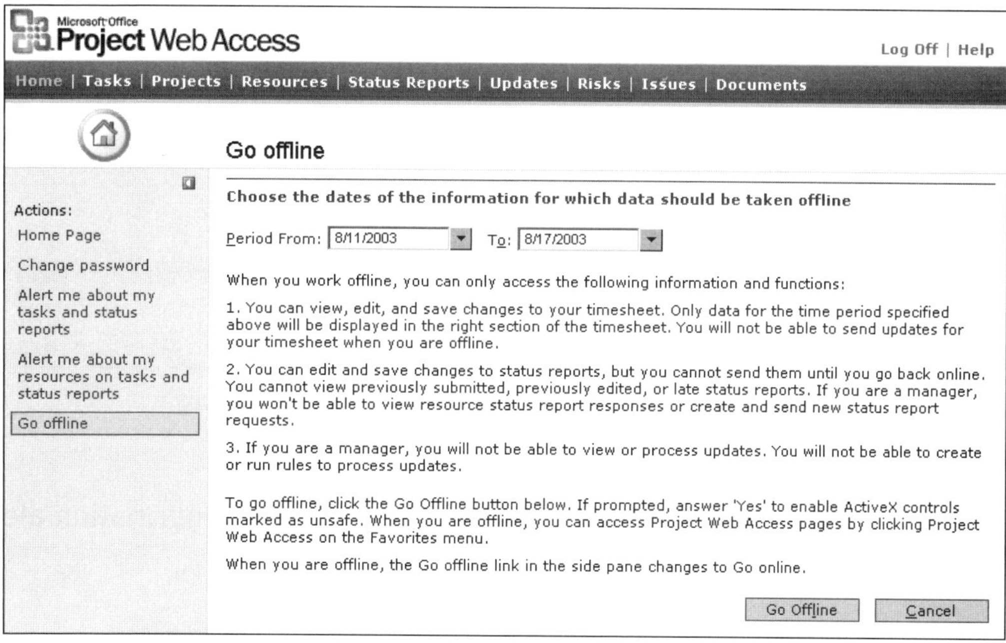

Figure 9-7: Go Offline page

To go offline with Project Web Access, select the date range desired by setting values in the *Period from* and *To* pick lists, then click the *Go Offline* button.

The system sets the initial dates in the *Period from* and *To* pick lists to the one-week period beginning with today. If your organization uses managed time periods, the system will not allow you to enter progress in your timesheet during closed time periods while working offline.

When you click the *Go Offline* button, the display continues to change while the system takes a snapshot of your Project Web Access information and copies it into your offline folders. The system reports progress as it saves each page, as shown in Figure 9-8.

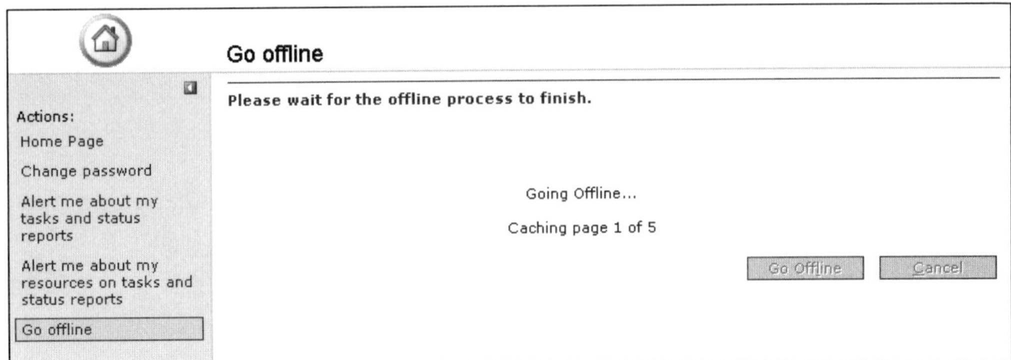

**Figure 9-8: Interim information while taking
Project Web Access pages offline**

Upon completion of the process, the system displays the confirmation alert
box shown in Figure 9-9.

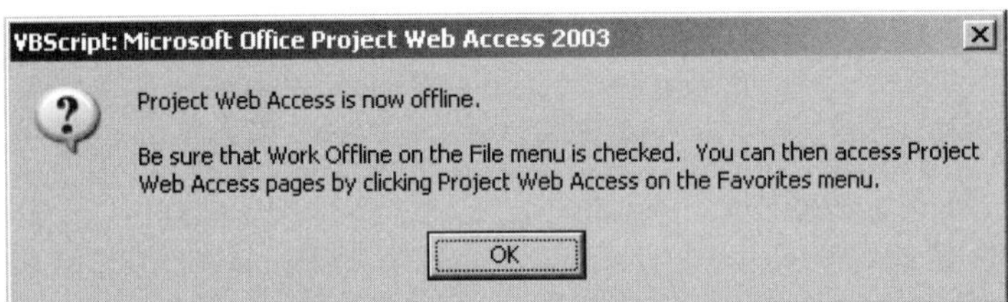

**Figure 9-9: Offline mode
confirmed**

Click the *OK* button in the alert dialog and the system will redisplay the
Home page, which now has a very limited menu selection available as shown
in Figure 9-10. Note that the system changed the *Go offline* link to the *Go
online* link instead.

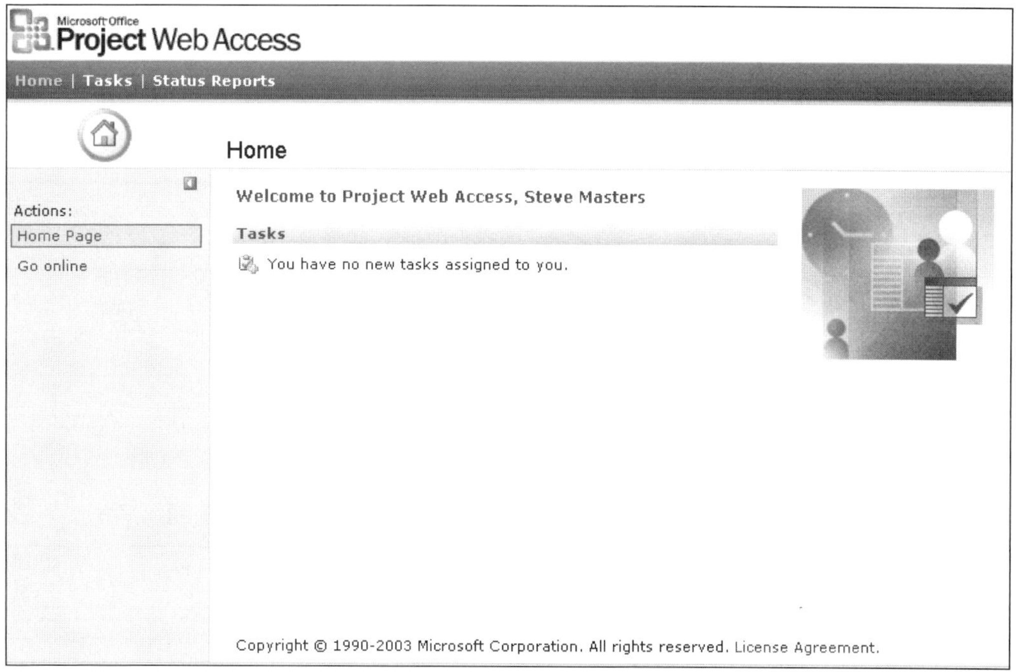

**Figure 9-10: Project Web Access Home page
while working Offline**

Taking Project Web Access offline adds a link to your *Favorites* menu shown in Figure 9-11. To access your offline pages, use this link.

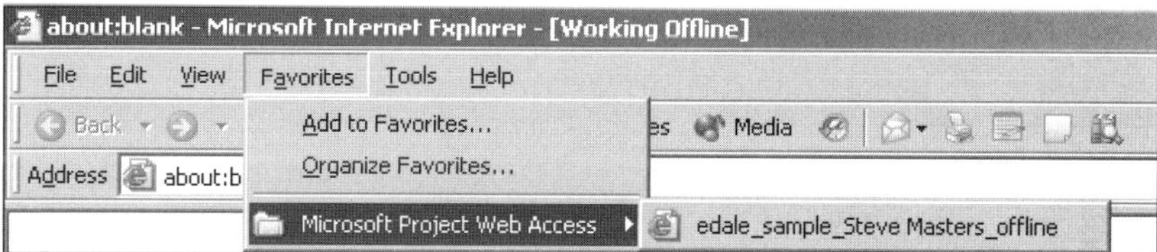

**Figure 9-11: Access offline pages
from the Favorites menu**

While working in Offline mode, you can enter progress in your timesheet in the View My Tasks page as shown In Figure 9-12. You can also edit and create status reports in the Status Reports page. These remain local to your machine until you reconnect to Project Server and choose to go online.

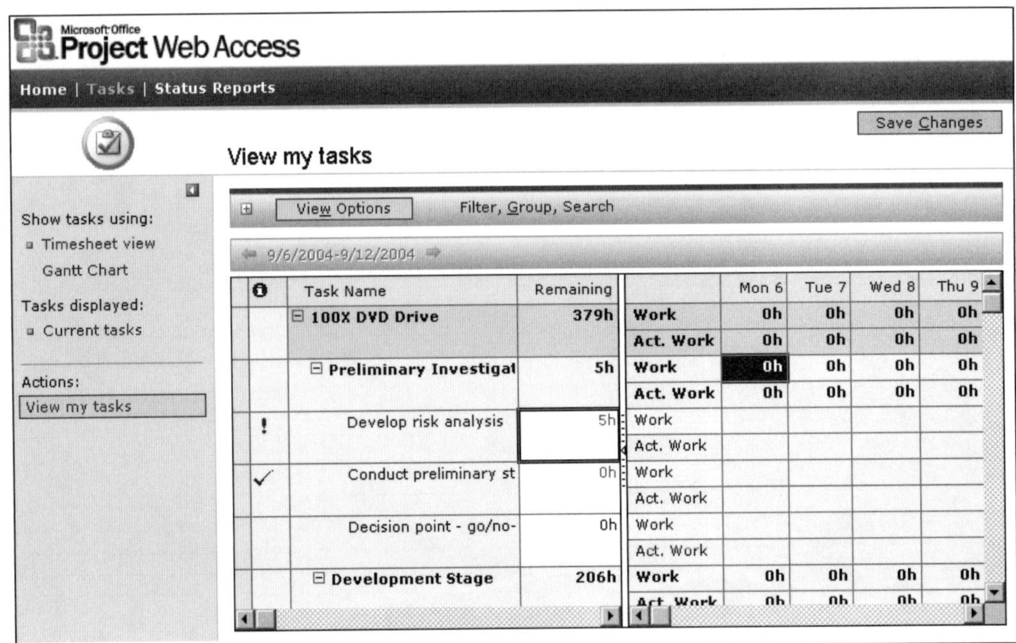

**Figure 9-12: View My Tasks page
while in Offline mode**

Once you are back in the office and can establish a connection with Project Server 2003, you can return to working online by clicking the Go online selection in the actions pane, previously shown in Figure 9-10. When you click the *Go online* link, the system displays the Offline Mode page shown in Figure 9-13.

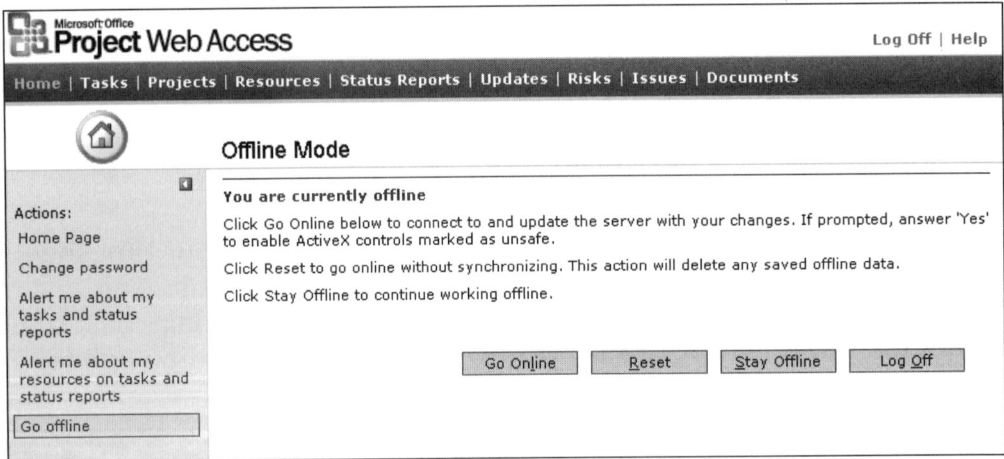

Figure 9-13: Offline Mode page

Click the *Go Online* button to update any data you have entered while in Offline mode and synchronize your data with the server. Keep in mind that although going online saves your data to the server, it doesn't automatically update time entries in your timesheet or send your offline status reports to their respective managers. You must perform these actions after the system is online.

Click the *Reset* button to discard any data entered while in Offline mode and reconnect as if you were never Offline. Click the *Stay Offline* button to remain in Offline mode. Click the *Log Off* button to log out of Project Web Access.

Hands On Exercise

Exercise 9-2

Take Project Web Access offline and then go back online again.

1. From the Home page, click the *Go Offline* link in the actions pane.

2. In the Go offline resulting display, select a date range for your offline activities.

3. Click the *Go Offline* button when done.

4. Click the *OK* button when the system prompts.

5. Explore the Offline version of Project Web Access.

6. Click the *Go online* link from the actions pane on the Home page.

7. Click the *Go Online* button from the resulting Offline Mode page.

8. Verify that you are back online with Project Web Access.

Module 10

Working with Risks, Issues, and Documents

Learning Objectives

After completing this module, you will be able to:

- Create and submit a new risk or issue
- Edit issues and risks
- Filter the Risks or Issues page
- Link risks to tasks, issues, documents, and other risks
- Link issues to tasks, risks, documents, and other issues
- Open a document library
- Create a new document library
- View documents contained in a document library
- Create new documents and upload documents to libraries
- View and use the project workspace for a selected project

Working with Risks, Issues, and Documents

The management of risks, issues, and documents is an important aspect of your organization's project management methodologies. Windows SharePoint Services (previously called SharePoint Team Services) provides the platform and services for managing risks, issues, and documents within Project Server 2003. All three services function correctly for users who have Windows credentials and use Windows authentication to access Project Server. Users who access Project Web Access with Project Server accounts are not able to access these services through Project Web Access.

When you log into Project Web Access, the Home page announces both active and changed risks, and active and changed issues. Notice in Figure 10-1 that I have one active risk and one active issue assigned to me.

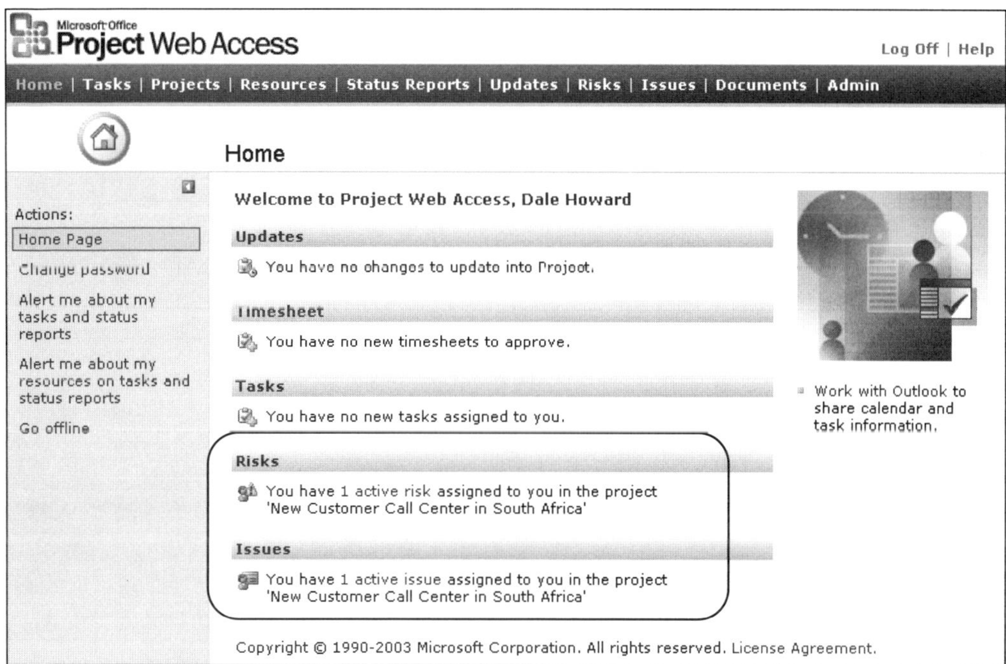

Figure 10-1: Home page with Risks and Issues information

Working with Risks

The Project Management Institute defines a risk as "an uncertain event or condition that, if it occurs, has a positive or negative effect on a project objective." Risks have both causes and consequences. If a risk occurs, the consequence can be either negative or positive. As a part of your organization's risk management methodologies, you may need to log and document anticipated risks to your project work.

257

Viewing Risks

On the Home page, you can either click the *Risks* link in the center of the page or click the *Risks* menu at the top of the page. To access the active risks assigned to you in a particular project, click the ____ *active risks* link located in the Risks section in the middle of the page. As you saw in the Tracking module, you can also access Risks through the timesheet interface in the View My Tasks page.

When you click either the *Risks* link or the *Risks* menu, the system displays the View and Submit Risks in All Projects page as shown in Figure 10-2.

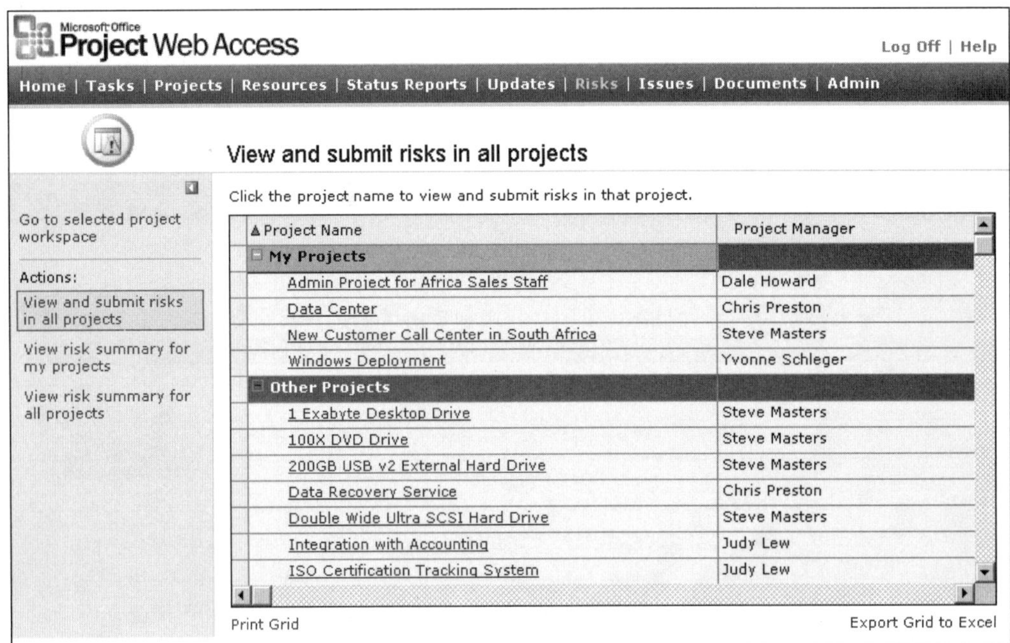

**Figure 10-2: View and Submit Risks
in All Projects page**

In the View and Submit Risks in All Projects page, the phrase "all projects" refers to the all of the projects to which you have access. The system automatically gives you access to any project in which you have an assignment or to any project for which you are the manager. In addition, the system may also give you access to additional projects based on your security permissions.

Notice in Figure 10-2 that there are two sections of projects: My Projects and Other Projects. The My Projects section contains projects in which you have an assignment or for which you are the manager. The Other Projects section contains projects to which you have access by your security permissions.

Click the *View risk summary for my projects* link in the actions pane to view the risk statistics for projects in the My Projects section. The system displays the View Risk Summary for My Projects page, as shown in Figure 10-3. This page gives you the latest statistics on Active, Postponed, and Closed risks in your projects. Notice that there is one Active risk and one Postponed risk in the New Customer Call Center in South Africa project.

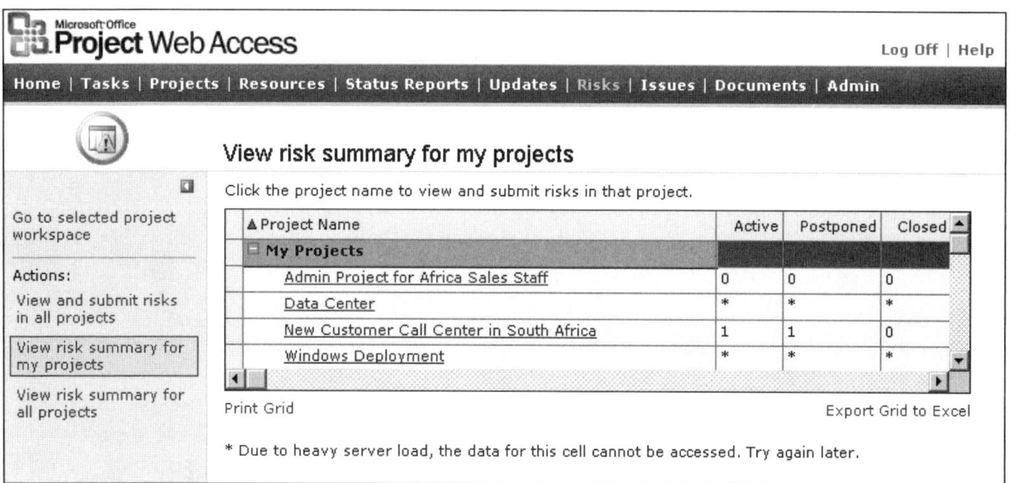

Project Name	Active	Postponed	Closed
My Projects			
Admin Project for Africa Sales Staff	0	0	0
Data Center	*	*	*
New Customer Call Center in South Africa	1	1	0
Windows Deployment	*	*	*

Figure 10-3: View Risk Summary for My Projects page

You can also click the *View risk summary for all projects* link in the actions pane to display a statistics page for the projects listed in both the My Projects and Other Projects sections.

Click the link for any project in the grid to display the Risks page for the selected project. As shown in Figure 10-4, the project name displays above the page title. In the Select a View section of the actions pane, notice that you can select a number of views based on standard criteria, such as all risks assigned to me or all risks owned by me. Click one of the links in the actions pane to redisplay the page with the conditions applied. Click the *All Risks* link in the actions pane to return the Risks page to the full selection of project risks.

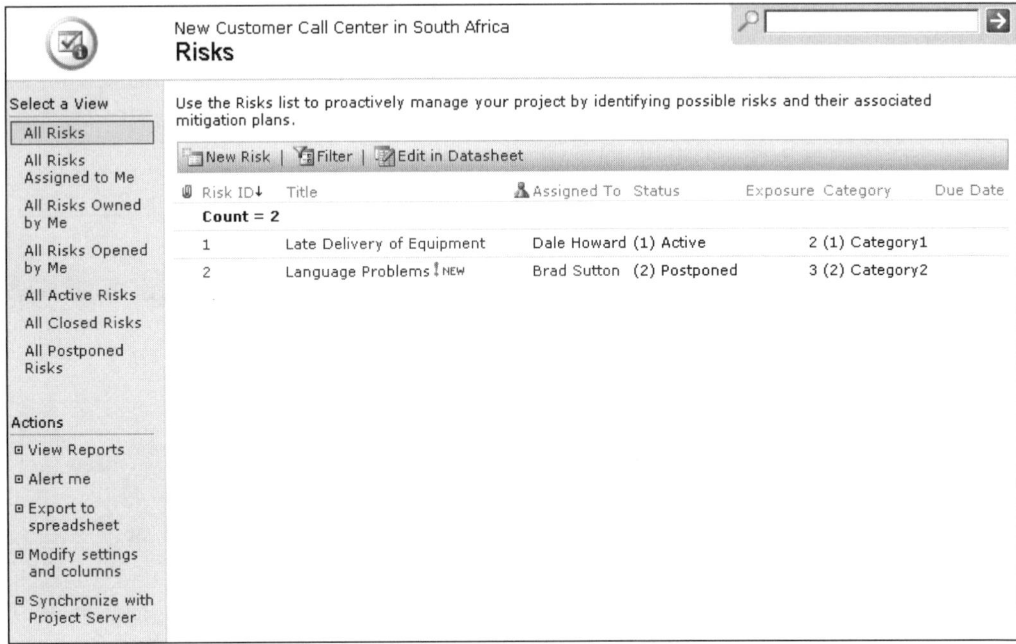

Figure 10-4: Risks page for a single project

You can use filtering to determine the list of risks displayed on the Risks page. Click the *Filter* button on the toolbar to activate autofiltering on the list of risks, as shown in Figure 10-5. Each field in the display becomes a pick list allowing you to set a value to filter on any column. Making a selection applies it to the view. Click the *Hide Filter Choices* button on the toolbar to cancel filtering.

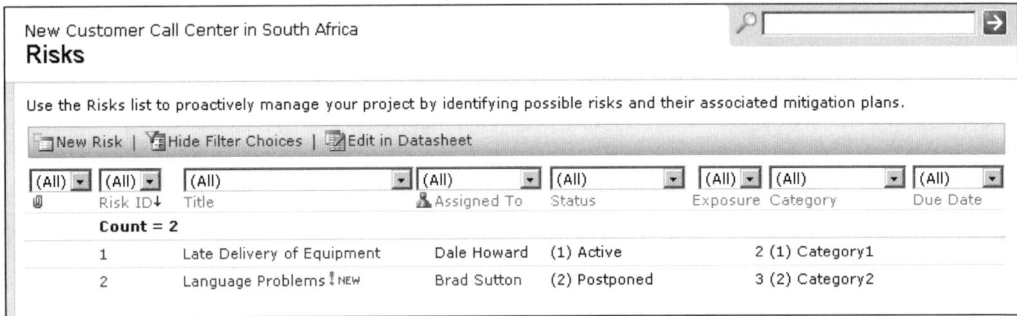

Figure 10-5: Risks page in ad hoc filter mode

You can also view the list of risks in an Excel-like view by clicking the *Edit in Datasheet* button on the toolbar. The system displays the list of risks in a grid of rows and columns, as show in Figure 10-6.

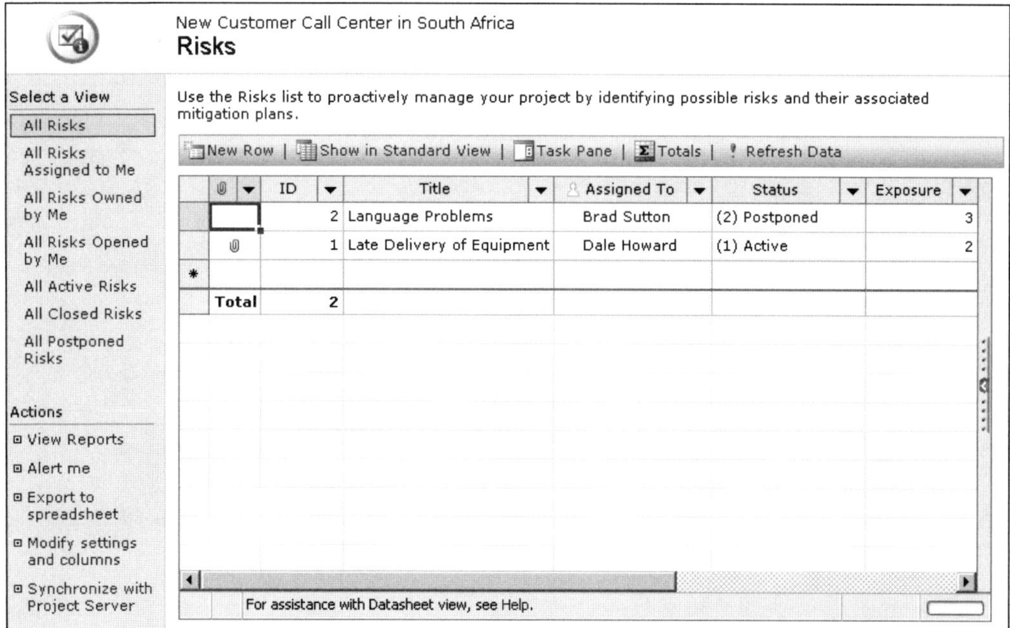

Figure 10-6: Risks page in Datasheet view

While in the Datasheet view of your project risks, you can create a new row and add a risk by clicking the *New Row* button. Click the *Task Pane* button to display a pane with choices for working with your datasheet in Excel or Access, as is shown in Figure 10-7. The choices available include being able to export and link the risk list to either an Excel spreadsheet or to an Access table. Click the *Totals* button to show and hide totals at the bottom of the datasheet.

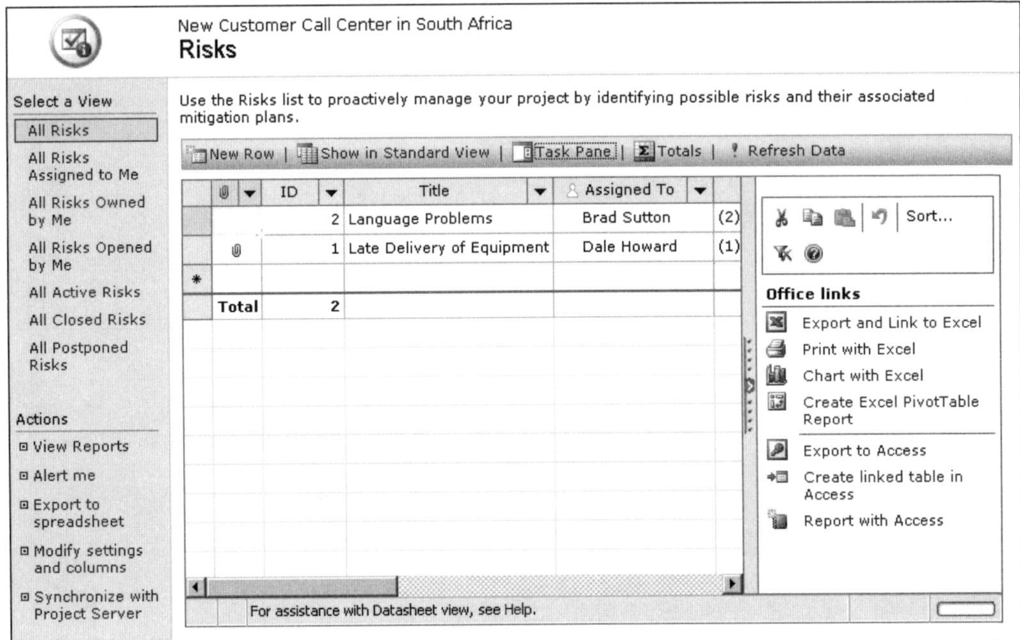

**Figure 10-7: Datasheet view of Risks page
with Task Pane displayed**

To return to the Standard view of your project risks, click the *Show in Standard View* button on the toolbar. Click the name of the risk in the list to display the risk details page shown in Figure 10-8.

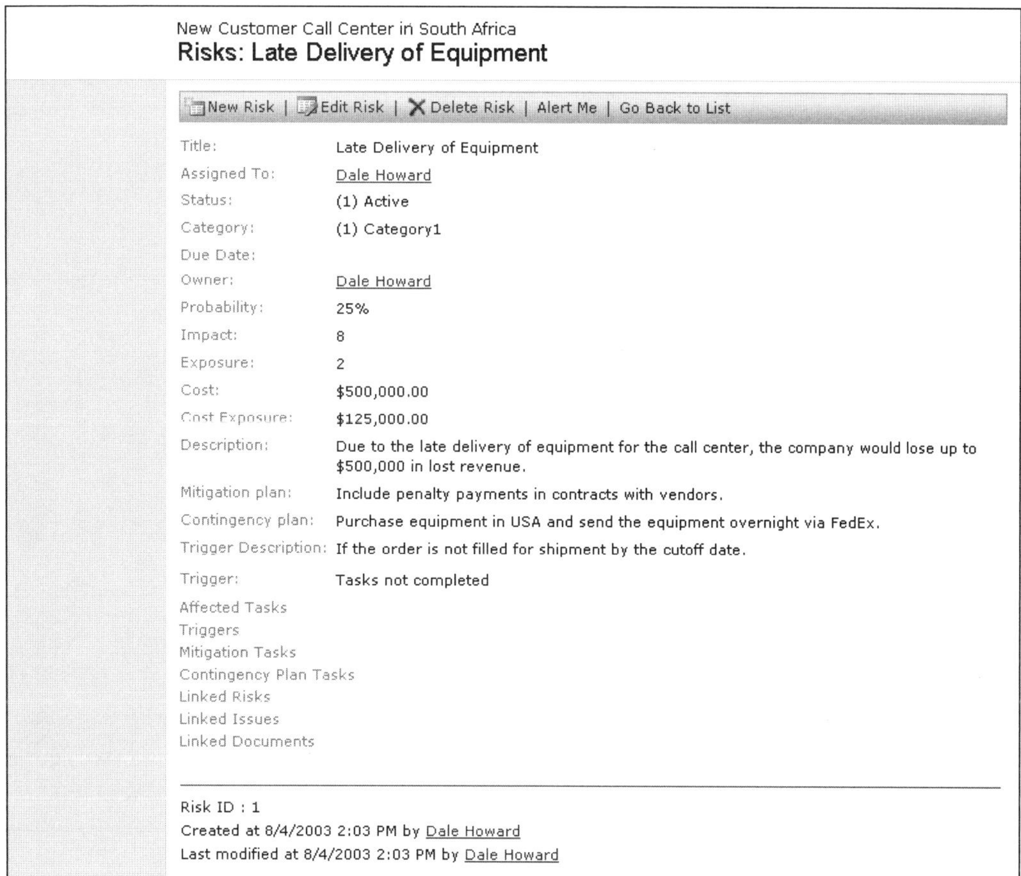

Figure 10-8: View risk details

Creating and Editing Risks

Click the *Edit Risk* button at the top to open the risk for editing as shown in Figure 10-9. You can make changes to any of the risk details from this page.

When you click the *New Risk* button, the system displays a page similar to the page shown in Figure 10-9, except the fields on the page are blank.

New Customer Call Center in South Africa
Risks: Late Delivery of Equipment

💾 Save and Close | 📎 Attach File | ✖ Delete Risk | Go Back to List

Title * Late Delivery of Equipment

Assigned To Dale Howard

Status (1) Active

Category (1) Category1

Due Date ▦ 12 AM 00
Enter date in M/D/YYYY format.

Owner Dale Howard

Probability * 25 %

Impact * 8
The magnitude of impact should the risk actually happen

Cost 500,000
The cost impact should the risk actually happen

Description
Due to the late delivery of equipment for the call center, the company would lose up to $500,000 in lost revenue.
The likely causes and consequences of the risk

Mitigation plan
Include penalty payments in contracts with vendors.
The plans to mitigate the risk

Contingency plan
Purchase equipment in USA and send the equipment overnight via FedEx.
The fallback plans should the risk occur.

Trigger Description
If the order is not filled for shipment by the cutoff date.

Trigger ⦿ Tasks not completed
○ Specify your own value:

The condition that triggers the contingency plan

Affected Tasks Select project tasks that are impacted by this risk
Triggers Select project tasks that are triggers for this risk
Mitigation Tasks Select project tasks that are part of the mitigation plan
Contingency Plan Tasks Select project tasks that are part of the risk contingency plan
Linked Risks Select other related risks in this project
Linked Issues Select project issues that are related to this risk
Linked Documents Select project documents that are related to this risk

* indicates a required field

Risk ID : 1
Created at 8/4/2003 2:03 PM by Dale Howard
Last modified at 8/4/2003 2:03 PM by Dale Howard

Related Risks

Risk ID	Title	Remove Related ID
2	Language Problems ❗NEW	Remove

Figure 10-9: Edit Risk page

Attaching Risks to Tasks, Issues, Documents, and Other Risks

In the Edit Risk page, click the *Attach file* button to attach documents to the risk. The system displays the page shown in Figure 10-10.

Figure 10-10: Attach file to a risk

To attach a file to a risk, click the *Browse* button to open the Choose File dialog. Navigate to the desired file, select the file, and then click the *Open* button as shown in Figure 10-11. Click the *OK* button to complete the attachment of the file.

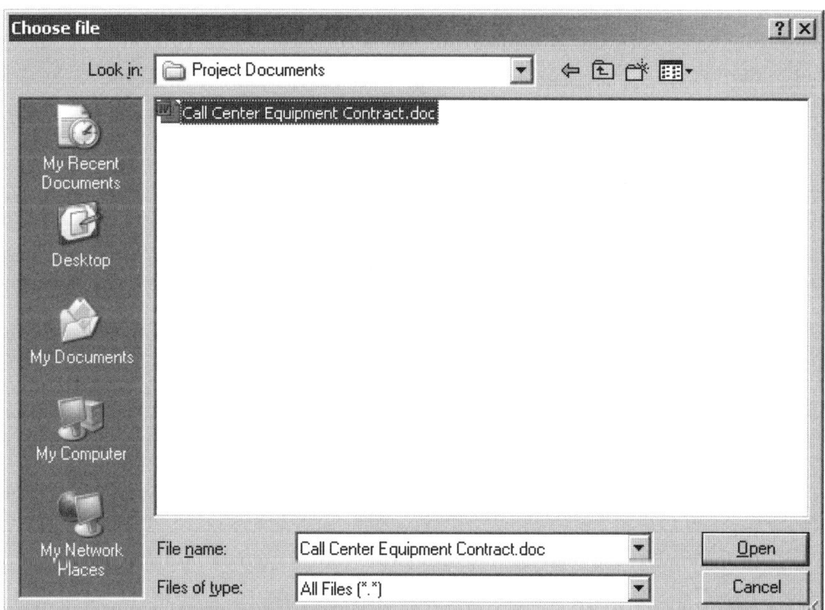

Figure 10-11: Choose File dialog

The system displays a paperclip icon on the Risks page for each risk with one or more attached files.

At the bottom of the Edit Risk page is a section of options that allow you to cross-link your risk to the following:

- Affected Tasks

- Triggers

- Mitigation tasks

- Contingency Plan Tasks

- Linked Risks

- Linked Issues

- Linked Documents

Selecting any of these options opens the appropriate dialog for the situation. For example, I have clicked the *Affected Tasks* link and the system opens the Link to the Selected Tasks dialog, as shown in Figure 10-12.

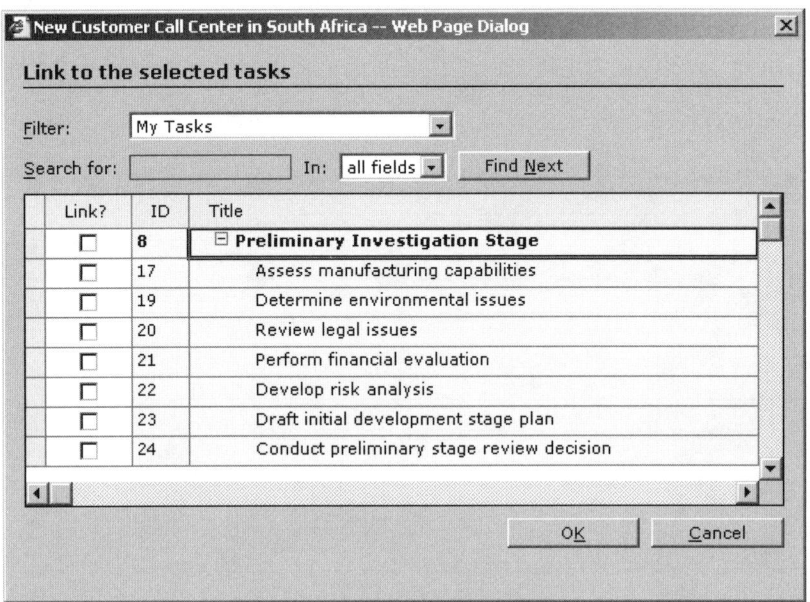

**Figure 10-12: Link to the
Selected Tasks dialog**

Note the filtering tools and search feature available to help you narrow the selection. Select the checkbox in the Link column for one or more items and then click the *OK* button.

While in the Edit Risk page, you can delete a risk by clicking the *Delete Risk* button. The system displays a confirmation dialog. Click the *OK* button in the confirmation dialog to delete the risk, or click the *Cancel* button to cancel the deletion.

When you have finished editing a risk, click the *Save and Close* button to save any changes you made. Click the *Go Back to List* button to abandon your changes without saving.

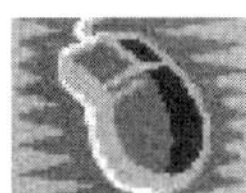 **Hands On Exercise**

Exercise 10-1

Create a new Risk in Project Web Access.

1. Click the *Risks* menu item from the Project Web Access main menu.
2. Click the name of a project that you created or to which you are assigned.
3. Click the *New Risk* button on the toolbar.
4. Enter relevant information about the new risk.
5. Click the *Save and Close* button on the toolbar.

Exercise 10-2

Edit and link a risk to a task.

1. Select the risk you created in Exercise 10-1.
2. Click the *Edit Risk* button on the toolbar.
3. Select the *Affected Tasks* link near the bottom of the page.
4. Select one or more tasks impacted by the risk.
5. Click the *OK* button when finished.
6. Click the *Save and Close* button on the toolbar.

Working with Issues

An issue is any type of problem or concern which you might have during the life of the project, and which you want to communicate to those who have an interest in the project. Examples of project issues could include a shortage of resources needed to complete the project on time, or an unanticipated hardware upgrade needed to move forward with project work.

Viewing Issues

Because the Risks, Issues, and Documents are very similar, you will find the features of the Issues pages very familiar. To access Issues, you can either click the *Issues* menu at the top of the page or the *Issues* link in the center of the Home page. The system displays the View and Submit Issues in All Projects page shown in Figure 10-13.

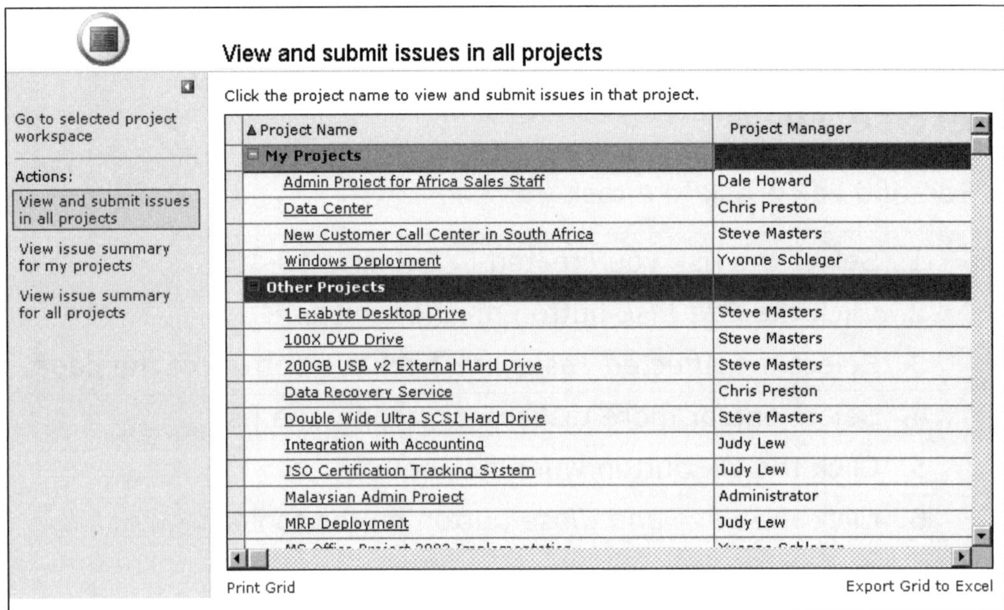

**Figure 10-13: View and Submit Issues
in All Projects page**

As with the Issues page, you can click the *View issues summary for my projects* link in the actions pane to view the issues statistics for projects in the My Projects section. You can also click the *View issues summary for all projects* link in the actions pane to display a statistics page for the projects listed in both the My Projects and Other Projects sections.

Click the name of any project in the grid to display the Issues page for the selected project, as shown in Figure 10-14. Similar to Risks, the Select a View section of the actions pane contains a number of views based on standard criteria.

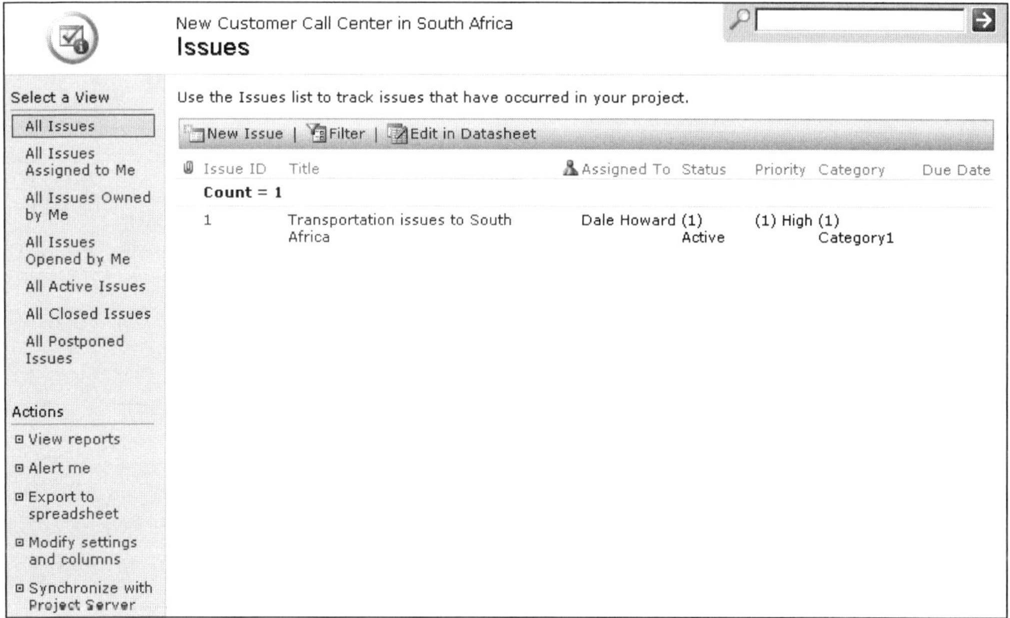

Figure 10-14: Issues page for a single project

You can click the *Filter* button on the toolbar to restrict the list of issues displayed on the Issues page. You can also view the list of issues in an Excel-like view by clicking the *Edit in Datasheet* button on the toolbar. Click the name of the issue in the list to display the issue details page, shown in Figure 10-15.

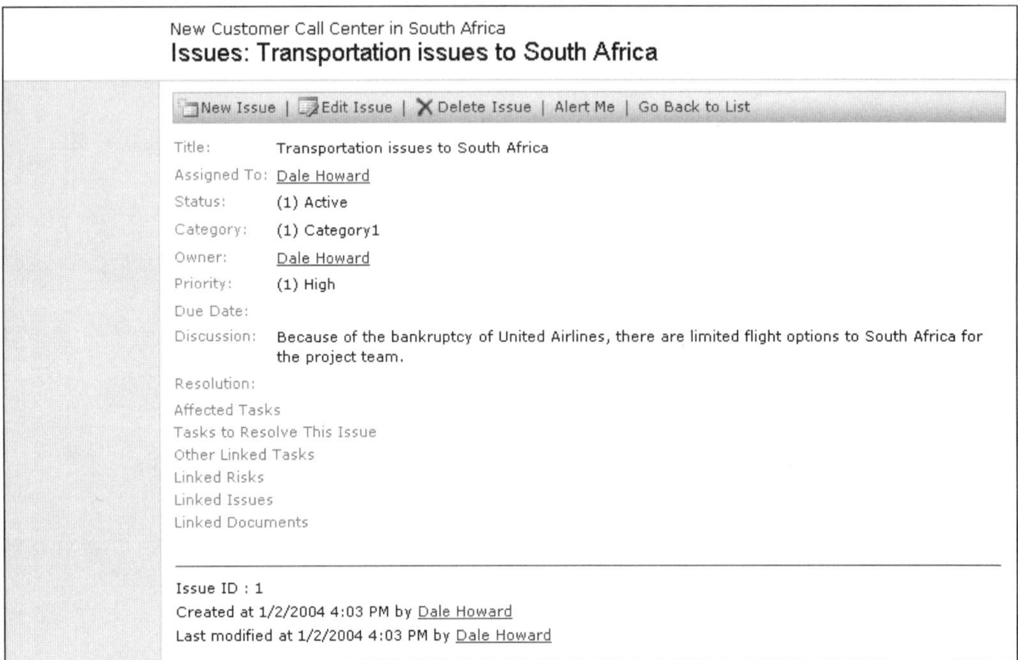

New Customer Call Center in South Africa
Issues: Transportation issues to South Africa

| New Issue | Edit Issue | X Delete Issue | Alert Me | Go Back to List |

Title:	Transportation issues to South Africa
Assigned To:	Dale Howard
Status:	(1) Active
Category:	(1) Category1
Owner:	Dale Howard
Priority:	(1) High
Due Date:	
Discussion:	Because of the bankruptcy of United Airlines, there are limited flight options to South Africa for the project team.
Resolution:	

Affected Tasks
Tasks to Resolve This Issue
Other Linked Tasks
Linked Risks
Linked Issues
Linked Documents

Issue ID : 1
Created at 1/2/2004 4:03 PM by Dale Howard
Last modified at 1/2/2004 4:03 PM by Dale Howard

Figure 10-15: View issue details

Creating and Editing Issues

Although there are a fewer number of details available for an issue than for a risk, the interface functions are the same. You can click the *Delete Issue* button to remove the issue, or click the *New Issue* button to create a new issue. Click the *Edit Issue* button to open the issue for editing, as shown in Figure 10-16. You can make changes to any of the issue details from this page.

When you click the *New Issue* button, the system displays a page similar to the page shown in Figure 10-16, except the fields on the page are blank.

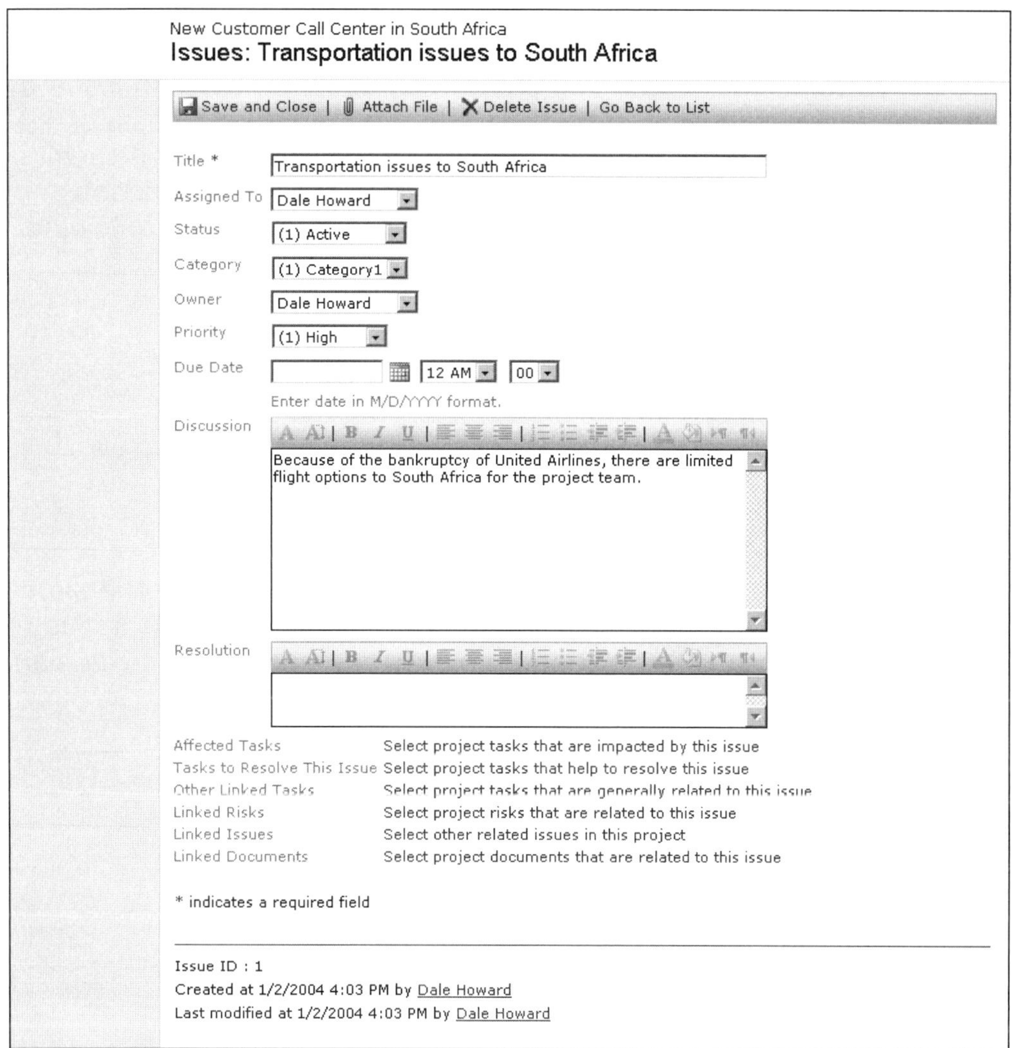

Figure 10-16: Edit Issue page

Attaching Issues to Other Issues, Tasks, Risks, and Documents

As you learned to do with risks, you can attach documents to an issue by clicking the *Attach File* button in the Edit Issue page. The process for attaching a document to an issue is identical to the process for attaching a document to a risk. At the bottom of the Edit Issue page is a section containing options that allow you to cross-link the issue to the following:

- Affected Tasks
- Tasks to Resolve this Issue
- Other Linked Tasks
- Linked Risks
- Linked Issues
- Linked Documents

Selecting any of these options opens the appropriate dialog for the situation. The dialogs displayed for linking issues are identical to those displayed for linking risks. When you have finished editing the issue, click the *Save and Close* button to save any changes made while editing. Click the *Go Back to List* button to abandon the changes without saving.

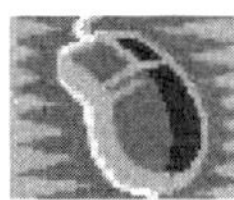

Hands On Exercise

Exercise 10-3

Create a new issue in Project Web Access.

1. Select the *Issues* menu item from the Project Web Access main menu.
2. Click the name of a project that you created or to which you are assigned.
3. Click the *New Issue* button on the toolbar.
4. Enter relevant information about the new issue.
5. Click the *Save and Close* button on the toolbar.

Exercise 10-4

Edit and link an issue to a task.

1. Select the issue you created in Exercise 10-3.
2. Click the *Edit Issue* button on the toolbar.
3. Select the *Affected Tasks* link near the bottom of the page.
4. Select one or more tasks impacted by the issue.
5. Click the *OK* button when finished.
6. Click the *Save and Close* button on the toolbar.

Working with Document Libraries

During the life cycle of a typical project, you may create multiple documents such as templates, deliverables, and items of information associated with the project. During project definition, you might create a Project Charter and a Statement of Work document. During the execution stage of the project, you might create Change Control documents and expense reports. At the closure of a project, you might create a Lessons Learned document to capture the knowledge gained during the life of the project, to name a few. Regardless of which type of project documents you create, each document is a part of your project's "electronic paper trail."

Viewing Document Libraries

To manage project documents, click the *Documents* menu at the top of the Project Web Access page. As you saw in the Tracking module, you can also access Documents through the timesheet interface in the View My Tasks page. When you click the *Documents* menu, the system displays the View and Upload Documents in All Projects page shown in Figure 10-17.

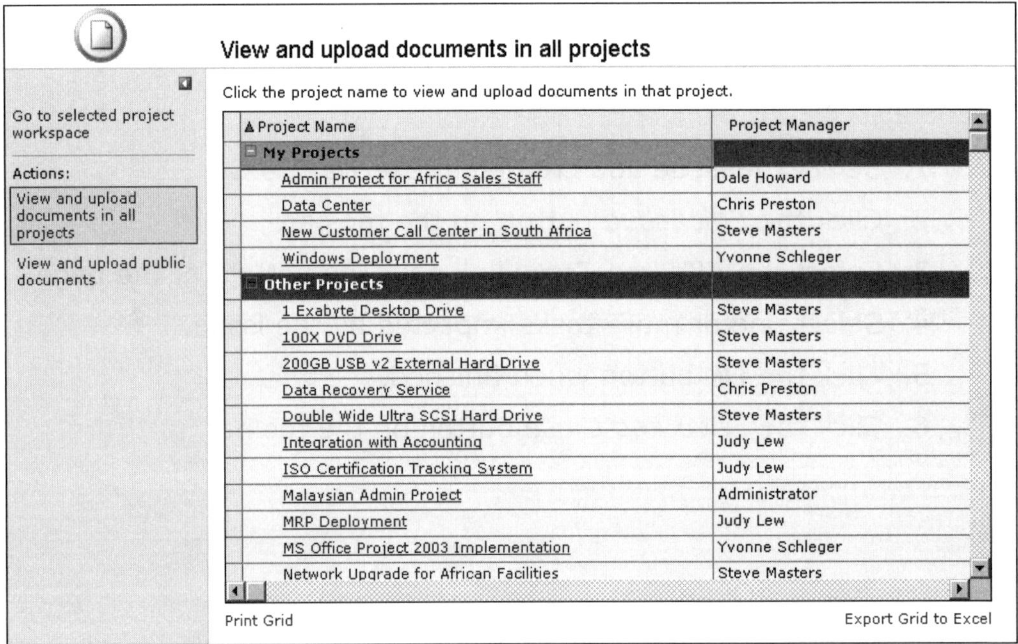

Project Name	Project Manager
My Projects	
Admin Project for Africa Sales Staff	Dale Howard
Data Center	Chris Preston
New Customer Call Center in South Africa	Steve Masters
Windows Deployment	Yvonne Schleger
Other Projects	
1 Exabyte Desktop Drive	Steve Masters
100X DVD Drive	Steve Masters
200GB USB v2 External Hard Drive	Steve Masters
Data Recovery Service	Chris Preston
Double Wide Ultra SCSI Hard Drive	Steve Masters
Integration with Accounting	Judy Lew
ISO Certification Tracking System	Judy Lew
Malaysian Admin Project	Administrator
MRP Deployment	Judy Lew
MS Office Project 2003 Implementation	Yvonne Schleger
Network Upgrade for African Facilities	Steve Masters

**Figure 10-17: View and Upload Documents
in All Projects page**

As with risks and issues, the system automatically grants you access to any project in which you have an assignment or to any project for which you are the manager. In addition, the system may also give you access to additional projects based on your security permissions and your position in your organization's RBS structure. Following he same pattern as risks and issues, notice in Figure 10-17 that there are two sections of projects: My Projects and Other Projects.

To give Windows users access to risks, issues, and document libraries for specific projects, give them a small assignment in each project. These are typically tasks with a token effort.

The actions pane of the View and Upload Documents in All Projects page offers two possible actions:

- View and upload documents in all libraries.
- View and upload public documents.

When you apply the first action, remember that the phrase "all libraries" refers to the libraries associated with all of the projects to which you have access. When you apply the second action, the phase "public libraries" refers to those that are available to every user in the system. To view the public libraries, click the *View and upload public documents* link and the system displays the Public Document Libraries page shown in Figure 10-18.

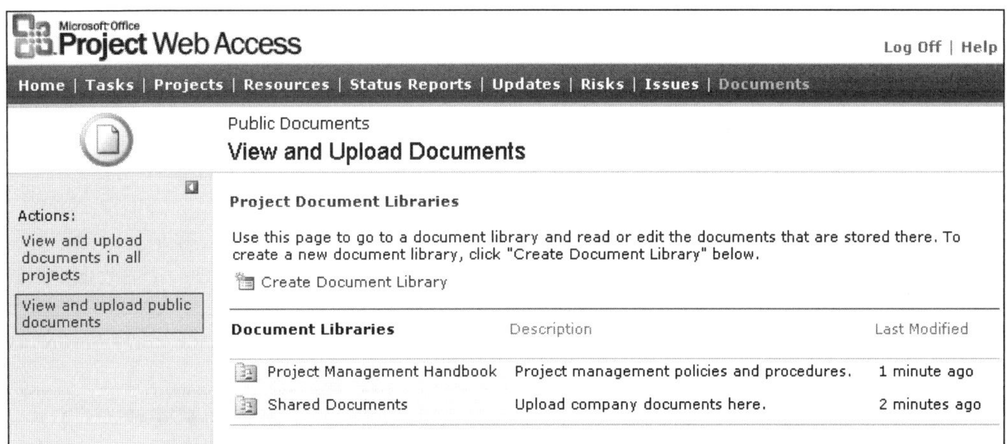

Figure 10-18: Public Document Libraries page

Figure 10-18 shows two public libraries to which I can upload documents. One Is the Project Management Handbook library, which is a custom library I created. The other is the Shared Documents library, which is the default public library for documents. To return to the all projects page, click the *View and upload documents in all projects* link in the actions pane.

Click the project name in the grid to open the Project Document Libraries page for the selected project, as shown in Figure 10-19. As with risks and issues, the name of the project displays above the page title.

**Figure 10-19: Project Document Libraries page
for a selected project**

Each project includes one default document library, which is the Shared Documents library. The Project Document Libraries page for each project displays this library and any other libraries that the team has added.

Creating a New Document Library

Click the *Create Document Library* link to generate a new library for your project. The system displays the New Document Library page shown in Figure 10-20. Give your new library a name and a description, and select your desired options in the Navigation and Document Versions sections of the page.

Document versioning is a new feature of Project Server 2003. This feature allows you to keep multiple versions of a document. If you enable this feature for your document library, the system automatically creates a new version of a document each time a user edits the document. If you need to reverse changes needs to a document, you can restore the previous version and continue working.

In the Document Template section, select the default template used for creating all new documents in the library. Your choice of templates includes the following:

- Microsoft Word document
- Microsoft FrontPage web page
- Microsoft Excel spreadsheet
- Microsoft PowerPoint presentation

- Basic page
- Web Part page
- None

The reason for selecting a blank template relates to features available only if you have a Microsoft Office 2003 client application license installed on your workstation. The full version of the Office 2003 web components, available only to users of Office 2003, allows you to create, open, and edit Office documents in the web browser, avoiding the need to download and upload the document each time. This feature will not work for users of earlier Office versions.

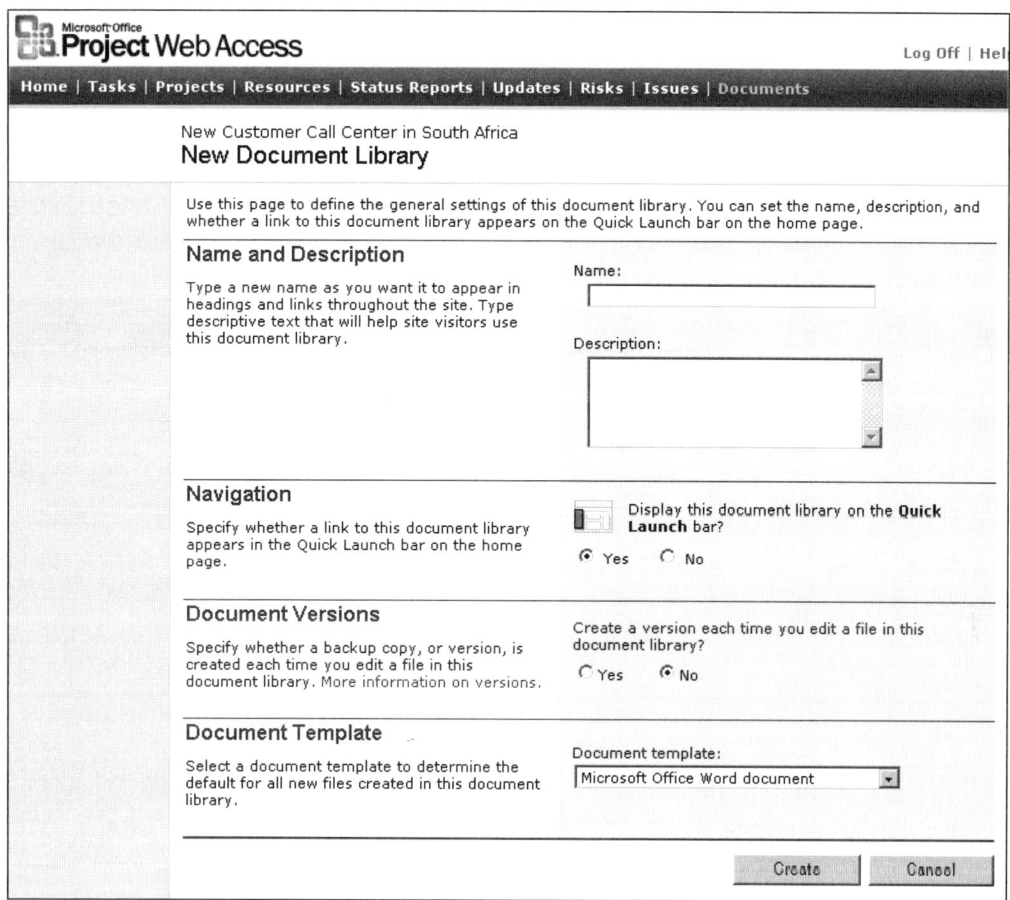

Figure 10-20: New Document Library page

When you click the *Create* button, the system creates the new library and adds it to your Project Document Libraries page, as shown in Figure 10-21.

Figure 10-21: New library added

Using a Document Library

Click the name of a document library to open it and view the documents in the library. The Shared Documents library shown in Figure 10-22 contains six documents related to the New Customer Call Center in South Africa project. Notice that the system flags the Project Budget spreadsheet as new since my last visit to the Shared Documents library.

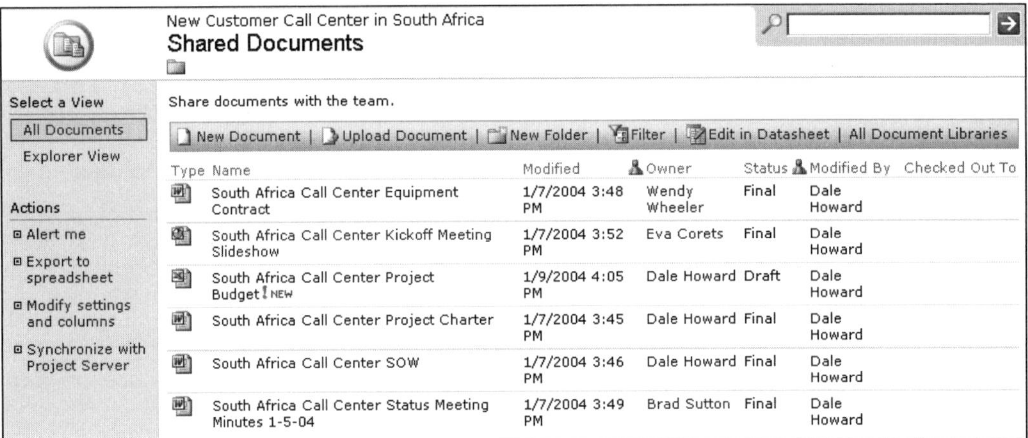

Figure 10-22: Documents in the Shared Documents library

The system offers you two default views of your document library through the Select a View section at the top of the actions pane. The default view for a documents library is the All Documents view. Click the *Explorer View* link to apply the folders view shown in Figure 10-23.

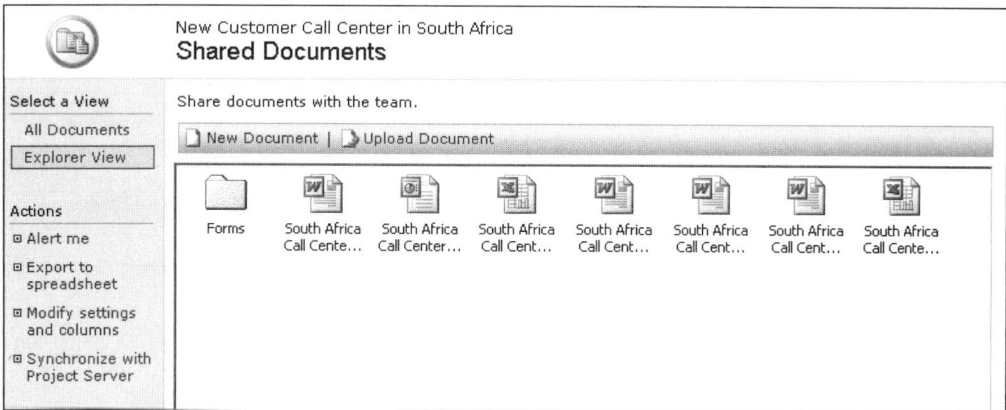

**Figure 10-23: Explorer View of
the document library**

Notice in Figure 10-23 that the toolbar for the document library contains only two buttons when you apply the Explorer view. When you apply the All Documents view, the toolbar for the document library contains several familiar buttons, such as the *Filter* button and the *Edit in Datasheet* button, which you saw in the Risks and Issues pages. The toolbar also offers buttons to create a new document in the library, upload an existing document to the library, to create a new folder within the library, and to return to the list of all document libraries.

Uploading Documents to a Library

Click the *Upload Document* button to upload an existing document to your project document library. The system displays the Upload Document page shown in Figure 10-24. As with linking documents to risks and issues, click the *Browse* button and navigate to the location of the document. Select the existing file in the Choose File dialog and then click the *Open* button.

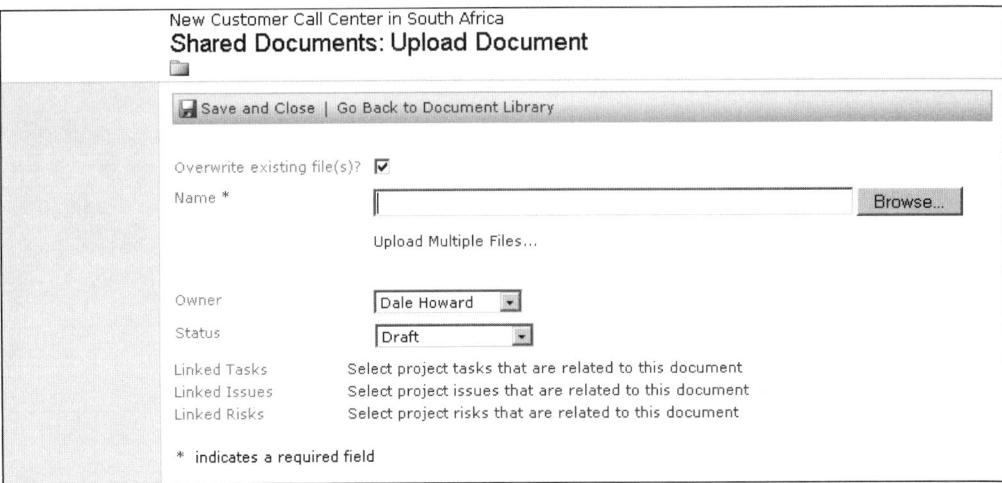

New Customer Call Center in South Africa
Shared Documents: Upload Document

Save and Close | Go Back to Document Library

Overwrite existing file(s)? ☑
Name *   Browse...

Upload Multiple Files...

Owner   Dale Howard
Status   Draft

Linked Tasks   Select project tasks that are related to this document
Linked Issues   Select project issues that are related to this document
Linked Risks   Select project risks that are related to this document

* indicates a required field

Figure 10-24: Upload Document page

When you have selected the file you wish to upload to the document library, you can also specify an Owner and a Status for the document. By default, the system sets the Owner value to your user account and the Status value to Draft. You can also link the document to any tasks, issues, and risks to which the document is related.

The system selects the *Overwrite existing files* option by default in the Upload Document page. If you are uploading an updated version of a document previously uploaded, you may wish to deselect the *Overwrite existing files* option to save multiple versions of your document.

If you wish to upload more than one document simultaneously, click the *Upload Multiple Files* link. The system displays the Upload Document page reconfigured to select multiple documents, as shown in Figure 10-25. You can upload multiple documents by navigating to the location of each document and then selecting the checkbox to the left of the document name.

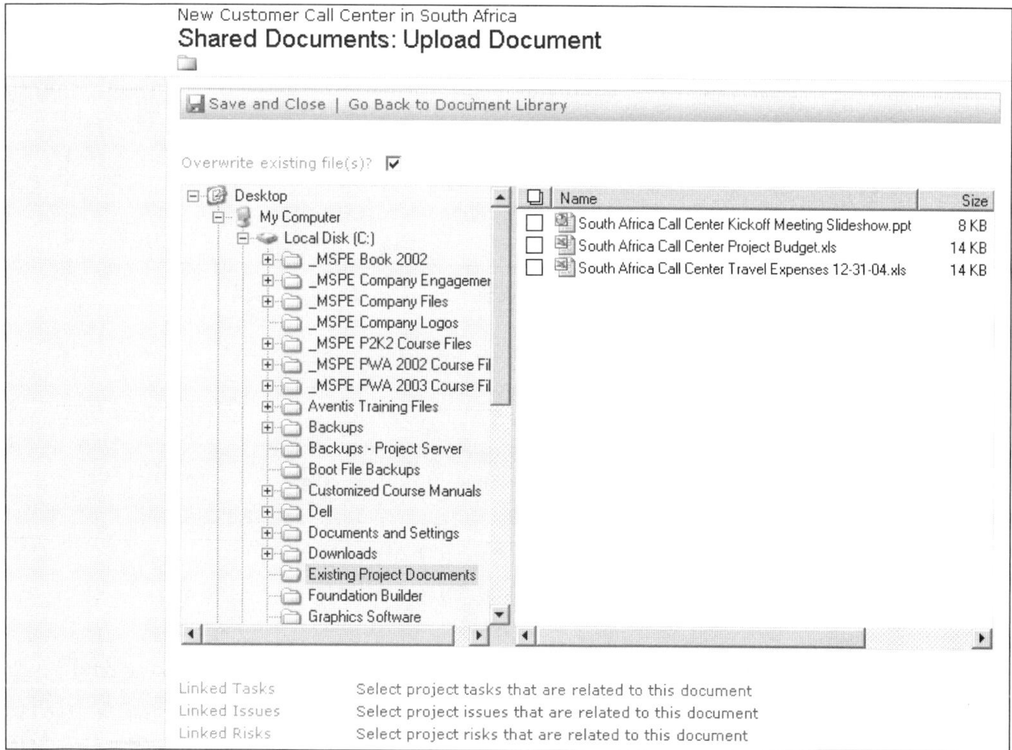

**Figure 10-25: Upload Document page
to upload multiple documents**

When you have selected the documents that you wish to upload, click the *Save and Close* button to return to the document library page. The system displays the newly uploaded documents and flags them as new documents.

When you upload multiple files simultaneously, the system sets the Owner value to None and the Status value to Draft for each document. If you wish to specify an Owner or Status value for these documents, you must edit the Properties for each document individually.

Creating a New Document in a Library

Click the *New Document* button on the toolbar to create a new document. The system automatically opens a new document based on the template type specified as the default for the document library. The default template in each project's Shared Documents folder is the Microsoft Word document template.

Create the document and then click the *Save* button in the application. The system displays the Save As dialog shown in Figure 10-26. Notice that the system pre-selects the Shared Documents folder in the *Save in* pick list.

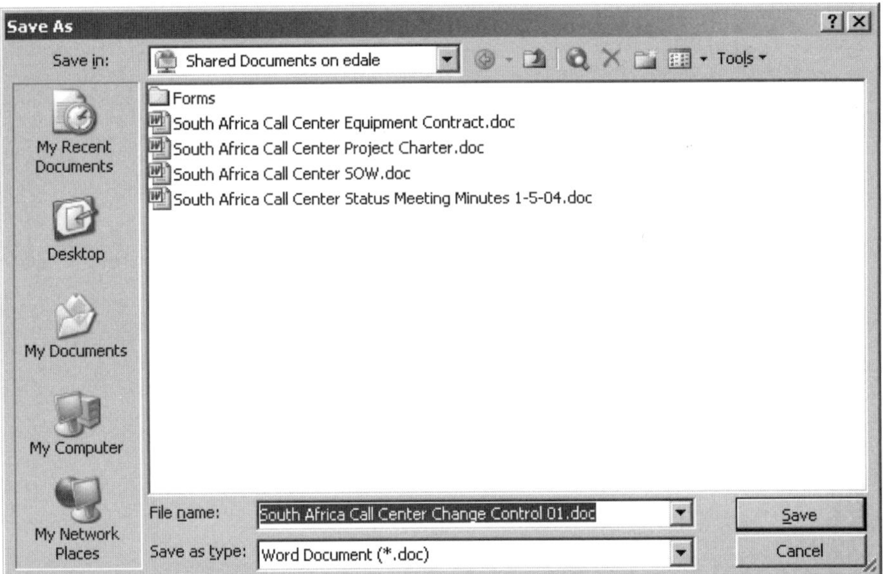

**Figure 10-26: Save As dialog
for new document in a library**

Click the *Save* button in the Save As dialog and the system presents the Web
File Properties dialog shown in Figure 10-27. Select the Owner and Status of
the new document and then click the *OK* button. The system displays the
new document in the document library and flags it as a new document.

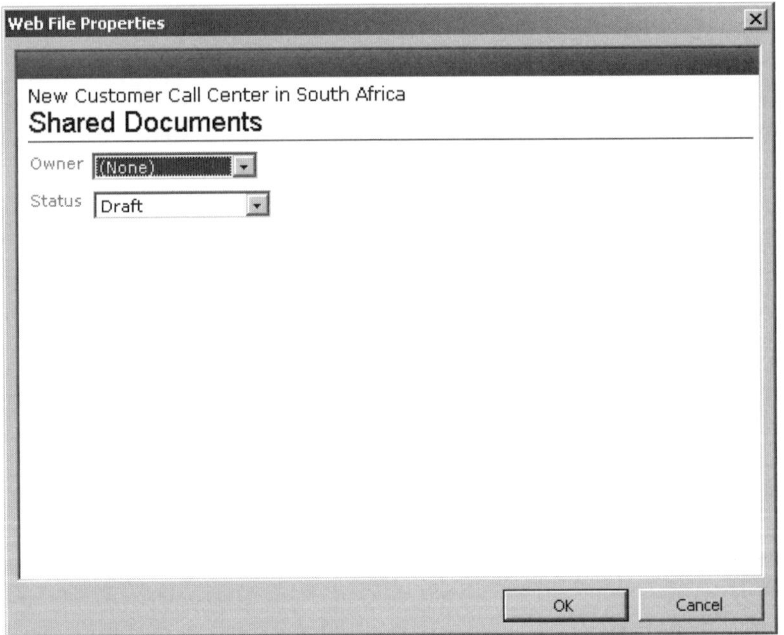

Figure 10-27: Web File Properties dialog

Creating a New Folder in a Library

It is now possible to create new folders within libraries in Project Server 2003.These function as sub-libraries to the libraries in which you create them. To create a folder in the project library, click the *New Folder* button on the toolbar. The system displays the New Folder page, shown in Figure 10-28.

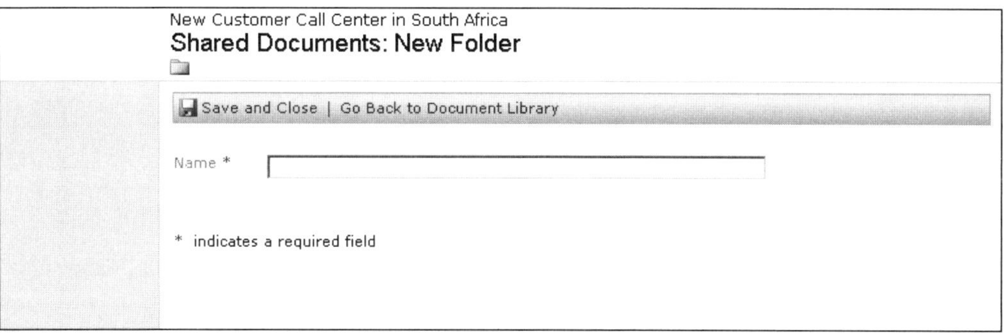

Figure 10-28: New Folder page

Give the folder a name and then click the *Save and Close* button. The system displays the new folder in the document library, as shown in Figure 10-29.

**Figure 10-29: New folder created
in document library**

To add documents in the new folder, simply click the folder to open it. The system displays a document library page for the new folder

Working with Existing Documents in a Library

To work with an existing document in a document library, float your mouse pointer over the name of the document. The system displays a pick list indicator for the selected project, as shown in Figure 10-30.

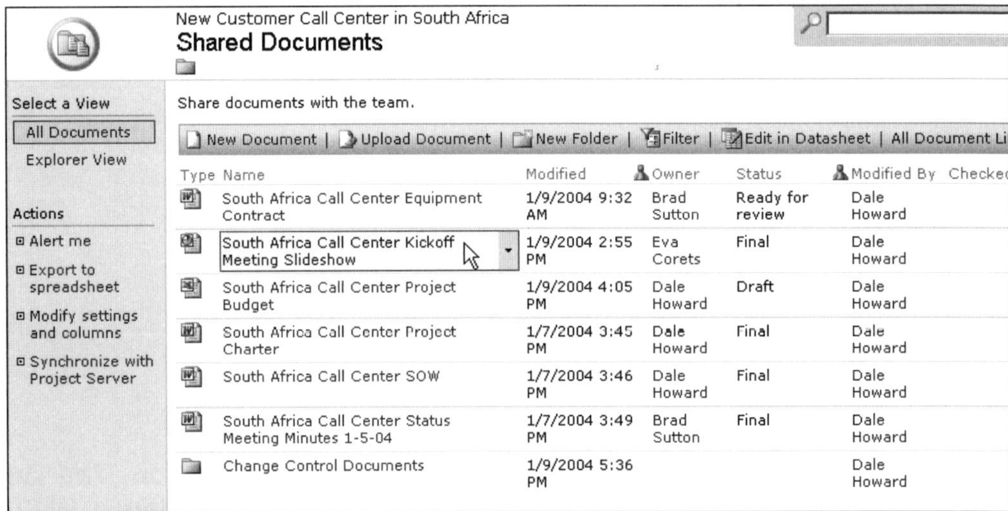

Figure 10-30: Preparing to edit a document

Click the pick list indicator to view the list of options for working with the document, as shown in Figure 10-31.

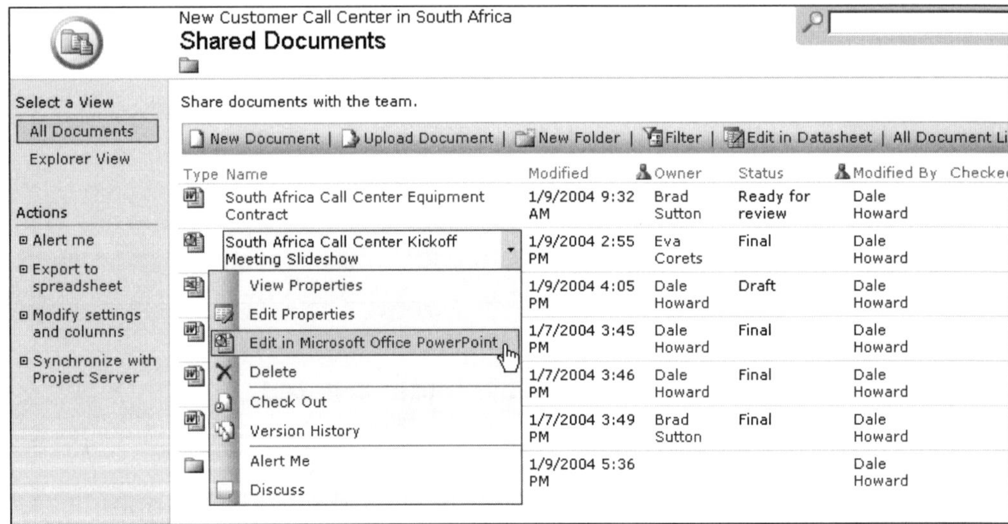

**Figure 10-31: Options for working
with a document in the library**

Viewing Document Properties

Click *View Properties* from the pick list for the selected project to view the Properties of the document, as shown in Figure 10-32. Notice that the buttons on the toolbar offer the remaining selections found on the pick list shown previously in Figure 10-31. Click the *Go Back to Document Library* button when you are finished.

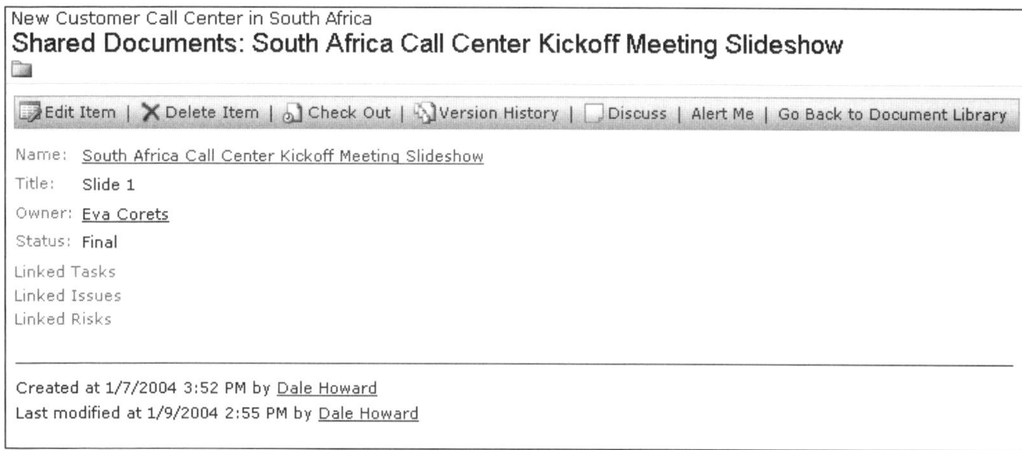

Figure 10-32: Properties of
the selected document

Editing Document Properties

Click *Edit Properties* from the pick list for the selected project to edit the selected document's Properties as shown in Figure 10-33. When you finish editing the document properties click the *Save and Close* button to save the changes and return to the document library. Click the *Go Back to Document Library* button to discard the changes and return to the document library.

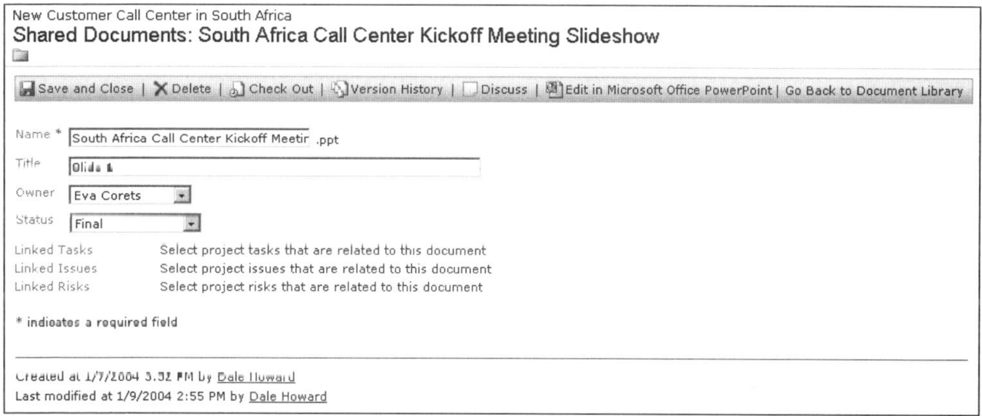

Figure 10-33: Edit the Properties
of the selected document

Editing in a Microsoft Office Application

Click *Edit in Microsoft Office application* from the pick list for the selected project to open the document in the application used to create it. The system opens both the application and the document, and displays the Shared Workspace sidepane on the right side of the screen, as shown in Figure 10-34.

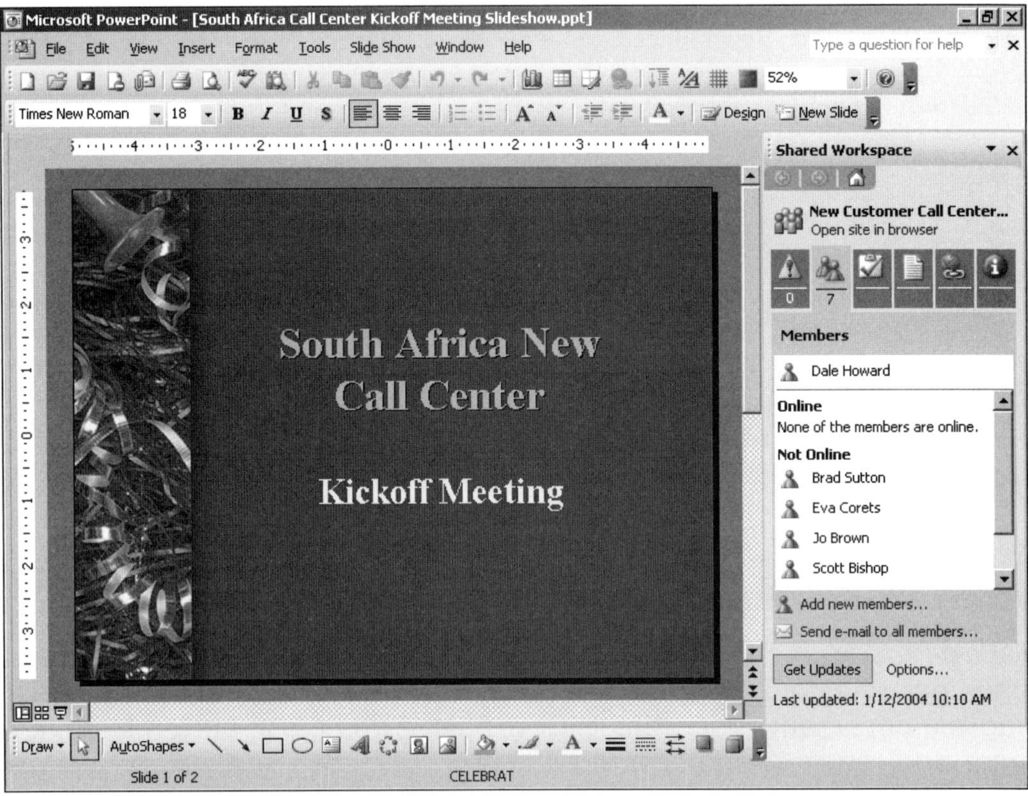

**Figure 10-34: PowerPoint slideshow in editing mode
with Shared Workspace sidepane on the right**

The Shared Workspace sidepane shows information about the status of your document, along with additional information such as presence of team members, related links, related documents, and tasks. The Shared Workspace feature also allows team collaboration in which multiple team members can open and edit the same document simultaneously. While editing the document, each team member can click the *Update* button to update their copy of the document with latest saved changes made by other team members.

As you work with the document in editing mode, click the *Save* button to save the latest changes to the document, and click File ➤ Close to close the document and click File ➤ Exit to close the application.

Deleting a Document

Click *Delete* from the pick list for the selected project to remove the selected document from the document library. The system displays a confirmation dialog to confirm your action. Click the *Yes* button to delete the document, or click No to cancel the action.

Checking Out/Checking In a Document

Click *Check Out* from the pick list for the selected project to prevent others from editing the document while you have it open. Because the system allows multiple users to edit a document simultaneously, you must check out the document if you wish to edit it exclusively. When you click the *Check Out* menu item, the system displays the document's checked-out status in the documents folder as shown in Figure 10-35.

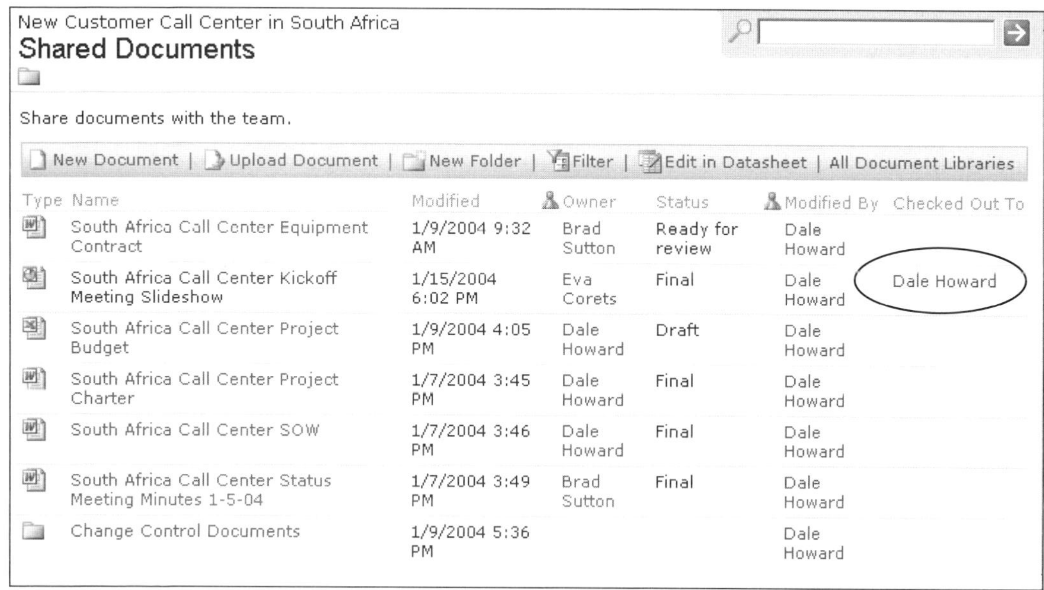

Figure 10-35: Document checked out

You will normally use the document check-out feature in conjunction with document editing, so click the *Edit in Microsoft Office application* menu item to open the document. The Shared Workspace sidepane shows the checked-out status of the document, as shown in Figure 10-36.

**Figure 10-36: Shared workspace
shows checked-out document**

 You can also check out a document by clicking File ➢ Check Out in the application used to open the document.

When you finish editing the checked-out document, click the *Save* button to save it. When you close the document, the system may display the Check In dialog as shown in Figure 10-37.

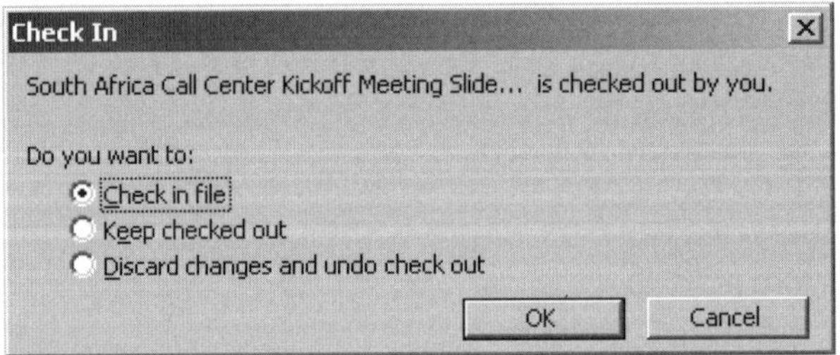

Figure 10-37: Check In dialog

The system automatically displays the Check In dialog when you close the file if you opened the document first and then checked out the document from the *File* menu. The dialog does not display if you checked out the document first and then opened it for editing.

Select the first option in the Check In dialog to check in the file. You can choose to leave the file in its checked-out condition if you plan to edit the file again later and do not want anyone to edit it in your absence. You can also choose to discard your changes and undo the checked-out condition of the document. Make your selection and click the *OK* button. The system displays the Check In Comments dialog shown in Figure 10-38. Add any comments you wish to make and click the *OK* button to return to the document library.

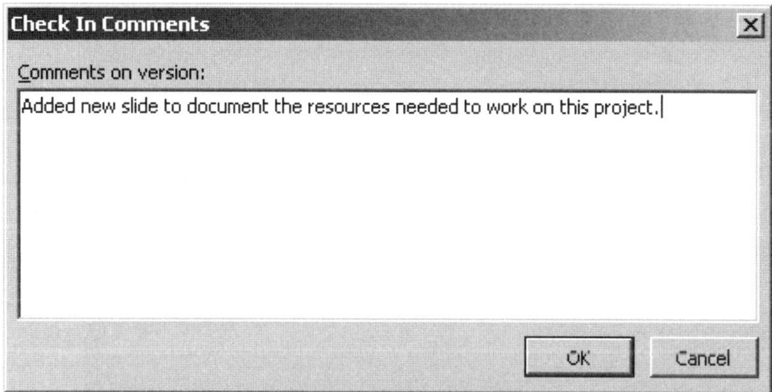

Figure 10-38: Check In Comments dialog

Prior to saving the document, you can also check in the document by clicking the *Check in* link in the Shared Workspace actions pane.

Working with the Versions History

Click *Version History* from the pick list for the selected project to view your document's version history. The system displays the Versions page with the version history by date in descending order. Notice in Figure 10-39 that there are four versions of the project budget spreadsheet file.

**Figure 10-39: Versions page for
the selected document**

The system always displays the current version of the document at the top of
the versions list. You can revert to a previous version of the document in just
a few steps. Float your mouse pointer over the version date to expose a pick
list selector. Click the pick list button to the right of the version date and
select the *Restore* menu item. In Figure 10-40, for example, I am preparing
to restore my PowerPoint slideshow version number three.

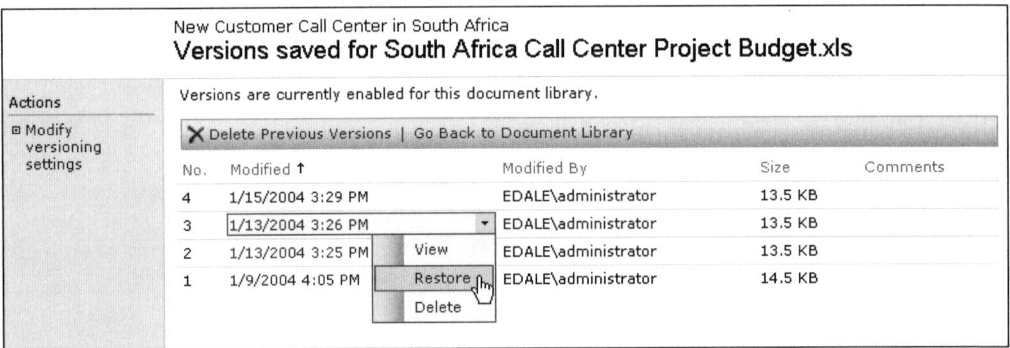

**Figure 10-40: Preparing to restore
the third version of the slideshow**

When you select the *Restore* menu item, the system displays the
confirmation dialog shown in Figure 10-41. Click the *OK* button to complete
the restoration of the version, or click the *Cancel* button to cancel the
operation.

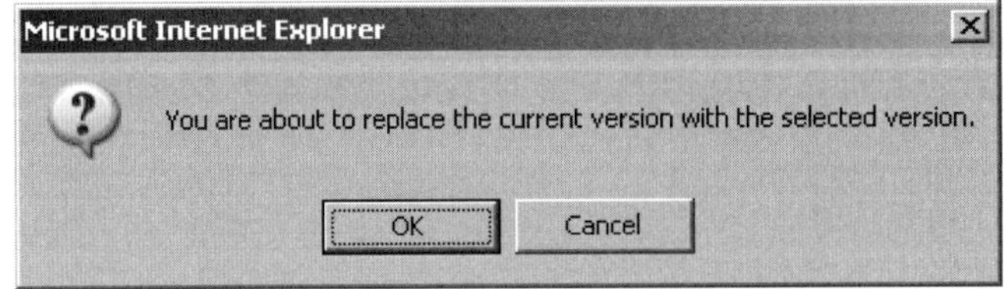

**Figure 10-41: Restore version
confirmation dialog**

When you restore a previous version of a document, the system adds the restored version at the top of the versions list. In Figure 10-42, what is now version 5 is actually the restored version 3.

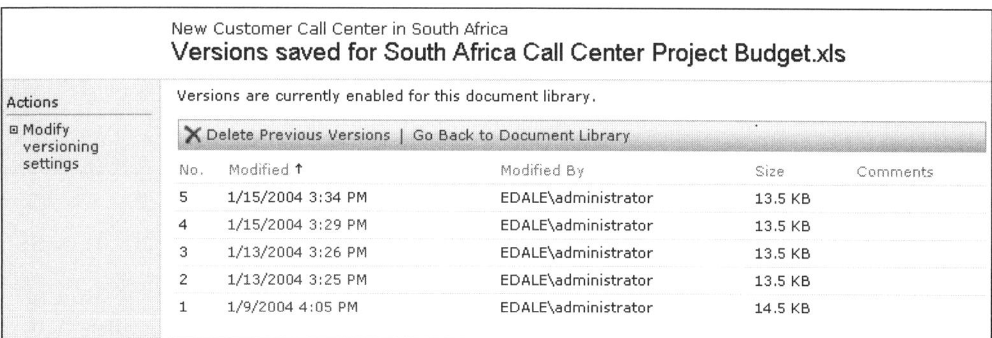

**Figure 10-42: Version 3 restored as
version 5 of the budget spreadsheet**

The system always opens the current version of a document when you click the *Edit in Microsoft Office application* pick list selection for any document in a document library. In the previous illustration, the system would open version 5 of the budget spreadsheet and you would not see the changes made in version 4.

Click the *Go Back to Document Library* button to return to your selected document library.

Before you can use version control with a document, your Project Server administrator must enable Versions for the selected document library.

Discussing a Document

You can only discuss a document from within the project workspace for the selected project. I will discuss the document discussions feature in the next section of this module.

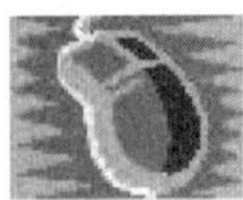

Hands On Exercise

Exercise 10-5

Create a new document library.

1. Select *Documents* menu item from the Project Web Access main menu.

2. Click the name of a project that you created or to which you are assigned.

3. Click the *Create Document Library* button on the toolbar.

4. Give your new library a name and description.

5. Make your desired selections in the Navigation, Document Versions, and Document Template sections.

6. Click the *Create* button.

Exercise 10-6

Upload a document to a Library.

1. Open the document library created in Exercise 10-5, if necessary.

2. Click the *Upload Document* button on the toolbar.

3. Use the *Browse* button to navigate to an existing file.

4. Set the Owner and Status values for the document.

5. If you care to do so, link the document to one or more tasks, issues, or risks.

6. Click the Save and Close when you are finished.

7. Verify that the uploaded document appears in the document library.

8. Notice the icon indicating that the document is new.

Using the Project Workspace

New to Project Server 2003 is full access to the SharePoint project workspace created by the system for each project published to the Project Server database. To access the project workspace for any project, select a project in the data grid on the Risks, Issues, or Documents page and then click the *Go to selected project workspace* link at the top of the actions pane, as shown in Figure 10-43.

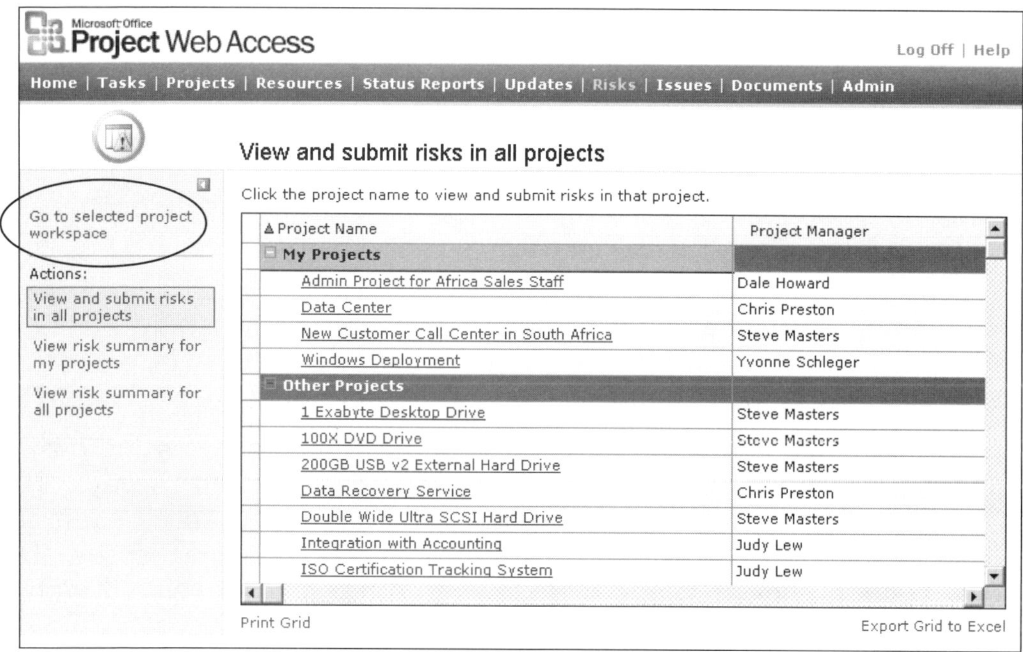

**Figure 10-43: View and Submit Risks page
with Project Workspace link**

Warning: When you select a project in the grid, do not click the hyperlink for the actual project. Instead, select either the row header to the left of the project name or the Project Manager cell to the right of the project name.

The system opens a new Internet Explorer window and displays the project workspace for the selected project, as shown in Figure 10-44.

293

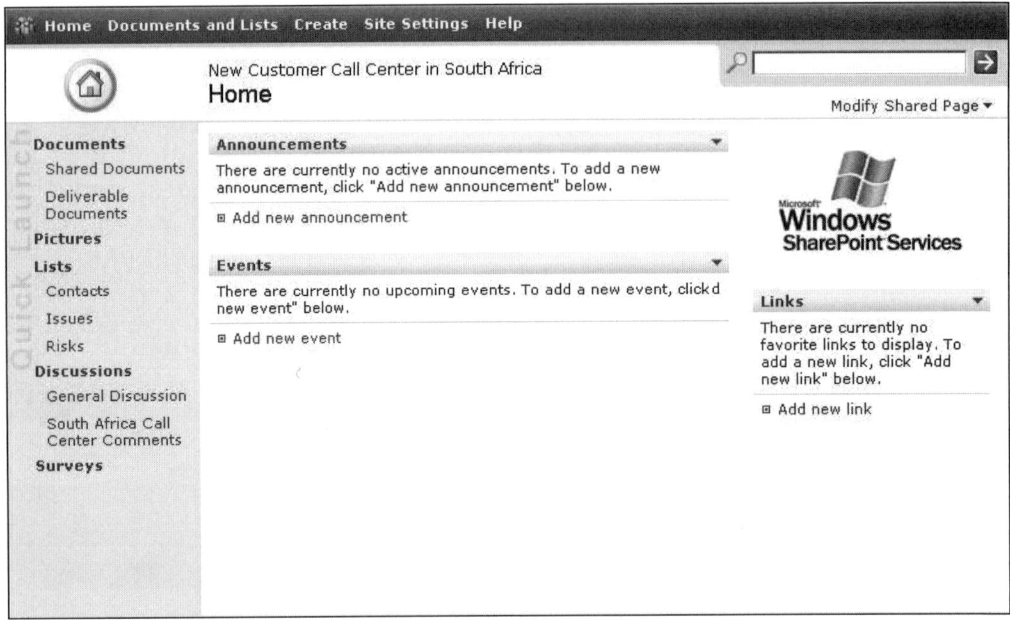

**Figure 10-44: Project workspace for the New Customer
Call Center in Africa project**

The project workspace page provides a single location for accessing project documents, pictures, contacts, issues, risks, discussions, and surveys. The page displays each of these options in the Quick Launch bar on the left side of the page. The project workspace page offers sections for project-related announcements and events, and even links to other project-related Web pages.

Your organization could use the project workspace page as a single point of communication within the Project Server environment.

Discussing a Document

To discuss a project document, select a document library in the Documents section of the Quick Launch bar. In the list of documents in the document library, float your mouse pointer over the desired document, click the pick list button and select the *Discuss* menu item. In Figure 10-45, notice that I am choosing to discuss the February 2004 Team Status Report document.

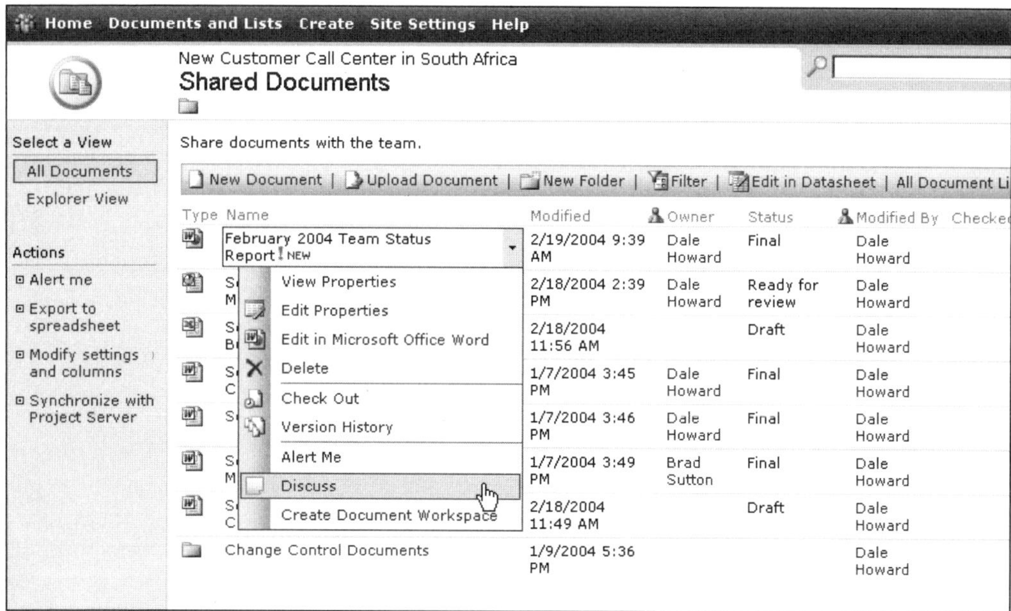

Figure 10-45: Discuss a document

The system displays the document with a Discussions toolbar at the bottom of the document, as shown in Figure 10-46. The Discussions toolbar allows you to insert discussions **in** the document or **about** the document. The difference between the two options is how the system handles the discussion thread, whether internally or externally to the document.

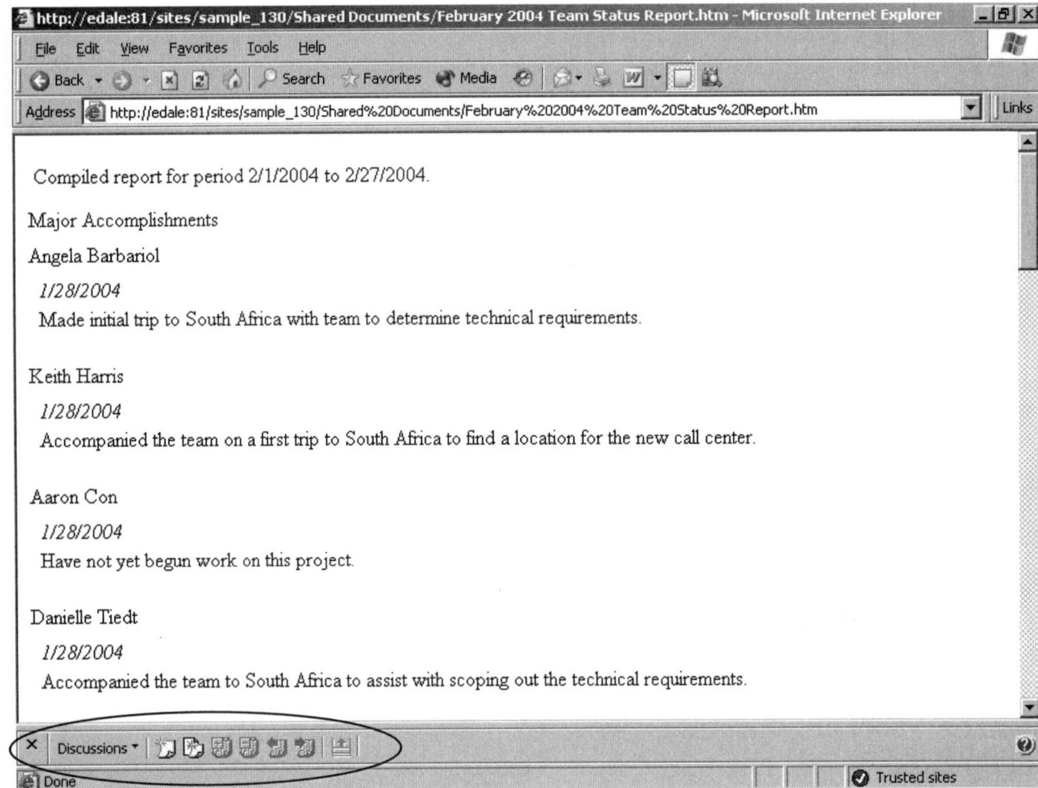

**Figure 10-46: Discussions toolbar
for the selected document**

To insert a discussion in the document, use either of the following options:

- Click the *Insert Discussion in the Document* button on the toolbar

- Click the *Discussions* button on the toolbar and then select the *Insert in the document* menu item

The system displays a Discussion marker in the document and also displays additional information in the Discussions toolbar, as shown in Figure 10-47.

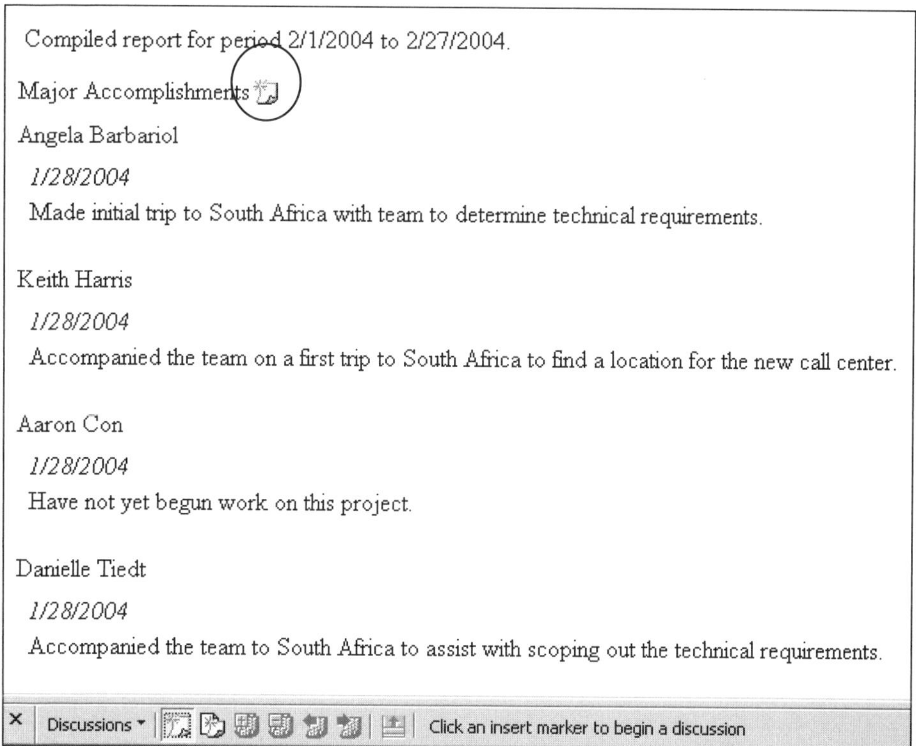

**Figure 10-47: Insert Discussion
in the document**

To add to the discussion in the document, click the discussion marker in the document. The system displays the Enter Discussion Text dialog as shown in Figure 10-48.

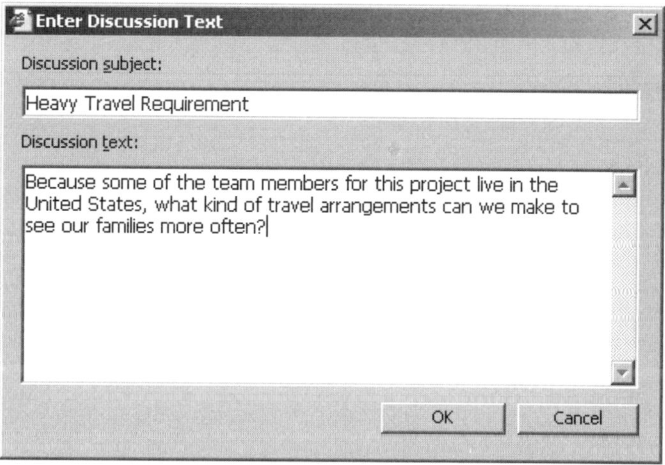

**Figure 10-48: Enter Discussion
Text dialog**

Enter your discussion text and then click the *OK* button. The system displays your discussion within the document, along with additional discussion buttons on the Discussions toolbar, as shown in Figure 10-49.

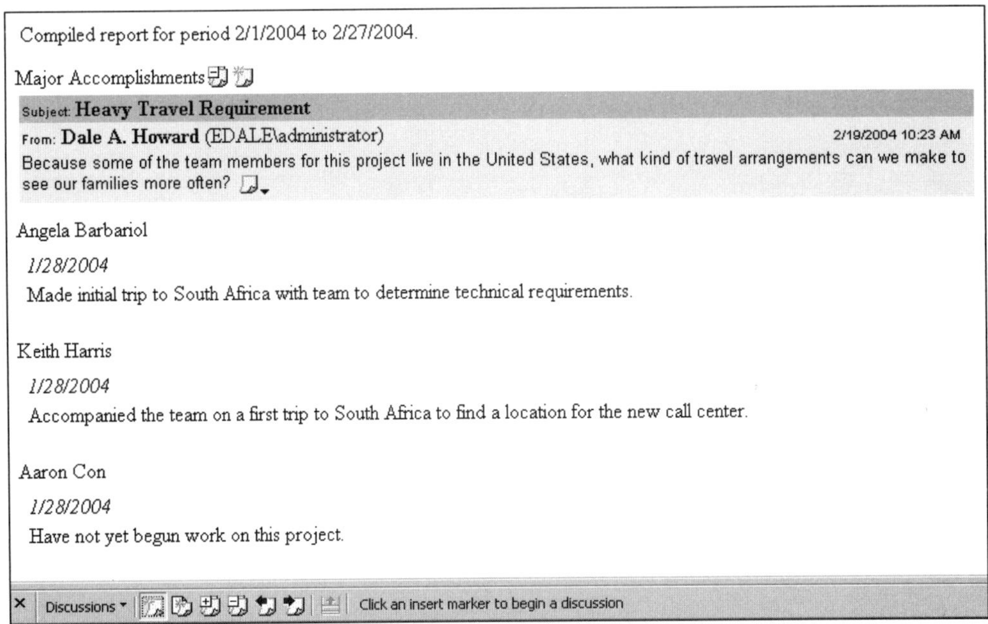

Figure 10-49: Discussion in a document

To view all discussions in the document, click the *Expand all discussions* button on the Discussions toolbar. To hide the discussions, click the *Collapse all discussions* button. Click the *Previous* button or the *Next* button to navigate between discussion items.

To add your thoughts to an existing discussion, click the *Show a menu of options* icon at the bottom of the existing discussion and select the *Reply* menu item, as shown in Figure 10-50. Notice that the system offers you several other options as well, such as editing, deleting, or closing the discussion.

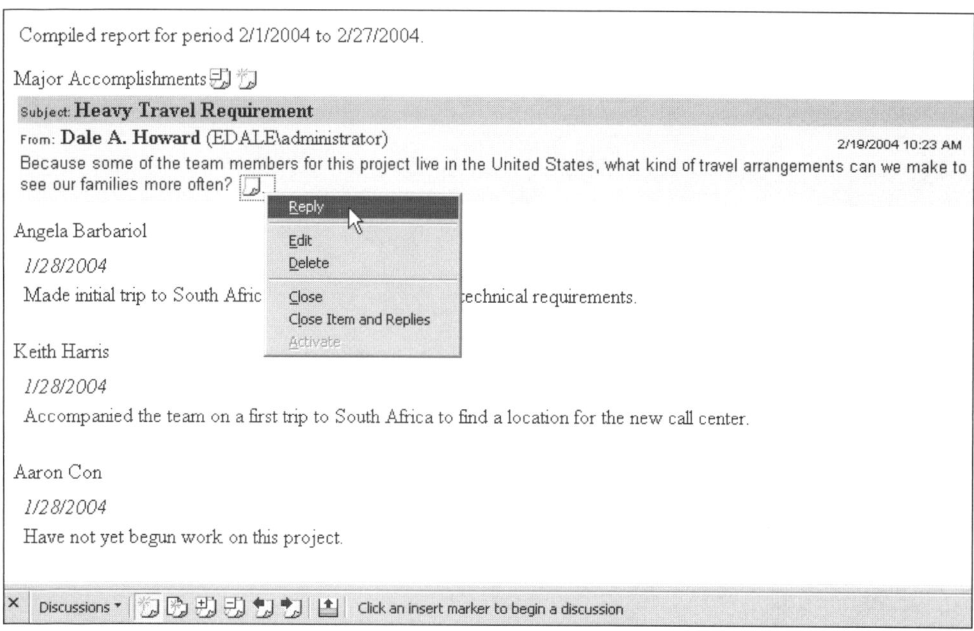

**Figure 10-50: Reply to an
existing discussion**

 **Warning**: You can only insert discussions **in** an HTML file or a text file. The system will generate an error message if you attempt to insert a discussion in any other type of document, such as in a PowerPoint slideshow. The system will allow you to insert discussions **about** any type of document, however.

To insert a discussion about the document, use either of the following options:

- Click the *Insert discussion about the document* button on the toolbar.

- Click the *Discussions* button on the toolbar and then select the *Insert about the document* menu item.

The system displays the Enter Discussion Text dialog previously shown in Figure 10-48. Enter your discussion text and then click the *OK* button. The system opens a discussion pane at the bottom of the document, as shown in Figure 10-51.

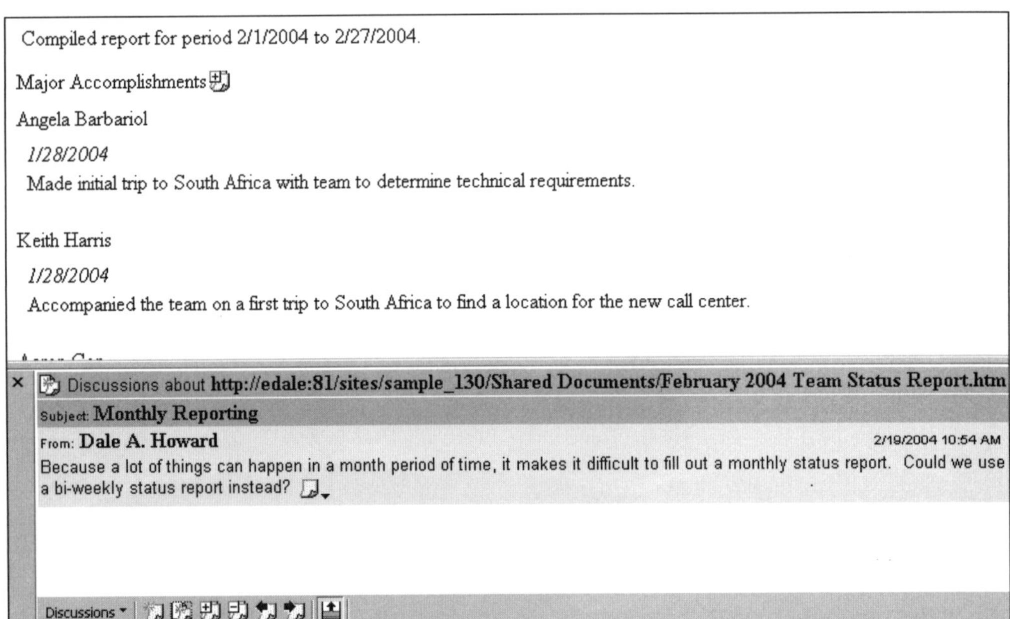

Figure 10-51: Discussion about the document

The system activates the *Show/Hide discussion pane* button on the Discussions toolbar. Click this button to show or hide the pane containing discussions about the document.

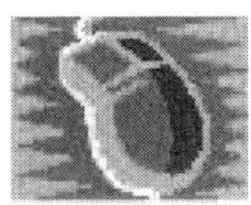 **Hands On Exercise**

Exercise 10-7

Explore the project workspace for a selected project.

1. Select the *Risks*, *Issues*, or *Documents* menu item from the Project Web Access main menu.

2. Select a project that you created or to which you are assigned.

3. Click the *Go to selected project workspace* link at the top of the actions pane.

4. Explore the project workspace for your selected project.

5. Close the project workspace window.

Module 11

Working with Advanced Features of Risks, Issues, and Documents

Learning Objectives

After completing this module, you will be able to:

- View reports for Risks, Issues, and Documents lists

- Set alerts for Risks, Issues, and Documents lists

- Export a list of Risks, Issues, or Documents to an Excel spreadsheet

- Modify settings and columns for Risks, Issues, and Documents lists

- Synchronize the Project Server database with Risks, Issues, and Documents lists that were exported as linked files to Excel or Access

Using Actions Pane Features

The Risks, Issues, and Documents pages of Project Web Access offer you a number of advanced features, such as exporting to Excel and modifying the layout of Views. You will find these features in the Actions section of the actions pane on the Risks, Issues, and Documents pages. These advanced features include:

- View Reports (Risks and Issues only)
- Alert Me
- Export to spreadsheet
- Modify settings and columns
- Synchronize with Project Server

Figure 11-1 shows the Actions section of the actions pane for the Risks page.

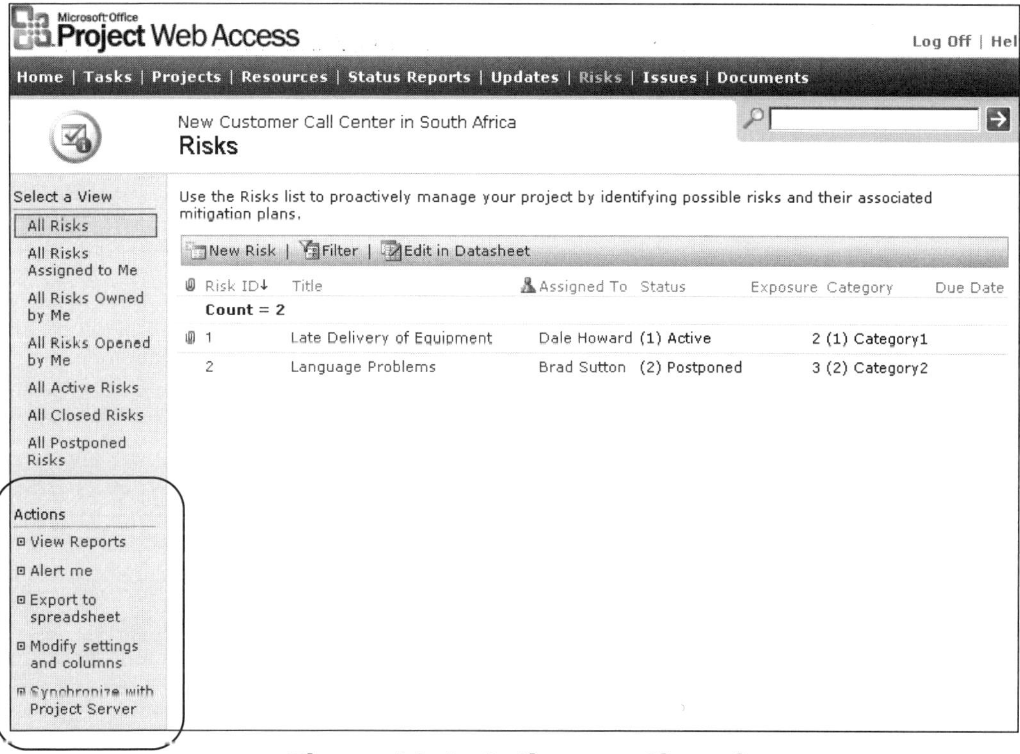

Figure 11-1: Actions section of actions pane on Risks page

Viewing Reports

Click the *View Reports* link to display the Reports page for either Risks or Issues. Figure 11-2 shows the Reports page for a selected project.

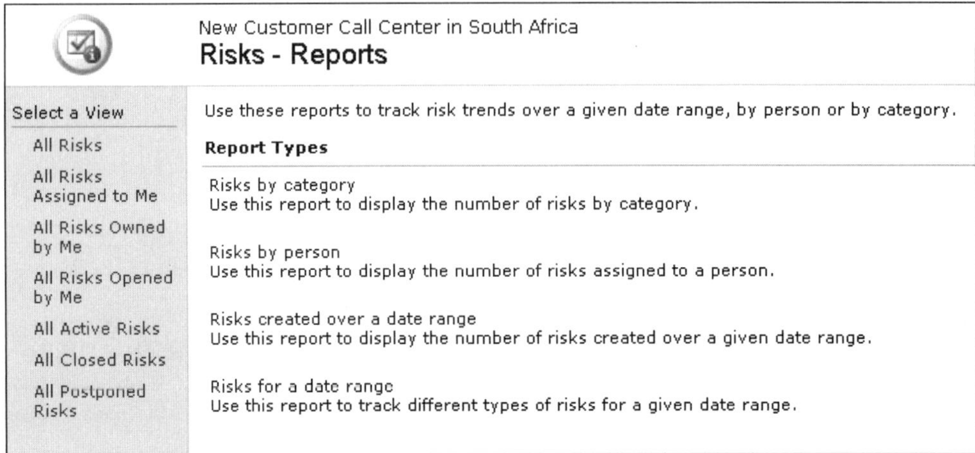

**Figure 11-2: Reports page for
a selected project**

The Report Type section of the Reports page for either Risks or Issues offers four options for creating a report in the selected project:

- By category
- By person
- Created over a date range
- For a date range

When you click the link for the type of Report you desire, the system displays the report in a grid of rows and columns. For example, I have selected the Risks by person report shown in Figure 11-3.

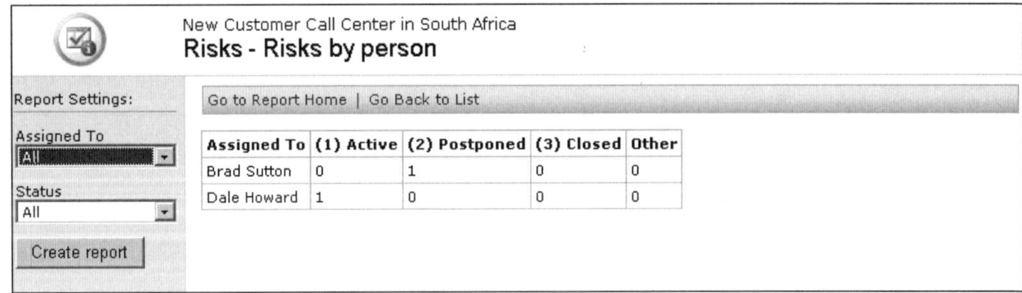

Figure 11-3: Risks by person report

For each type of report, the Report Settings section of the actions pane displays two or more pick lists that you can use to customize your report. Notice in Figure 11-4 that I can narrow the number of names displayed in the report by selecting a value from the *Assigned To* pick list. After you select an item from any of the pick lists, click the *Create report* button to create your customized report.

**Figure 11-4: Customize the
Risks by person report**

Click the *Go to Report Home* button on the toolbar to return to the Reports page for either Risks or Issues. You can also click the *Go Back to List* button to return to the Risks page for the selected project.

Hands On Exercise

Exercise 11-1

View a Report for a Risks or Issues list.

1. Click either the *Risks* or *Issues* menu item from the Project Web Access main menu.

2. Select a project which you created or to which you are assigned.

3. In the actions pane, click the *View Reports* link.

4. Select one of the Report Types.

5. Modify the Report, if necessary.

Setting Alerts

Click the *Alert Me* link in the actions pane of the Risks, Issues, or Documents pages to display the New Alert page shown in Figure 11-5.

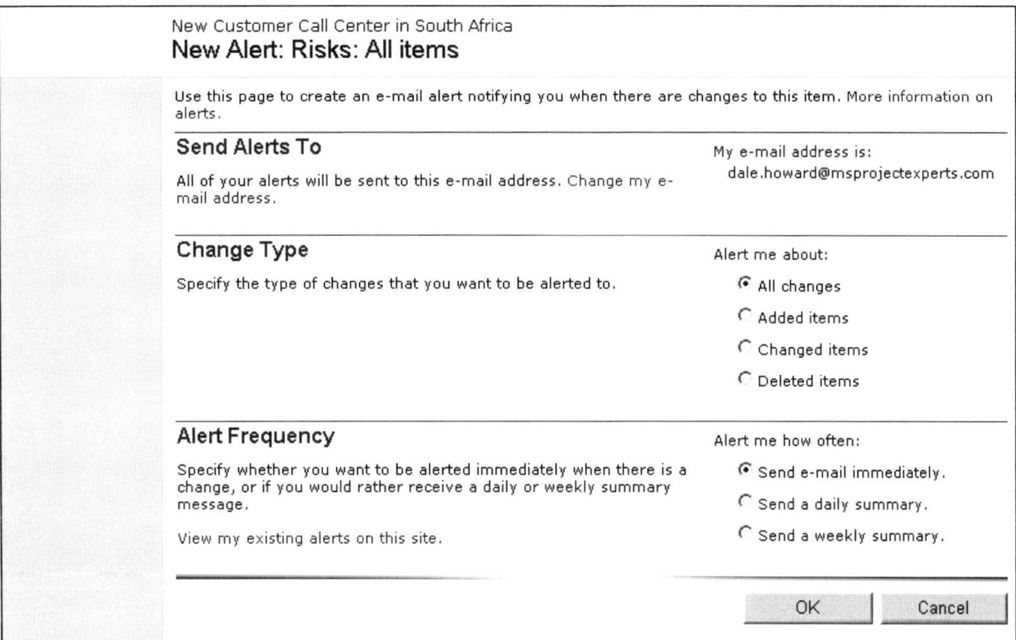

Figure 11-5: New Alert page

Select an option in the Change Type section to determine what type of activity will trigger an e-mail alert to you. These activities include the following:

- All changes
- Added items
- Changed items
- Deleted items
- Web discussion updates (Documents only)

Select an option in the Alert Frequency section to determine how often you want the system to send you alerts. The system can alert you immediately, or send you a daily or weekly summary of changes. Click the *OK* button to confirm your alert selections, or click the *Cancel* button to cancel the alert.

Exporting to an Excel spreadsheet

Click the *Export to spreadsheet* link in the actions pane to export the selected project's list of Risks, Issues, or Documents to an Excel workbook. The system creates an Excel query file and then displays the File Download dialog shown in Figure 11-6.

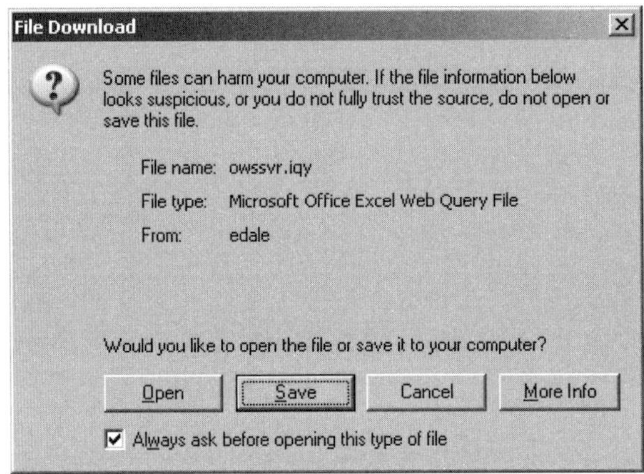

**Figure 11-6: File Download
dialog**

Click the *Save* button to save the file, and open it later in Excel. If you click the *Open* button to open the query file in Excel, the system displays the Opening Query dialog shown in Figure 11-7. Click the *Open* button to open the query file in Excel.

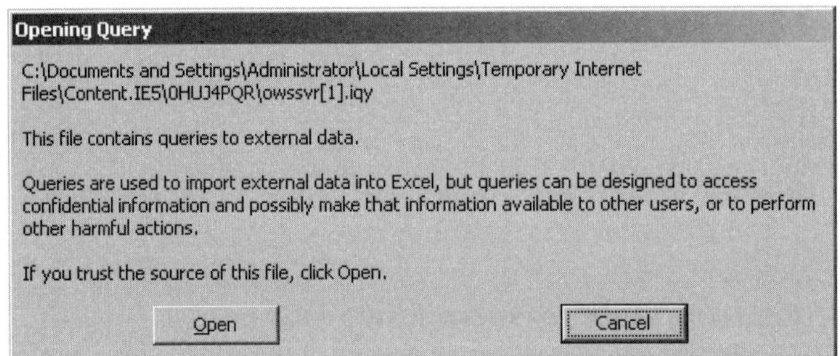

Figure 11-7: Opening Query dialog

The system opens the query file in Excel and displays a floating List toolbar to help you manipulate the query data. Figure 11-8 shows the exported Risk list for a project as an Excel query file.

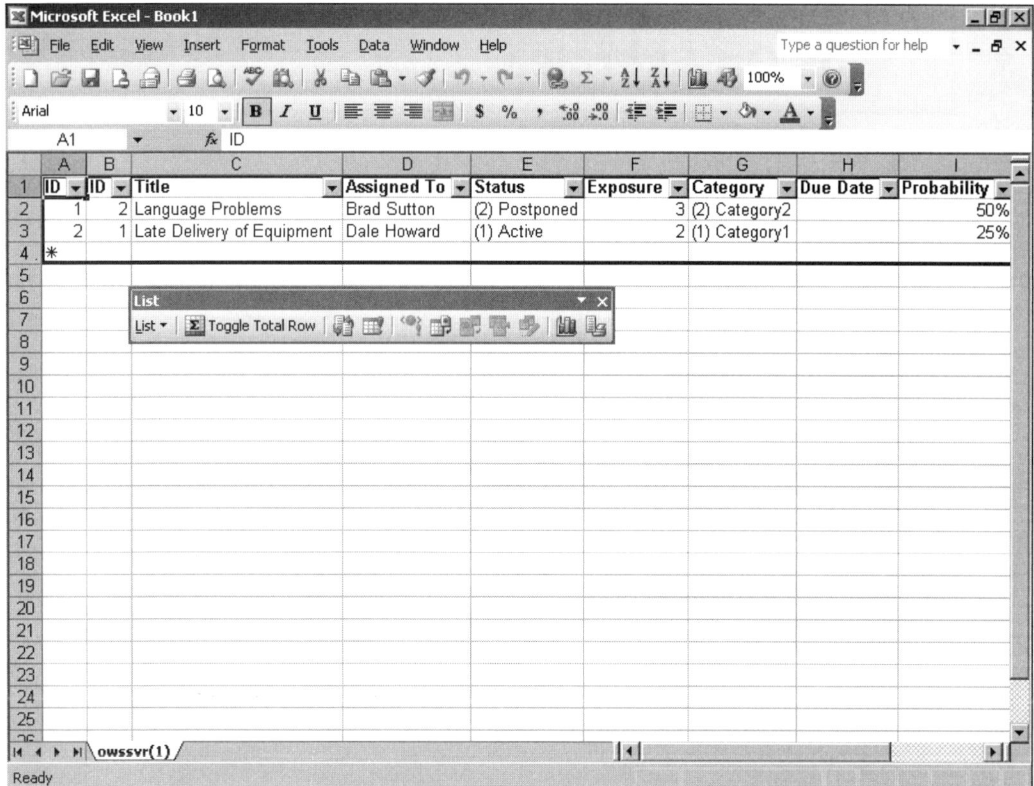

**Figure 11-8: Risk query for a selected project
opened as an Excel workbook**

When you export a Document library list to Excel, the system displays the warning dialog shown in Figure 11-9. The warning indicates that you can edit rows of information in the query, such as the information contained in the Status or Owner fields, but you may not add additional records to the query.

Figure 11-9: Excel warning dialog

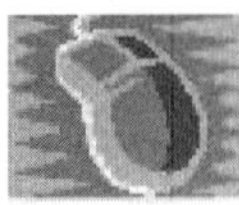

Hands On Exercise

Exercise 11-2

Export a Risks or Issues list to an Excel spreadsheet.

1. Click either the *Risks* or *Issues* menu item from the Project Web Access main menu.

2. Select a project which you created or to which you are assigned.

3. In the actions pane, click the *Export to spreadsheet* link.

4. In the File Download dialog, click the *Open* button.

5. In the Opening Query dialog, click the *Open* button.

6. Examine the spreadsheet file in Excel.

7. Close the spreadsheet file and exit Excel.

Modifying Settings and Columns

Click the *Modify settings and columns* link in the actions pane to customize the display characteristics of the Risks, Issues, or Documents pages. Clicking this option on the Risks page displays the Customize Risks page shown in Figure 11-10.

The Customize page for Risks, Issues, and Documents contain the same three sections: General Settings, Columns, and Views. Naturally, the options in each section are slightly different and vary according to the function of the page.

The options available in the General Settings section for both Customize Risks and Customize Issues are:

- Change general settings
- Change permissions for this list

The options available in the General Settings section for Customize Documents are:

- Change general settings
- Save document library as template
- Change permissions for this document library
- Delete this document library

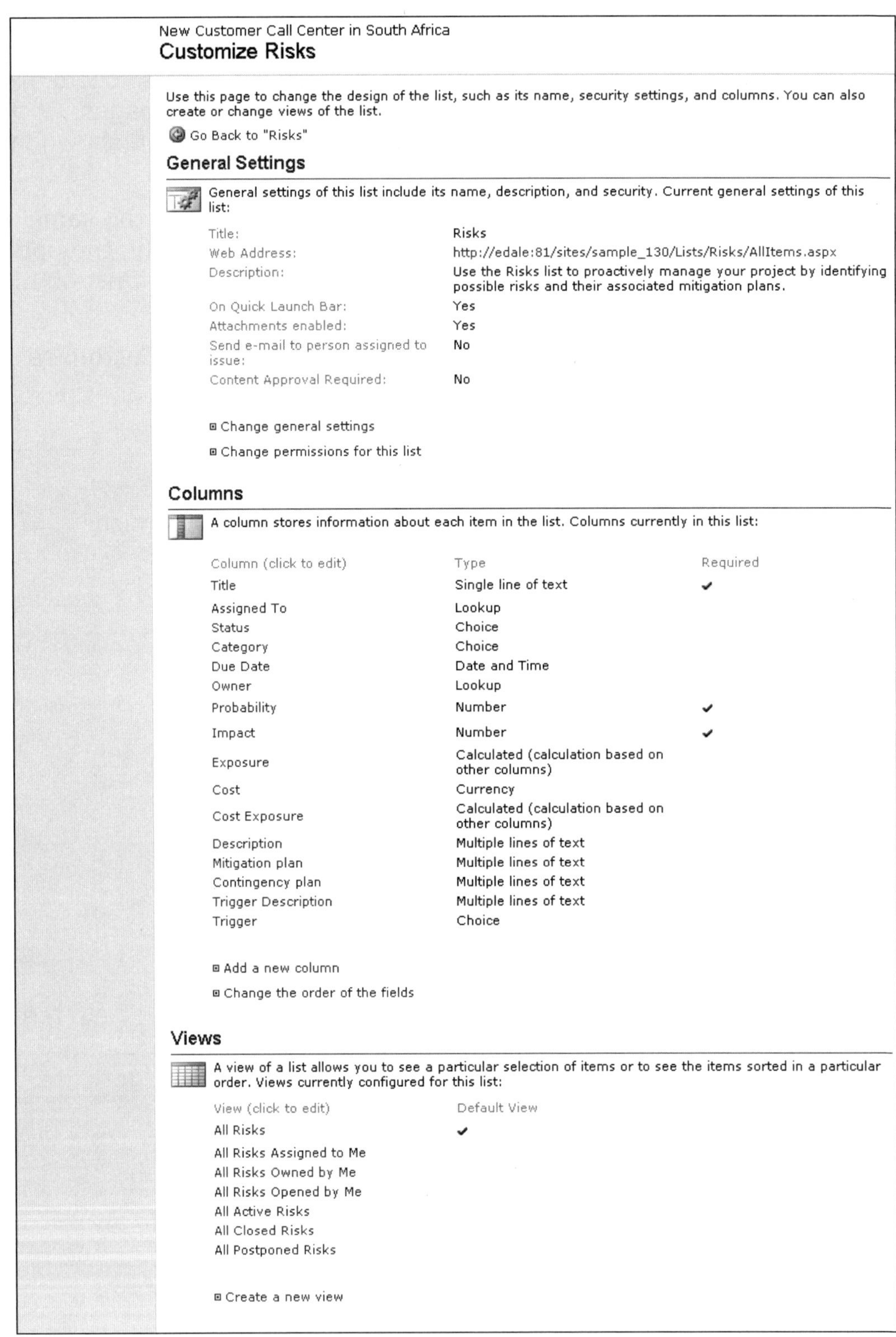

Figure 11-10: Customize Risks page

Modifying General Settings for Risks and Issues

In the General Settings section for Risks or Issues, click the *Change general settings* link and the system displays the List Settings page shown in Figure 11-11.

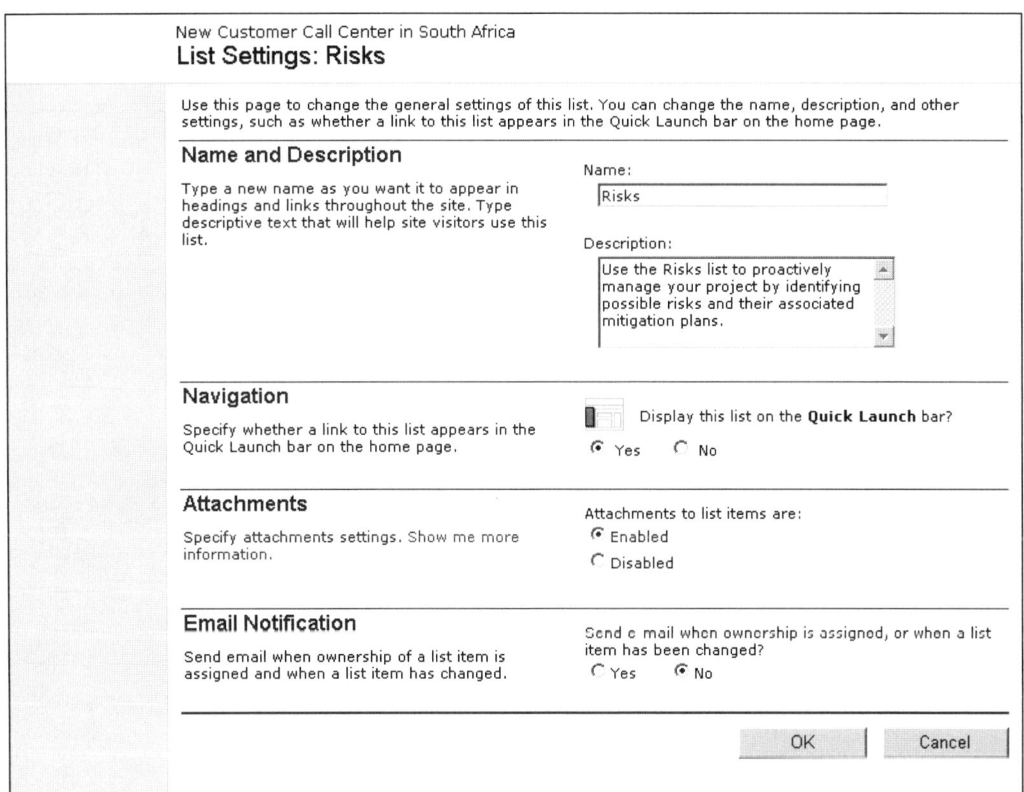

Figure 11-11: List Settings page for Risks

The options in the List Settings page allow you to specify the name and description of the Risks or Issues page, and to determine how the system handles navigation, attachments, and e-mail notifications for the selected project only. Select your desired options and then click the *OK* button to apply the changes or click the *Cancel* button to discard the changes.

The Navigation section of the List Settings page offers the option to display the list on the Quick Launch bar. You can find the Quick Launch bar in the project workspace page for the selected project.

In the General Settings section for Risks or Issues, click the *Change permissions for this list* link to open the Change Permissions page shown in Figure 11-12. Use this page to determine who has access to the Risks page for the selected project. The page displays a description of each user group to which you can assign users. The description lists the permissions for each group. To edit the permissions for any of the groups listed, click the name of the group or select the checkbox for the desired group and then click the *Edit Permissions of Selected Users* button on the toolbar. After selecting a group, you can also add users to the group by clicking the *Add Users* button on the toolbar. You can delete user groups by selecting the checkbox for the desired group and then clicking the *Remove Selected Users* button. Click the *Go Back to List* button to return to the Risks page for the selected project.

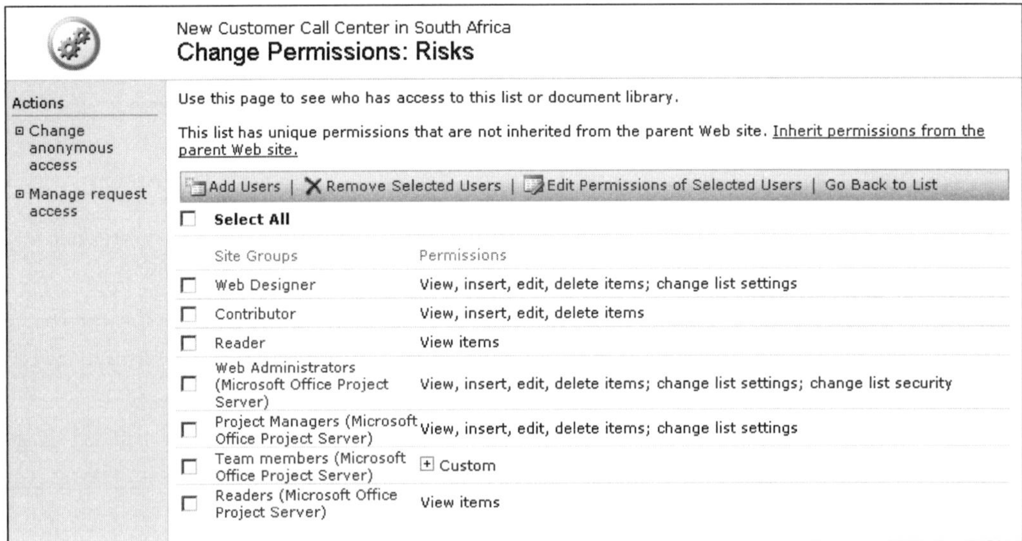

Figure 11-12: Change Permissions page

Because making changes in permissions potentially affects many users in your organization, msProjectExperts recommends that your Project Server administrator be responsible for making all changes to permissions.

Modifying General Settings for Documents

In the General Settings section for Documents, click the *Change general settings* link and the system displays the List Settings page. The List Settings page for Documents contains sections at the bottom of the page for Document Versions and the Document Template, as shown in Figure 11-13. I previously discussed the options on this page in Module 10 in the section on creating a new document library.

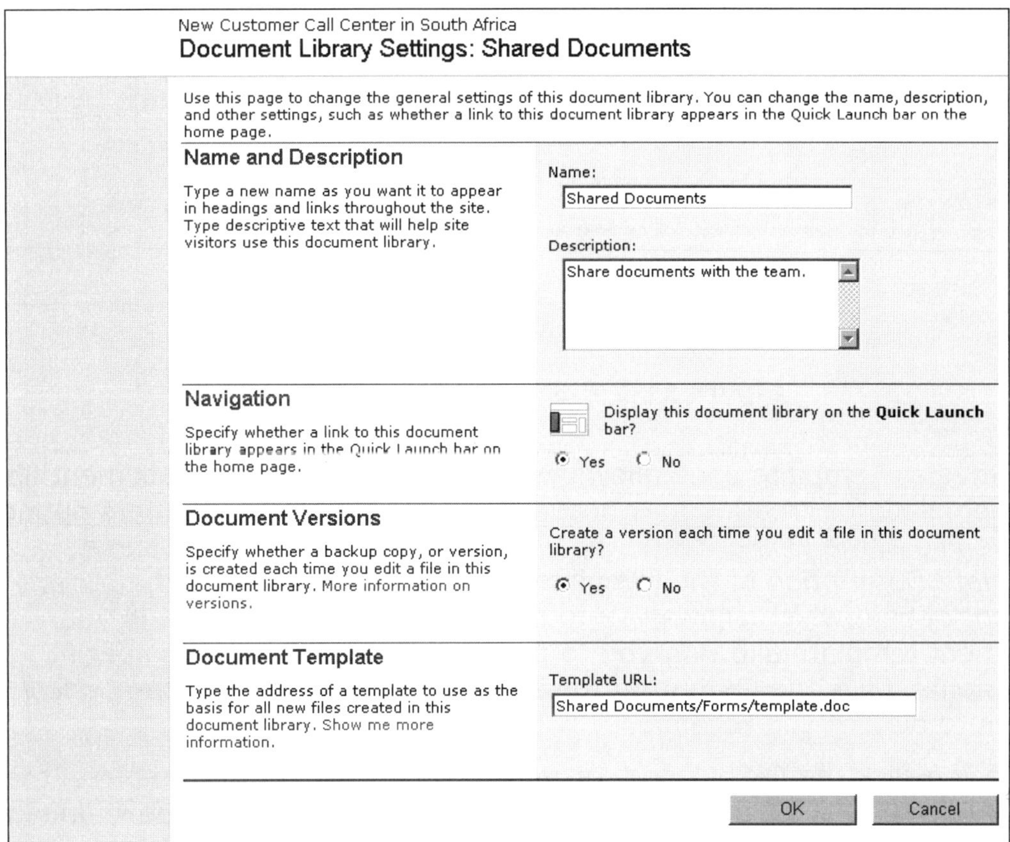

Figure 11-13: List Settings page for Documents

In the General Settings section for Documents, click the *Save document library as template* link and the system displays the Save as Template page, as shown in Figure 11-14.

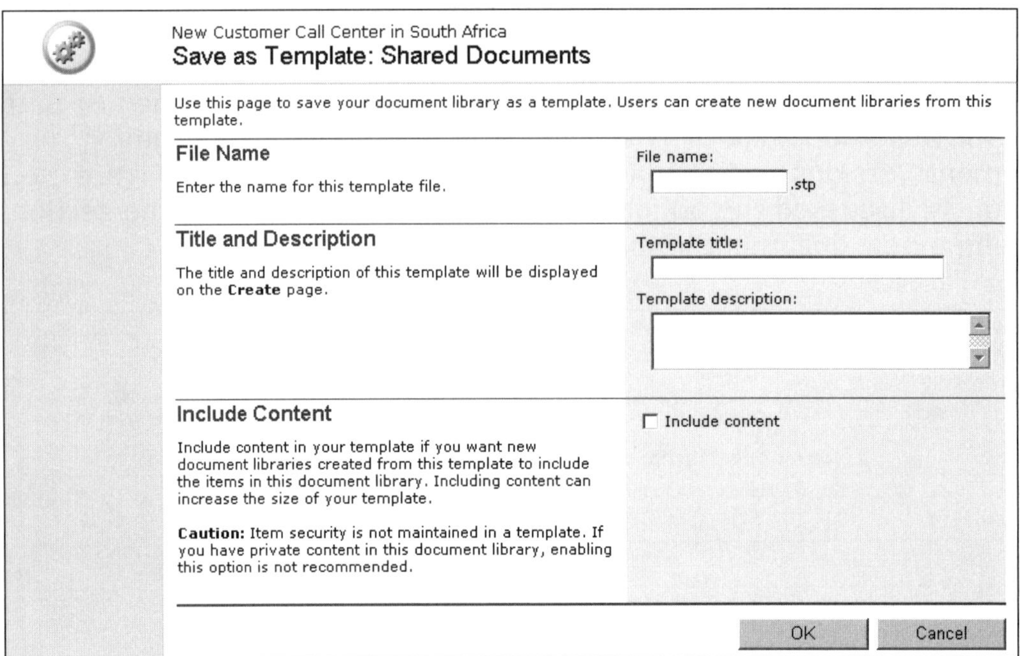

Figure 11-14: Save as Template page

The Save as Template page allows you to save the selected document library as a template for creating new document libraries. The page offers options for the *File Name* of the template, along with a *Template Title* and a *Template Description* of the template. An important option is the *Include content* option, which allows you to include specific documents in your document template allowing you to pre-populate a library with specific documents. Click the *OK* button to save the template or click the *Cancel* button to discard your changes.

When you click the *OK* button to save the document library template, the system displays the Operation Completed Successfully page shown in Figure 11-15.

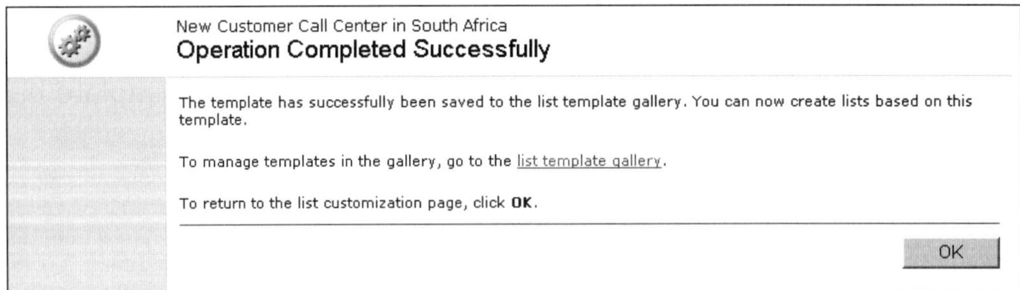

Figure 11-15: Operation Completed Successfully page

To return to the list customization page, click the *OK* button. To manage the templates in the gallery, click the *List template gallery* link. The system displays the List Template Gallery page for the selected project shown in Figure 11-16.

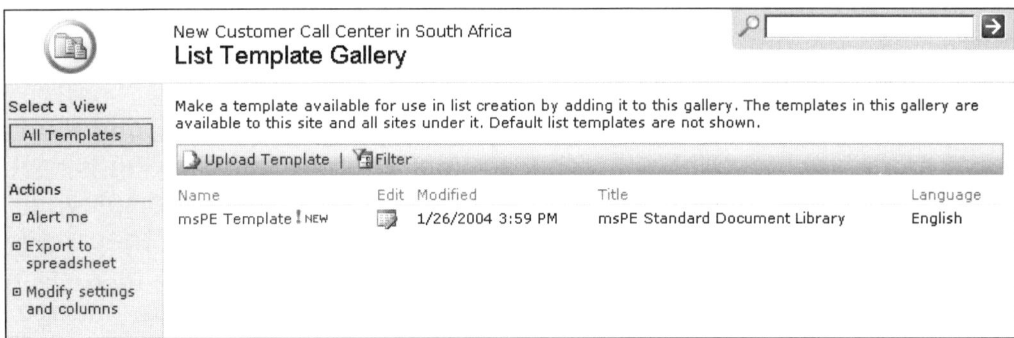

Figure 11-16: List Template Gallery page

Use the options on the List Template Gallery page to take the following actions:

- Upload a new template to the gallery.

- Apply filtering to the templates in the gallery.

- Set up alerts.

- Export the gallery to an Excel spreadsheet.

- Modify the settings and columns for the gallery.

In the General Settings section for Documents, you can change the user permissions for the library by clicking the *Change permissions for this document library* link. The options on the Change Permissions page are identical to the options available for Risks and Issues list.

In the General Settings section for Documents, click the *Delete this document library* link to remove the library for the selected project. The system displays the confirmation dialog shown in Figure 11-17. Click the *OK* button to delete the document library or click the *Cancel* button to cancel the deletion process.

**Figure 11-17: Confirmation dialog to
delete a document library**

Modifying Columns Settings

You make changes to any of the columns displayed on the Risks, Issues, or Documents pages by clicking the link for the name of the column. Figure 11-18 shows the Change Column page for the Status column. To get this display, you click the Status column in the Risks page. The system displays options in the Change Column page according to the type of column you select.

Notice in Figure 11-18 that the system gives you options to change the column's name and description, to determine whether information is required in the column, and to determine what information the system displays in the column as well as how it displays the information. You can see that the system displays information in the Risks Status column using a pick list with selections for Active, Postponed, and Closed. If you want to add, change or delete a status value, you do it here. Edit the column to your liking, and then click the *OK* button to save the changes for the selected column or click the *Cancel* button to discard the changes.

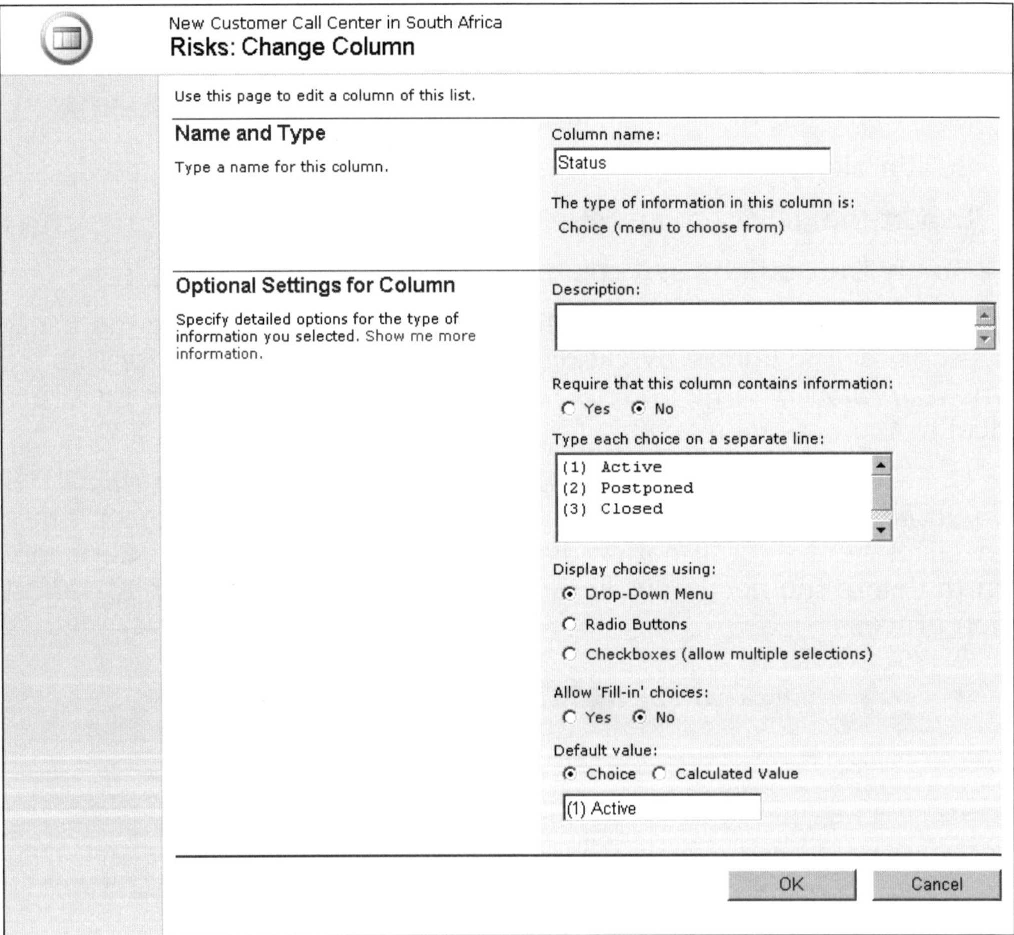

**Figure 11-18: Change Column page
for the Status column**

When you click the *Add a new column* link in the Columns section, the system opens the Add Column page shown in Figure 11-19. This page is virtually identical to the Change Column page and requires you to enter the name of the column along with the type of type of information displayed in the column. Based on the type of column you choose, the system redraws the page to include options for the column type. Notice in the figure that I selected the *Choice (menu to choose from)* option as my information type and the system displayed the selections in the Optional Settings for Column section accordingly. Make your selections about the new column and then click the *OK* button to add the new column, or click the *Cancel* button to discard the changes.

**Figure 11-19: Add Column page
with Choice information selected**

Click the *Change the order of the fields* link in the Columns section to open the Change Field Order page shown in Figure 11-20. Notice that the page displays the current order of fields listed in the Risks page for the selected project. A numbered pick list to the right of each field name indicates the position of the field from the top of the list. When you change the position number for a field, the system automatically renumbers the remaining fields. Make any changes you desire to the order of the fields, and then click the *OK* button to save the changes. Click the *Cancel* button to discard the changes.

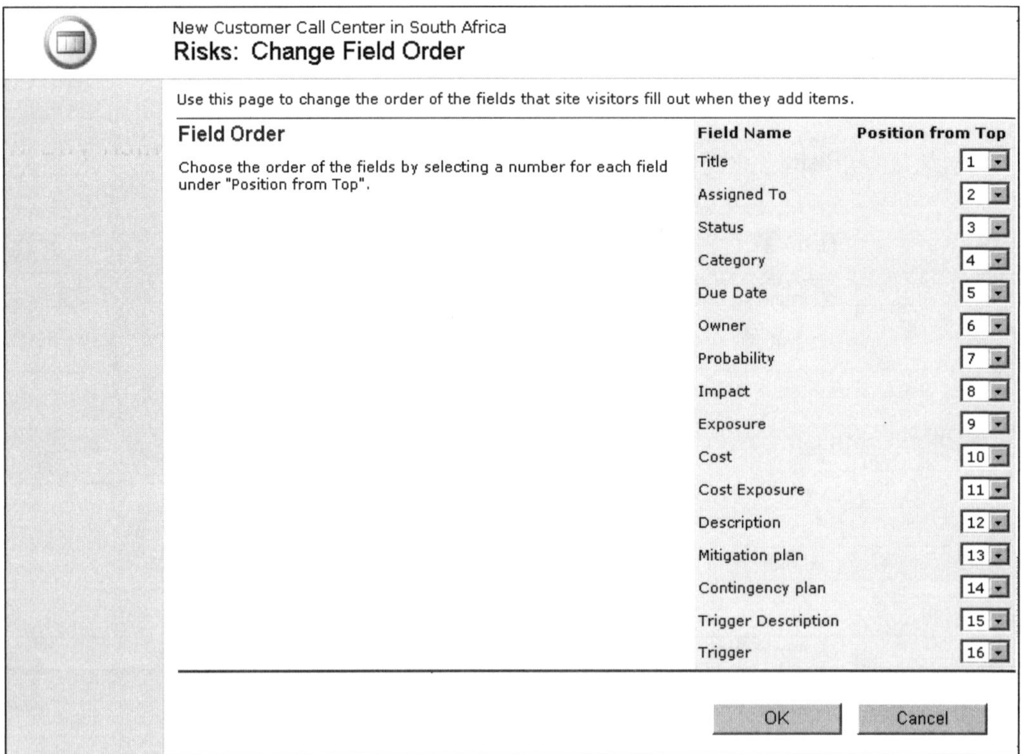

Figure 11-20: Change Field Order page

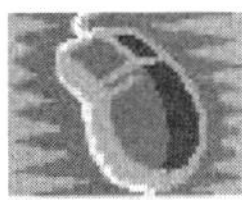 **Hands On Exercise**

Exercise 11-3

Add an extra column to a Document library.

1. Select the *Documents* menu item from the Project Web Access main menu.
2. Select a project and click the document library which you wish to modify.
3. Click the *Modify settings and columns* link in the actions pane.
4. In the Columns section, click the *Add a new column* link.
5. Enter a name for your column and choose a data type.
6. Set optional settings for the column.
7. Click the *OK* button when done.
8. View the new column in the document library.

Modifying Views

When you a click a View listed in the Views section, the system presents the Edit View page shown in Figure 11-21. Notice that I selected the All Risks Assigned to Me view for editing. The Name section of the Edit View page allows you to rename the view, specify the Web address for the view, or set this view as the default view. The Columns section of the Edit View page allows you to select which columns the system displays in the view and in what order. The Sort section allows you to apply two levels of sorting to the selected view. The Filter section allows you to apply multiple levels of filtering to the view. By default, the system displays only two levels of filtering, but you can click the *Show More Columns* link to add more columns to the filter.

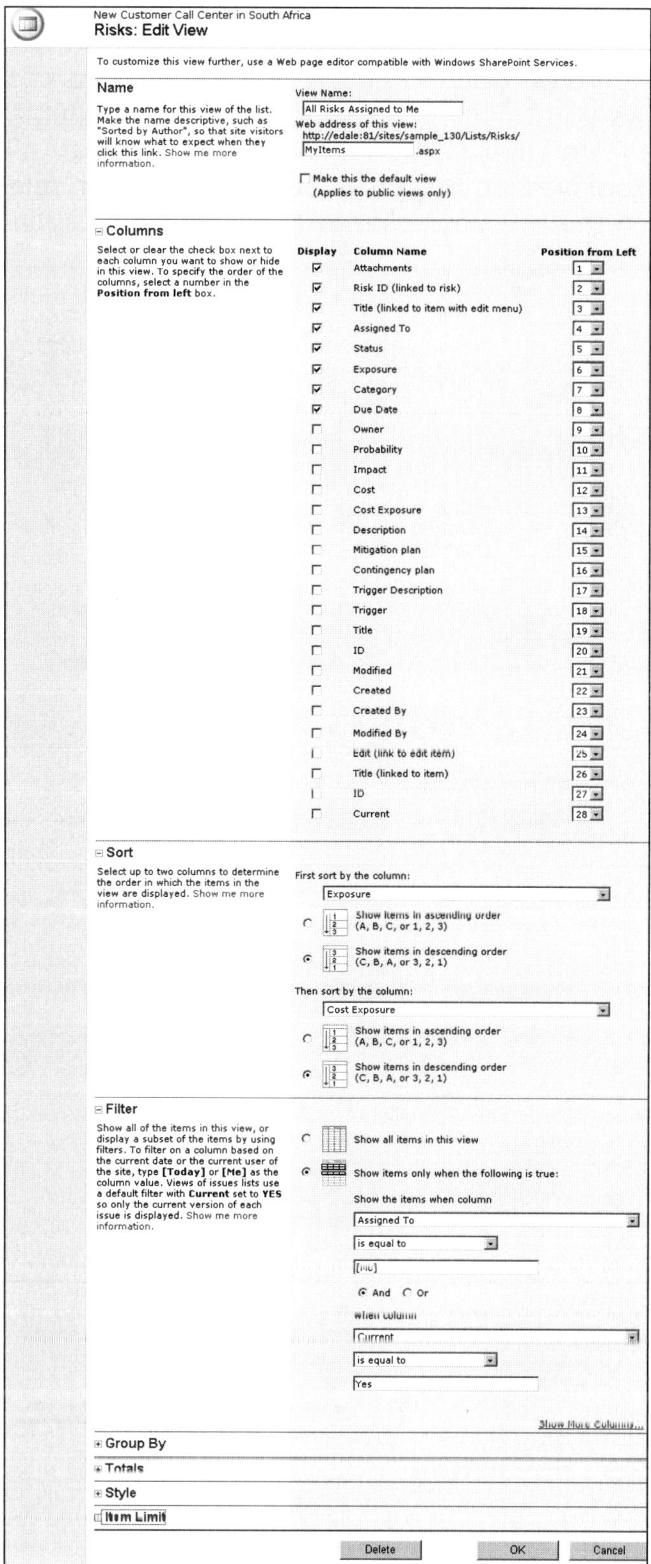

Figure 11-21: Edit View page

By default, the system displays the Group By, Totals, Style, and Item Limit sections collapsed. In Figure 11-22, I expanded the contents of these four sections. The Group By section allows you to apply up to two levels of grouping, while the Totals section allows you to add totals to the display. The Style section allows you to select from one of eight available styles for the display, while the Item Limit section allows you to specify a limit on the number of risks displayed on the Risks page. Make your selections and then click the *OK* button to save your changes, or click the *Cancel* button to discard your changes.

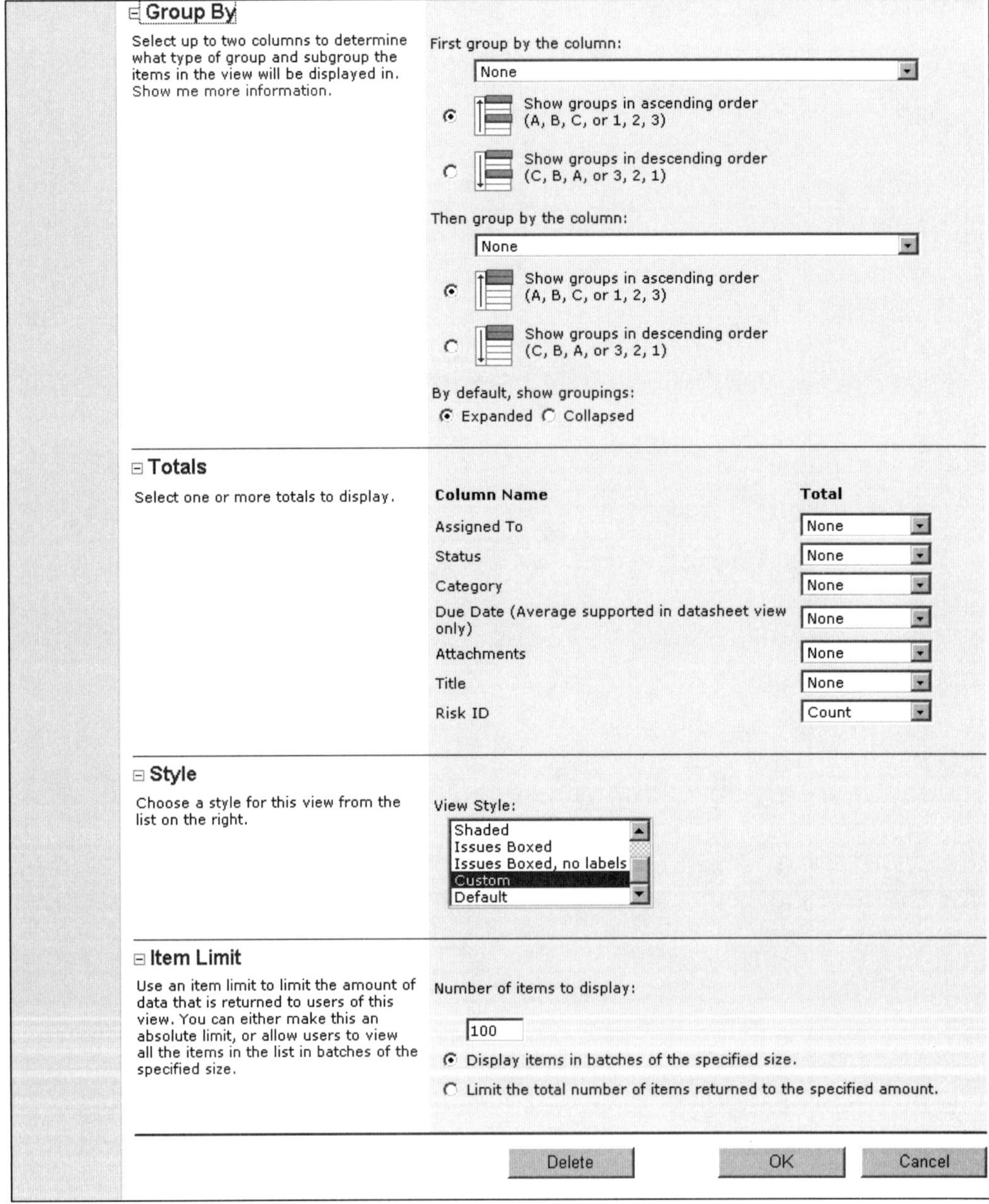

**Figure 11-22: Last four sections
expanded on the Edit View page**

 You can also delete the current view while in the Edit View page by clicking the *Delete* button. The system displays a confirmation dialog to make certain you want to delete the view.

When you click the *Create a new view* link in the Views section, the system presents the Create View page shown in Figure 11-23. The system allows you to create three kinds of Views: Standard, Datasheet, and Calendar.

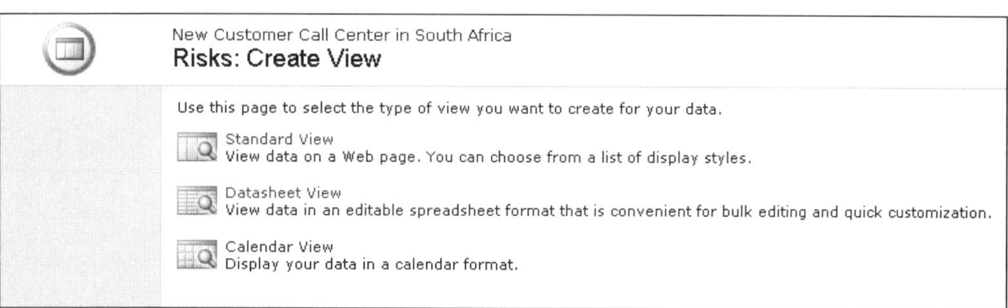

Figure 11-23: Create View page

All default view selections in the actions pane are Standard views for Risks, Issues, and Documents. Click the *Standard View* button to create a new Standard view, or click the *Datasheet View* link to create a new Datasheet view. Because the Create View pages for both selections are virtually identical to the Edit View pages with which you are already familiar, I will not go into depth on how to create new Standard and Datasheet views.

If the source list for which you want to create a custom view contains a column with date information, you can create a Calendar View to display information on a standard calendar. Click the *Calendar View* link to display the Create Calendar View page shown in Figure 11-24. In the Name section of the page, enter a name for your new Calendar view and select the *Make this the default view* option if you wish to make this new view the default view for the list page where you are applying it. In the Audience section, select either the *Create a Personal view* option or the *Create a Public view* option. Personal views are for your own personal use, while Public views are available to everyone within the system.

 The *Make this the default view* option applies only to Public views. The system will not allow you to set a Private view as the default view.

New Customer Call Center in South Africa
Risks: Create Calendar View

Use this page to create a view of this list.

Name

Type a name for this view of the list. Make the name descriptive, such as "Sorted by Author", so that site visitors will know what to expect when they click this link. Show me more information.

View Name:

☐ Make this the default view
(Applies to public views only)

Audience

Select the option that represents the intended audience for this view. Show me more information.

View Audience:

○ Create a Personal View

Personal Views are intended for your use only. However, if given the correct URL, others may use, modify or delete your personal view.

◉ Create a Public View

Public views can be visited by anyone using the site.

⊟ Columns

Select the column(s) on which the calendar will be based.

◉ Base calendar on: Due Date / Modified / Created

○ Base calendar on the following interval:
Between [Due Date / Modified / Created] and [Due Date / Modified / Created]

⊟ Calendar Settings

Choose the calendar settings for this view.

Calendar opens in: ◉ Month View
○ Week View
○ Day View

You can change this at any time while using the calendar.

⊟ Filter

Show all of the items in this view, or display a subset of the items by using filters. To filter on a column based on the current date or the current user of the site, type **[Today]** or **[Me]** as the column value. Views of issues lists use a default filter with **Current** set to **YES** so only the current version of each issue is displayed. Show me more information.

○ Show all items in this view

◉ Show items only when the following is true:

Show the items when column

Current ▼

is equal to ▼

Yes

○ And ◉ Or

When column

None ▼

is equal to ▼

Show More Columns...

OK   Cancel

Figure 11-24: Create Calendar View page

In the Columns section, select an option to base the calendar on a single date or on a date range. Both options allow you to choose whether to display the Risk, Issue, or Document according to date criteria. In the Calendar Settings section, you choose whether to display a monthly, weekly, or daily calendar. The Filter section, gives you options to display all items or to apply a filter to the list. If you select the option to filter your list, create the filter with one or two columns of data. When you have finished creating your custom Calendar view, click the *OK* button to save your view or click the *Cancel* button to discard the view.

When your new custom view is complete, it appears in the actions pane for the Risks, Issues, or Documents page. Click on your new view to apply it. Figure 11-25, shows the new custom Calendar view I created to show all risks in a calendar format, based on the creation date of the risk.

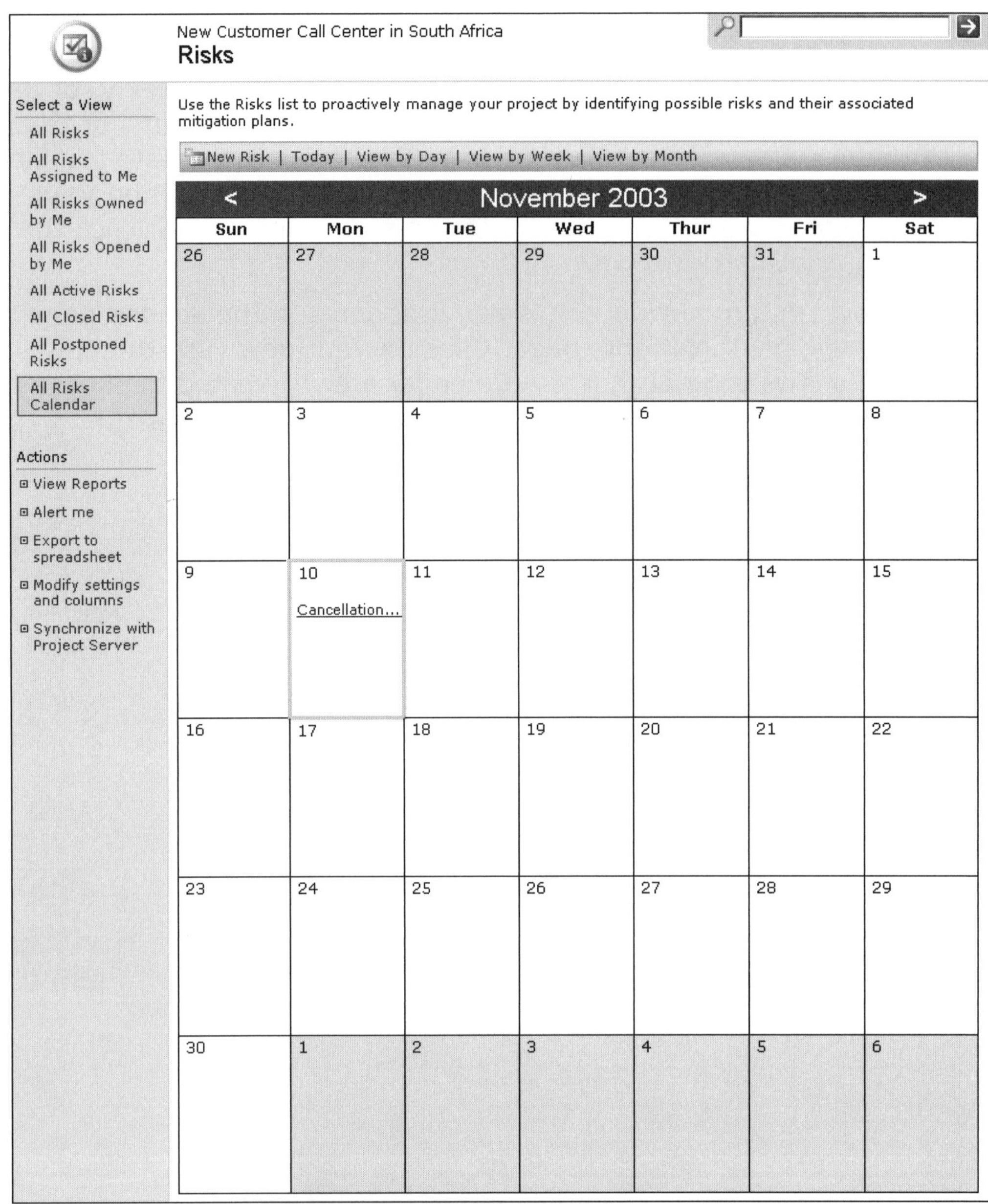

Figure 11-25: Custom Calendar view

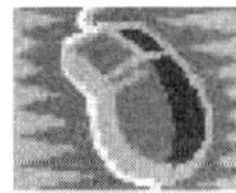

Hands On Exercise

Exercise 11-4

Add a new view to a Document library.

1. Select the *Documents* menu item from the Project Web Access main menu.

2. Select a project and then select the document library in which you wish to create a new view.

3. Click the *Modify settings and columns* link in the actions pane.

4. In the Views section, click *Create a new view* link and select a Standard View.

5. Enter a Name for your new view, select an Audience, and determine the columns to display and the order to display them.

6. Select additional options as you desire.

7. Click the *OK* button when you are finished creating the new view.

8. Try your new view in the document library.

Synchronizing with Project Server

Project Server 2003 gives you the means to export and link a Risks, Issues, or Document list to an Excel spreadsheet or to an Access table. To use this feature, apply the Datasheet view of any project's Risk, Issue, or Documents list and then click the *Task Pane* button in the toolbar to display the Task Pane shown in Figure 11-26.

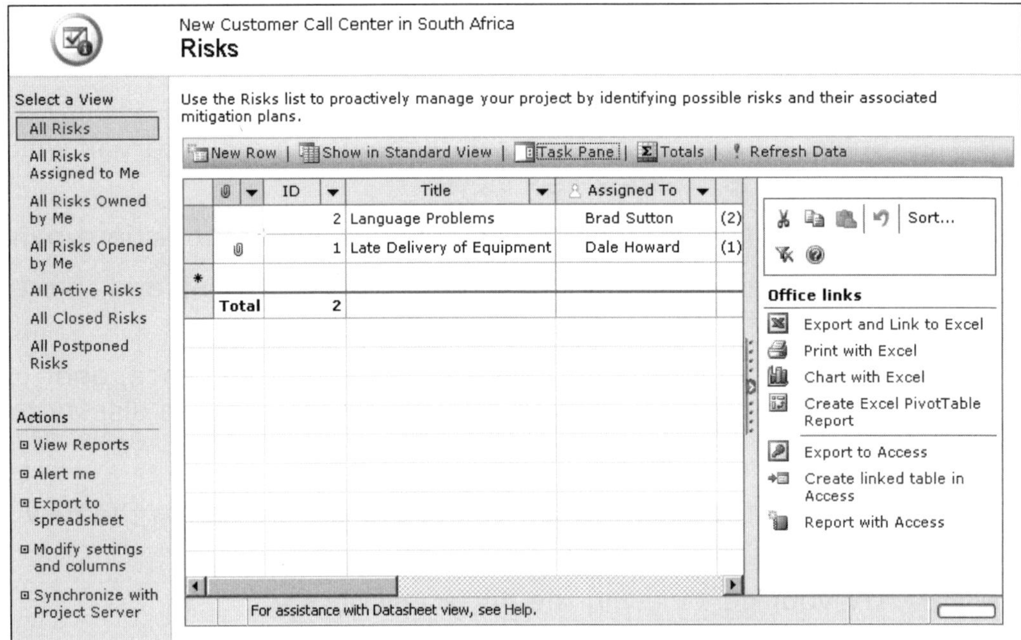

Figure 11-26: Task pane for Risks list

If you export a Risks, Issues, or Documents list to either Excel or Access, and subsequently make changes to the exported file in these applications, you can synchronize the changes with the SharePoint database. In fact, both Excel and Access warn you at the time you save by displaying the dialog shown in Figure 11-27.

**Figure 11-27: Synchronization
warning dialog**

To synchronize the changes in a linked Excel spreadsheet or Access table, click the *Synchronize with Project Server* link at the bottom of the Actions list in the actions pane. The system displays a confirmation dialog shown in Figure 11-28. Click the *OK* button to synchronize the data.

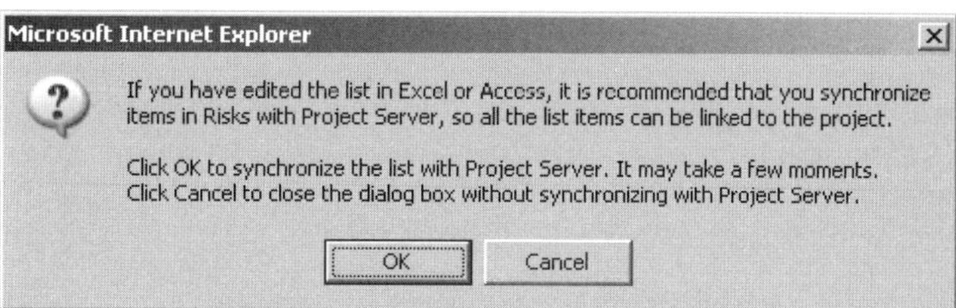

**Figure 11-28: Synchronize to
Project Server dialog**

Once the system synchronizes the changes between Excel or Access and the SharePoint database, it displays the confirmation dialog shown in Figure 11-29.

**Figure 11-29: Synchronization
is successful**

Module 12

Working with Status Reports

Learning Objectives

After completing this module, you will be able to:

- Create a new status report request
- Save and send a status report request
- Edit and delete a status report
- Respond to a status report request
- Submit an unrequested status report
- View individual status report responses
- View a merged team status report
- View unrequested status reports

Requesting a Status Report

Click the *Status Reports* menu item on the main menu in Project Web Access to begin working with the Status Reports Overview page shown in Figure 12-1. Team members do not see the Request a Status Report section in the page or the option in the actions pane.

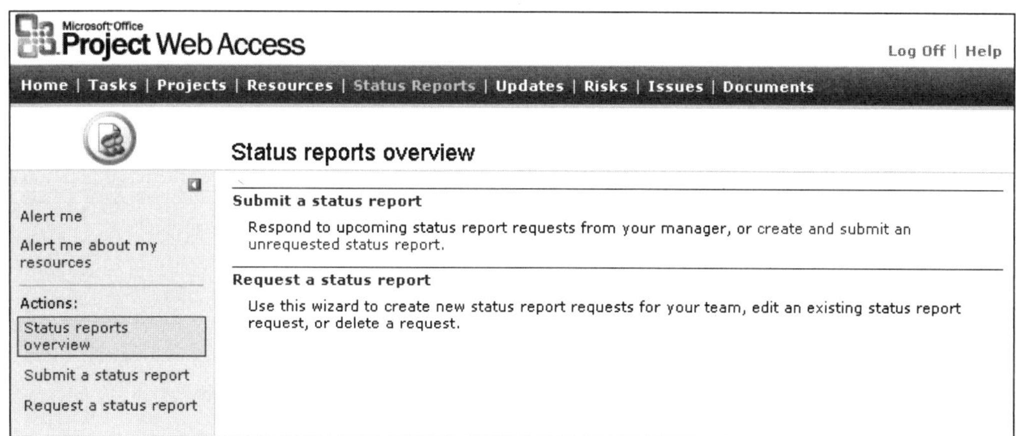

Figure 12-1: Status Reports Overview page

The Request a status report feature is dependent on permissions granted in Groups in Project Web Access. By default, it is available only to the following Groups: Executives, Project Managers, Resource Managers, Team Leads, and Administrators.

You can use the Request a status report feature to create periodic Status Reports due on a regular basis. Click the *Request a status report* link to display the Request a Status Report page shown in Figure 12-2. Note that the selections on this page not only allow you to create a new status report request, they also allow you to modify or delete an existing status report request. You must select an action before continuing.

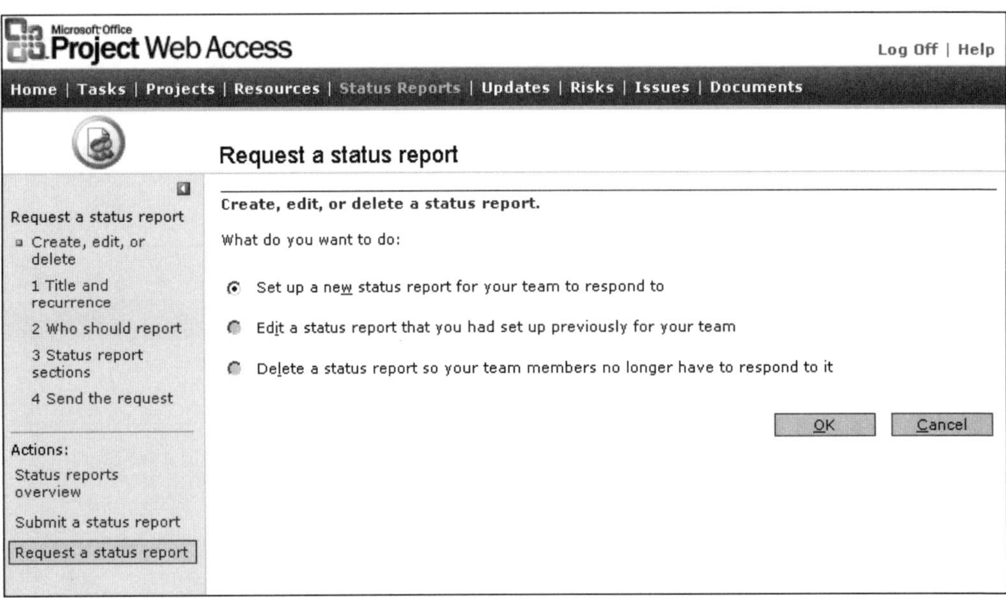

Figure 12-2: Request a Status Report page

Creating a New Status Report Request

To create a new status report request, select Set up a new status report for your team to respond to on the Request a Status Report page previously shown in Figure 12-2, and click the *OK* button. The system displays the Step 1 page of a four-step wizard, as shown in Figure 12-3. Give the status report a name, determine its recurrence rate and due date, and set the start date of the first reporting period on this page. Notice in Figure 12-3 that my new status report is due on a monthly basis on the last Friday of every month and the first reporting period begins February 1, 2004. In other words, team members must submit their first response on or before the last Friday of February.

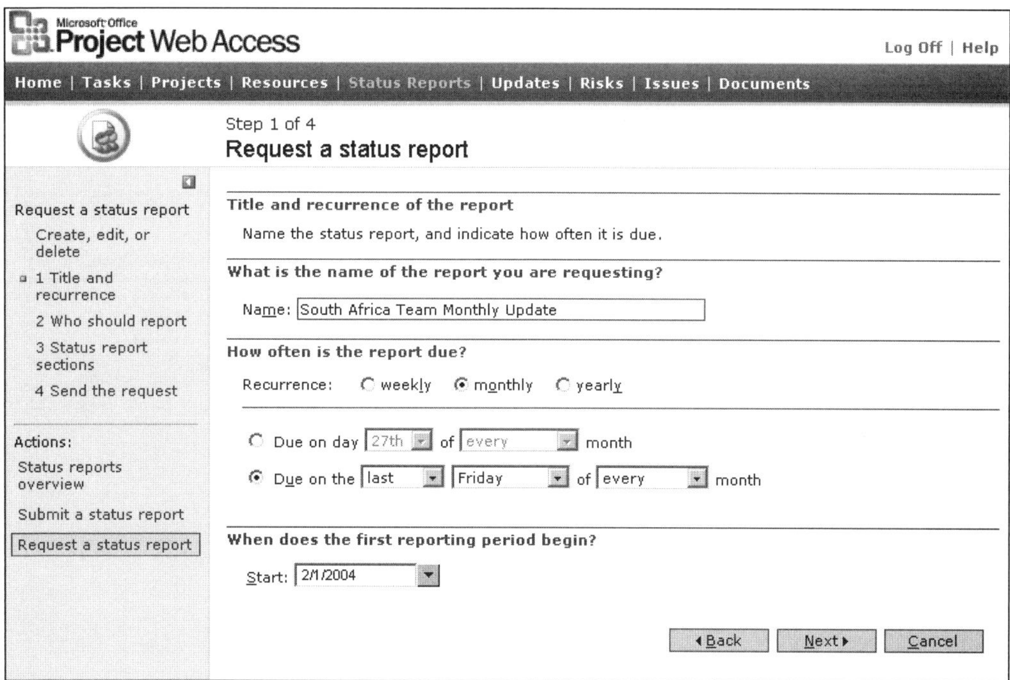

**Figure 12-3: Request a Status Report – Step 1
Set the Title and Recurrence**

Click the *Next* button to display the Step 2 page and select the resources who must respond to the status report. Notice in Figure 12-4 that I selected four resources. Notice that the system selects the checkbox to the left of each name by default as you add resources to the respondent list. The checkbox is an indication to the system to merge the responses from each individual resource into a single consolidated Status Report. Deselecting the checkbox removes the individual from the merged report.

**Figure 12-4: Request a Status Report – Step 2
Select the resources who should respond
to the status report request**

Click the *Next* button to display the Step 3 page, where you configure the status report's topical sections. By default, the system offers the three sections shown in Figure 12-5. You can delete, reorder, rename, add to them, or accept them as they are.

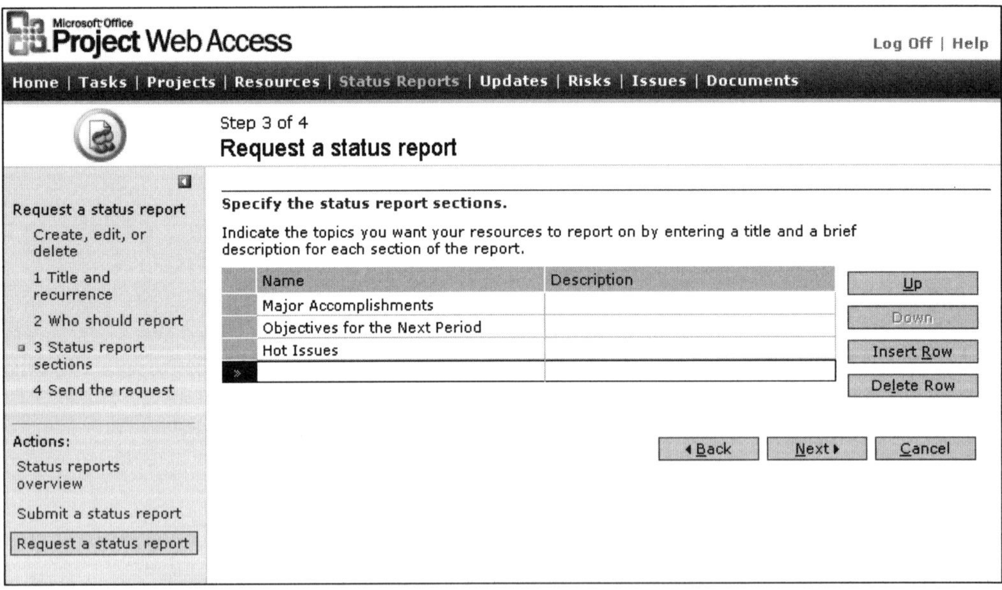

**Figure 12-5: Request a Status Report – Step 3
Specify the status report sections**

Click the *Next* button to display Step 4 shown in Figure 12-6. This page gives you an opportunity to go back and edit your selections, or to confirm the Status Report creation. Click the *Save* button to create and save the status report in the system without sending it to the respondents or click the *Send* button to save the status report and send it to the respondents immediately. If you save without sending, you can send the report later. Click the *Cancel* button to cancel the operation.

Figure 12-6: Request a Status Report – Step 4
Confirm status report creation

After you save or send your status report the system redisplays the Status Reports Overview page as shown in Figure 12-7. Notice that your new status report request displays in the Requested Reports section.

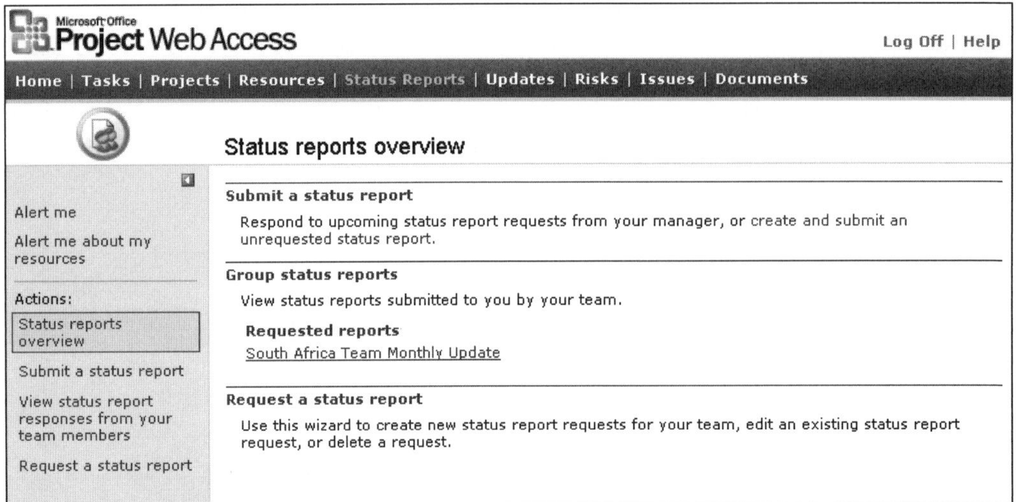

**Figure 12-7: Status Reports Overview page
with new status report request**

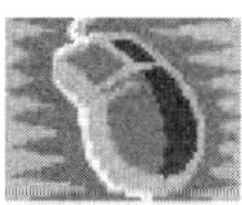

Hands On Exercise

Exercise 12-1

Create a new Status Report request.

1. Click the *Status Reports* menu item from the Project Web Access main menu.

2. Click the *Request a Status Report* link.

3. Select the *Set up a new Status Report for your team* option and click the *OK* button.

4. Set the *Name* and *Recurrence* options for the new status report and click the *Next* button (use a past date for the first reporting period).

5. Select yourself and members of your class as resources who must respond to the Status Report.

6. Verify that the *Merge* checkbox is selected for each name, and then click the *Next* button to continue.

7. Specify the section headings for the Status Report and click the *Next* button to continue.

8. Click the *Send* button to send the Status Report.

9. Navigate to the Home page in Project Web Access to verify the status report request.

Editing and Deleting Status Reports

To edit an existing status report, you must first click the *Request a status report* link on the Status Reports Overview page. The system displays the Request a Status Report page. When you click the *Edit a status report that you had set up previously for your team* option the system displays a pick list of your previously created status reports. Notice in Figure 12-8 that I am selecting the Steve Masters Team Weekly Report for editing. Once you select a status report for editing, click the *OK* button to continue through all four steps of the wizard.

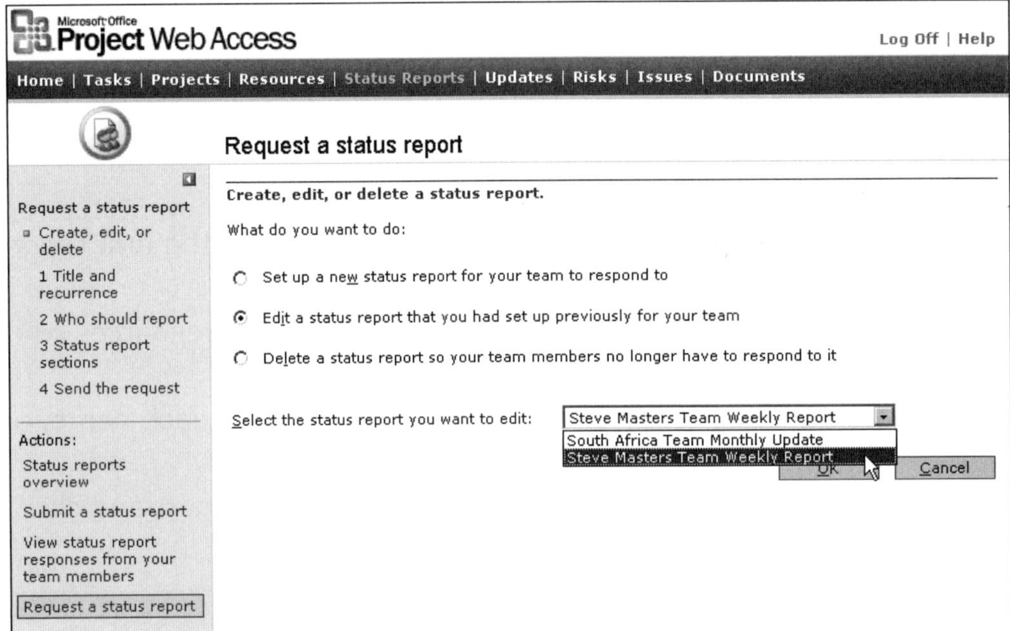

Figure 12-8: Edit a status report request

To delete a status report request, select the *Delete a status report so your team members no longer have to respond to it* option. As with the Edit a status report selection, the system displays your previously created status reports in a pick list. Select a status report for deletion and click the *OK* button. The system displays the confirmation dialog shown in Figure 12-9.

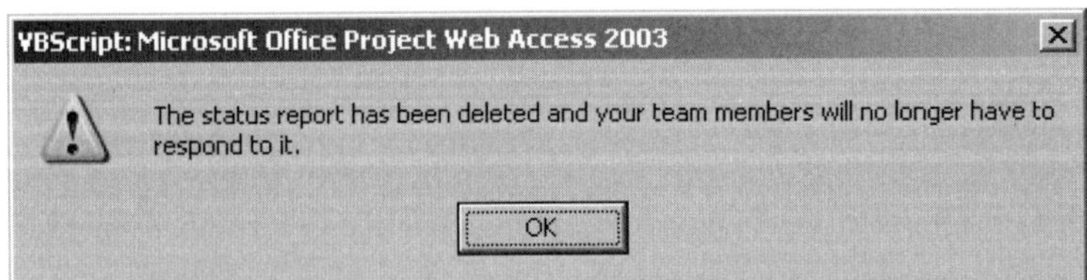

Figure 12-9: Status report deleted

Responding to a Status Report Request

When a project manager sends a status report request, the selected resources see it in the Status Reports section of their Home page, as shown in Figure 12-10. Resources may see multiple status report requests created by multiple managers.

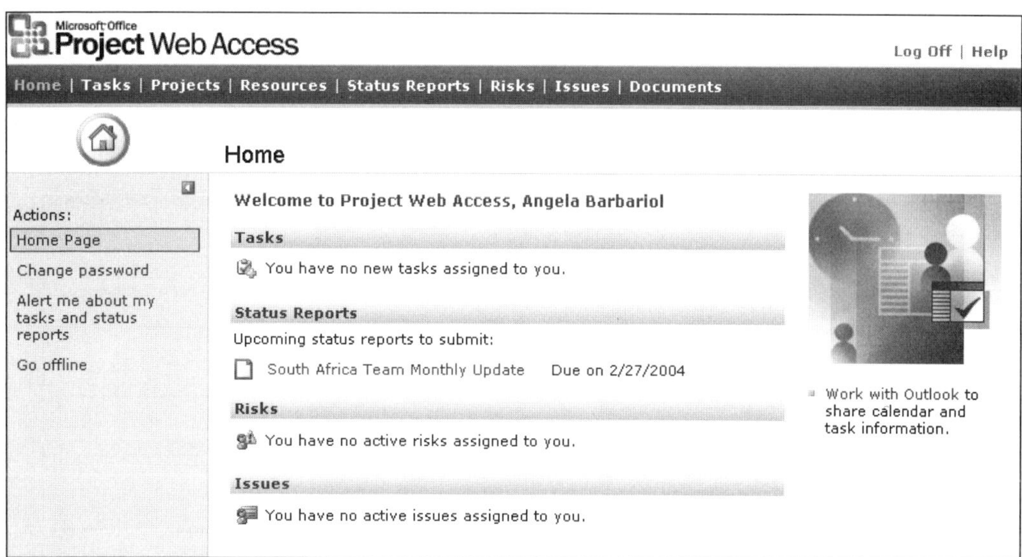

**Figure 12-10: Project Web Access Home page
Upcoming status report**

To respond to a status report request, click the *Status Reports* menu item on the Project Web Access main menu or click the *Status Reports* link in the main content area of the Home page, which allows you to navigate to the Status Reports Overview page or to select a specific status report. If you select either of the first two methods, the system displays your personalized Status Reports Overview page with a list of all upcoming status reports shown in Figure 12-11.

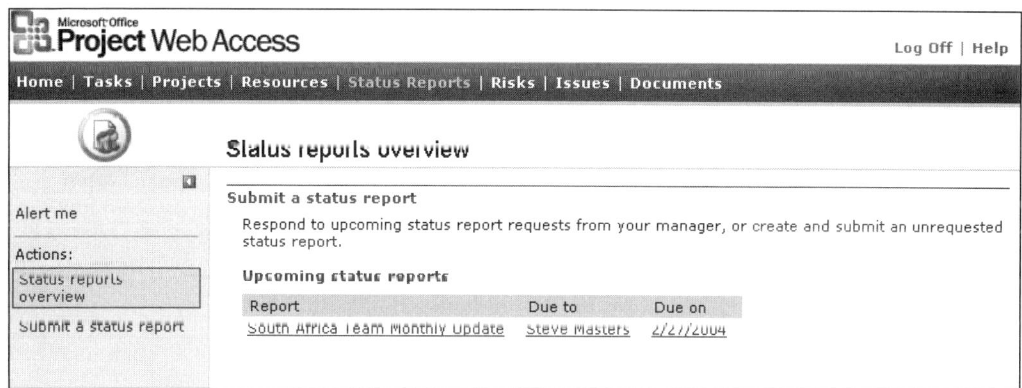

**Figure 12-11: Status Reports
Overview page**

To respond to a specific status report request from the Home page, click the named status report link.

When you click the link for a specific status report from your Home page or Status Reports Overview page the system displays the Submit a Status Report page shown in Figure 12-12.

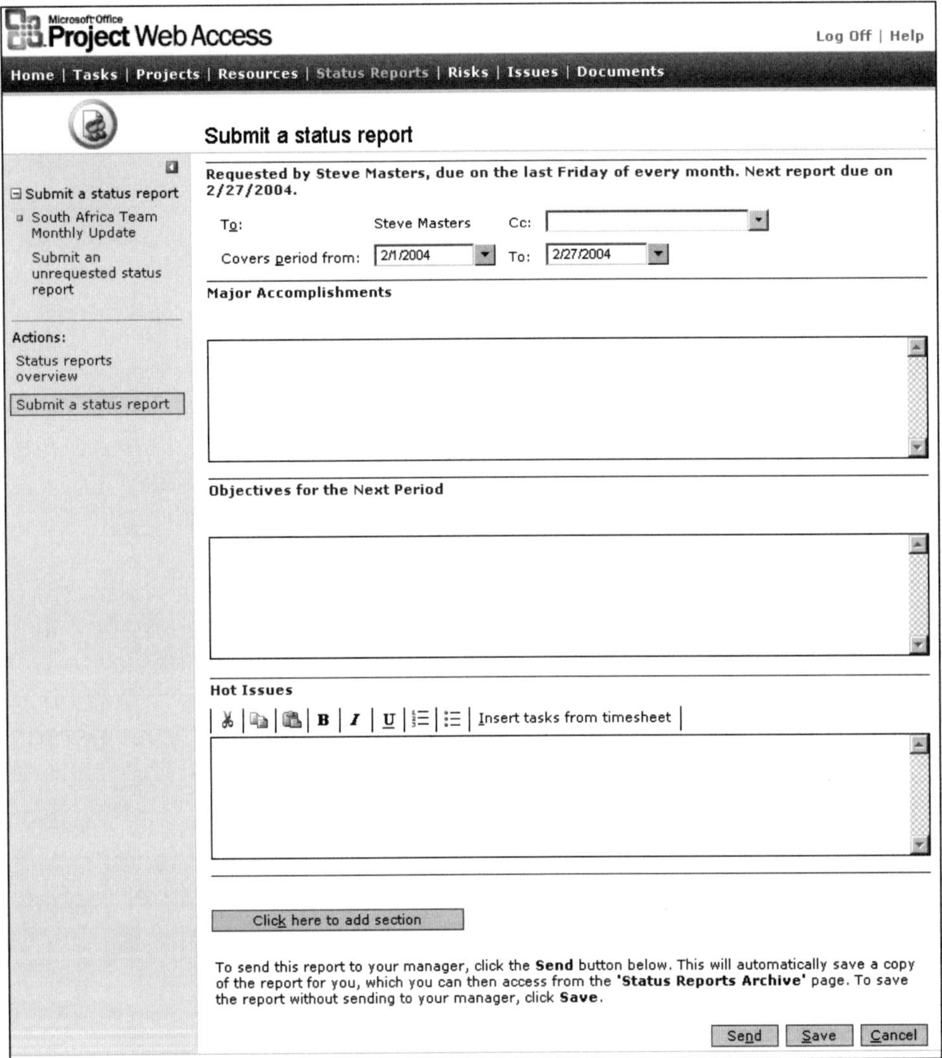

Figure 12-12: Submit a Status Report page

Text in the upper section of the Submit a Status Report page describes the status report and indicates the manager requesting it. You can select one or more names from the *Cc:* pick list to send a carbon copy of the status report. If you desire, you can select a reporting period different from the one indicated by selecting different dates in the Covers Period From or To fields.

 To select multiple values from the *Cc:* pick list, select the first name, press the Control key on your keyboard, and then select the additional names.

To enter information into your status report, click the text field in any of the topic sections. When you do, the editing toolbar displays for that section. Notice in Figure 12-13 that I selected the Major Accomplishments text field.

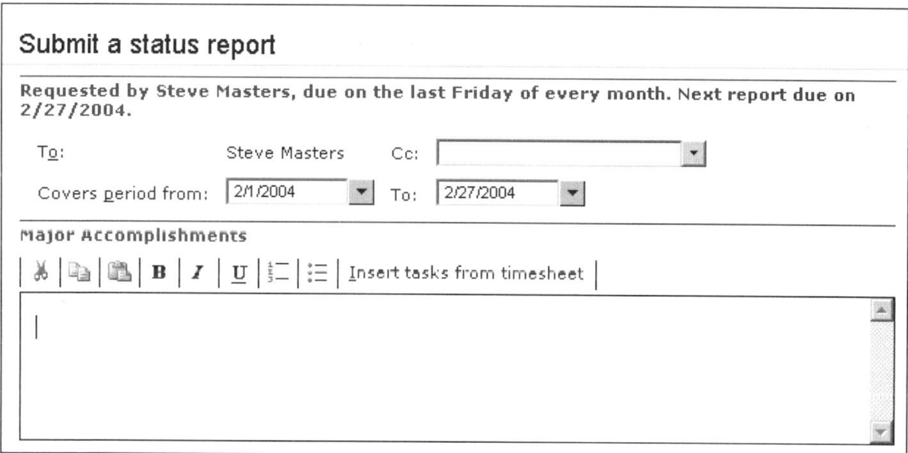

**Figure 12-13: Ready to enter text
in the Major Accomplishments field**

Use the toolbar for each text field to apply rich text formatting to your entries. Click the *Insert tasks from timesheet* button to display your timesheet in the Submit a Status report page. Select the checkbox to the left of each task you want displayed in your status report, and then click the *Insert Tasks* button at the bottom of the page. Notice in Figure 12-14 that I have selected and inserted each of the tasks in the Review Current Infrastructure section of my timesheet.

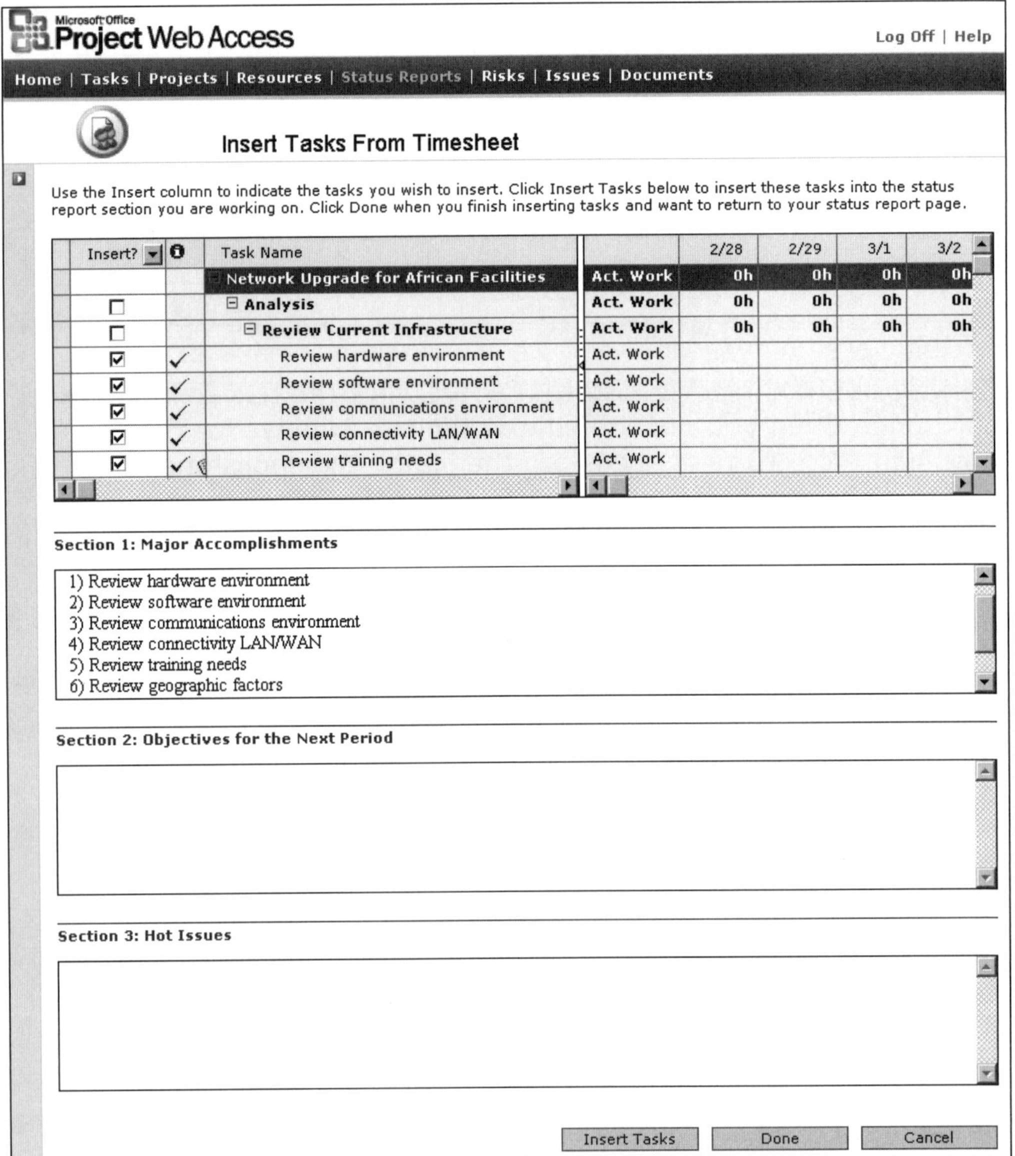

Figure 12-14: Insert Tasks from Timesheet page

Click the *Done* button to close the Insert Tasks from Timesheet page and return to the Submit a status report page.

At the bottom of the Submit a Status Report page, click the *Click here to add section* button to create an additional topic section. Name the new topic section and then click the *OK* button. A new topic section will appear at the bottom of the page. Click the *Send* button when you are ready to submit the status report or click the *Save* button to save the Status Report to send later.

Submitting an Unrequested Status Report

You can create and send an ad hoc status report without a manager requesting a status report from you. To submit an unrequested status report, first click the *Status Reports* menu to display the Status Reports Overview page. Click the *Create and submit an unrequested status report* link in the Submit a Status Report section of the page. The system displays the Submit a Status Report page, shown in Figure 12-15, allowing you to create your own custom status report.

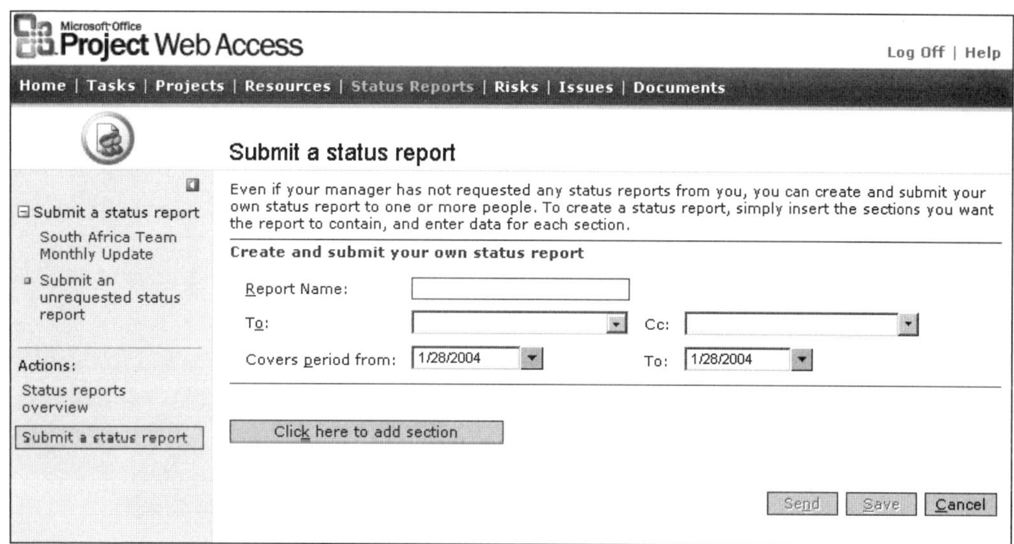

Figure 12-15: Submit a Status Report page
Create an unrequested status report

To create the unrequested status report, first give your status report a name and then select the primary status report recipient as well as anyone else you wish to receive a carbon copy from the respective pick lists. Next, select the reporting period that your status report covers. Click the *Click here to add section* button and give your new topic section a name, and then click the *OK* button. Insert additional topic sections as you wish. Enter data into your status report the same way you enter data into a requested status report using the same system-provided tool set. Click the *Send* button when you are ready to submit the status report. Otherwise, click the *Save* button to save the status report and send it later.

Viewing the Status Reports Archive

The Status Reports Archive page provides you access to view your saved status reports and any previously submitted status reports. Click the *Status Reports* menu and then click the *Status Reports Archive* link in the actions pane of the Status Reports Overview page. Note that this link does not appear on your Status reports overview page until you submit your first status report. The system displays the Status Reports Archive page shown in Figure 12-16, indicating that there are two status reports in the archive. The first is a submitted status report for the February 2004 reporting period while the second is a saved status report not yet submitted for the March 2004 reporting period. Icons appearing in the report column below the status report name indicate the status of the reports. In the figure, I'm floating my mouse over the indicators to reveal their meaning in a popup display.

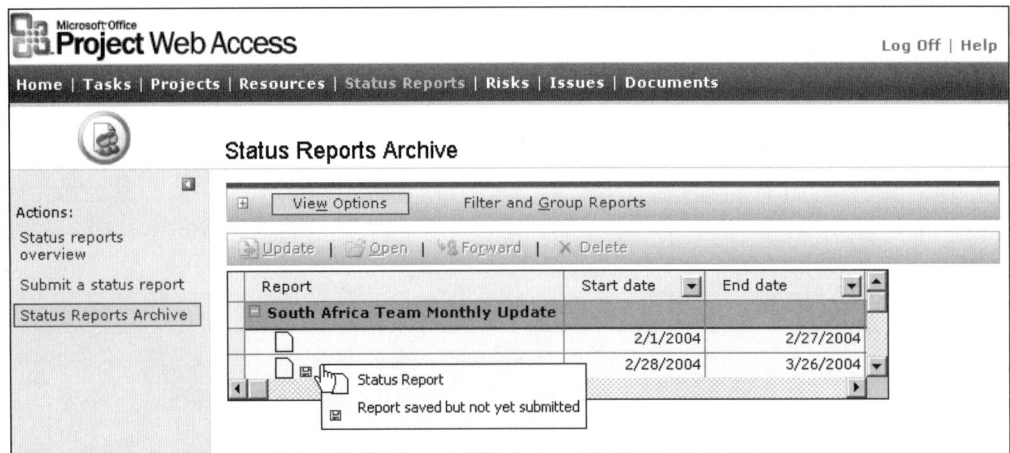

Figure 12-16: Status Reports Archive page

To view either status report, click its icon in the Report column. The system displays the status report, as shown in Figure 12-17.

Figure 12-17: Submitted status report

If you wish to edit the status report and then resubmit it, click the *Update* button on the toolbar. The system opens the status report, ready for editing. Click the *Save* button or the *Send* button when you are finished. If you simply wish to forward the status report to another manager, click the *Forward* button on the toolbar. Select one or more people from the *Forward To* pick list and then click the *Send* button.

To submit a saved status report, first open the status report in the Status Reports Archive page by clicking its icon in the Report column. Finish editing your report as necessary and then click the *Send* button.

Hands On Exercise

Exercise 12-2

Respond to a Status Report request.

1. Click the *Status Reports* menu item on the Project Web Access main menu.

2. Select the Status Report request created for this class session.

3. Fill out the Status Report using your own data.

4. Click into one of the topic sections, click the *Insert tasks from timesheet* button on the toolbar, and experiment with inserting tasks.

5. Click the *Send* button when you have completed your Status Report response.

Viewing Status Report Responses

The system alerts managers to new status report responses on their Home page in Project Web Access. Figure 12-18 shows the relevant alert section of the Home page.

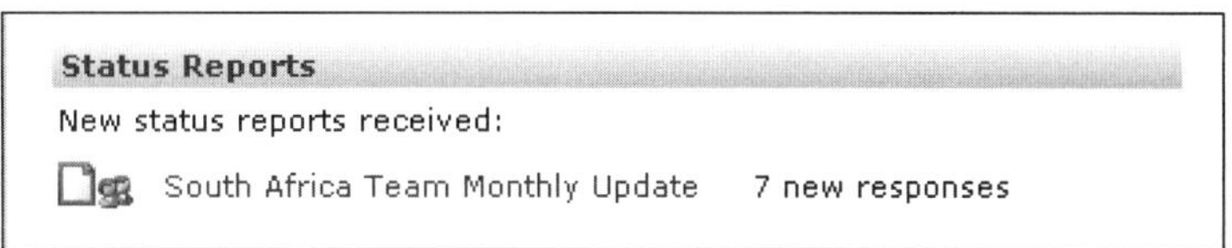

**Figure 12-18: Status Reports
section of Home page**

To view status report responses, click the link for the specific status report on the Home page. You can alternately click the *Status Reports* menu to navigate to the Status Reports Overview page and then select the specific status report. Selecting a status report opens the View Status Report Responses from Your Team Members page shown in Figure 12-19. Note the title of the report displays at the top of the page.

**Figure 12-19: View Status Report Responses
from Your Team Members page**

This page uses a data grid to show the responses from each resource for each reporting period. The data grid lists resources by name in the Resource Name column and indicates the date range for each reporting period in the column header at the top of each response column. As the months accrue, you see more columns in the display representing additional reporting periods. You can scroll through the columns for each reporting period to view previously submitted reports. The data grid indicates a response to the status report request in each cell using an icon that looks like a blank piece of paper and indicates no response from a resource with a blank cell. The top row in the data grid is the merged Team Status Report.

Notice that Figure 12-19 shows that there are responses from all of the team members except for Lynn Tsoflias. At the bottom of the page, in the Unmatched Reports section, notice that Lynn did respond to the status report request, however, she reported for a non-standard reporting period.

Before viewing the compiled team report, I want to bring Lynn's report into the team report. To do this, I click the *Match To* pick list, select a standard reporting period, and then click the *Match* button. Notice in Figure 12-20 that I selected the standard reporting period for the February 2004 status report.

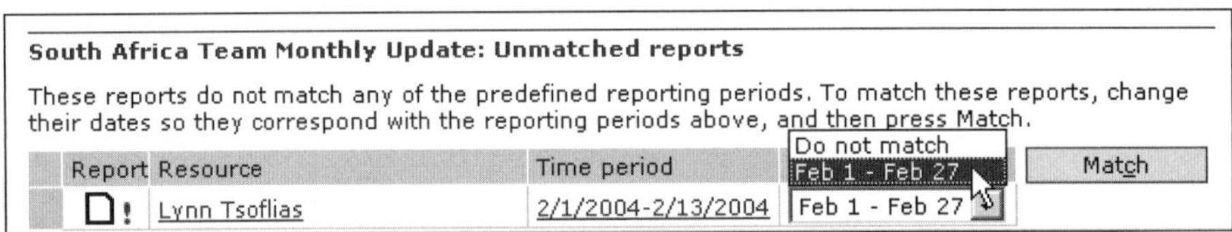

**Figure 12-20: Match an unmatched report
to a standard reporting period**

When I click the *Match* button, the system brings Lynn's report into the list with the rest of the status reports for that reporting period. In Figure 12-21 the system now displays an icon for Lynn's status report grayed out with a red exclamation mark. Floating my mouse pointer over the icon indicates that the report has not been merged with the others.

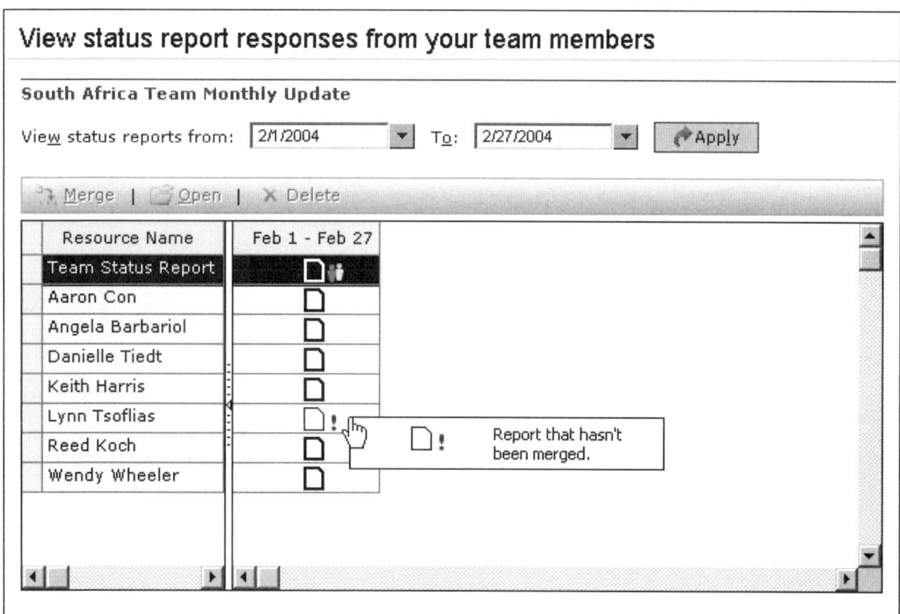

Figure 12-21: Unmerged status report response

To merge Lynn's status report with the others, I click the icon for her Feb 1 – Feb 27 reporting period. The system displays Lynn's individual status report, as shown in Figure 12-22. When I click the *Merge* button in the toolbar at the top of the status report, the system merges her report into the combined Team Status Report.

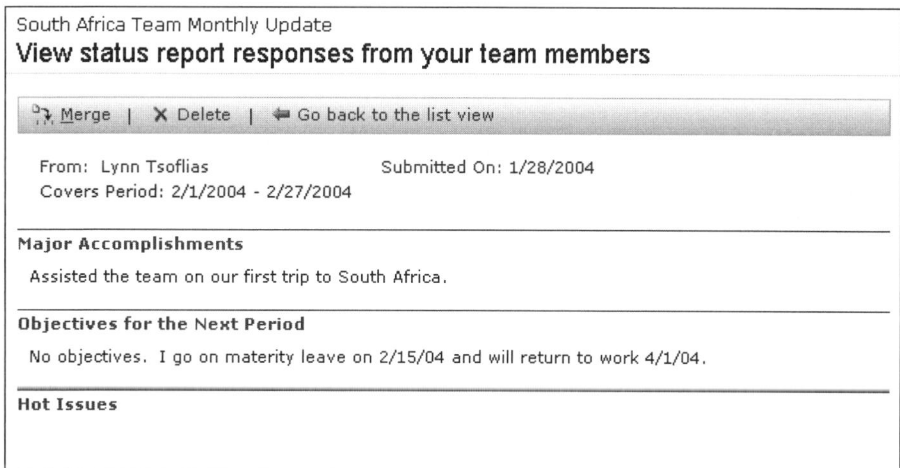

**Figure 12-22: Click the Merge button
to merge this status report**

As with opening an individual's status report, you open the merged team status report by clicking the icon in the Team Status Report row. The system merges the reports based on the options you chose when you selected the responding resources for the status report request.

Figure 12-23 displays the merged Team Status Report for the South Africa Team Monthly Update. Each section of the report display contains each team member's response listed by name and date. Scroll down the page to read responses in all sections.

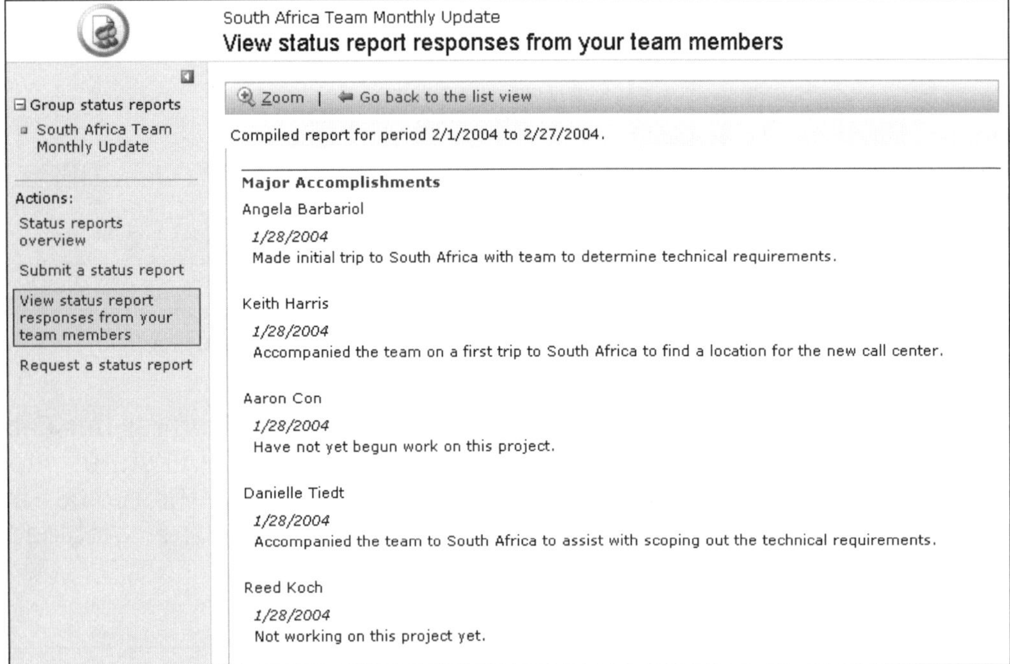

Figure 12-23: Team Status Report

Click the *Zoom* button at the top of the compiled Status Report to open the report in a new window. In the new window, select File ➢ Save As and save the Team Status Report in HTML format. You can then open this file in Word or FrontPage for editing.

MSProjectExperts recommends that you upload the saved copy of the Team Status Report to the document library for the project team. Doing so will allow you to share the status reports with the team and with other stakeholders. You can also distribute these reports by email.

How do I e-mail a combined Team Status Report to one or more recipients?

To forward a combined team Status Report via e-mail to one or more recipients, complete the following steps:

1. On the Home page of Project Web Access, select the status report you want to forward.

2. On the View Status Report Responses From Your Team Members page, click the Team Status Report icon for the desired reporting period.

3. In the combined report page, click the *Zoom* button.

4. In the new Internet Explorer window containing the zoomed Team Status Report, click File ➢ Send ➢ Page by E-mail.

5. Select the recipients of the message and send it.

Viewing Unrequested Status Reports

When a team member sends you an unrequested status report, the system does not alert you in the Status Reports section the Project Web Access Home page. In fact, the only indication you will receive is an additional link in the actions pane for the Status Reports Overview page. The *Miscellaneous reports* link shown in Figure 12-24, appears only when you receive unrequested status reports.

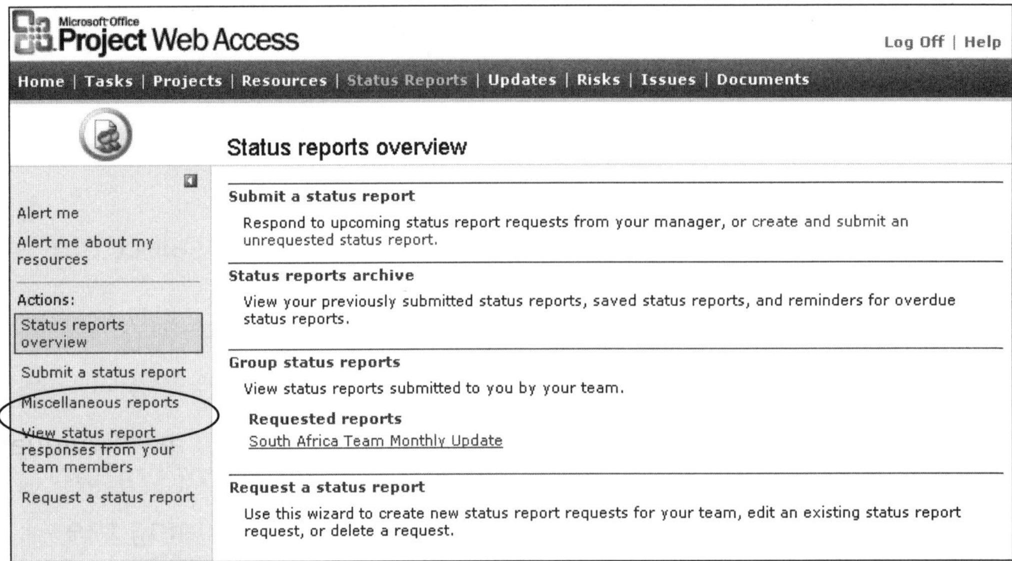

**Figure 12-24: Miscellaneous reports link
in actions pane**

To view unrequested status Reports, click the *Miscellaneous reports* link. The system opens the Miscellaneous Reports page shown in Figure 12-25. To view the report, click the links in any of the columns of the report. You cannot merge unrequested reports into any previously requested status reports.

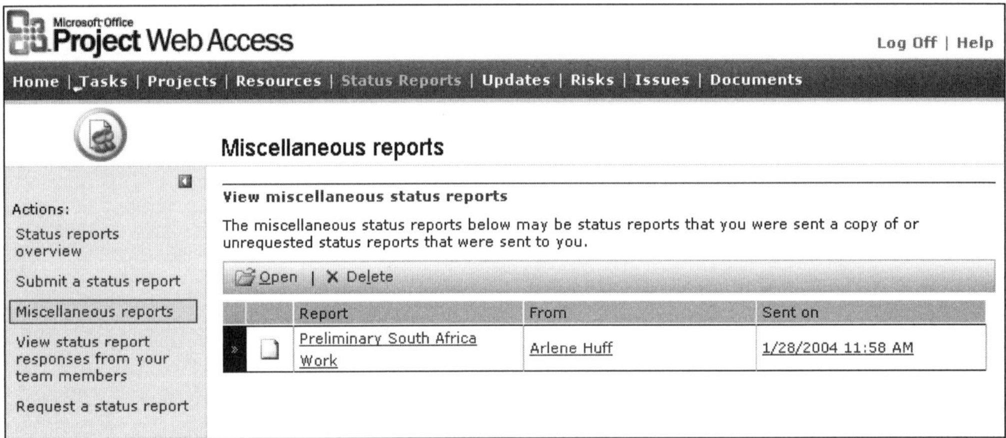

Figure 12-25: Miscellaneous Reports page

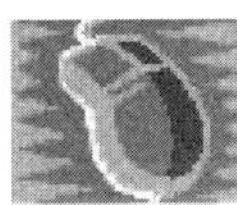 **Hands On Exercise**

Exercise 12-3

View Status Report responses.

1. Click the *Status Reports* menu item on the main menu.

2. Select a Status Report to view.

3. Click the icon for an individual resource to view an individual report.

4. Click the icon for the Team Status Report to view the merged team status report.

5. Click the *Zoom* button on the tool bar.

6. In the new Internet Explorer window, click File ➢ Save As and save the zoomed report as an html document.

Module 13

Working in the Resource Center

Learning Objectives

After completing this module, you will be able to:

- Apply Resource Center views
- View resource availability
- Edit resource details
- Open a resource for editing in Project Server 2003
- View resource assignment information
- Adjust actuals for your resources
- View a timesheet summary for your resources

Using the Resource Center

When you click the *Resources* menu item on the Project Web Access main menu, the system displays the Resource Center page shown in Figure 13-1. The Resource Center contains a data grid that displays all of the resources your security permissions allow you to see in the Enterprise Resource Pool. The default display lists all resources in the system.

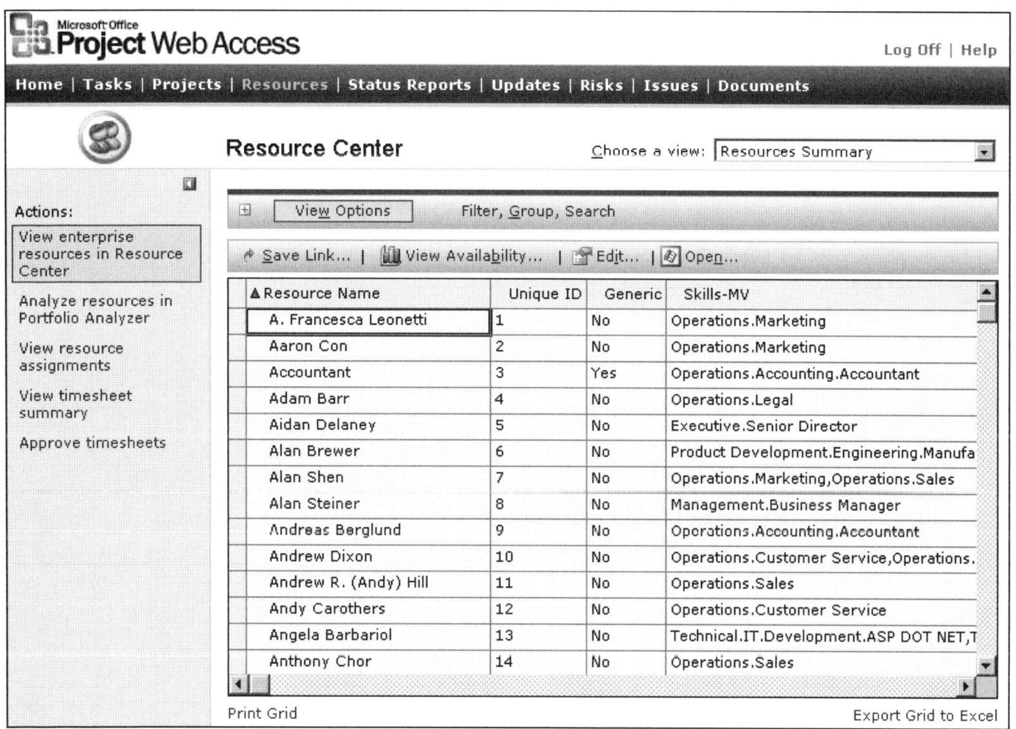

Figure 13-1: Resource Center page

The Resource Center displays only enterprise resources. It does not display local resources.

To select a view, click the *Choose a view* pick list in the upper right corner of the page. You can choose any view defined in the system for the Resource Center that you have permission to see. The Resources Summary view is the only view included in the Resource Center by default.

Your Project Server administrator controls the views available in the Resource Center. If you need a custom view in the Resource Center, contact your Project Server administrator.

Viewing Resource Availability

You can use the Resource center to analyze the availability of one or more resources by first selecting the resources in the data grid, and then clicking the *View availability* button on the toolbar. The system displays the View Resource Availability page shown in Figure 13-2.

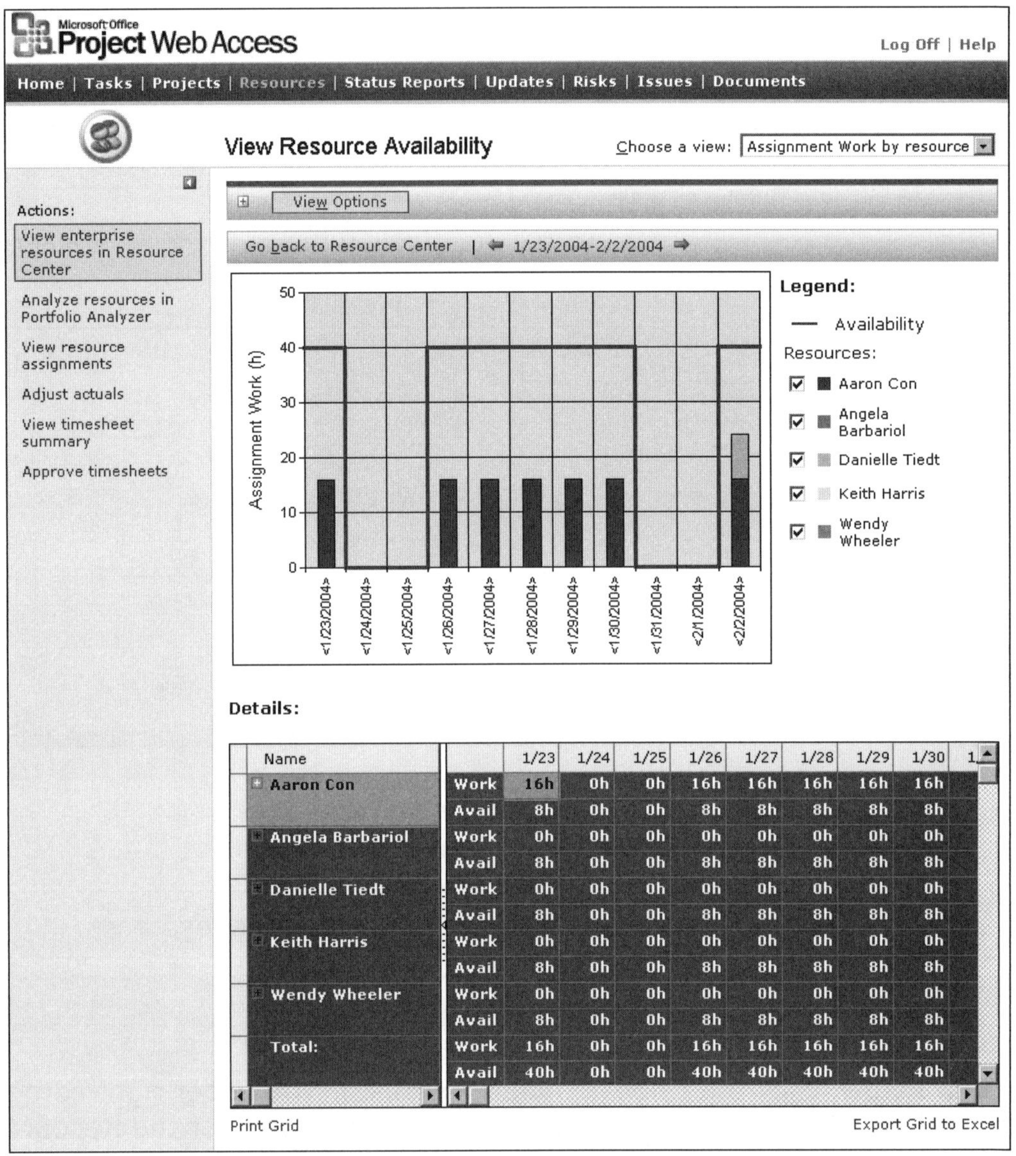

**Figure 13-2: View Resource Availability page
Assignment Work by Resource view**

The page contains two sections: a chart and a timesheet. The chart displays a graphic representation of the data displayed in the timesheet. By default, the chart shows Assignment Work and Availability for each resource across time.

The *Choose a view* pick list displayed in the View Resource Availability page allows you to select one of four default views:

- Assignment Work by Resource

- Assignment Work by Project

- Remaining Availability

- Work

The Assignment Work by Resource view displays a stacked bar chart for each time period, with each bar portion representing the assignment work of an individual resource. This view also displays a line chart representing the total Availability for all of the selected resources. Shown previously, Figure 13-2 displays the Assignment Work by Resource view.

Figure 13-3 shows the Assignment Work by Project view. This view displays a stacked bar chart for each time period, with each bar portion representing the total assignment work for the selected resources in an individual project. The line chart in the view represents the total Availability for all of the selected resources.

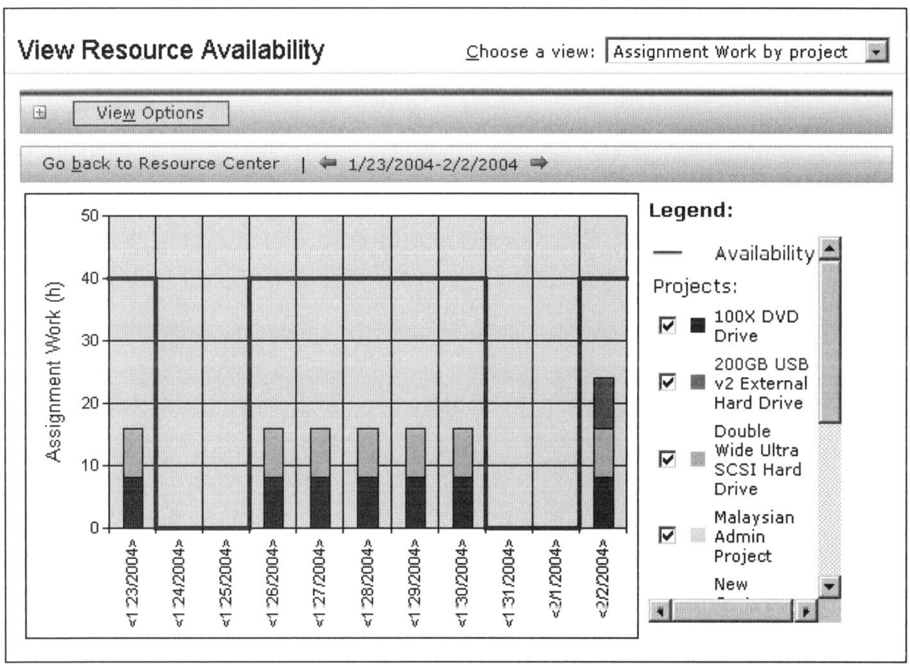

**Figure 13-3: View Resource Availability page
Assignment Work by Project view**

Figure 13-4 shows the Remaining Availability view that displays a line chart for each selected resource, with each line showing the remaining availability for each resource during each time period.

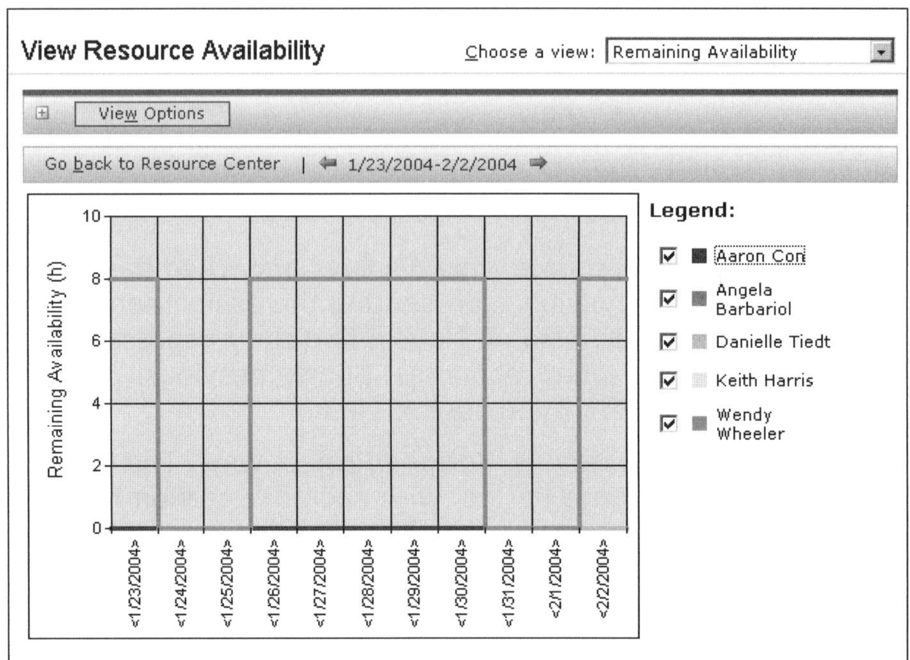

Figure 13-4: View Resource Availability page
Remaining Availability view

 It can be difficult to see the remaining availability for a specific resource when you select multiple resources. To make it easier you can deselect one or more resources using the checkboxes in the Legend section until you see the line chart for your specific resource.

 As referenced at the end of Module 03, you can use the Remaining Availability view to avoid creating overallocations at the time you make resource assignments.

Figure 13-5 shows the Work view. This view displays a line chart for each resource representing the total amount of work assigned to the resource during each time period.

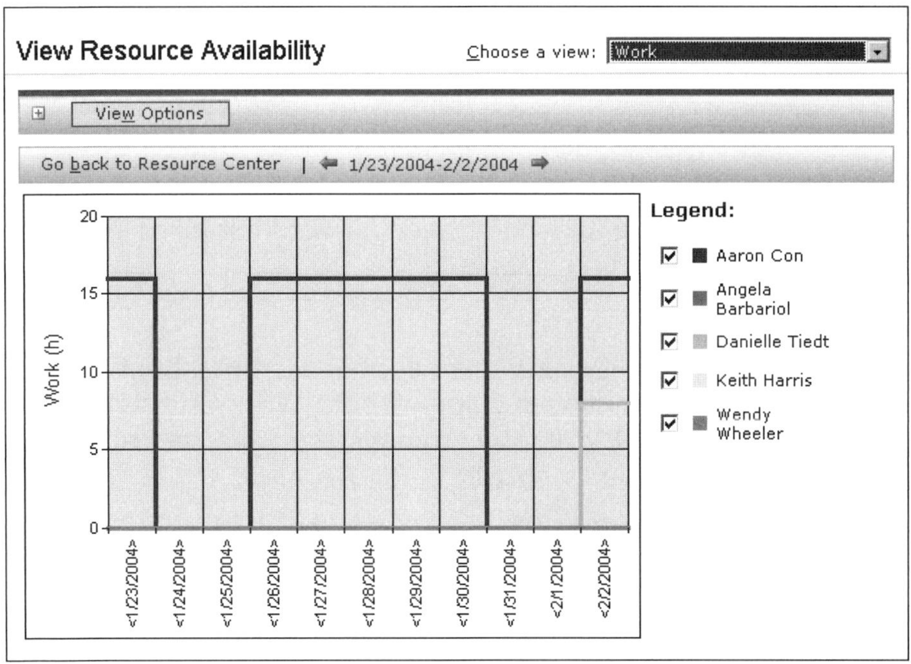

**Figure 13-5: View Resource Availability page
Work view**

While you work in the View Resource Availability page, you can change the date range of the view using the date selector tool on the toolbar. Click the *View Options* tab shown in Figure 13-6 to broaden or narrow the date window thereby changing the scale of thc graph. Select the *Include Proposed Bookings* option to include proposed bookings for the selected resources in the graph and timesheet.

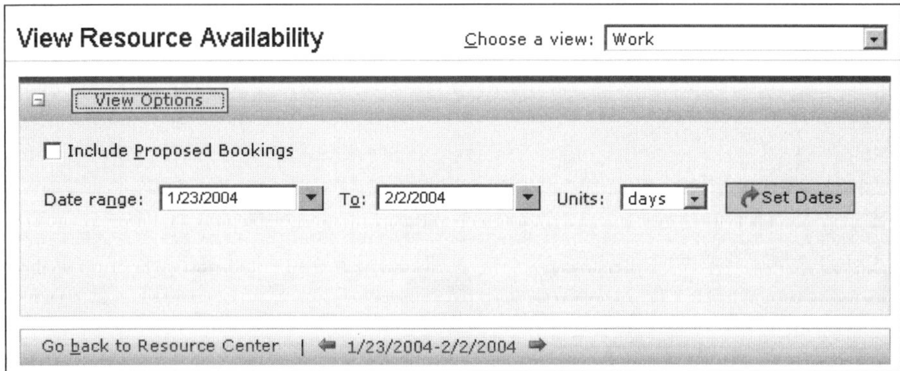

Figure 13-6: View Options tab

> **Warning:** You may occasionally see a message in red text at the bottom of the chart stating, "Availability data has not been published for one or more resources in the selected date range." This message indicates that your Project Server administrator must update the resource availability tables before you can see information for some or all of the dates in the range that you selected.

The View Resource Availability page also contains a timesheet grid at the bottom of the page. The timesheet displays both Work and Availability values for each selected resource. By default, the system collapses each resource's task assignments, as previously shown in Figure 13-2.

To expand the task assignments for each resource, click the expand symbol (+) to the left of the resource's name. The system displays each project in which the resource has assignments along with a line showing the resource's Availability. Expand one or more projects to see specific resource assignments. Notice in Figure 13-7 that I expanded the New Server Farm for Africa Region project for Danielle Tiedt.

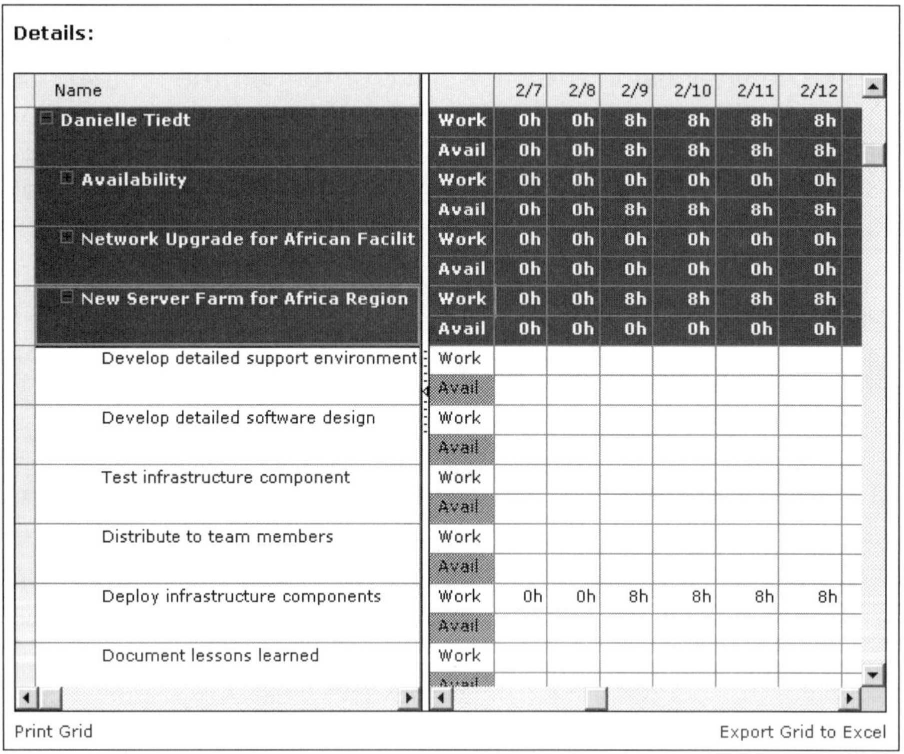

Details:

Name		2/7	2/8	2/9	2/10	2/11	2/12
⊟ **Danielle Tiedt**	Work	0h	0h	8h	8h	8h	8h
	Avail	0h	0h	8h	8h	8h	8h
⊟ **Availability**	Work	0h	0h	0h	0h	0h	0h
	Avail	0h	0h	8h	8h	8h	8h
⊟ **Network Upgrade for African Facilit**	Work	0h	0h	0h	0h	0h	0h
	Avail	0h	0h	0h	0h	0h	0h
⊟ **New Server Farm for Africa Region**	Work	0h	0h	8h	8h	8h	8h
	Avail	0h	0h	0h	0h	0h	0h
Develop detailed support environment	Work						
	Avail						
Develop detailed software design	Work						
	Avail						
Test infrastructure component	Work						
	Avail						
Distribute to team members	Work						
	Avail						
Deploy infrastructure components	Work	0h	0h	8h	8h	8h	8h
	Avail						
Document lessons learned	Work						
	Avail						

Print Grid   Export Grid to Excel

**Figure 13-7: Timesheet grid with
resource assignments expanded**

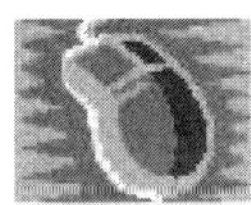

Hands On Exercise

Exercise 13-1

Explore the Resource Center and then determine current work levels and availability for a resource.

1. Click the *Resources* menu item on the Project Web Access main menu.

2. Select one or more resources by clicking in the grid. Press and hold the Control key to select multiple resources.

3. Click the *View Availability* button on the toolbar.

4. Click the *Choose a view* pick list and select different availability views.

5. Select and deselect projects or resources in the various detailed displays.

6. Select each of the available views and examine the information presented about each resource or project.

Editing Resource Details

If you have the proper Project Server security permissions, you can edit the custom enterprise details for a resource by selecting a single resource and then clicking the *Edit* button on the Resource Center toolbar. The system displays the Resource Details page for the selected resource as shown in Figure 13-8.

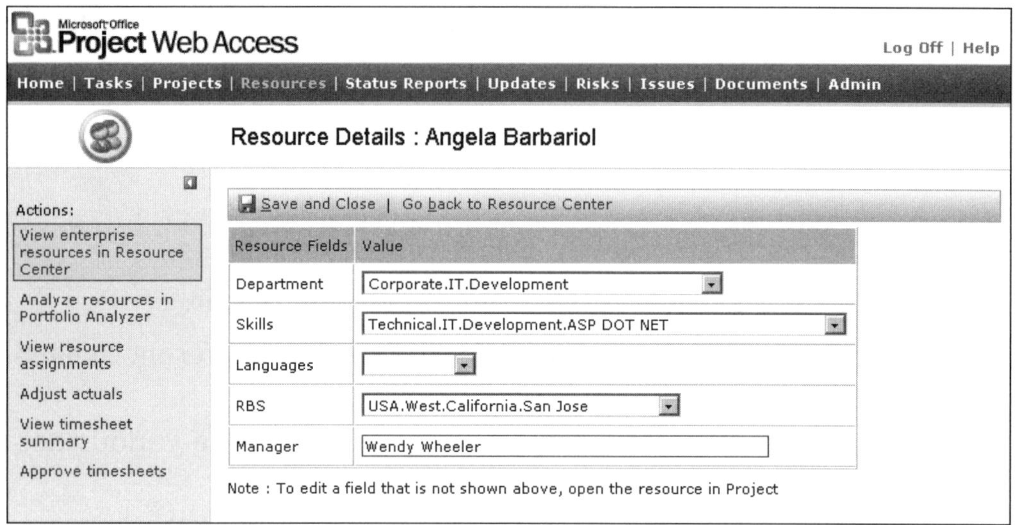

**Figure 13-8: Resource Details page
for a selected resource**

The Resource Details page displays all your organization's custom enterprise Resource outline codes and only those custom enterprise Resource fields that **do not** contain a formula or a value list. Edit your fields and/or outline codes for a resource, and then click the *Save and Close* button to commit the changes. Click the *Go back to Resource Center* button to discard the changes.

To edit any Resource fields not displayed on the Resource Details page, you must check out the resource for editing in the Enterprise Resource Pool using Project Professional 2003.

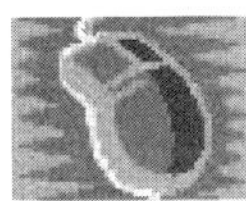

Hands On Exercise

Exercise 13-2

Edit resource details for a selected resource.

1. Click the *Resources* menu item on the Project Web Access main menu.

2. Select a resource in the data grid.

3. Click the *Edit* button on the toolbar.

4. Note which enterprise Resource outline codes and fields can be edited in this area.

Opening a Resource for Editing

If you have the proper Project Server security permissions, you can open a resource for editing in Project Server 2003 by selecting a single resource and clicking the *Open* button on the toolbar. The system launches Project Professional 2003 and checks out the single resource for editing in the Enterprise Resource Pool file as shown in Figure 13-9. Edit the resource as desired, then save and close the checked-out resource.

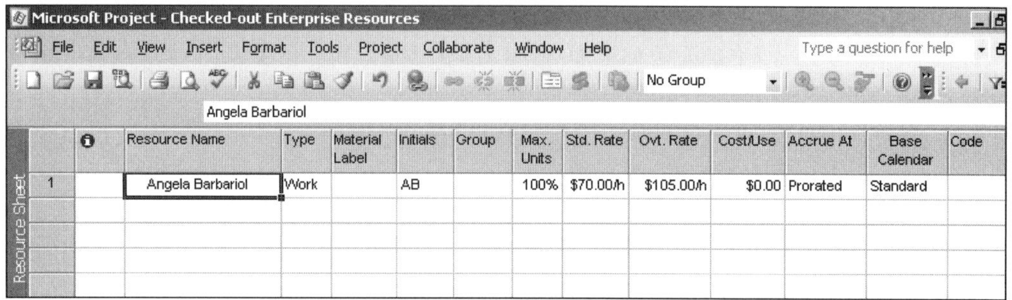

**Figure 13-9: Single resource
checked out for editing**

When a resource is open for editing in Project Professional 2003, you can change both standard and custom information about the resource. You can change the information in standard fields such as Group and Standard Rate and can change the information in enterprise custom fields and outline codes established for your organization.

Viewing Resource Assignments

Select the *View resource assignments* link in the actions pane of the Resource Center to display the View Resource Assignments page shown in Figure 13-10. The View Resource Assignments page allows you to select up to 100 resources for viewing. Select your desired resources from the Available resources list on the left and copy them to the Resources to display list on the right by clicking the *Add* button. Click the *Add All* button to add all of the resources to the Resources to display list.

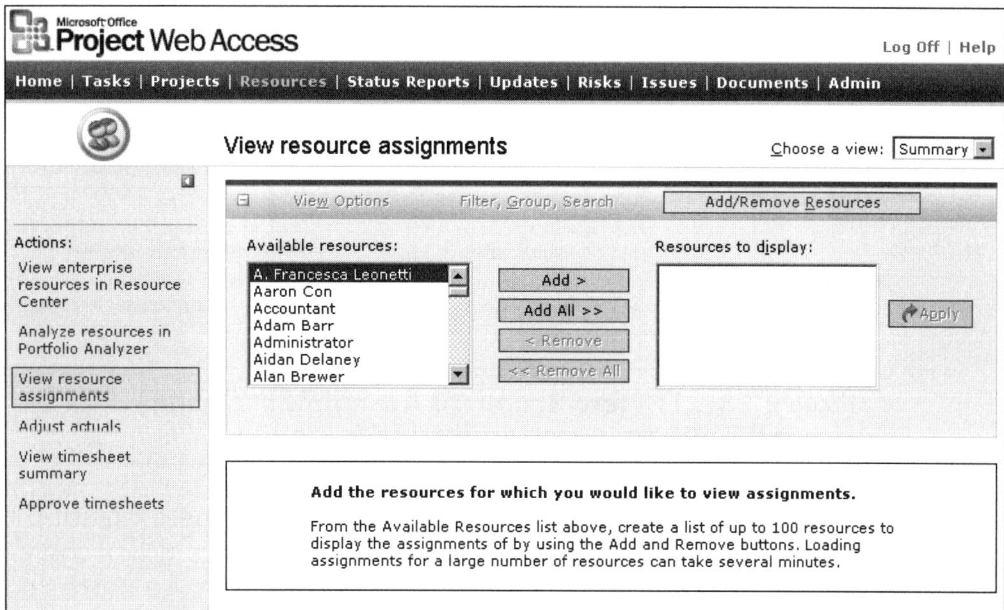

Figure 13-10: View Resource Assignments page

After selecting your list of resources to display, click the *Apply* button. The View Resource Assignments display changes as shown in Figure 13-11.

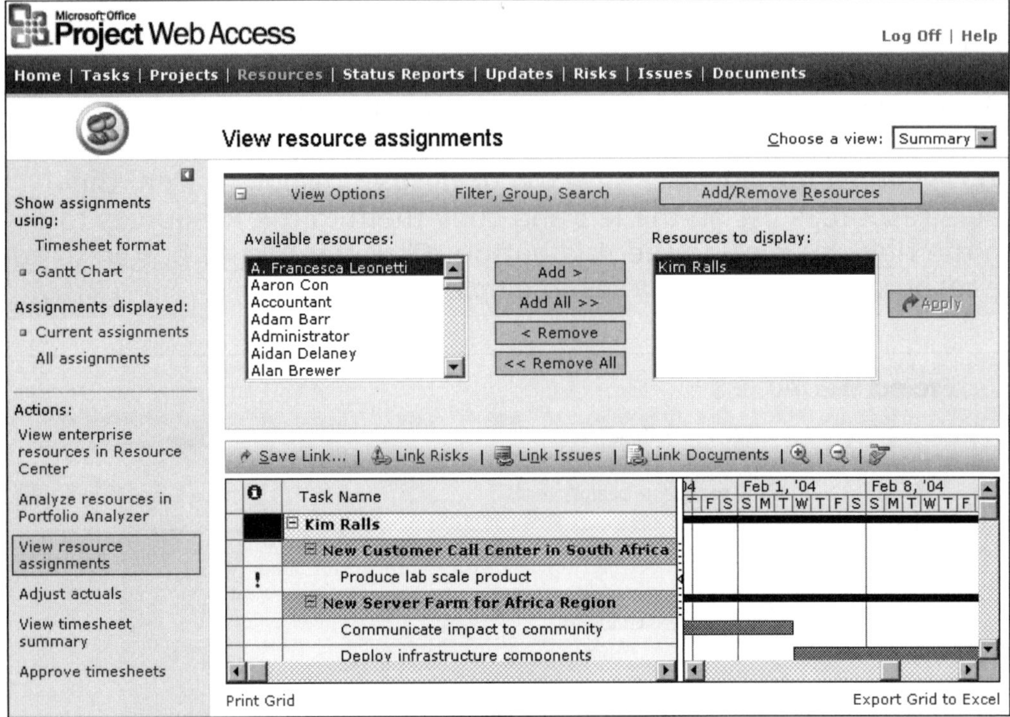

**Figure 13-11: View Resource Assignments page
with one resource selected for viewing**

Notice in Figure 13-11 that the system activates all three customization tabs at the top of the page upon displaying resource assignments. Click the *Add/Remove Resources* tab to collapse the tab options to make more room for displaying assignments.

The links in the actions pane on the left side of the page allow you to apply a Timesheet or Gantt Chart format to the assignments, and to show either Current assignments or All assignments. By default, the system displays Current assignments and applies the Gantt Chart format. Click the Timesheet format to view each resource's timesheet. Click the *All assignments* link if you want to see both completed and future assignments, as well as current assignments.

The View Resource Assignments page includes a toolbar with buttons to link Issues, Risks, or Documents to an assignment. You can link risks, issues, and documents to tasks in exactly the same way as in the View My Tasks page or the Updates page. The system displays additional toolbar buttons that are appropriate to either the Gantt Chart or Timesheet format.

The *View Options* tab allows you to select the *Show scheduled work* option to show the planned work for each task assignment in a separate row for each task. The default grouping in the *Filter, Group, Search* tab is by Resource and then by Project. Figure 13-12 shows the View Resource Assignments page with *Timesheet format*, *All assignments*, and *Show scheduled work* options selected.

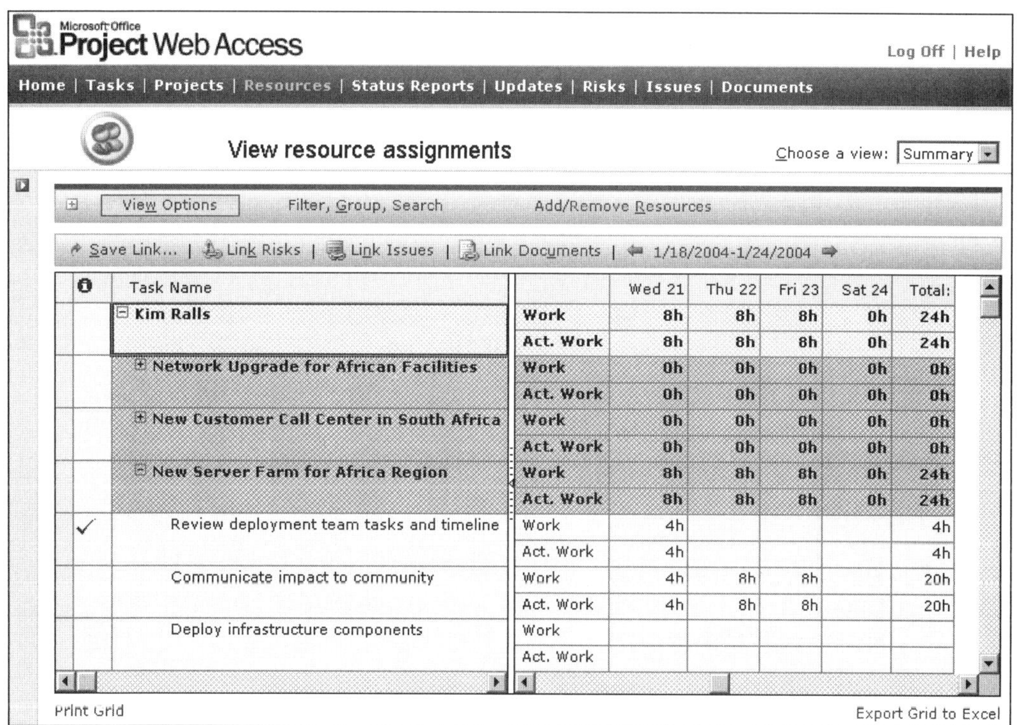

**Figure 13-12: View Resource Assignments page
configured for ease of use**

By default, the Summary view is the only available selection on the *Choose a view* pick list unless your Project Server administrator has created additional views for your organization. Notice that the same task indicators that display in the View My Tasks page and Updates page also appear in this view. This is not surprising since the View Resource Assignments page is a window into user assignments and timesheet information.

**How do I determine which team members
have not submitted their timesheets
for the current reporting period?**

If your organization does not use Managed Time Periods
with Project Server 2003, you can use the View Resource
Assignments page to determine timesheet compliance. The
Submitted On and Status columns contain the relevant
information about timesheet compliance, and the
timesheet grid contains the supporting information.
Following is how to interpret the information shown in
these columns:

- If a team member submitted an update and the
  project manager updated the changes into the
  Microsoft Project plan, the date they submitted the
  update appears in the Submitted on column and "No
  change since last update" appears in the Status
  column.

- If a team member submitted an update but the
  project manager has not yet approved the update,
  the date they submitted the update appears in the
  Submitted on column and "Changes submitted"
  appears in the Status column.

- If a team member saves timesheet changes but
  doesn't submit them to the project manager, "NA"
  appears in the Submitted on column and "Changes
  not yet submitted" appears in the Status column.

- If a team member fails to enter any progress during
  the current reporting period, the timesheet grid
  shows Work scheduled during that time period but
  does not show any Actual Work for a task.

Saving a Link to a Resource Assignment View

Click the *Save Link* button on the toolbar to save a link that can recall your view with the custom grouping and filtering you applied in the *Filter, Group, Search* tab. Enter a name for your new link in the Save Link dialog shown in Figure 13-13. When you subsequently click the link, the system displays the view with your custom formatting changes.

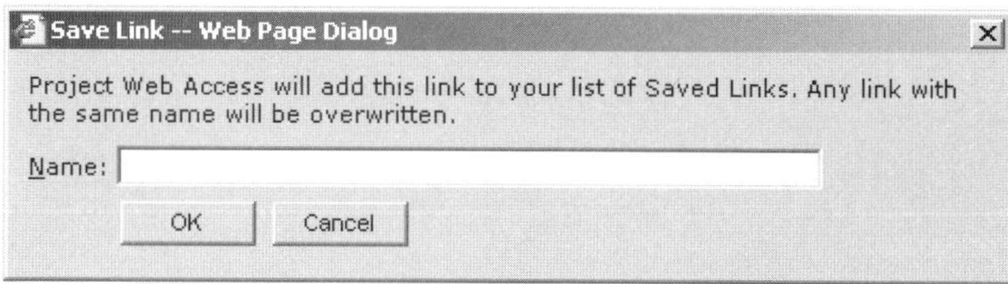

Figure 13-13: Save Link dialog

When you save a link in any page, the system displays two new menu items in the actions pane adding a Saved Links section near the top of the actions pane and an *Organize your saved links* link at the bottom as shown in Figure 13-14.

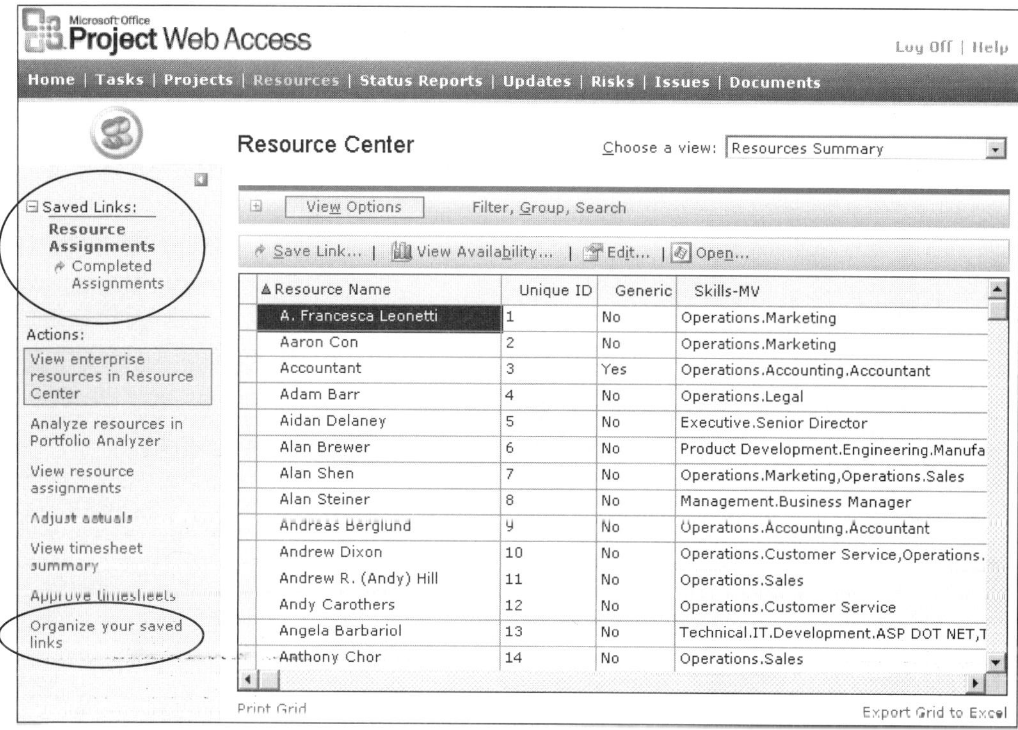

Figure 13-14: Saved links options

Click the *Organize your saved links* link in the actions pane to display the Organize Your Saved Links page shown in Figure 13-15. You can delete or rename your links from this page. Note you cannot reverse a link deletion.

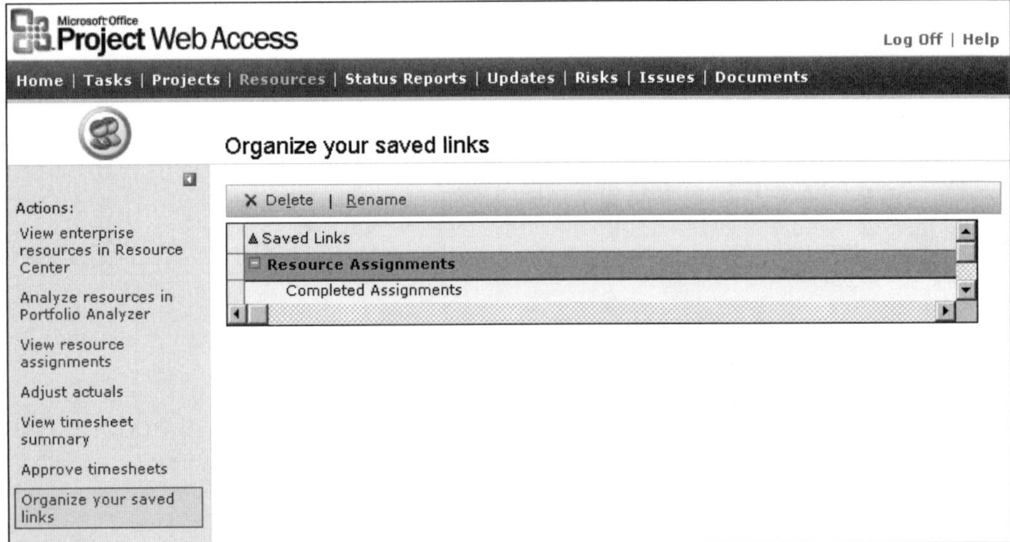

Figure 13-15: Organize Your Saved Links page

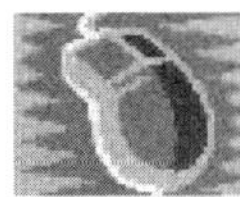

Hands On Exercise

Exercise 13-3

View resource assignments.

1. Click the *Resources* menu item on the Project Web Access main menu.

2. Select the *View resource assignments* link in the actions pane.

3. Select one or more resources from the Available resources list, then click the *Add* button and the *Apply* button.

4. Click the *Add/Remove resources* tab to collapse the tab options.

5. Click the *Timesheet format* link and the *All assignments* link in the actions pane.

6. Examine the resource assignments for your resources.

Adjusting Actuals for Resources

Project Server 2003 allows resource managers and other authorized individuals to enter and adjust actual progress for their resources. This is useful to your organization if you use Project Server's timesheet approval process, as it allows you to correct errors on timesheets prior to approving them.

To adjust actuals for a resource, click the *Adjust actuals* link in the actions pane in the Resource Center. The system displays the Adjust Actuals page shown in Figure 13-16. Notice that the layout of this display is very similar to the View Resource Assignments page.

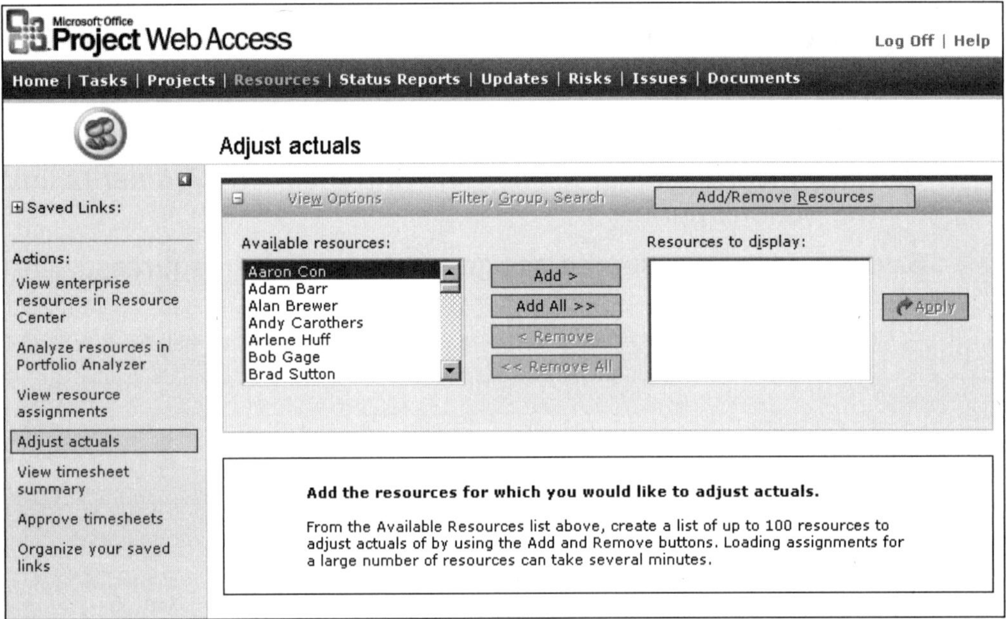

Figure 13-16: Adjust Actuals page

As with the View Resource Assignments page, the Adjust Actuals page allows you to pre-select up to 100 resources. Select resources from the Available resources list on the left and copy them to the Resources to display list on the right by clicking the *Add* button. Click the *Add All* button to add all of the resources to the Resources to display list. Click the *Apply* button to display your resources and then click the *Add/Remove Resources* tab to collapse the options on the tab to increase the page area available to display data as shown in Figure 13-17.

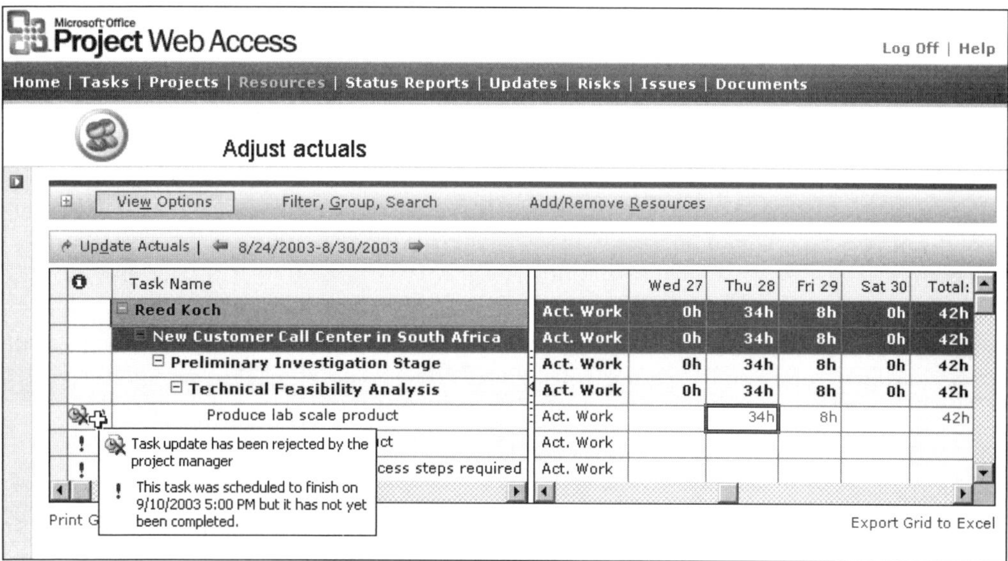

**Figure 13-17: Adjust Actuals page
"fat finger" error on Thursday 28**

Notice in Figure 13-17 that the project manager rejected Reed Koch's task update on the task Produce lab scale product. You can see the reason for the rejection in the timesheet portion of the page, in which the resource has accidentally "fat fingered" 34 hours of Actual Work on August 28, when he intended to type 4 hours. This is the type of situation where it is appropriate for a manager to intervene and adjust a resource timesheet.

To adjust actuals for any resource select the task assignment and the date in the timesheet, and edit the numbers entered by the resource. When finished, click the *Update Actuals* button on the toolbar. The system displays the confirmation dialog shown in Figure 13-18. Click the *OK* button to complete the adjusting actuals process.

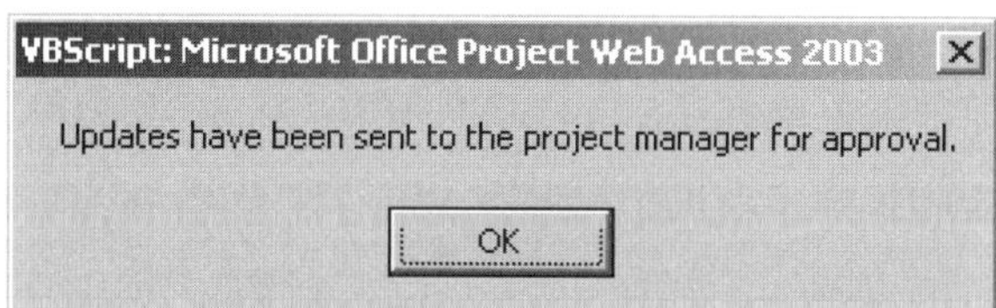

**Figure 13-18: Updated actuals
sent to project manager**

Viewing the Timesheet Summary

Project Server 2003 allows individuals with the proper authority, such as resource managers, to view resource timesheets. This may be useful to your organization, as it allows managers to oversee resource entry of actual work in the system. To view a timesheet summary for your resources, click the *View timesheet summary* link in the actions pane in the Resource Center. The system displays the View Timesheet Summary page shown in Figure 13-19.

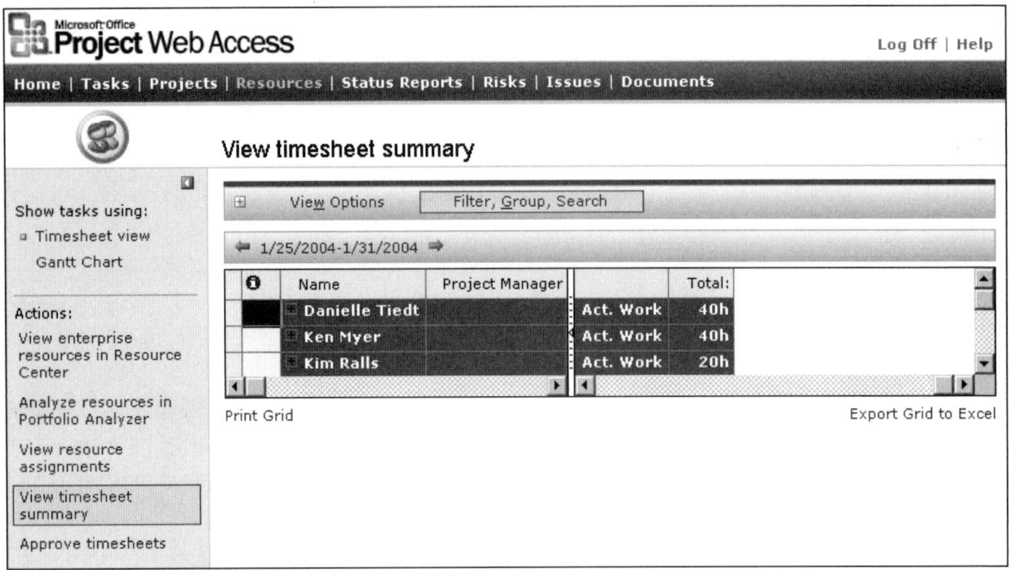

Figure 13-19: View Timesheet Summary page

The View Timesheet Summary page is for viewing timesheet information only. You must perform actions such as approving timesheets or adjusting actuals on other pages. To make best use of the View Timesheet Summary page set up your page as follows:

1. Collapse the actions pane to see more of the timesheet.

2. Expand the name of each resource whose timesheet you wish to see.

3. Collapse any project assignments you do not wish to see.

4. Position the split bar as you desire between the resource list and the timesheet.

5. Use the date selector tool to select the desired date range for the timesheet summary.

6. Using the scroll bar in the timesheet portion of the grid, scroll to the left until you see the days in the desired time period.

7. Apply a filter from the *Filter, Group, Search* tab.

The *Filter* pick list on the *Filter, Group, Search* tab contains five preformatted filters, such as the All Unsubmitted Timesheets filter, that allow you to view only the timesheets meeting the criteria you choose. Notice in Figure 13-20 that I am selecting the All Approved Timesheets filter.

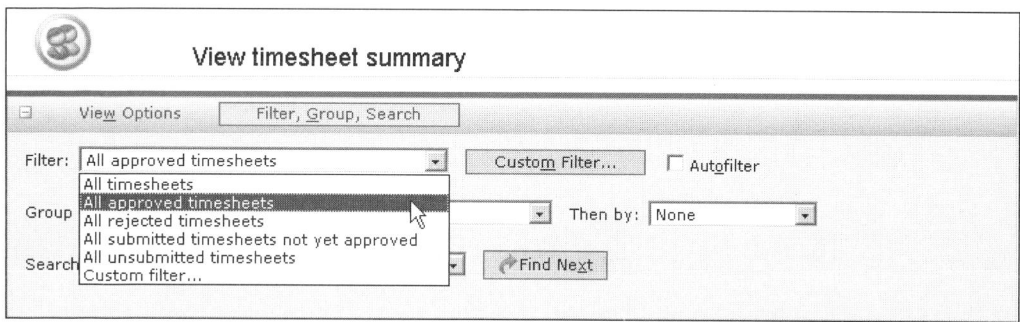

Figure 13-20: Expanded Filter, Group, Search tab

Figure 13-21 shows the View Timesheet Summary page after configuring it to optimize viewing. Notice that I expanded the timesheets for two resources, Danielle Tiedt and Kim Ralls, and I collapsed the timesheet for Ken Myer.

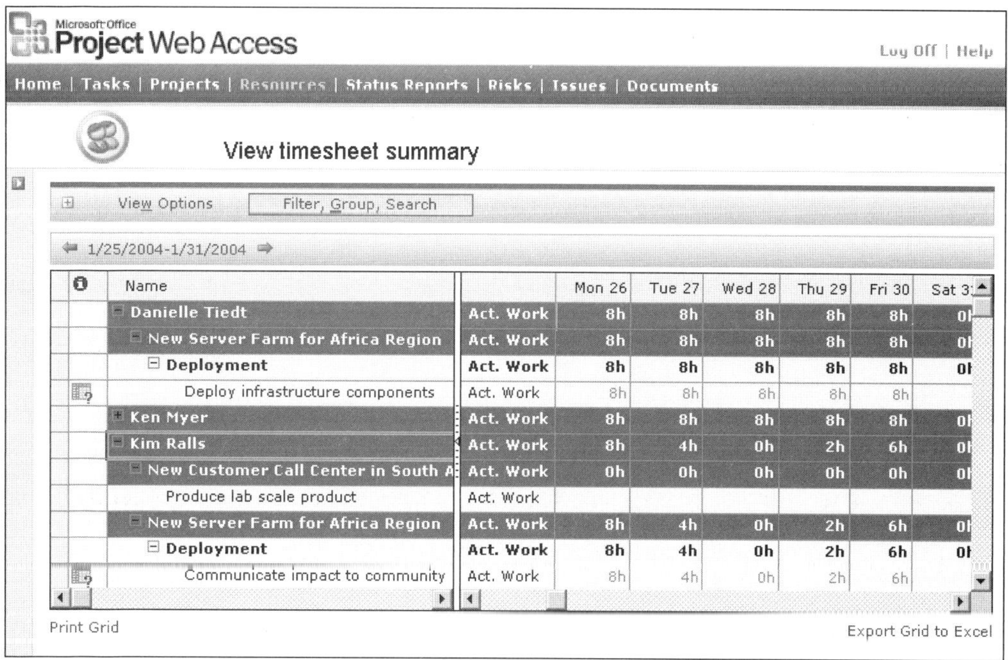

**Figure 13-21: View Timesheet Summary page
configured for best viewing**

Working in the Project Center

Learning Objectives

After completing this module, you will be able to:

- Work in the Project Center
- Access Risks, Issues, and Documents from the Project Center
- Work with Project Center views
- Build a project team in the Project Center
- Edit project details and open a project in the Project Center
- Check in a project
- Work with detailed Project views
- Organize and manage saved links
- Create and manage to-do lists

Working in the Project Center

The Project Center is the distribution hub for project information and project analysis in Project Web Access. The Project Center page displays portfolio-level views across all projects in your organization's portfolio. In addition, you can select an individual project from any Project Center view to open a detailed project view allowing you to drill down into the project detail. You can also access core Project Server analysis features from the Project Center using the Portfolio Analyzer and the Portfolio Modeler. Figure 14-1 shows the Project Center page with Steve Master's portfolio of projects displayed.

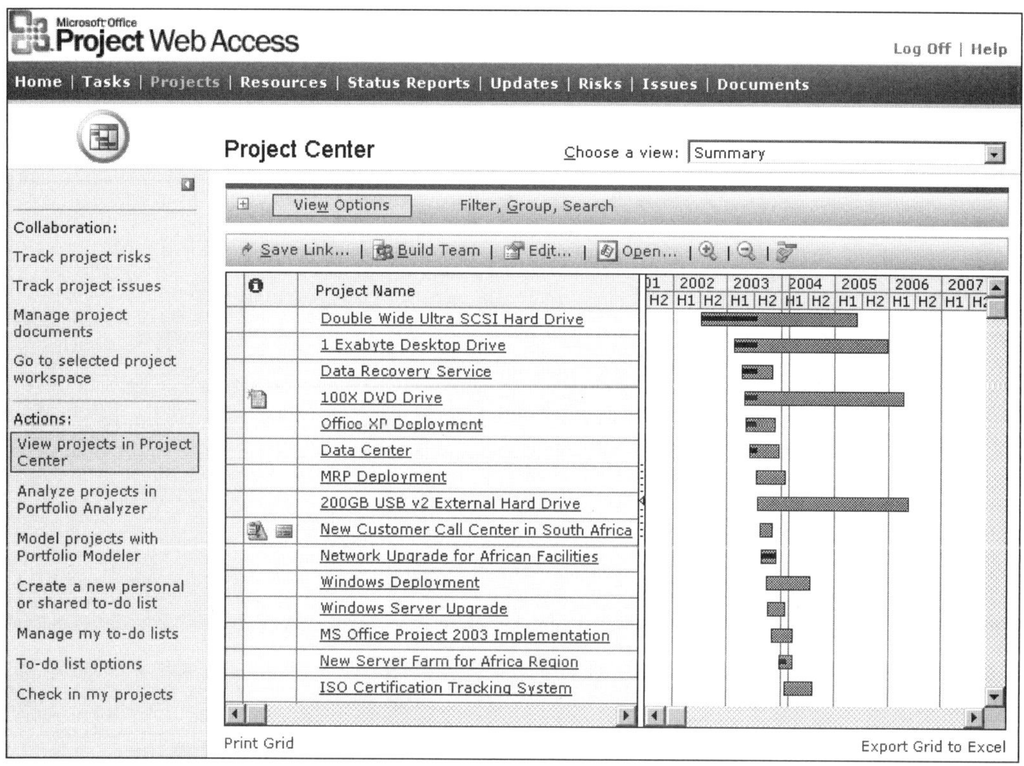

Figure 14-1: Project Center page

The Project Center page displays a data grid with a project list on the left and a Gantt Chart on the right. The project list displays a single line of information about each project with multiple columns of information about each project, depending on the current view selected from the *Choose a view* pick list.

The Gantt Chart displays one or two Gantt bars representing the life span of the project. When the system displays two Gantt bars, one represents the baseline schedule while the other represents the current schedule of the project.

Accessing Risks, Issues, and Documents from the Project Center

You can use the Project Center page to access Risks, Issues, or Documents for any of the projects in the portfolio. Notice in Figure 14-1 that the Indicators column reveals that 100X DVD Drive project has Documents associated with it, while the New Customer Call Center in South Africa project has Risks and Issues associated with it. You can quickly see the meaning of the indicators by floating your mouse over the Indicators column for any project, as shown in Figure 14-2.

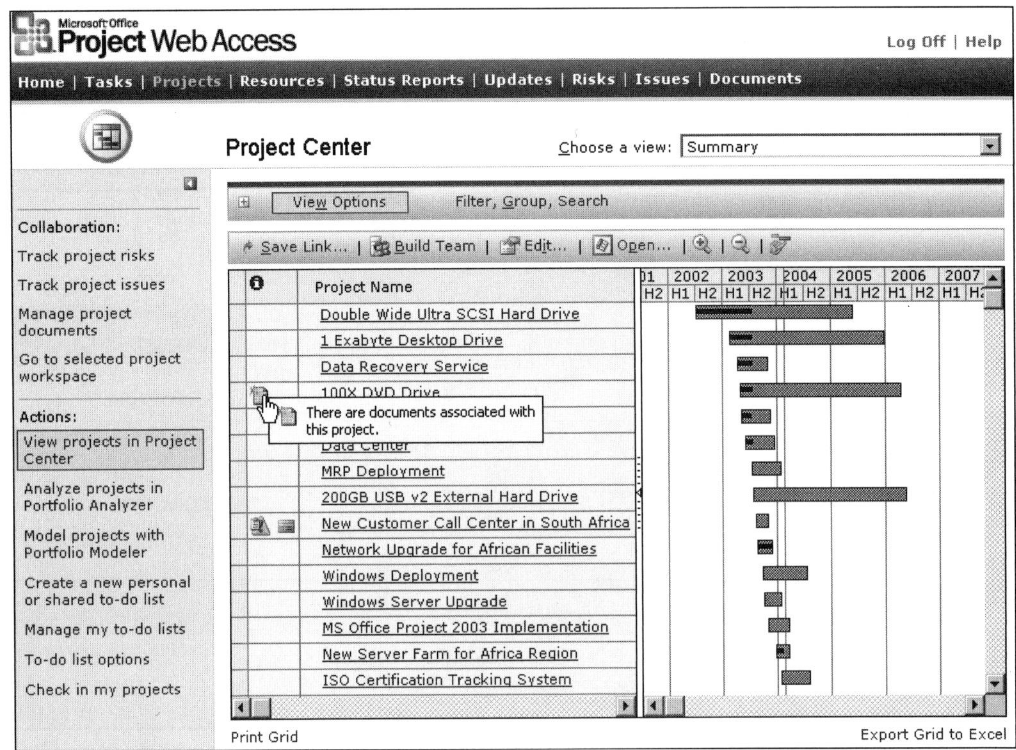

**Figure 14-2: Documents associated with
the 100X DVD Drive project**

To access the Risks, Issues, or Documents page for any project, do one of the following:

- Click the Risk, Issue, or Document icon in the Indicators column to the left of the project.

- Select any cell for a project in any column other than the Project Name column, and then click one of the first three links in the Collaboration section of the actions pane.

The Collaboration section of the actions pane also contains a link that takes you to the project workspace for the selected project.

Using Project Center Views

The Project Center page is your primary source for a two-dimensional presentation of your project portfolio. The system provides five standard views that you select from the *Choose a view* pick list in the upper right corner of the page:

- Summary
- Tracking
- Cost
- Earned Value
- Work

The Project Center **Summary** view displays the "vital statistics" for each project, with columns showing the project's Version, Duration, Start date, Finish date, Percent Complete, and Owner. The Summary view includes a Gantt Chart with a single Gantt bar for each project, using a unique color for each project version, and a black stripe indicating project progress. Notice in Figure 14-3 that the system displays the 200GB USB v2 External Hard Drive project twice, once for the Target (baseline) version and once for the Published (production) version of the project. Notice also that the system displays a different-colored Gantt bar for each version.

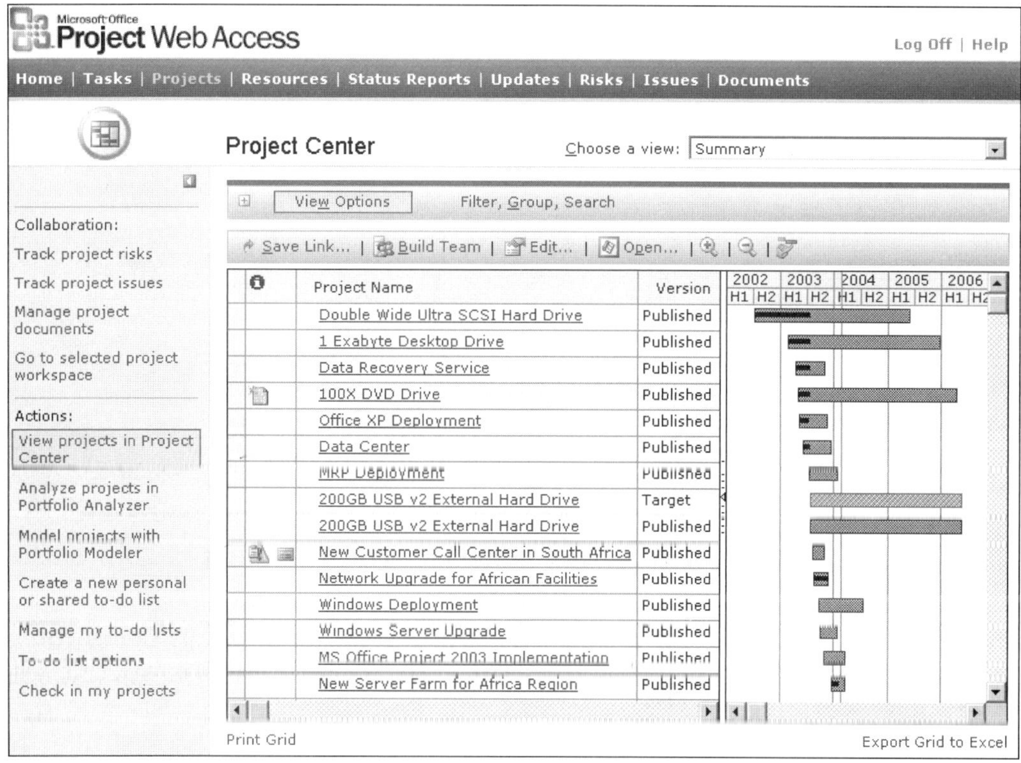

Figure 14-3: Project Center Summary view

To use the Version feature in Project Server 2003, your Project Server administrator must first set up versions according to your company's methodologies.

The Project Center **Tracking** view displays schedule variance information about each project, including the Scheduled Start and Finish dates, Actual Start and Finish dates, Baseline Start and Finish dates, Percent Complete, Duration, Actual Duration, Remaining Duration, Actual Cost, and Actual Work fields. The Tracking view shown in Figure 14-4 displays a Tracking Gantt Chart with two Gantt bars for each project. The top Gantt bar represents the current schedule for each project, while the bottom Gantt bar represents the baseline schedule for each project. The black stripe in the top Gantt bar indicates project progress.

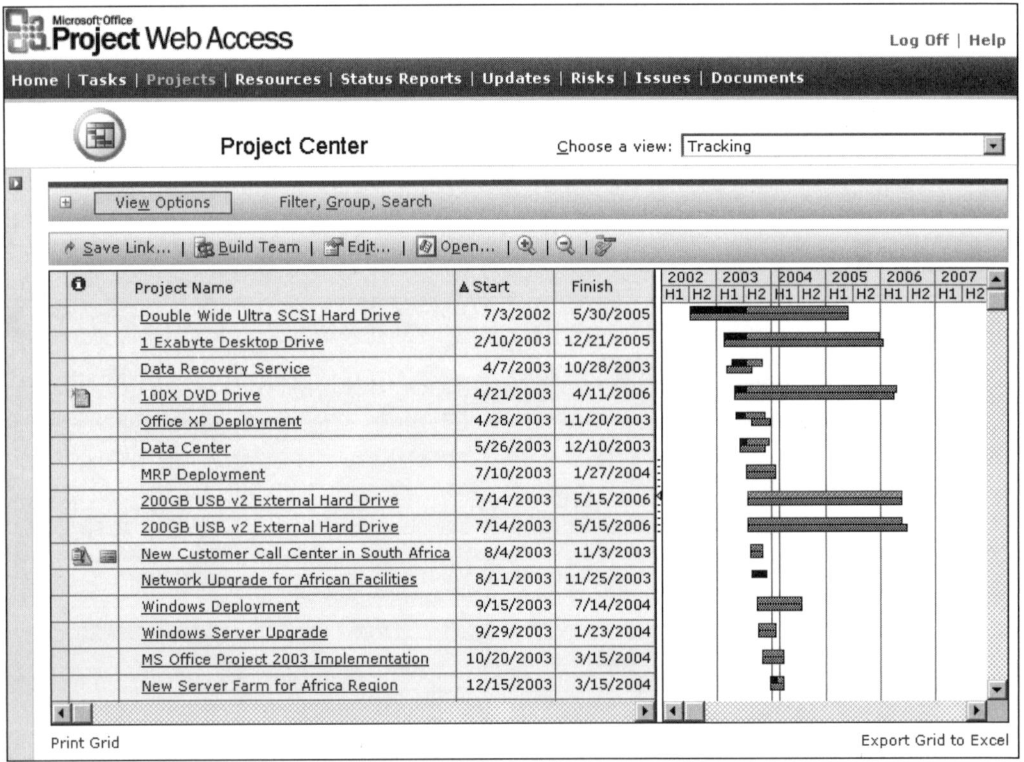

Figure 14-4: Project Center Tracking view

The Project Center **Cost** view shown in Figure 14-5 displays information about project costs, including columns for Fixed Cost, Cost, Baseline Cost, Cost Variance, Actual Cost, Remaining Cost, and the project's Start and Finish dates. The Cost view also displays a Tracking Gantt Chart similar to the one shown in the Tracking view.

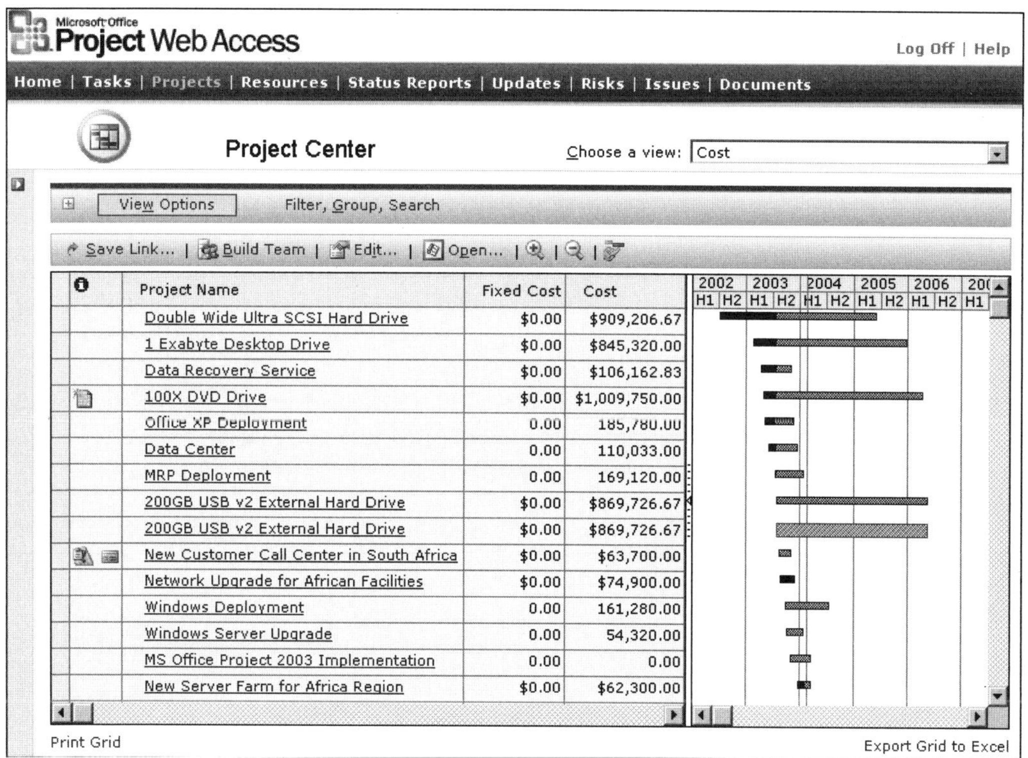

Figure 14-5: Project Center Cost view

The Project Center **Earned Value** view displays the calculated earned value at the project level for each project. This view includes columns for BCWS, BCWP, ACWP, SV, CV, Cost, Baseline Cost, VAC, and the Start and Finish dates. The Earned Value view shown in Figure 14-6 includes the same Tracking Gantt Chart as the Cost view. Notice in the figure that only the Published version of any project displays tracking information.

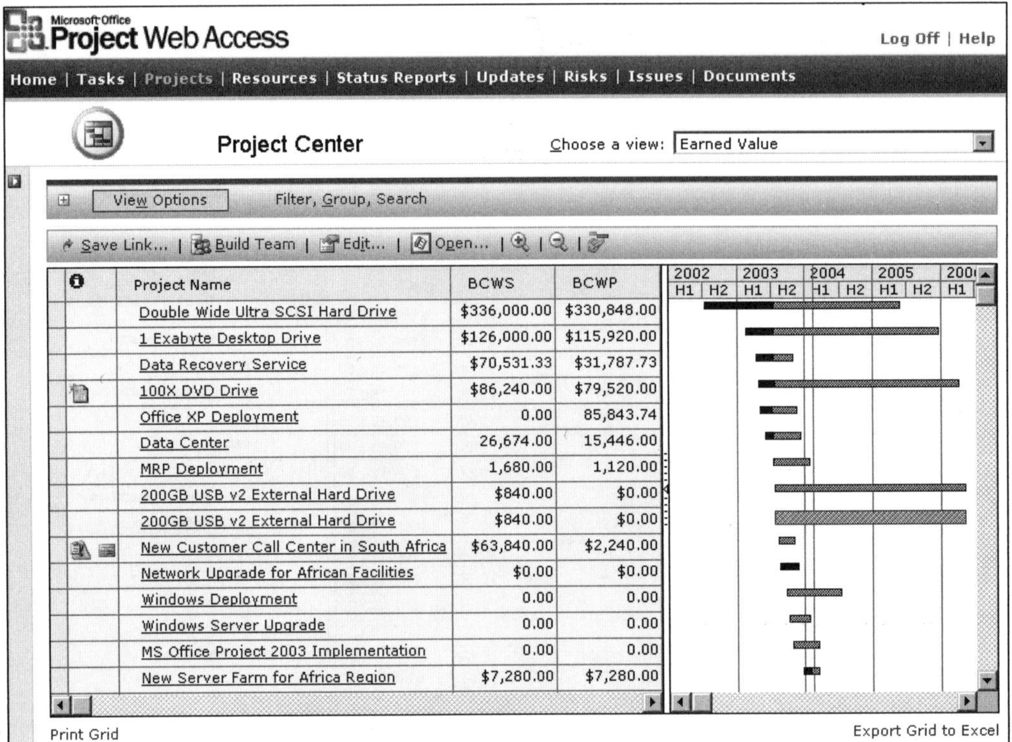

❶	Project Name	BCWS	BCWP
	Double Wide Ultra SCSI Hard Drive	$336,000.00	$330,848.00
	1 Exabyte Desktop Drive	$126,000.00	$115,920.00
	Data Recovery Service	$70,531.33	$31,787.73
	100X DVD Drive	$86,240.00	$79,520.00
	Office XP Deployment	0.00	85,843.74
	Data Center	26,674.00	15,446.00
	MRP Deployment	1,680.00	1,120.00
	200GB USB v2 External Hard Drive	$840.00	$0.00
	200GB USB v2 External Hard Drive	$840.00	$0.00
	New Customer Call Center in South Africa	$63,840.00	$2,240.00
	Network Upgrade for African Facilities	$0.00	$0.00
	Windows Deployment	0.00	0.00
	Windows Server Upgrade	0.00	0.00
	MS Office Project 2003 Implementation	0.00	0.00
	New Server Farm for Africa Region	$7,280.00	$7,280.00

**Figure 14-6: Project Center
Earned Value view**

The Project Center **Work** view displays information about the expenditure of project work hours, including columns for Work, Baseline Work, Work Variance, Actual Work, Remaining Work, % Work Complete, and the project's Start and Finish dates. The Work view displays the same Tracking Gantt Chart found in the Cost and Earned Value views, as shown in Figure 14-7.

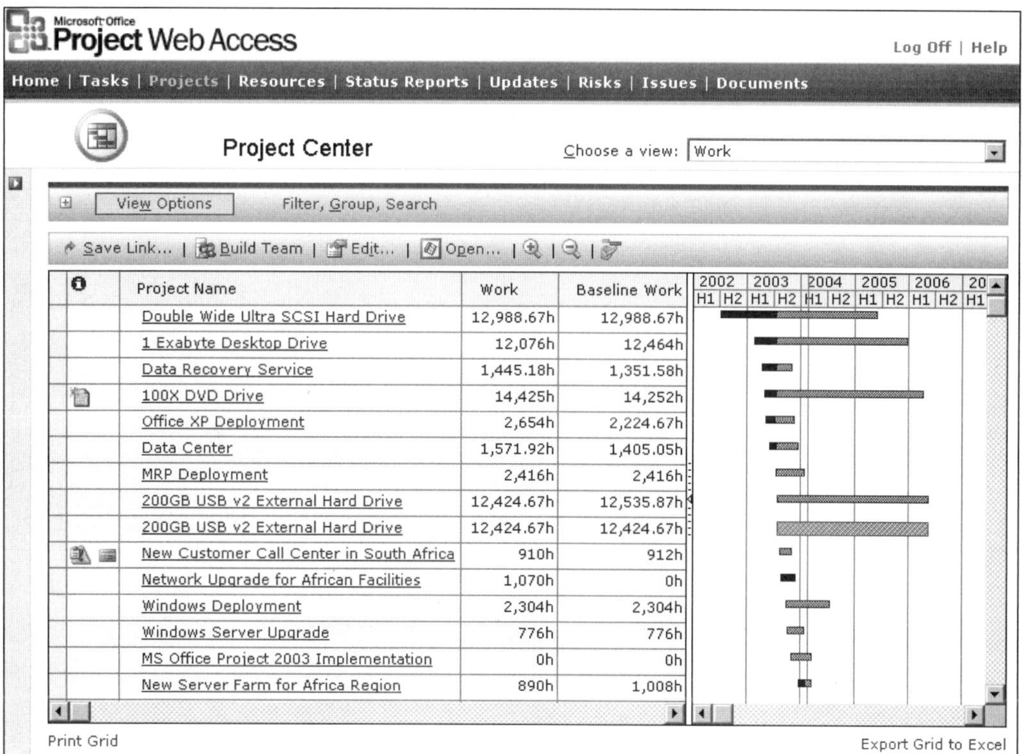

Figure 14-7: Project Center Work view

In addition to the five standard views, the *Choose a view* pick list may also include custom views added by your Project Server administrator. The Project Center is a great forum for the use of graphical indicators in custom views. Figure 14-8 shows the A Datum Executive Summary view that displays several columns containing custom graphical indicators.

The Budget column shows the cost variance for each project using a red, yellow, or green stoplight indicator. The Schedule column reveals schedule variance for each project using the same three stoplight indicators. The Exposure column contains a red, yellow, or green flag indicating High, Medium, or Low exposure for each project.

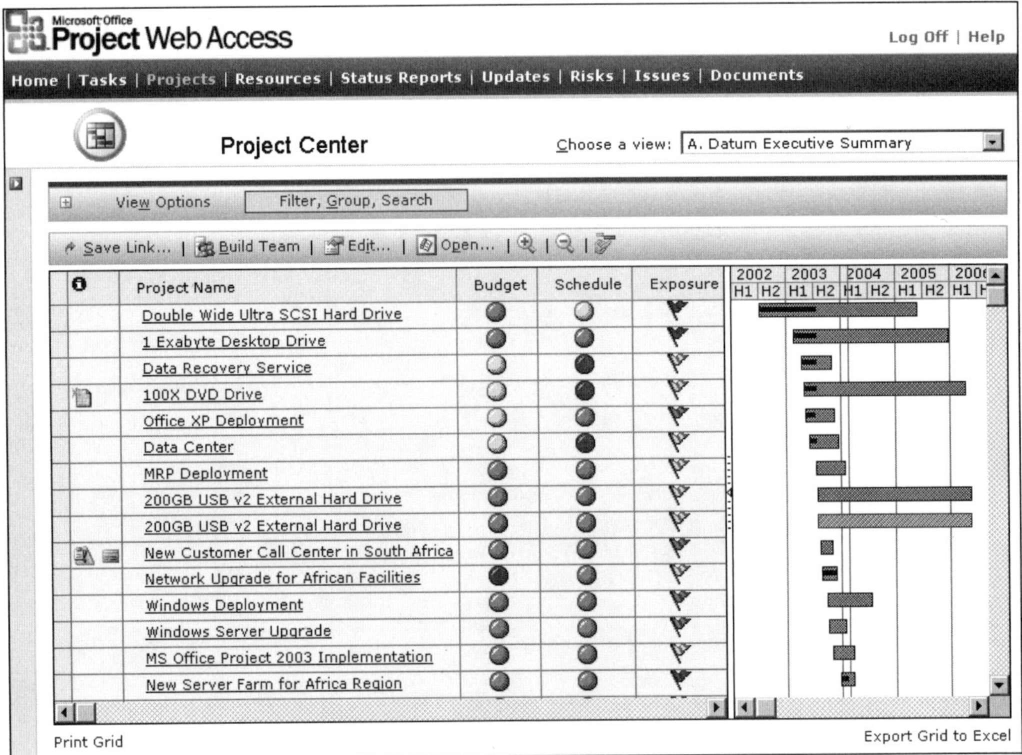

Figure 14-8: Custom Project Center view

As with the Resource Center, you can apply filtering and grouping to the Project Center views using the options on the *Filter, Group, Search* tab. In Figure 14-9, I have grouped the projects by Owner and filtered for all High exposure projects. Notice that two project managers, Chris Preston and Steve Masters, handle the lion's share of the difficult projects from an exposure perspective. Contrary to what you might expect, most of the projects for each of these project managers are on track from both a budget and a schedule perspective. This fact might reveal a high level of competency for these two project managers.

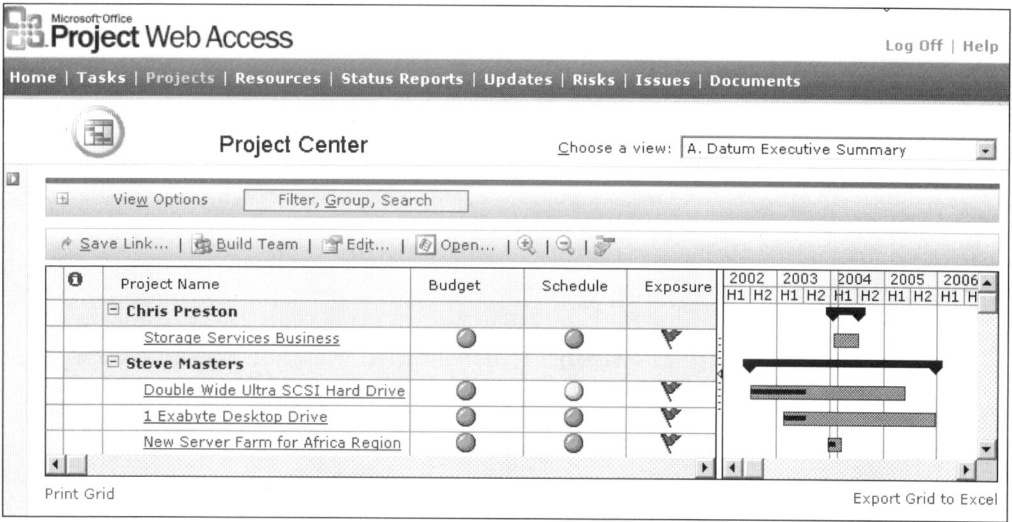

**Figure 14-9: A. Datum Executive Summary view
with grouping and filtering applied**

When you use the Save Link feature in the Project Center,
your saved link will include both the Group and the Filter that
you have applied.

Use the *Zoom In* and *Zoom Out* buttons to change the timescale of the Gantt
Chart. You can change the timescale to periods as small as 15-minute
intervals or as large as years. Use the *Go To Task* button, represented on the
far right-hand icon on the tool bar above the data grid, to scroll the Gantt
Chart to the start date of the selected project.

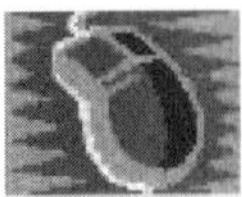

Hands On Exercise

Exercise 14-1

Explore the Project Center views.

1. Click the *Projects* menu item on the Project Web Access main menu.

2. Click the *Choose a view* pick list and apply each of the five default Project Center views individually.

3. Explore the information shown in each Project Center view.

4. Reapply the Summary view.

5. Click the *Filter, Group, Search* tab.

6. Click the *Group by* pick list and select the Owner field.

7. Note that the display changes to the grouped view.

8. Create your own custom Filter and note the results.

Building a Project Team

The Project Center includes a Build Team feature that you can use to build a project team from within Project Web Access. This feature is especially useful for Resource Managers who do not have the full version of Project Professional 2003. In the 2002 version, you could only build a team for a project using the full client tool.

To use the Build Team feature, to which Microsoft refers as Team Builder Lite, select a project in the Project Center view and then click the *Build Team* button on the toolbar. The system displays the Build Team page shown in Figure 14-10.

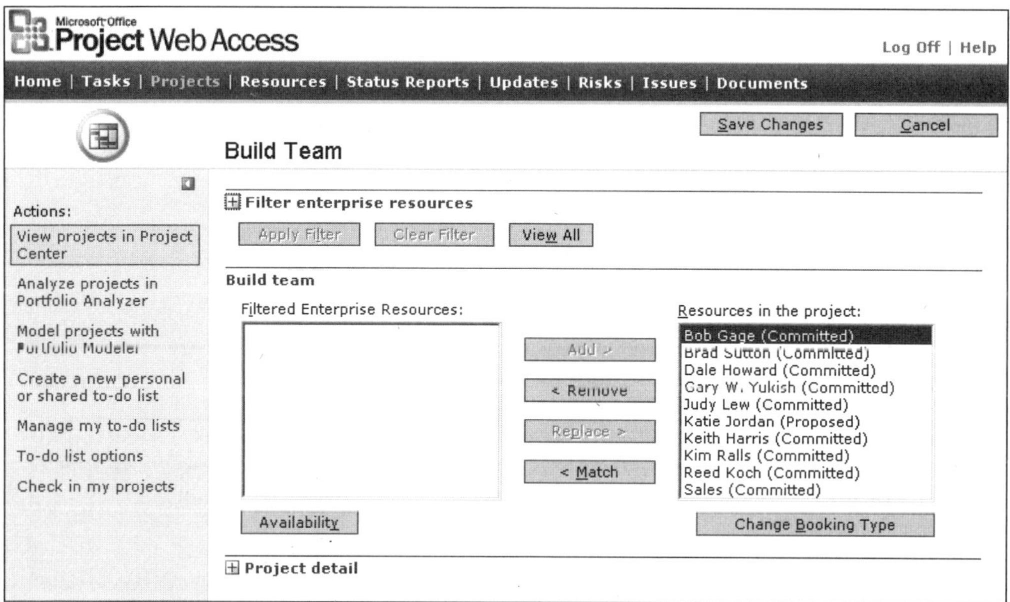

Figure 14-10: Build Team page

By default, the Build Team page does not display any resources in the Filtered Enterprise Resources list on the left side of the page. Click the *View All* button to display all of the resources in the Enterprise Resource Pool. If you wish to pre-filter the list of resources that the system displays, click the *expand* button (+) in the Filter Enterprise Resources section. The system displays the Filter Enterprise Resources section shown in Figure 14-11.

If your organization has a large resource pool, the Filter Enterprise Resources section allows you to narrow the list using the custom attributes assigned to your resources. Loading many hundreds of resources into the selection list can consume a lot of time. Use filtering to speed up the performance of the tool.

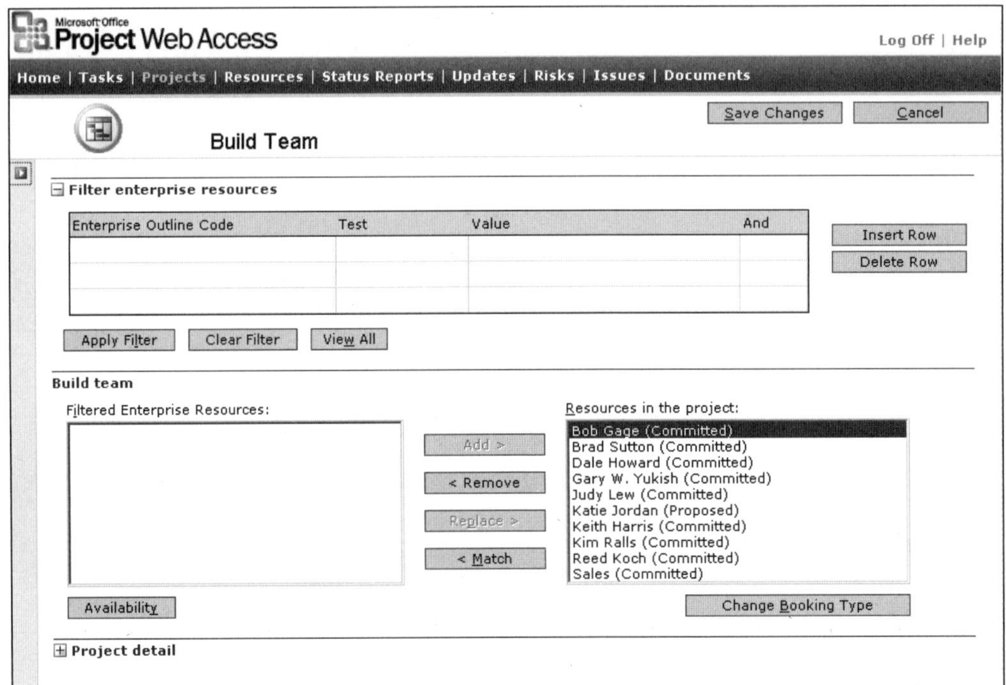

**Figure 14-11: Build Team page with
Filter Enterprise Resources section expanded**

To filter the list of enterprise resources, build a custom filter by setting values in the Enterprise Outline Code, Test, and Value columns. Build a compound filter using multiple lines of fields, tests, and values along with and/or values in the And column. Click the *Apply Filter* button to apply the filter. In Figure 14-12, I filtered the list of resources to show only those in the Corporate Marketing Department.

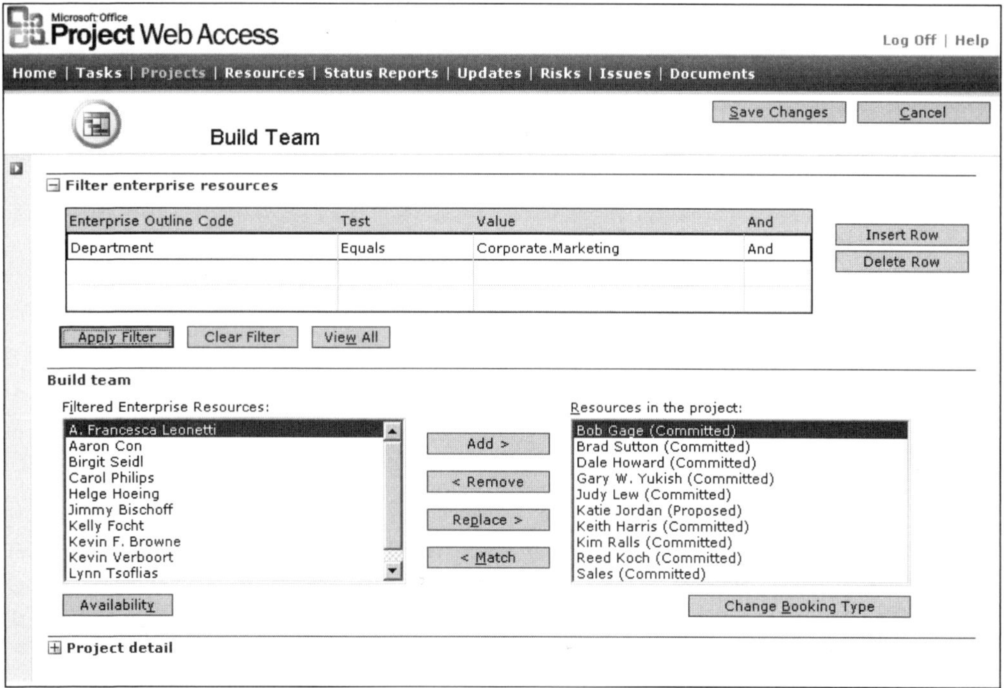

**Figure 14-12: Build Team page
with a filter applied**

When using Build Team, you may wish to see the selected project as a guide in selecting team members. Click the *expand* button (**+**) in the Project Detail section at the lower left corner of the page and the system displays project details as shown in Figure 14-13. The project details displayed include the Task Name, Duration, Start and Finish dates, % Complete, and Resource Names for each task in the project.

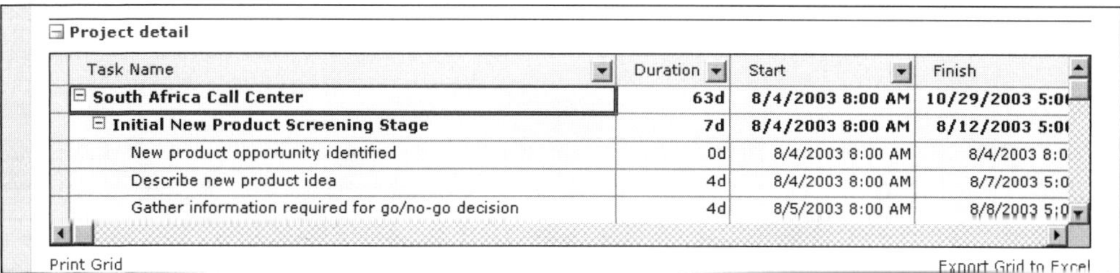

**Figure 14-13: Project Detail section
expanded on Build Team page**

To build your project team, select the names of resources in the Filtered Enterprise Resources list and click the *Add* button. To remove members from the team, select the names of team members in the Resources in the project list and click the *Remove* button. If you remove a team member who has not reported progress on any task assignments, the system displays the confirmation dialog shown in Figure 14-14.

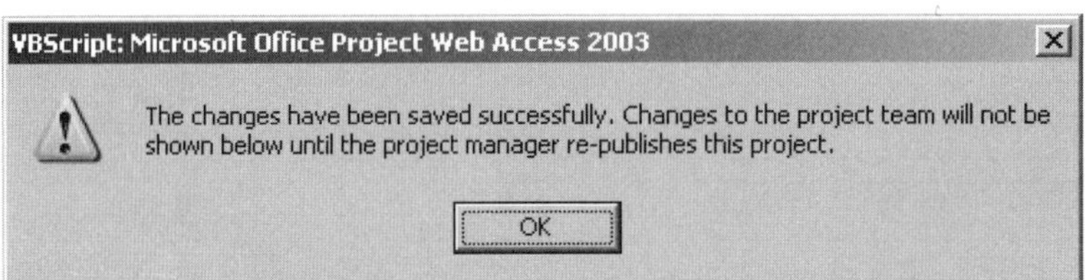

**Figure 14-14: Changes to project
team saved successfully**

If you attempt to remove a team member who has reported progress on any task assignments, or who has actual progress pending, the system will deny the removal with the dialog shown in Figure 14-15. At this point, your only option is to use the Assign Resources dialog in Project Professional 2003 to replace the resource only on task assignments with remaining work.

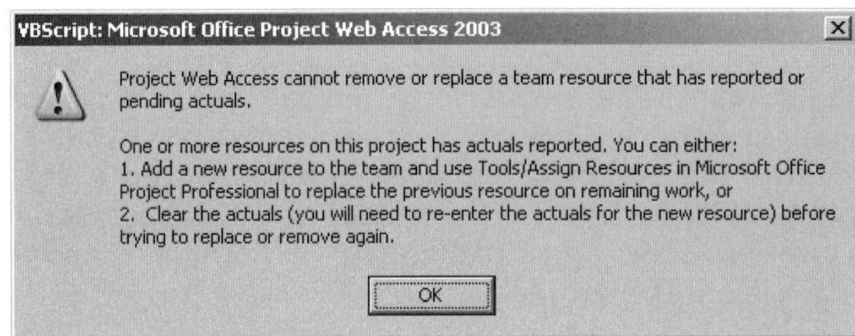

**Figure 14-15: Cannot remove or
replace a team member with actuals**

To replace an existing team member, select the resource in the Resources in the project list, select the replacement in the Filtered Enterprise Resources list, and then click the *Replace* button. If you attempt to replace a team member who has reported progress on any task assignments, or who has actual progress pending, the system will deny the replacement with the dialog shown previously in Figure 14-15.

To match the skills of a team member such as a Generic resource, select the Generic resource from the Resources in the project list and click the *Match* button. The system builds a temporary filter that matches the resource attributes defined for the Generic resource. This temporary filter will replace any filter that you have already built, and will display only those resources who match the attributes of the Generic resource.

To change the booking type for any member of the project team, select the resource from the Resources in the project list and then click the *Change Booking Type* button. The system toggles the Booking Type for the selected resource, such as changing a resource from Committed to Proposed.

Remember from Module 3 that a Proposed booking indicates a tentative commitment for the resource, while a Committed booking indicates a firm commitment. The default Booking type for each project team member is Committed.

Editing Project Details and Opening Projects

If you have the proper security permissions, you can edit the enterprise custom fields for any project you can see in the Project Center. Select a single project in the data grid and then click the *Edit* button on the Project Center toolbar. The system displays the Project Details page shown in Figure 14-16.

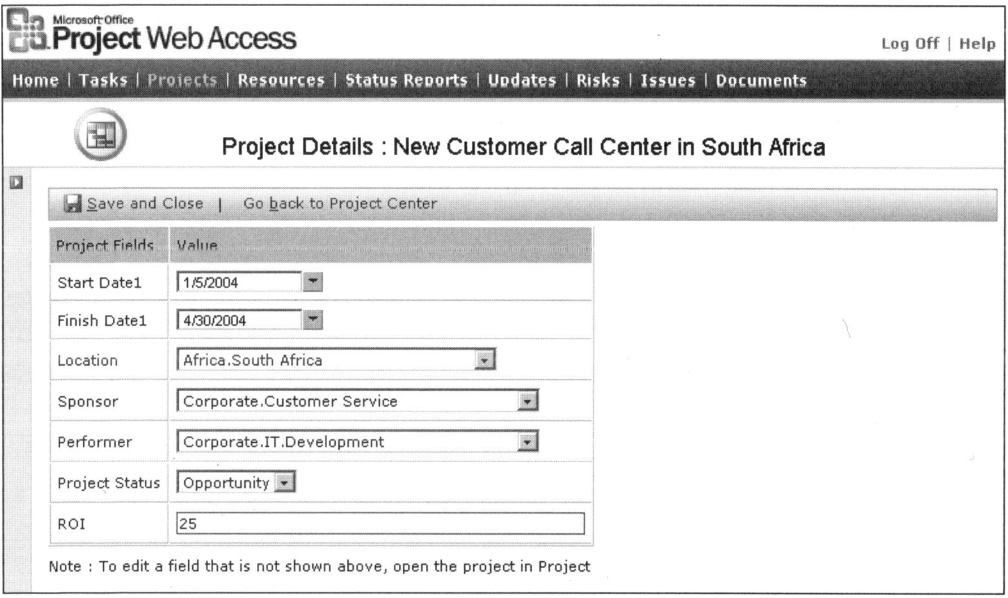

**Figure 14-16: Project Details page
for a selected project**

The Project Details page displays all custom enterprise Project outline codes plus only those enterprise Project fields that **do not** contain a value list or a formula. Enterprise Project outline codes and fields are the only project-level information that you can edit through Project Web Access. Edit any of the displayed fields and then click the *Save and Close* button to commit the changes. Click the *Go back to Project Center* button to return to the Project Center page.

To edit any custom enterprise project field not displayed in the Project Details page, you must open the project in Project Professional 2003, and then click Project ➢ Project Information. You must edit custom enterprise project fields that contain a value list or formula using this method.

Clicking the *Open* button on the toolbar launches Project Professional 2003 (if you have not already launched it), and then checks out and opens the project that you selected in the grid. After completing the logon ritual according to the preferences you set, you can proceed to edit your project.

Because you can access Project Center views from within Project Professional 2003, you can use the Open feature to locate and open files in a very large portfolio. The Open dialog in Project Professional 2003 allows you to group only on a single outline code, and does not provide any filtering capabilities. If you want to group on multiple outline codes or to filter on fields or outline codes, use the grouping and/or filtering capabilities of the Project Center views, and then open your project from the Project Center page using the *Open* button.

If you select multiple projects in the grid using the Control key and then click the *Open* button, Project Server 2003 will create a master project in Project Professional 2003 with each of the selected projects as subprojects. You can use a master project to set cross-project dependencies between tasks in the selected projects, or to analyze trends in the portfolio of selected projects. Figure 14-17 shows a master project consisting of five subprojects managed by Steve Masters.

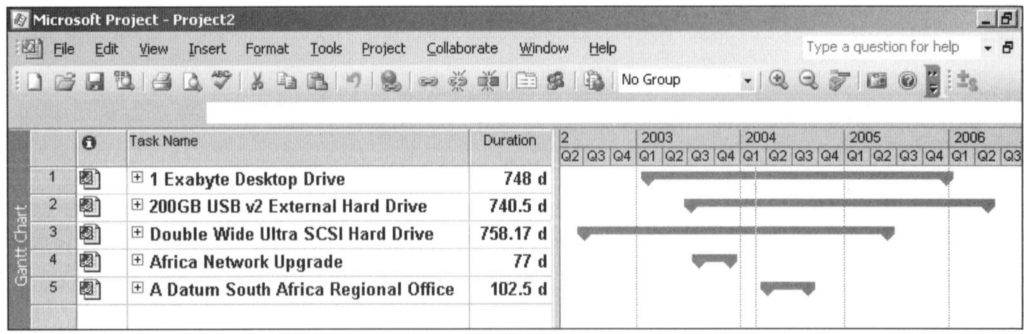

**Figure 14-17: Master project with five
subprojects managed by Steve Masters**

Hands On Exercise

Exercise 14-2

Edit the Project Details for a project.

1. Click the *Projects* menu item on the Project Web Access main menu.

2. Select a project in the grid.

3. Click the *Edit* button on the toolbar.

4. Examine the fields available for editing.

5. Click the *Go back to Project Center* button.

Checking In Projects

Project Server 2003 allows you to check in projects that you own. Occasionally you may find that the system leaves a project in a checked-out state because of network problems or a workstation crash. To check in a project, click the *Check in my projects* link at the bottom of the actions pane. The system displays the Check In My Projects page shown in Figure 14-18.

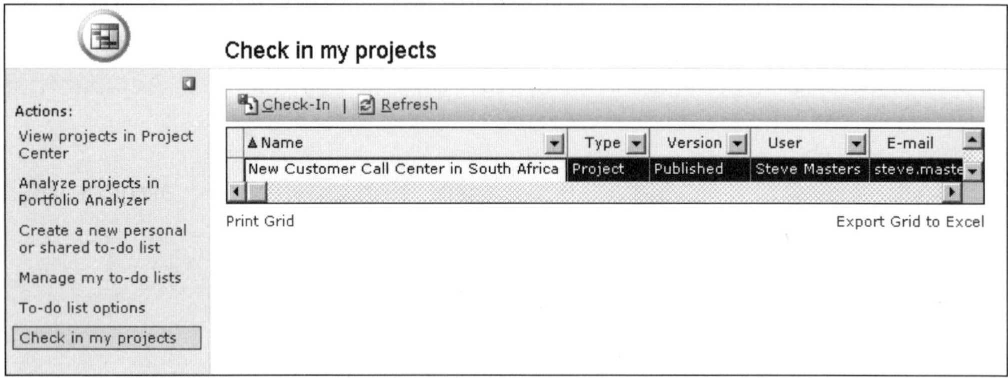

Figure 14-18: Check In My Projects page

Notice that the system indicates that Steve Masters has checked out the New Customer Call Center in South Africa project, even though he does not have the project currently open in Project Professional 2003. To check in a project, select the desired project and click the *Check-In* button on the toolbar. The system displays the warning message shown in Figure 14-19.

**Figure 14-19: Warning dialog about
checking in a checked-out project**

If you accidentally check in a project that you currently have checked out in Project Professional 2003, the warning dialog shown in Figure 14-20 displays when you attempt to save or close the project.

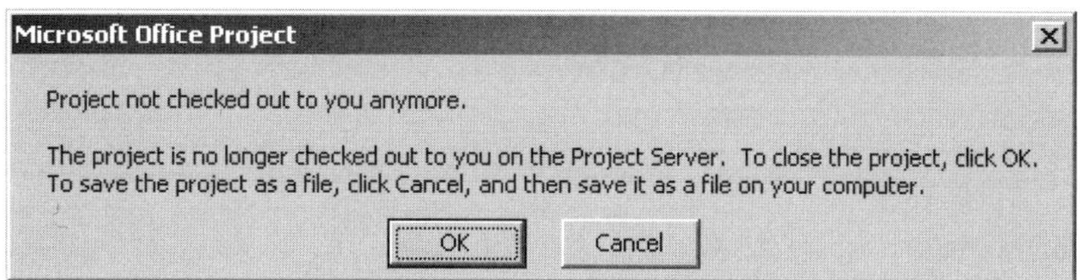

**Figure 14-20: Project not
checked out warning**

Working with Detailed Project Views

In addition to viewing a single line of information about each project in the portfolio, the Project Center gives you the ability to view the details of any project. Click the name of any project in the data grid of the Project Center page. The system displays a detailed Project view as shown in Figure 14-21.

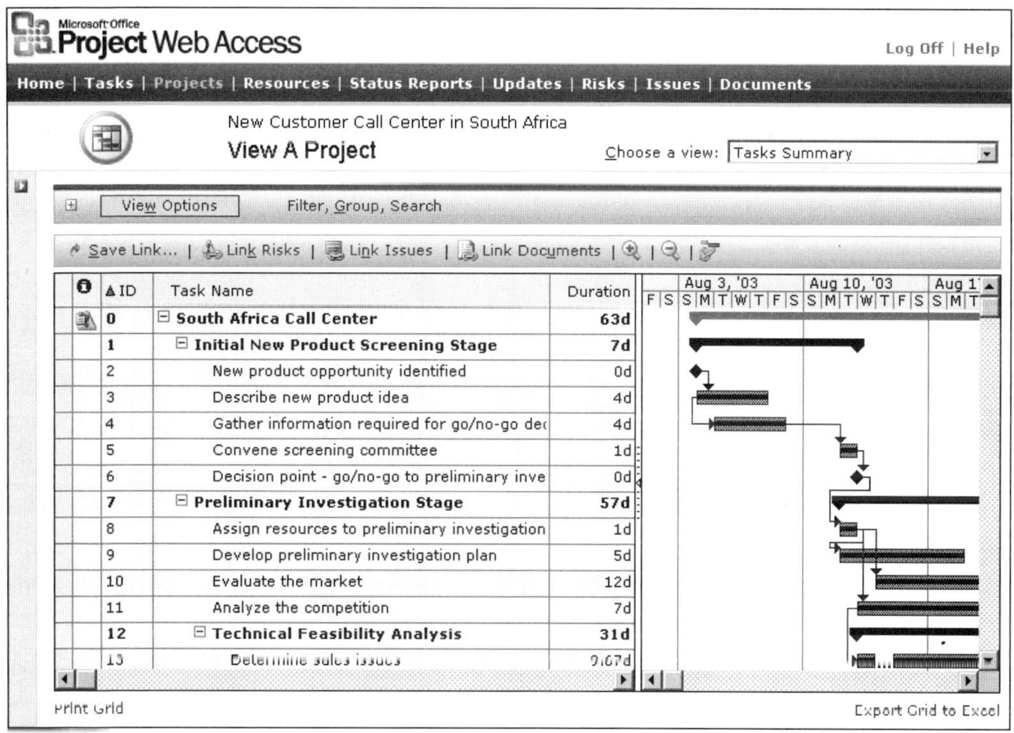

❶	▲ID	Task Name	Duration
	0	⊟ **South Africa Call Center**	**63d**
	1	⊟ **Initial New Product Screening Stage**	**7d**
	2	New product opportunity identified	0d
	3	Describe new product idea	4d
	4	Gather information required for go/no-go dec	4d
	5	Convene screening committee	1d
	6	Decision point - go/no-go to preliminary inve	0d
	7	⊟ **Preliminary Investigation Stage**	**57d**
	8	Assign resources to preliminary investigation	1d
	9	Develop preliminary investigation plan	5d
	10	Evaluate the market	12d
	11	Analyze the competition	7d
	12	⊟ **Technical Feasibility Analysis**	**31d**
	13	Determine sales issues	9.67d

**Figure 14-21: Detailed Project view
of the selected project**

405

The *Choose a view* pick list offers three types of detailed Project views consisting of tasks, assignments, and resources. The system includes nineteen default views organized within the three types as shown in Table 14-1.

Task Views	Assignment Views	Resource Views
Tasks Summary	Assignments Summary	Resources Summary
Tasks Top-Level		
Tasks Detail	Assignments Detail	
Tasks Leveling		
Tasks Tracking	Assignments Tracking	
Tasks Cost	Assignments Cost	Resources Cost
Tasks Earned Value	Assignments Earned Value	Resources Earned Value
Tasks Schedule		
Tasks Work	Assignments Work	Resources Work

Table 14-1: Detailed Project views

The system remembers which detailed Project view you selected the last time you displayed the page, and defaults to that view when you select another project from the Project Center.

Like Project Center views, you can apply grouping and filtering to any detailed Project view. You can also use the Save Link feature to save your preferred grouping and filtering of these views.

Use the *Zoom In* and *Zoom Out* buttons to change the timescale of the Gantt Chart. You can change the timescale to periods as small as 15-minute intervals or as large as years. Use the *Go To Task* button to scroll the Gantt Chart to the start date of the selected task.

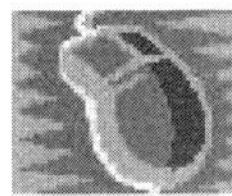

Hands On Exercise

Exercise 14-3

Explore detailed Project views from the Project Center.

1. Click the *Projects* menu item on the Project Web Access main menu.
2. Click the name of a project in the grid.
3. Select any Tasks view from the *Choose a view* pick list.
4. Select any Assignments view from the *Choose a view* pick list.
5. Select any Resources view from the *Choose a view* pick list.
6. Click the *View projects in the Project Center* link in the actions pane to return to the Project Center page.

Organizing Your Saved Links

After you create your first saved link in any page, the system displays two new menu items in the actions pane. A Saved Links section appears at the top of the actions pane and an *Organize your saved links* link appears at the bottom as shown in Figure 14-22.

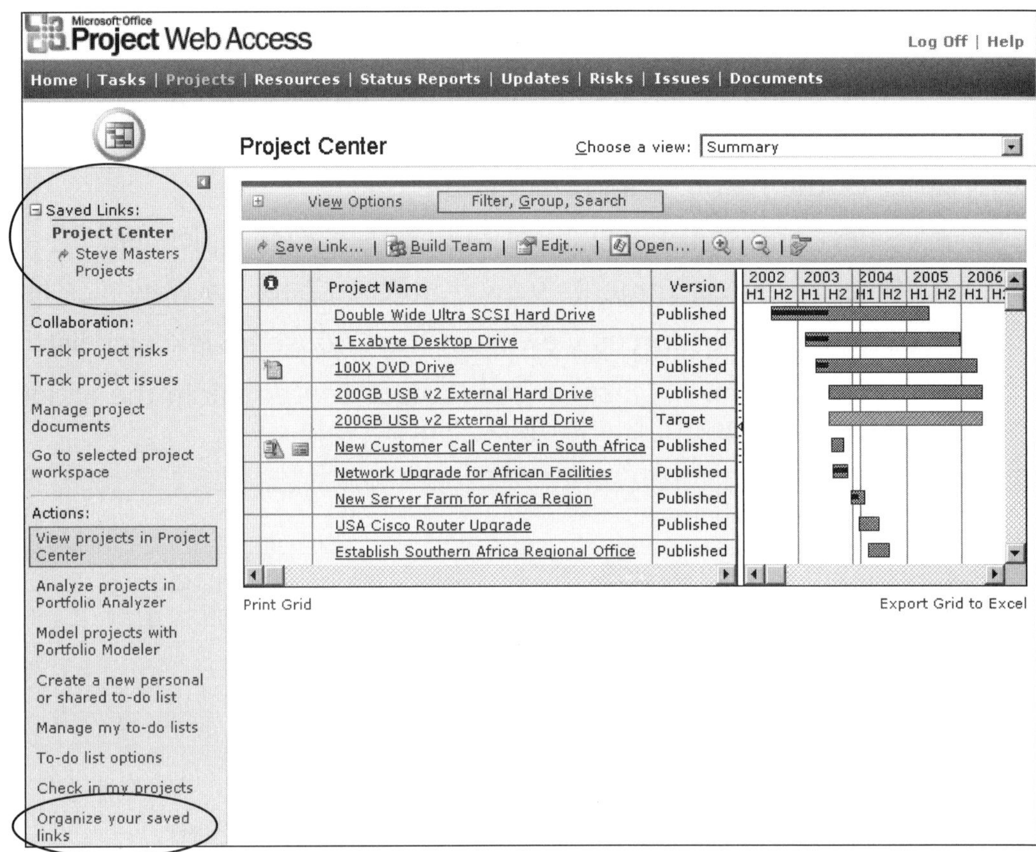

Figure 14-22: Saved links options

Notice in Figure 14-22 that I have clicked the *expand* button (**+**) to the left of the Saved Links section to display my Saved Links in the Project Center page. Click the *Organize your saved links* link and the system displays the Organize your saved links page shown in Figure 14-23. You can delete or rename your links from this page. Once you delete a link, you cannot undo the deletion.

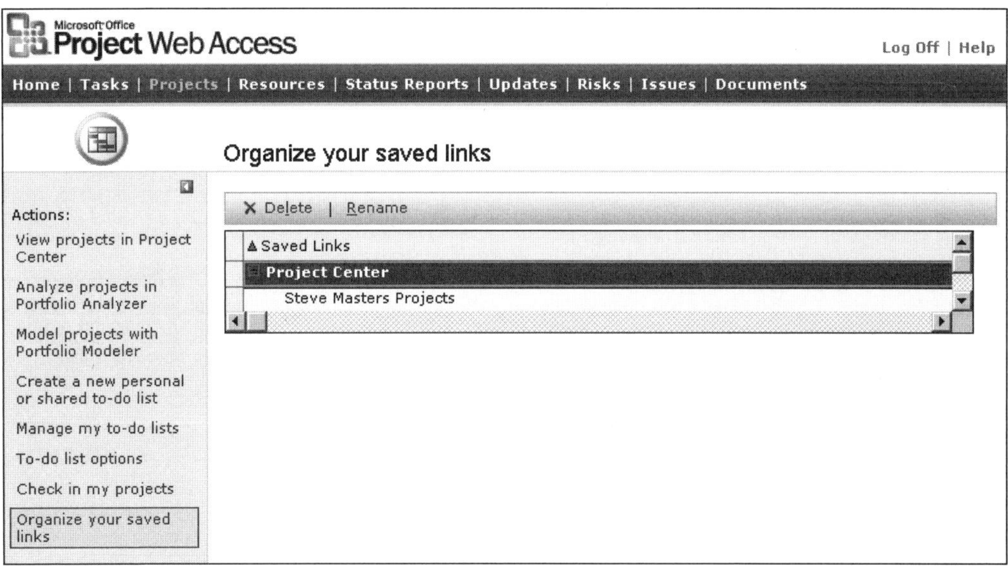

Figure 14-23: Organize Your Saved Links page

Working with To-Do Lists

To-Do lists provide an informal task management tool within a formal project management tool. To-Do lists provide a flexible forum for managing task work significant enough that you want to formally record it, but do not want to formally manage it. Although tasks created on to-do lists appear in the timesheet in the View My Tasks page, to-do list tasks do not accept progress reporting like project tasks.

Click the *Create a new personal or shared to-do list* link from the actions pane and the system displays the Create a New Personal or Shared To-Do List page shown in Figure 14-24.

**Figure 14-24: Create a New Personal
or Shared To-Do List page**

To create a new To-Do list, follow these steps:

1. Enter a name for your new to-do list.

2. Select the access rule to apply to Anyone, to All resources who are assigned tasks from this to-do list, or Me (only) by selecting the corresponding option.

3. Click the *Next* button to display the Create a New Task page shown in Figure 14-25.

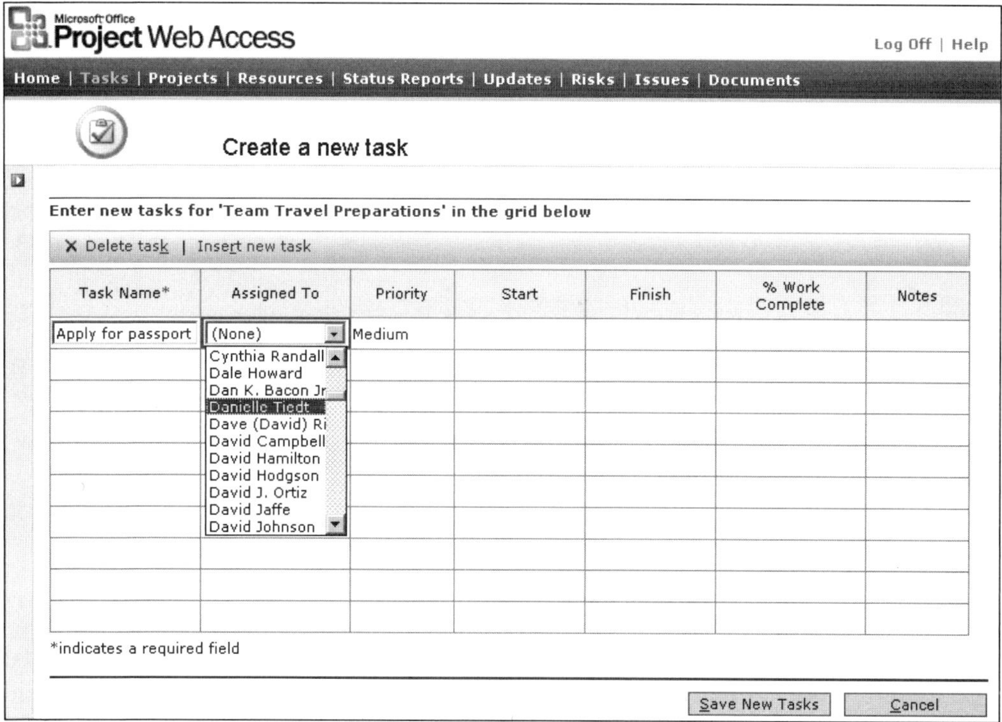

Figure 14-25: Create a New Task page

The Create a New Task page is specific to creating tasks for to-do lists. Create new to-do list tasks by entering information in the respective columns of the data grid. The only required field is the Task Name column. Insert and delete tasks in the grid using the corresponding tools on the toolbar. Note that you can assign a resource to a task by selecting the resource name from the *Assigned To* pick list as shown previously in Figure 14-25.

4. Click the *Save New Tasks* button to complete your entries.

The system accepts and saves your to-do list tasks and displays the Manage My To-Do Lists page shown in Figure 14-26. Notice that the system represents to-do lists as groupings of tasks in this view. You can also access this view directly by clicking the *Manage my to-do lists* link in the actions pane.

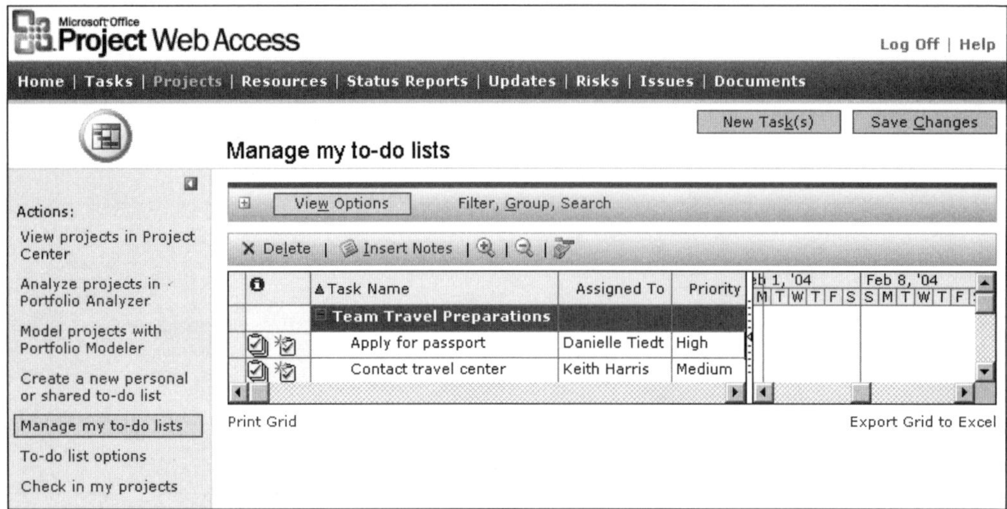

Figure 14-26: Manage My To-Do Lists page

Notice the icons displayed in the Indicators column in the display. The stacked clipboards icon indicates a to-do list task. The other icon indicates that the to-do task is a new assignment. To insert a note on any to-do list task, select the task and then click the *Insert Notes* button on the toolbar. Click the *New Tasks* button at the top of the page to add more tasks in the Create a New Task page shown previously in Figure 14-24. Click the *Save Changes* button to save your to-do list to the Project Server database. The system displays the confirmation dialog shown in Figure 14-27.

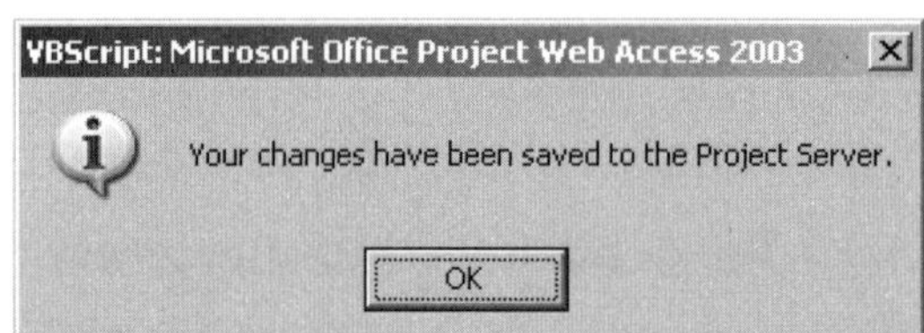

**Figure 14-27: To-do list
saved to Project Server**

The remaining To-Do list item in the actions pane is the *To-do list options* link. Click this selection and the system opens the To-Do List Options page shown in Figure 14-28.

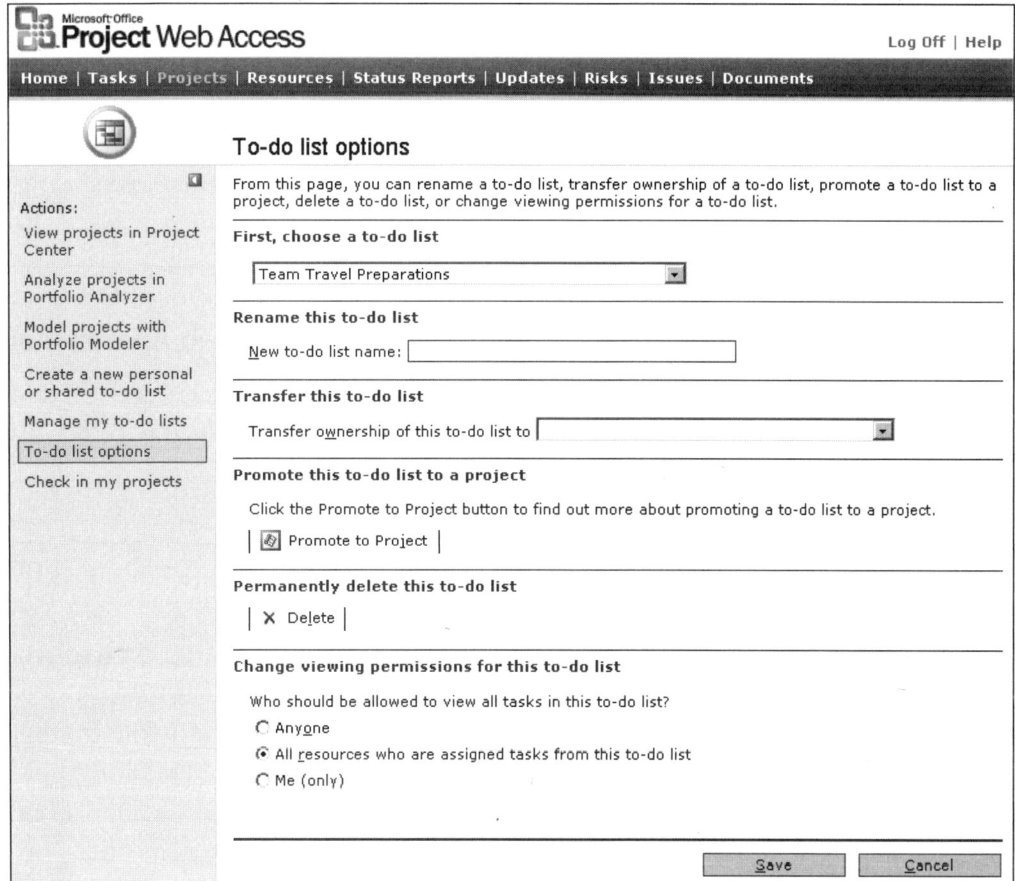

Figure 14-28: To-Do List Options page

Before you can use the options on this page, you must first select a to-do list. Once you select the to-do list, the system offers the following actions:

- **Rename this to-do list** allows you to change the to-do list name.

- **Transfer this to-do list** allows you to transfer ownership of the to-do list to another system user by selecting their name from a pick list.

- **Promote this to-do list to a project** opens Project Professional 2003 if it is not open and writes all the tasks and resource information in the to-do list into a new project file that you can then save to Project Server.

- **Permanently delete this to-do list** allows you to delete the to-do list.

- **Change viewing permissions for this to do list** allows you to change who may see the tasks in the to-do list.

Click the *Save* button when you are satisfied with your to-do list changes.

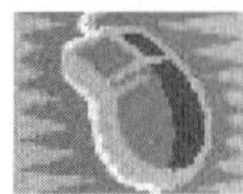

Hands On Exercise

Exercise 14-4

Create a new to-do list.

1. Click the *Projects* menu item on the Project Web Access main menu.

2. Click the *Create a new personal or shared to-do list* link in the actions pane.

3. Give your new to-do list a name.

4. Select who will be allowed to view tasks in the to-do list and click the *Next* button to continue.

5. Add a task in the grid, give it a name, assign it to a resource, and then enter Priority, Start and Finish information.

6. Click the *Save New Tasks* button.

Exercise 14-5

Manage to-do lists and then promote a to-do list to a project.

1. Click the *Projects* menu item on the Project Web Access main menu.

2. Click the *To-do list options* link in the actions pane.

3. Select the to-do list you created in the previous exercise.

4. Notice the options available.

5. Click the *Promote to Project* button.

6. Click the *Yes* button when prompted.

Module 15

Working with Project Server Analysis

Learning Objectives

After completing this module, you will be able to:

- Understand the need for Project Server analysis
- Use Portfolio Analyzer views
- Create a custom Portfolio Analyzer view and save a link to it
- Create, use, and modify Portfolio Models
- Compare Portfolio Models

The Need for Project Analysis

You will likely want to perform two types of analysis in your organization's project management environment: project analysis and resource analysis. You can use project analysis to understand what is happening across your project portfolio. For example, you might want to compare actual costs against baseline costs for a portfolio of projects in a single region.

You can use resource analysis to study resource allocation across a portfolio of projects. For example, you might want to analyze the total resource hours committed to a portfolio of projects within a single IT department.

Project Server 2003 offers you the ability to do both project analysis and resource analysis using the Portfolio Analyzer and the Portfolio Modeler. You can find Links for both the Analyzer and Modeler in the actions pane of the Project Center page and you will find a link to the Analyzer in the Resource Center as well.

You can access Analyzer views from either the Project Center or the Resource Center. In the Project Center, click the *Analyze projects in Portfolio Analyzer* link. In the Resource Center, click the *Analyze resources in Portfolio Analyzer* link. Both links take you to the Portfolio Analyzer where you can perform either type of analysis.

Using Portfolio Analyzer Views

Because Portfolio Analyzer views are highly dependent on enterprise custom data, Project Server 2003 does not include any of these views by default. Instead, the Project Server administrator must create unique Portfolio Analyzer views to meet your organization's enterprise project analysis needs.

Portfolio Analyzer views can be used dynamically, which means that they can be modified for "on the fly" analysis. You can literally delete everything from a view and then start over, as if you were creating a new view from scratch. Because you can change anything in an analyzer view, you can create new personal views and save them simply by clicking the *Save Link* button.

Warning: Project Server 2003 uses Office 2003 Web Components to provide the functionality of the Portfolio Analyzer. You must have a license on your PC for Microsoft Office 2003, or Microsoft Project 2003 Standard or Professional, to get the full functionality of analyzer views. Otherwise, you will not be able to create your own personal analyzer views.

To view the Portfolio Analyzer, click the *Projects* menu, then click the *Analyze projects in Portfolio Analyzer* link in the actions pane. A Portfolio Analyzer view consists of two sections: a PivotChart and a PivotTable as shown in Figure 15-1. The PivotTable functions like an Excel worksheet, and contains the underlying data for the view. The data in the PivotTable displays graphically in the PivotChart.

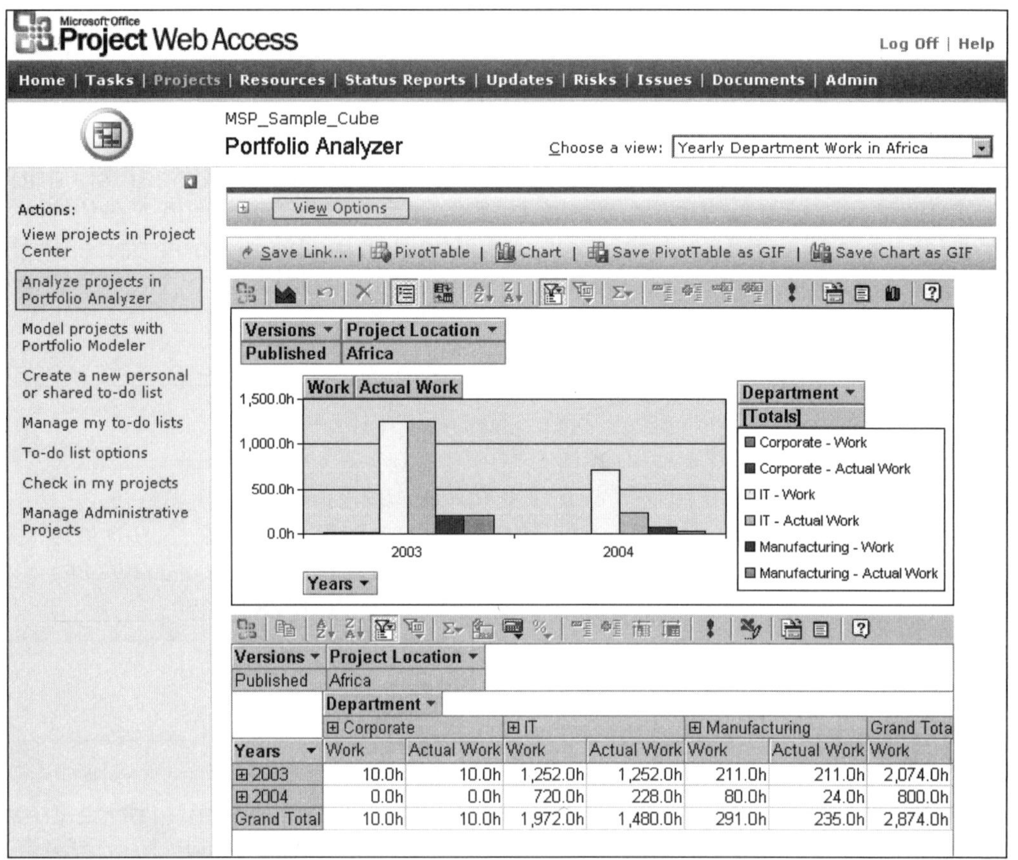

Figure 15-1: Portfolio Analyzer view
Yearly Department Work in Africa

To make best use of the Portfolio Analyzer, collapse the actions pane on the left side of the page.

In addition to the PivotTable and PivotChart areas of the view, you can access the PivotTable Field List dialog and the Portfolio Analyzer toolbar as well. These additional features give you the ability to customize any existing Portfolio Analyzer views "on the fly" and save the new view as your own personal custom view.

You must be a Project Server administrator to create a new Portfolio Analyzer view that is available to everyone through the *Choose a View* pick list. The original view creator can set view options that determine the initial state of the view, such as whether the toolbar and field list display by default or whether the view displays both the pivot table and chart or only one of these by default.

Regardless of the initial view presentation parameters, you can display the toolbar and field list by clicking the *View Options* tab at the top of the page and selecting the appropriate options. Figure 15-2 shows the expanded *View Options* tab. Select the *Show Field List* and *Show toolbar* options, then click the *View Options* tab to collapse it. Note that once you display the toolbar, you can toggle the display through chart and pivot table, pivot table only, or chart only.

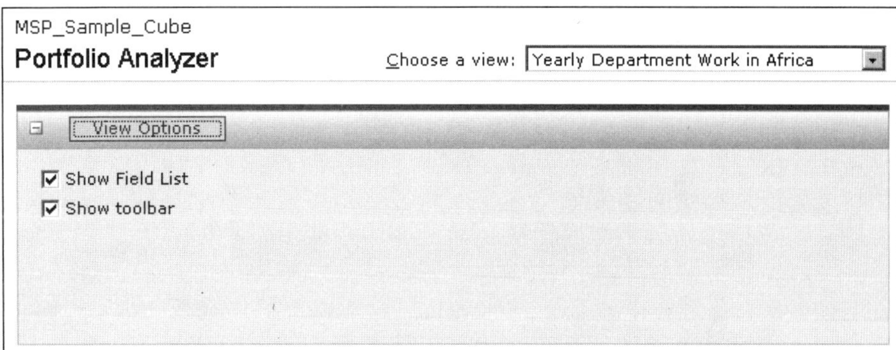

**Figure 15-2: View Options tab on the
Portfolio Analyzer page**

When you select the *PivotTable Field List* option, the Field List dialog floats over the Portfolio Analyzer view, as shown in Figure 15-3.

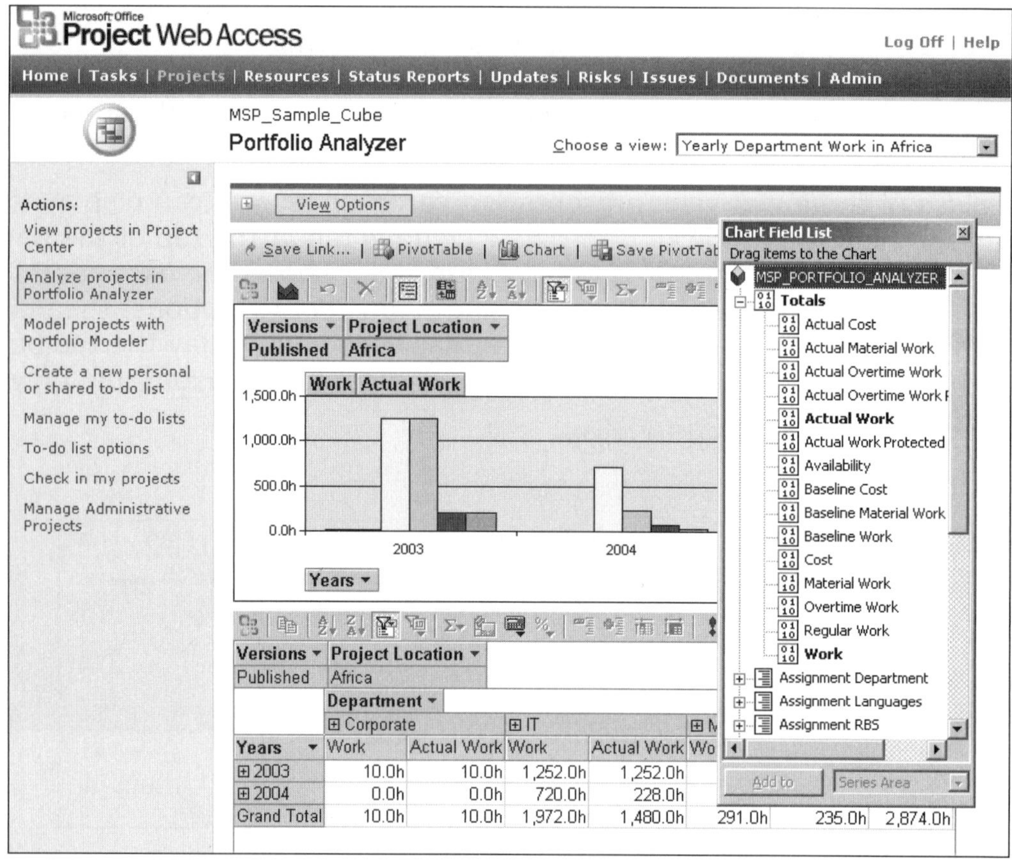

**Figure 15-3: Portfolio Analyzer view
with PivotChart Field List dialog**

If you accidentally hide the Field List dialog, you can
redisplay this dialog by clicking the *Field List* button on either
the PivotTable or PivotChart toolbars.

In Figure 15-3, notice that there are two types of icons in the PivotChart
Field List dialog. The icons resembling dominos in the Totals section
represent totals that you can drag into the PivotChart area. In OLAP terms,
these are fact charts and contain totals for project work, availability, and
costs. Figure 15-4 shows the complete list of Totals. Notice that some of the
fields and dimension in the display appear in bold type; this indicates that
the total or dimension is already part of the view.

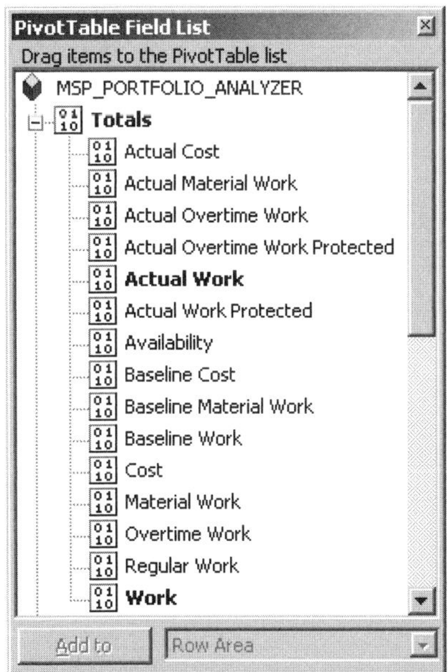

**Figure 15-4: Field List with
Totals list expanded**

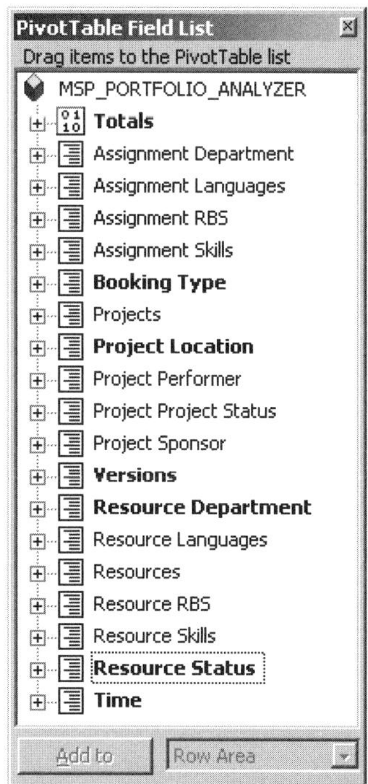

**Figure 15-5: Field List
shows all available fields
and dimensions**

The icons resembling the right-justify format text button in Word, shown in Figure 15-5, represent dimensions available in the OLAP cube. Except for a handful of default dimensions, these are the custom enterprise project outline codes and enterprise resource outline codes created by your Project Server administrator. You can drag any of the fields or dimensions into the PivotTable or PivotChart area to create your own Portfolio Analyzer view. The default dimensions available in the OLAP Cube are:

- **Projects dimension** contains the names of all projects in the system.

- **Versions dimension** contains each project and version combination.

- **Time dimension** contains time settings, years, quarters, months, and days.

- **Resources dimension** contains all resource names.

- **Resource Status dimension** contains the types of resource information available, including Enterprise Active, Enterprise Generic Active, Local Resources, Project Fixed Costs, and Task Only Work.

- **Booking Type dimension** contains both Booking types (Proposed and Committed).

When a Portfolio Analyzer view contains both PivotTable and PivotChart data, the information contained in the PivotTable determines the graph in the PivotChart. The PivotTable contains four "drop areas" into which you can drop fields and dimensions. Figure 15-6 shows a blank PivotTable with each of these drop areas.

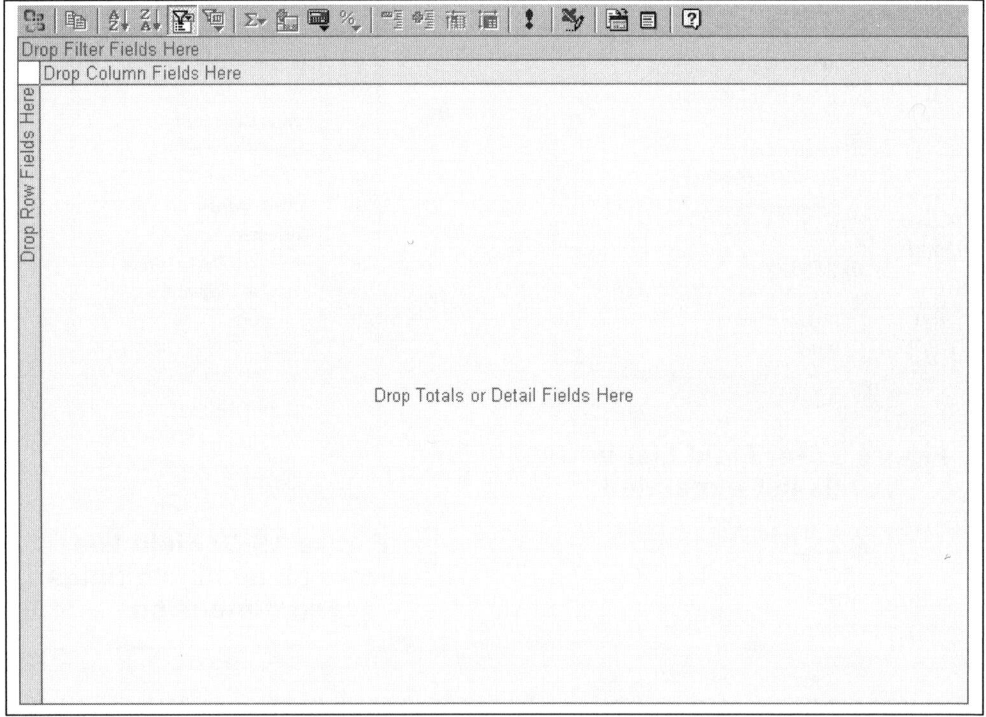

Figure 15-6: Blank PivotTable

The use of each of these drop areas is as follows:

- **Filter Fields** – Drag dimensions and total fields here to filter the data in the PivotTable.

- **Column Fields** – Drag dimensions and total fields here to group data in columns.

- **Row Fields** – Drag dimensions and total fields here to group data in rows.

- **Data Fields** – Drag total fields here to display the data grouped by row and column dimensions.

To create the PivotTable view shown in Figure 15-7, the Project Server administrator did the following:

- Dragged the Versions dimension and the Project Location field into the Filter Fields drop area.

- Dragged the Department field into the Column Fields drop area.

- Dragged the Years time dimension into the Row Fields drop area.

- Dragged the Work and Actual Work total fields into the Data Fields drop area.

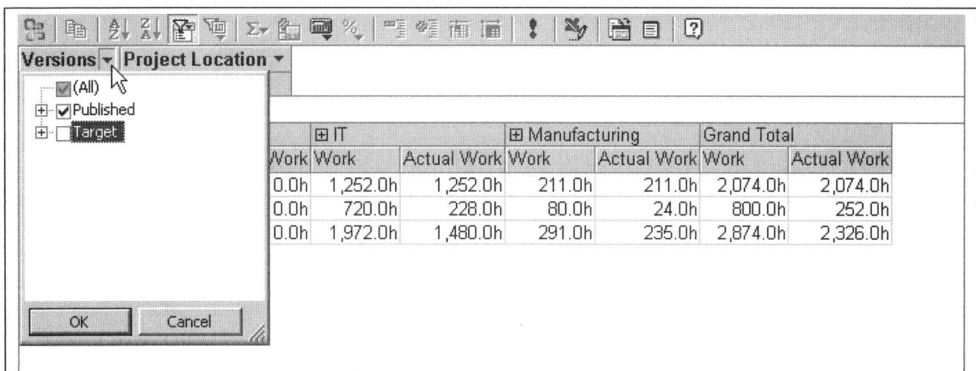

Figure 15-7: PivotTable

In addition, the Project Server administrator also filtered the PivotTable data for the Versions dimension, Project Location field, and the Department field. To filter the PivotTable data, click the pick list button on any field or dimension. In Figure 15-8, notice that I clicked the *Versions* pick list and filtered the data displayed in my PivotTable view to only Published projects by deselecting the checkbox for the Target version.

**Figure 15-8: Select only Published projects
in the Versions dimension**

What Is the Resource Status Dimension?

The five leaves of the Resource Status dimension allow the Portfolio Analyzer to account for every hour of Work and every dollar of Cost in the project portfolio. These five leaves function within the system as follows:

Enterprise Active refers to human resources (non-Generic and non-Local resources) assigned to tasks in all enterprise projects. In the Enterprise Active column, the Cost field displays the total costs and the Work field displays the total work for all human resources in all projects.

Enterprise Generic Active refers to Generic resources assigned to tasks in all enterprise projects. In the Enterprise Generic Active column, the Cost field displays the total costs and the Work field displays the total work for all Generic resources in all projects.

Local Resources refers to Local resources (non-enterprise resources) assigned to tasks in all enterprise projects. In the Local Resources column, the Cost field displays the total costs and the Work field displays the total work for all Local resources in all projects.

Project Fixed Costs is not a resource dimension at all, but rather, is a project dimension. It refers to the fixed costs added to each project in the Fixed Costs column of the Cost table. In the Project Fixed Costs column, the Cost field displays the total Fixed Cost for all projects.

Task Only Work is not a resource dimension at all, but rather, is a project dimension. It refers to any task in any project in which you estimated the Work for the task but did not assign a resource to the task. In the Task Only Work column, the Work field displays the total Work for tasks to which no resource is assigned in all projects.

Creating Custom Portfolio Analyzer Views

To do "on the fly" customization of any Portfolio Analyzer view, you can take a number of actions, including:

- Remove dimensions and fields from the PivotTable drop areas.

- Add new dimensions and fields to the PivotTable drop areas.

- Limit the data displayed in any dimension or field in the PivotTable.

- Format the data in the PivotTable or the PivotChart.

For example, suppose that you want to create a new custom Portfolio Analyzer view that shows project costs by project location and department, and filtered to present Published projects for 2004 only. In addition, you would like to format the resulting PivotChart as an exploded 3D pie chart.

To create this new custom Portfolio Analyzer view, first remove the Work and Actual Work fields from the Data Fields drop area. To remove a field, click and hold the gray field name and drop it anywhere outside of the PivotTable. While doing so, the mouse pointer includes a large red "X" symbol. Notice in Figure 15-9 that I am removing the Work field from the Data Fields drop area.

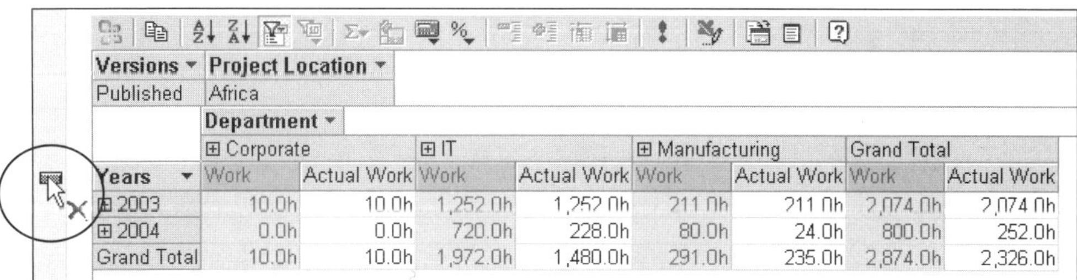

Versions ▾	Project Location ▾							
Published	Africa							
	Department ▾							
	⊞ Corporate		⊞ IT		⊞ Manufacturing		Grand Total	
Years ▾	Work	Actual Work	Work	Actual Work	Work	Actual Work	Work	Actual Work
⊞ 2003	10.0h	10.0h	1,252.0h	1,252.0h	211.0h	211.0h	2,074.0h	2,074.0h
⊞ 2004	0.0h	0.0h	720.0h	228.0h	80.0h	24.0h	800.0h	252.0h
Grand Total	10.0h	10.0h	1,972.0h	1,480.0h	291.0h	235.0h	2,874.0h	2,326.0h

**Figure 15-9: Drag the Work field from
the Totals drop area of the PivotTable**

After removing the Work and Actual Work fields from the PivotTable, you must add the Cost field to the Data Fields drop area. Select the Cost field in the PivotTable Field List dialog, and drag it to the Data Fields drop area. Note that you can also double click a field or dimension to add it to the view. Double-clicking a total field adds it to the Column Fields area while double-clicking a dimension adds it to the Row Fields area. Once a field or dimension is in your view, you can drag it to a new position by clicking and dragging. As you drag and drop the field, the system displays the field as a floating box and highlights the selected drop area, as shown in Figure 15-10.

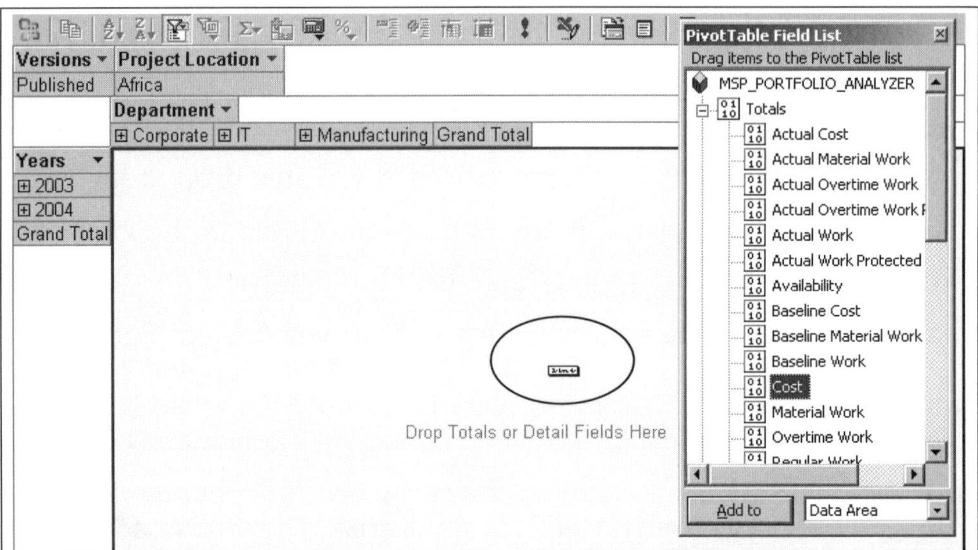

**Figure 15-10: Drag the Cost total field from the
Field List dialog to the Data Fields drop area**

Dragging total fields into drop areas in an Analyzer view is a very straightforward process. Either you drag a total field to the Data Fields drop area or you do not do so. Dragging dimensions is another story. With dimensions, you can select the entire dimension or a single leaf.

Next, move the Years dimension to the Filter Fields drop area, and move the Project Location field to the Row Fields drop area by dragging and dropping each of them to their new location in the PivotTable. Because the Project Location field filters the view to show Africa projects only, you need to select the other project locations you wish to display by clicking the pick list button on the Project Location field and selecting all four locations. Click the *OK* button when your selections are complete, as shown in Figure 15-11.

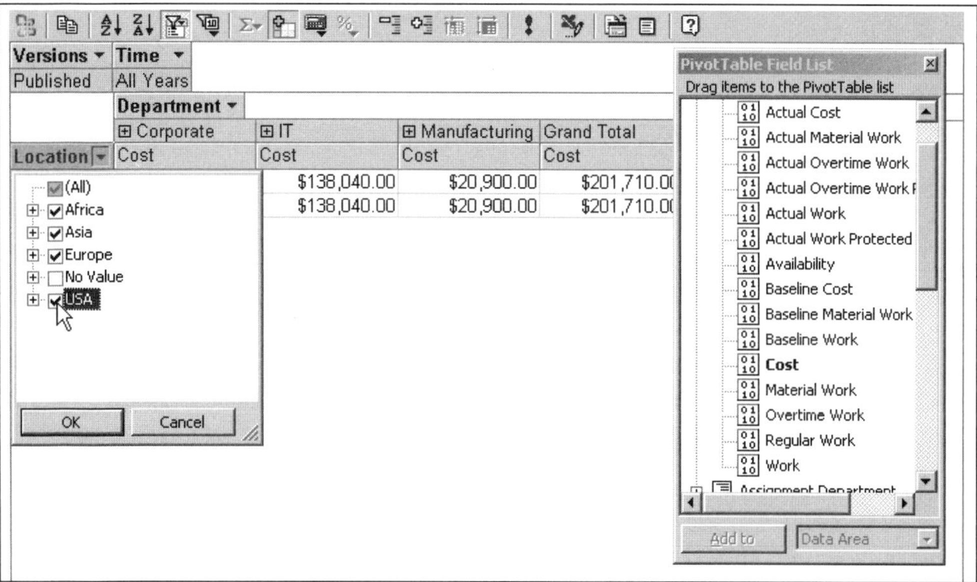

**Figure 15-11: Select the desired
project locations in the Locations field**

To show project costs for 2004 only, you must filter the Time dimension to display 2004. To do so, click the pick list button on the Quarters field, deselect all years other than 2004, and then click *OK*.

As you complete each step, not only does the PivotTable data refresh automatically, the system redraws the PivotChart as well. Figure 15-12 displays the completed PivotTable and PivotChart.

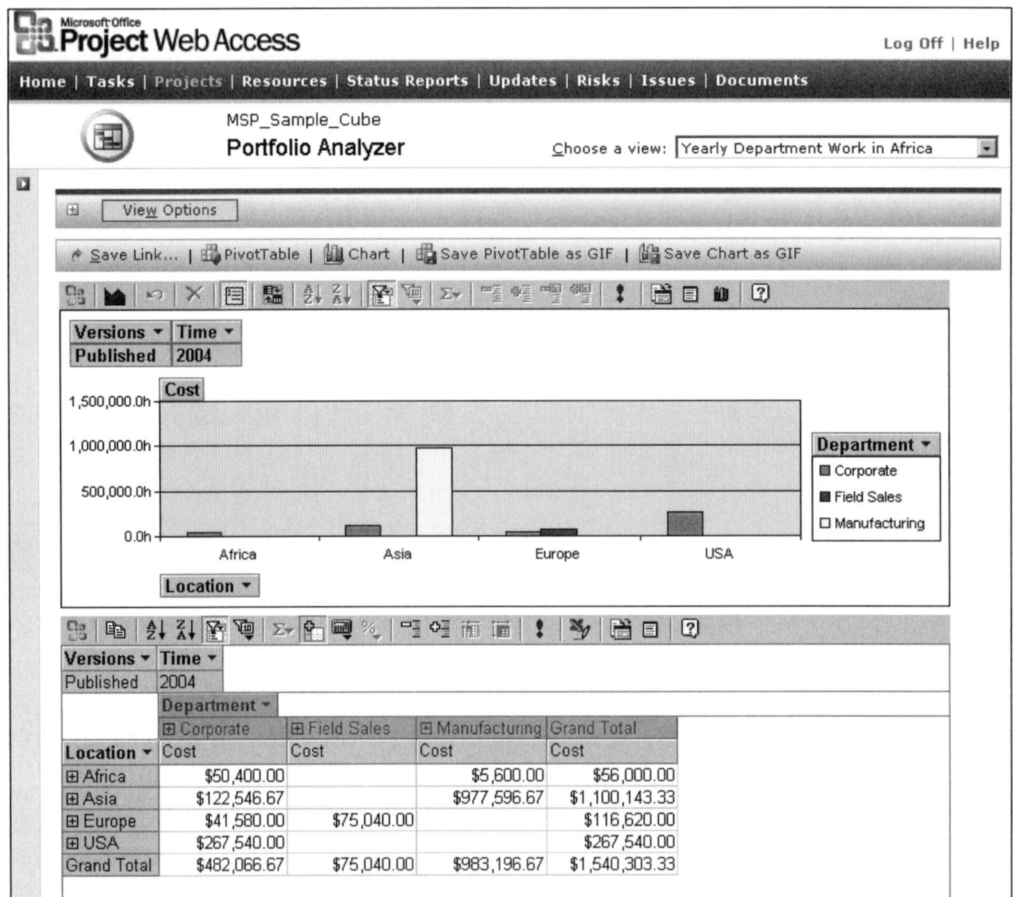

**Figure 15-12: Set Quarters field to
show FY 2004 project costs only**

To complete your custom Portfolio Analyzer view, you must convert the
PivotChart display from a standard bar chart to an exploded 3D pie chart.
Click the *Chart Type* button on the PivotChart toolbar shown in Figure 15-13.

Figure 15-13: PivotChart toolbar

When you click the *Chart Type* button, the system opens the Commands and
Options dialog and displays the Type page, as shown in Figure 15-14. Select
the desired chart type and sub-type, which in this case is the exploded pie
chart. Notice that the PivotChart reformats immediately when you make the
change.

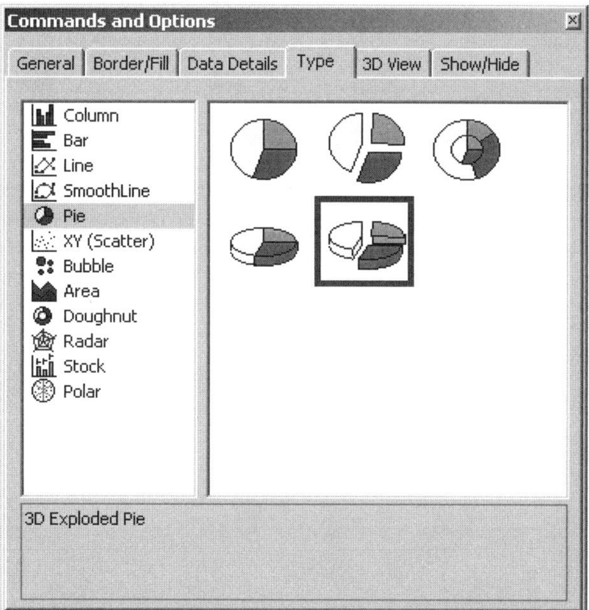

**Figure 15-14: Change the chart type
in the Commands and Options dialog**

After you select the new chart type for the PivotChart, close the Commands
and Options dialog. Figure 15-15 shows your completed custom Portfolio
Analyzer view.

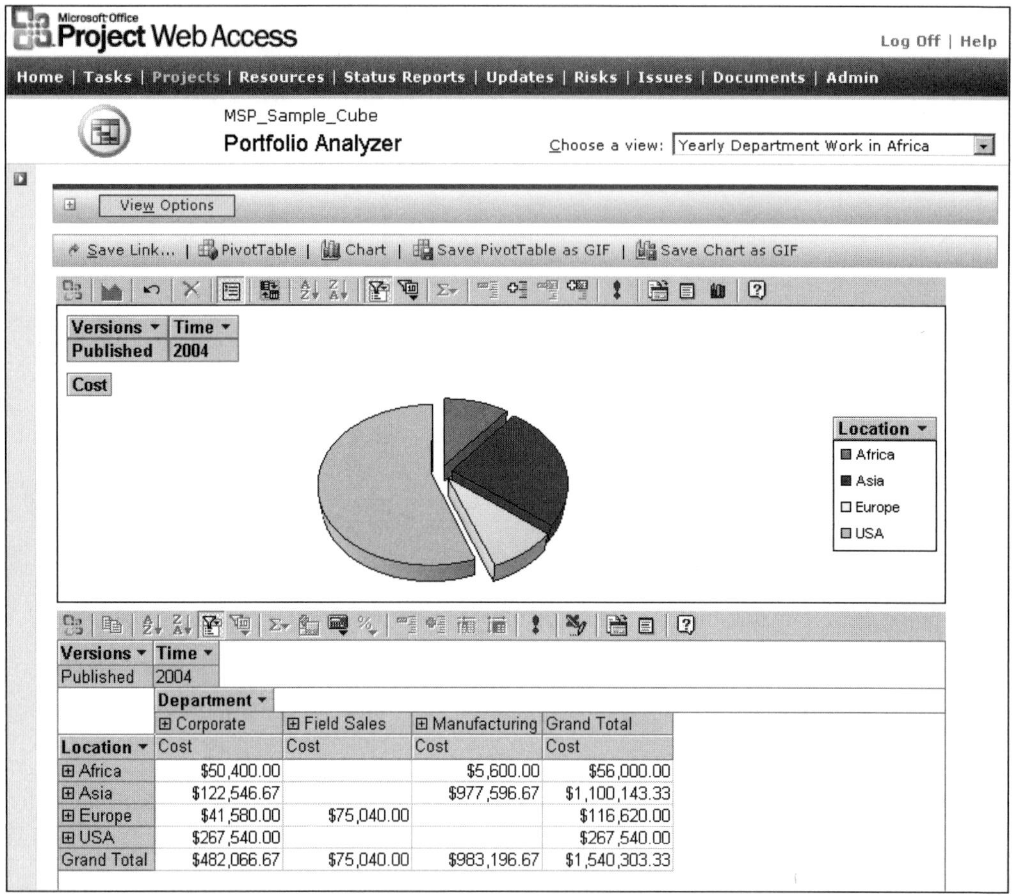

Figure 15-15: Custom Portfolio Analyzer view

To save this customized Portfolio Analyzer view as a personal view, click the *Save Link* button on the Portfolio Analyzer toolbar and give your view a name. Once you save the link, your new personal view is visible in the Saved Links section of the actions pane.

If you create a custom Portfolio Analyzer view that would be useful to others in your organization, ask your Project Server administrator to create an enterprise Portfolio Analyzer view based on your specifications.

Additional Portfolio Analyzer Options

Like the Project Center, the Portfolio Analyzer page contains a toolbar at the top of the page. Figure 15-16 shows the Portfolio Analyzer toolbar.

Figure 15-16: Portfolio Analyzer toolbar

The Portfolio Analyzer toolbar offers you the following actions:

- Click the **Save Link** button to save the current view as a customized Portfolio Analyzer view.

- Click the **PivotTable** button to display only the PivotTable.

- Click the **Chart** button to display only the PivotChart.

- Click the **PivotTable and Chart** button to display both the PivotTable and the PivotChart. This option is available when only the Chart or the PivotTable is displayed, but not both.

- Click the **Save PivotTable as GIF** button to save the PivotTable area as an image file in GIF format.

- Click the **Save Chart as GIF** button to save the PivotTable area as an image file in GIF format.

If you elect to save your PivotTable or PivotChart as a GIF file, the system displays the dialog shown in Figure 15-17. Give your GIF image file a name and click the *OK* button.

**Figure 15-17: Confirmation to save
the PivotTable as a GIF image file**

Before the system saves your GIF image file to your Desktop folder, it displays the warning dialog shown in Figure 15 18. Click the *Yes* button to confirm the save or click the *No* button to cancel the action.

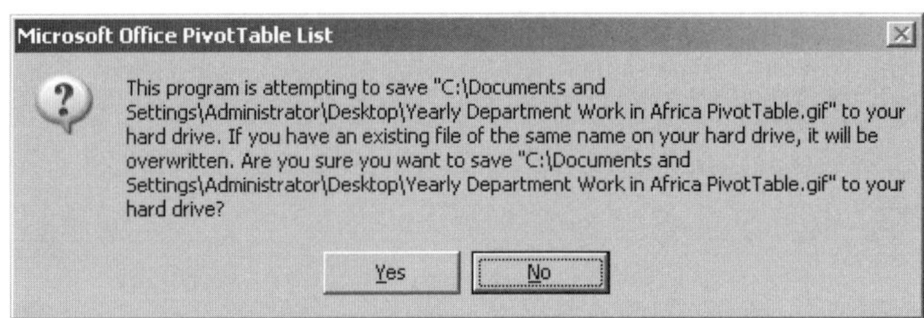

**Figure 15-18: Save GIF image file
to the My Documents folder**

The PivotTable and PivotChart each have their own unique toolbar. Figures 15-19 and 15-20 show the PivotChart and PivotTable toolbars.

Figure 15-19: PivotChart toolbar

Figure 15-20: PivotTable toolbar

The PivotChart toolbar offers a variety of helpful options, such as changing the Chart Type, showing or hiding the Legend, and running the Chart Wizard to format the Chart. The PivotTable toolbar offers helpful options, such as applying sorting and filtering to the PivotTable data, adding subtotals and totals to the data, creating custom formulas, and exporting the data to Excel.

The *Commands and Options* button is available on either toolbar. Click this button to open the respective Commands and Options dialog. Use this dialog to apply additional formatting or to change the layout of either the PivotChart or the PivotTable. Figures 15-21 and 15-22 show the Commands and Options dialogs for both the PivotChart and the PivotTable areas of the Portfolio Analyzer.

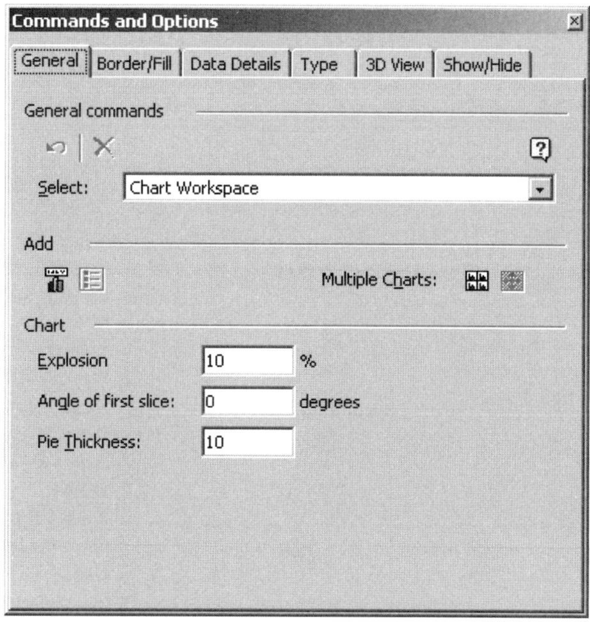

**Figure 15-21: PivotChart
Commands and Options dialog**

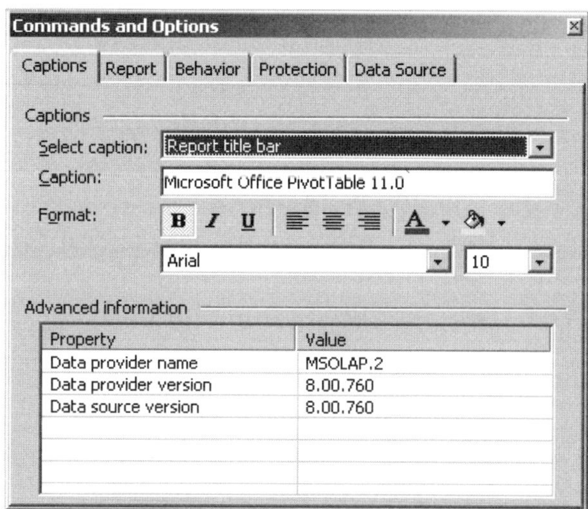

**Figure 15-22: PivotTable
Commands and Options dialog**

Tips for Using the Portfolio Analyzer

Problem: When I drag a field to a drop area, the system does not display the field's real name. Instead, it displays a generic name, such as Level02, as shown in Figure 15-23.

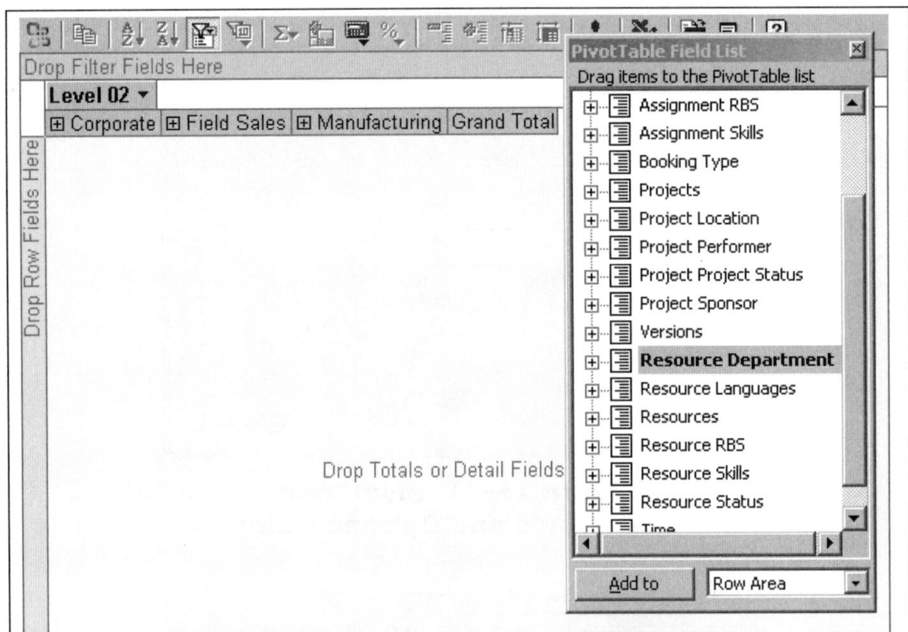

**Figure 15-23: Field name displays
as Level02 instead of Department**

Solution: Right-click the Level02 field name and select the *Commands and Options* menu item from the shortcut menu. Select the *Captions* tab as shown in Figure 15-24. Change the Caption value to your desired name for the field and then close the Commands and Options dialog.

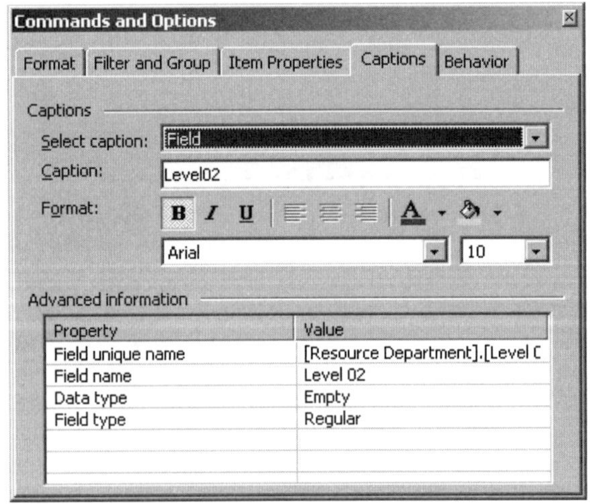

**Figure 15-24: Commands and Options
dialog, Captions page**

Problem: The formatting of a field name is not correct for the type of data displayed in the field. For example, in Figure 15-25 the system has left aligned the text of the Work and Actual Work field names, while the data in each field is right justified naturally.

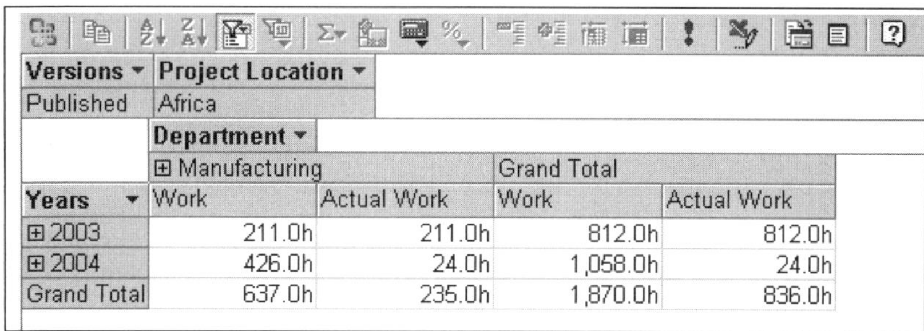

**Figure 15-25: Left aligned formatting of
Work and Actual Work field names**

Solution: Right-click the Work or Actual Work field name and select the *Commands and Options* menu item from the shortcut menu. Select the Captions tab shown in Figure 15-26. Click the *Align Right* button in the Format section and then close the Commands and Options dialog.

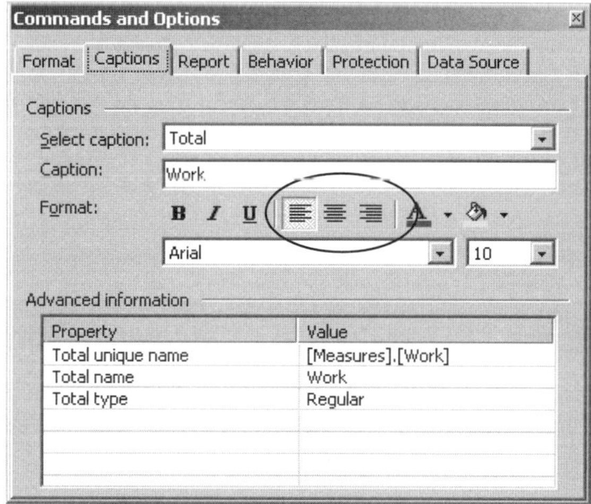

**Figure 15-26: Commands and
Options dialog, Captions page**

Problem: I created a new Portfolio Analyzer view, but the Legend does not display on the right side of the PivotChart.

Solution: By default, the Legend does not display in the PivotChart when you create a new Portfolio Analyzer view. To display the Legend, click the *Show/Hide Legend* button on the PivotChart toolbar shown in Figure 15-27.

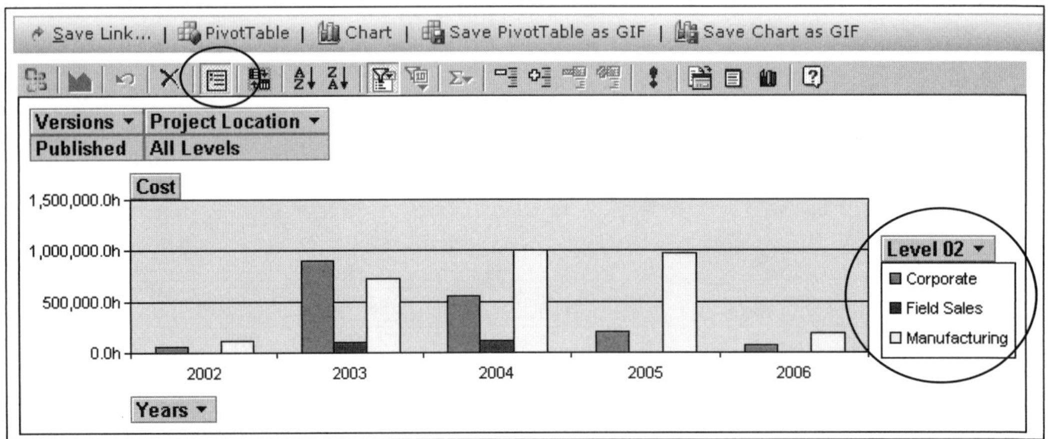

Figure 15-27: PivotChart with Legend

Problem: How can I create a custom formula in the Data Fields drop area of the PivotTable?

Solution: To create a custom formula, click the *Calculated Totals and Fields* button on the PivotTable toolbar and select *Create Calculated Total* from the menu as shown in Figure 15-28.

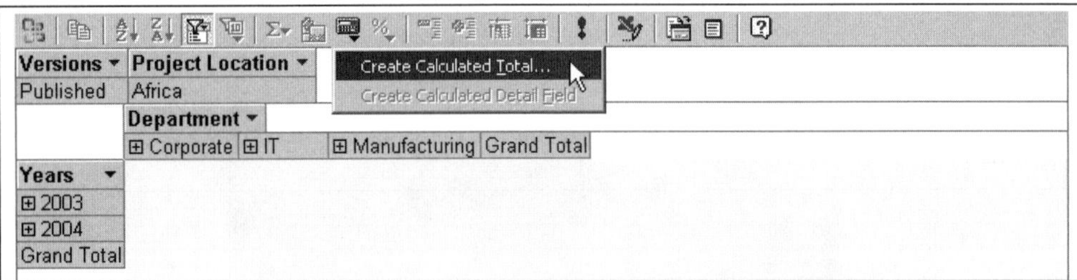

Figure 15-28: Create a Calculated Total

The system displays the Commands and Options dialog with the Calculation tab selected shown in Figure 15-29.

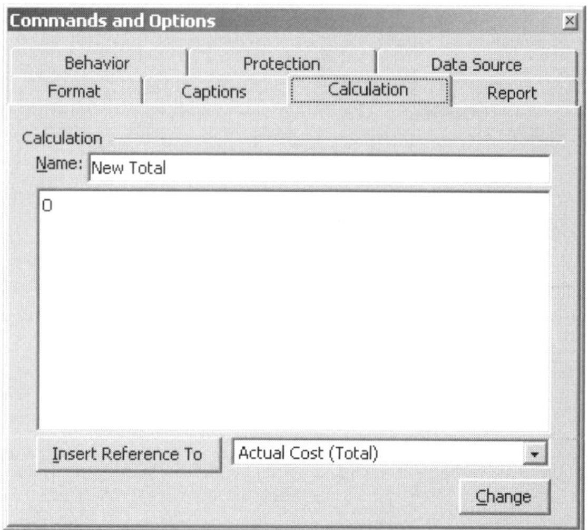

**Figure 15-29: Commands and Options
dialog, Calculation page**

To create the custom calculation, complete the following steps:

1. Give the calculation a meaningful name, such as Remaining Availability.

2. Click the field list to the right of the *Insert Reference To* button and select a field, such as the Availability (Total) field.

3. Click the *Insert Reference To* button to enter the selected field in the Calculation section.

4. Select the text area of the Calculation section and enter any mathematical operators needed to perform a calculation, such as the minus sign to subtract a value from the Availability field.

5. Continue adding fields and mathematical operators as needed to create the final formula.

6. Click the *Change* button when you have completed the formula to display the results in the Data fields drop area.

Notice in Figure 15-30 that I created a custom formula to calculate the Remaining Availability for resources in the system.

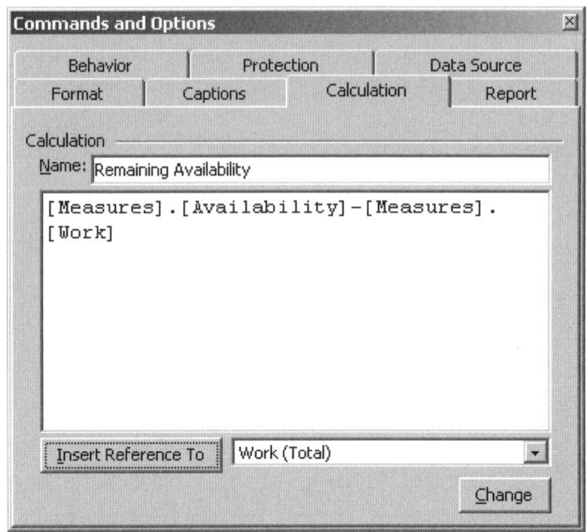

**Figure 15-30: Commands and Options
dialog, Calculation page with
Remaining Availability formula**

Figure 15-31 displays the Remaining Availability field in the PivotTable.

Years	⊞ Corporate Remaining Availability	⊞ IT Remaining Availability	⊞ Manufacturing Remaining Availability	Grand Total Remaining Availability
⊞ 2002	16896	54912	39072	240768
⊞ 2003	33398	107324	77045	473990
⊞ 2004	33536	107192	77126	475030
⊞ 2005	33280	108160	76960	474240
⊞ 2006	15744	51168	36408	224352
Grand Total	132854	428756	306611	1888380

**Figure 15-31: Remaining Availability
custom formula**

When you create a custom formula, the system displays the values using the
General number format. To apply a different number format, click the Format
tab in the Commands and Options dialog and select a format from the
Number pick list in the Text Format section of the dialog. For example, a
better number format for the values shown previously in Figure 15-31 would
be the Standard format, which displays commas in each number.

Using the Portfolio Modeler

The Portfolio Modeler provides a workspace to do "what if" analysis for making changes to staffing and timelines for plans. It features a resource optimization engine driven by parameters you define through its interface. You can use the Portfolio Modeler to build models and explore scenario-based scheduling alternatives by comparing them to each other.

To launch the Portfolio Modeler, click the *Model Projects with Portfolio Modeler* link on the actions pane of the Project Center. The system displays the Model Projects with Portfolio Modeler page shown in Figure 15-32. In the figure, notice that I collapsed the actions pane, which allows me to see the complete information about the two existing models in the grid. All of the functions you activate from this page are on the toolbar above the grid.

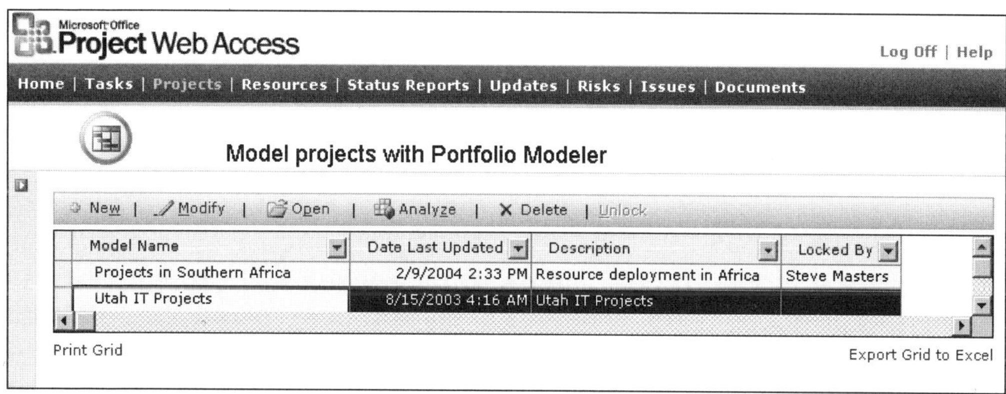

**Figure 15-32: Model projects with
Portfolio Modeler page**

The functions of the buttons on the Portfolio Modeler toolbar are as follows:

- **New** launches a series of steps to create a new model.

- **Modify** allows you to make changes to the existing model you select in the grid.

- **Open** allows you to open an existing model.

- **Analyze** compares resource demand and availability in the model's plans.

- **Delete** permanently removes a model from the system.

- **Unlock** resets a locked model, which is similar to checking in resources and projects.

Warning: You cannot perform any of the functions on the Portfolio Modeler toolbar on a locked model. The only people who can unlock a model are the person who locked it and a Project Server administrator.

Creating a New Model

Click the *New* button and the system displays the Model Projects with Portfolio Modeler page shown in Figure 15-33. Enter a name and description for your new model, select the projects you want to include in your model, and then select the resources you want to consider in your new model. You have three choices for selecting resources:

- Use the resources that already have assignments in the selected projects.

- Select an RBS level at or below which the system should consider resources.

- Choose your specific resources by selecting them in the Available resource pane and moving them to the Selected resources pane.

I want to create a model to help me determine when A. Datum's manufacturing projects in Malaysia are likely to finish, given the fact that there are a number of overallocations in these projects. I want the model to locate and substitute available resources for overallocated resources in an attempt to optimize the schedule of each Malaysia manufacturing project.

Notice in Figure 15-33 that I selected three Malaysia manufacturing projects and selected resources at or below the Malaysia RBS level. Selecting an RBS level allows the system to select other resources in the Enterprise Resource Pool and potentially ignore the current assignments in the three projects.

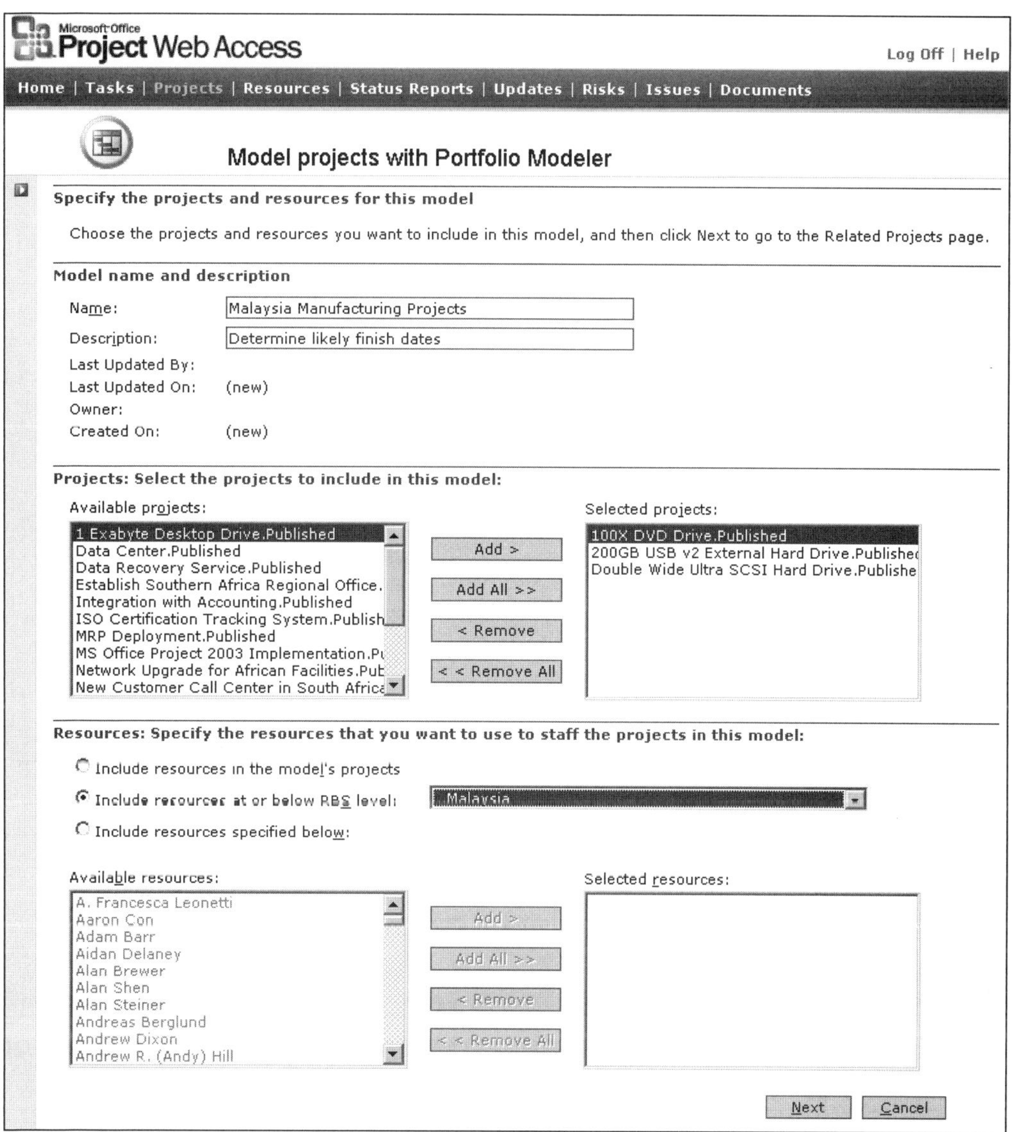

**Figure 15-33: Create a new model
projects and resources page**

Click the *Next* button and the system displays the Include Related Projects page. The system identifies other projects in the system with direct and indirect relationships to the selected projects, and displays them as shown in Figure 15-34. As with the Resource Substitution Wizard, a project has a direct relationship when it shares resources with one of the selected plans. A project has an indirect relationship when it shares resources with a project that shares resources with one of the selected model projects. In the figure, notice that I did not select any related projects for my new model.

**Figure 15-34: Select related projects to
include in your new Portfolio Model**

Click the *Next* button and the system displays the scheduling options page, shown in Figure 15-35. For each project in the model, you can set a Priority number, select Scheduling Options, and set a Start no earlier than date. Setting a Priority number for each project allows the system to determine which project receives preference when resolving scheduling conflicts for resources.

The Scheduling Options allow you to select the scheduling behavior for each included project. Notice the *Schedule Options* pick list shown in Figure 15-35. These options are:

- **Keep dates and assignments** instructs the Portfolio Modeler not to change dates and assignments in the selected project. The system will not optimize dates or reassign resources to assignments.

- **Use current assignments** keeps the current assignments in the plan as set, but allows the Portfolio Modeler to change dates and attempt to resolve overallocated resource assignments.

- **Reassign resources in project** instructs the Portfolio Modeler that it may reassign resources for the selected project only. The modeler substitutes resources based on capacity and skill if the system is able to optimize the schedule in doing so.

- **Reassign resources in model's pool** allows the Portfolio Modeler to use resources included in the virtual resource pool formed by the combination of resources in the model's projects and any additional resources you included based on the combination of this selection and the steps you took in specifying resources for the model.

Setting a Start no earlier than date allows you to set a threshold date before which the modeler does not attempt to reschedule the project. You can use any combination of dates here.

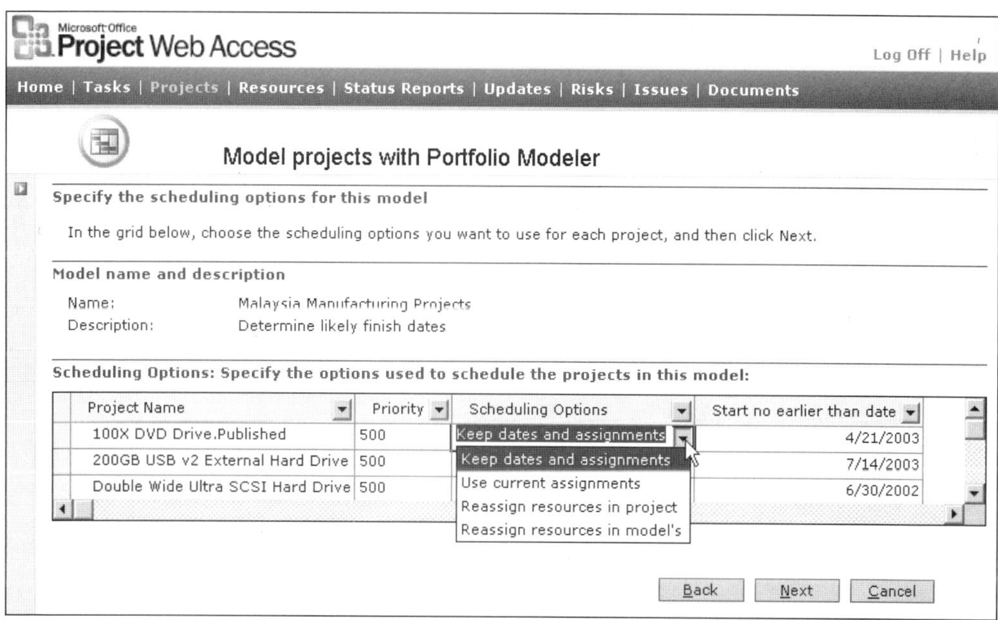

**Figure 15-35: Set scheduling options, priorities
and start date thresholds**

For comparison purposes, I selected the *Keep dates and assignments* option for each project in my model. Doing so allows me to see the "big picture" on the projects I select for the model. Click the *Next* button and the system redisplays the new model in the Model Projects with Portfolio Modeler page.

Opening a Model

To open your Portfolio Model, select the model in the grid and click the *Open* button. Figure 15-36 displays the model I created. The model consists of three sections:

- The Model name and Description section gives general information about the model.

- The Project Scheduling section shows each project in the model, along with a Gantt bar representing the resource utilization in the project.

- The Resource Assignments section displays resource utilization information for each resource in the selected project.

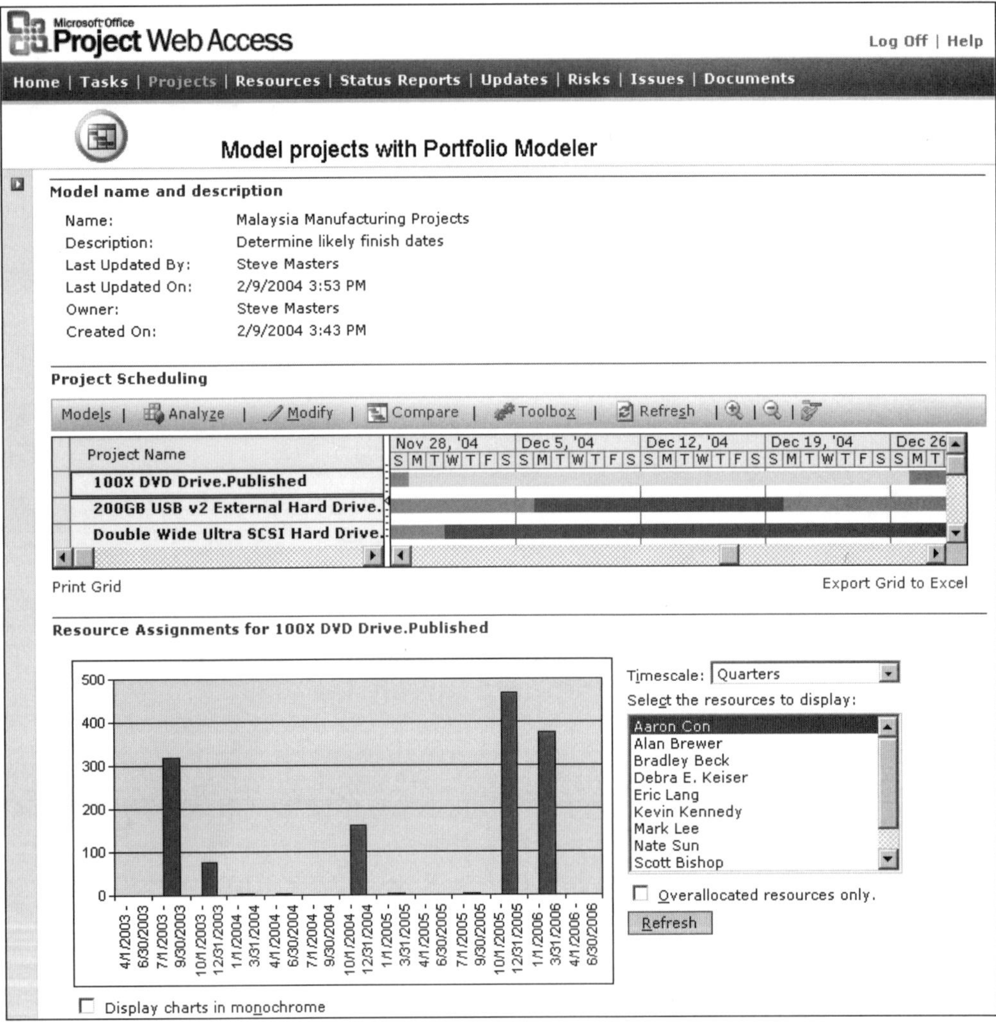

Figure 15-36: An open model

In Figure 15-36, I dragged the divider bar in the grid to the left to give myself a better view of the Gantt bar for each project. The bar colors display green, yellow, or red. In the figure, the 100X DVD Drive project shows a yellow bar portion in December 2004, while the other two projects show red bars during the same period. The meaning of the green, yellow, and red bars is as follows:

- **Green** indicates that there are no resources over allocations occurring during the time period spanned.

- **Yellow** indicates that resources are overallocated, but there are no overallocations more than 10% of demand over availability.

- **Red** indicates that there are resources overallocated at a rate of 10% or greater of demand over availability.

In this case, the results are clear: all three projects are suffering from overallocations that will affect the finish date of each project. To further study resource allocation for a selected project in the model, examine the Resource Assignments section. This section of the page allows you to look at resource loading in the project to help you pinpoint the trouble spots.

Use the *Timescale* pick list to set the timescale on the chart. By default, the Timescale value is set to Auto, which means that the system selects the earliest project start date and latest project finish date, and then selects the best date formatting for the data. Select one or more names from the Select the resources to display list to graph an individual resource or a group of resources. Select the *Overallocated resources only* option to view only overallocated resources. Click the *Refresh* button to redisplay the graph based on any selection changes that you make.

I took the following actions to create the stacked bar chart shown in Figure 15-37:

- Selected the 200GB USB v2 External Hard Drive project in the Project Scheduling section.

- Set the *Timescale* option to Auto.

- Selected the *Overallocated resources only* option.

- Selected all of the resources listed in the Select the Resources to Display list.

- Clicked the *Refresh* button.

- Hovered the mouse pointer over one of the stacked bar sections to display a screentip containing information about the overallocated resource.

Notice that the screentip for the stacked bar section reveals that the project manager has severely overallocated Scott Bishop with a 292% allocation during the last quarter of 2005.

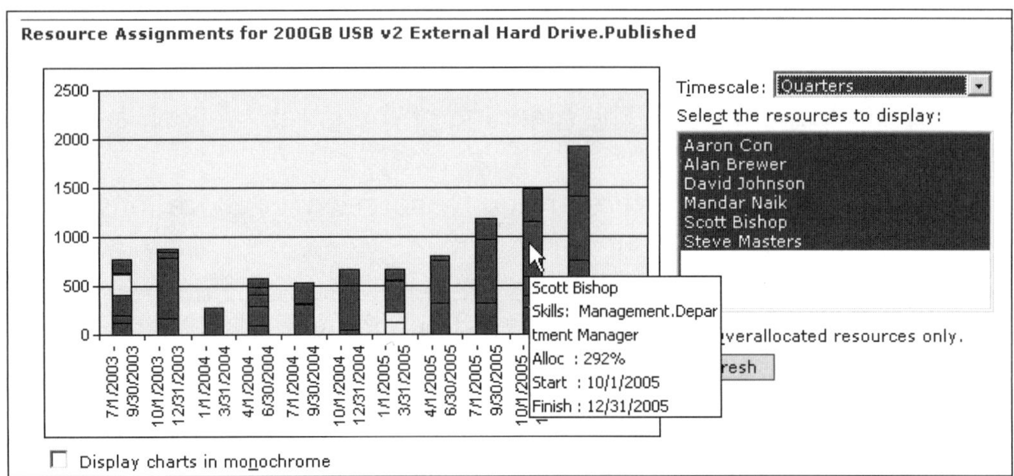

**Figure 15-37: Resource Assignments
for Selected Project section of the model**

Modifying your Model

Whether you select modify from the Model Projects with Portfolio Modeler home page or select it from the toolbar in the single model display shown in the previous two figures, the system takes you through the same series of screens you worked through when you created your model. In other words, refer back to the Creating a New Model section of this module to review the steps for modifying a model.

Select a project from the Project Scheduling section, previously shown in Figure 15-36, and then click the *Toolbox* button on the toolbar to open the Portfolio Model Property Toolbox shown in Figure 15-38. Although you cannot change the name of the model using this dialog, you can change almost every parameter in the model. For each project in the model, I changed the parameters to allow the modeler to make reassignments of resources using all the resources in the model.

To change the parameters of each project in the model without closing the Portfolio Model Property Toolbox dialog, make changes to the first project and click the *Apply* button, then select the next project from the grid. This dialog is a bit unusual, in that it allows you to select objects outside of the dialog.

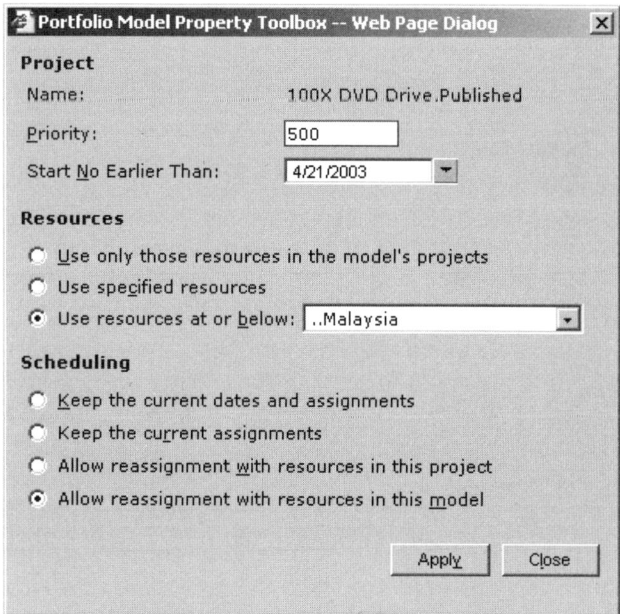

**Figure 15-38: Portfolio Model
Property Toolbox dialog**

After applying my changes, the modeler was able to resolve resource overallocations across all three projects, as shown in Figure 15-39. Allowing the system to substitute available resources for overallocated resources certainly solved the overallocation problem, but what impact has this action had on the finish dates of the three projects in the model?

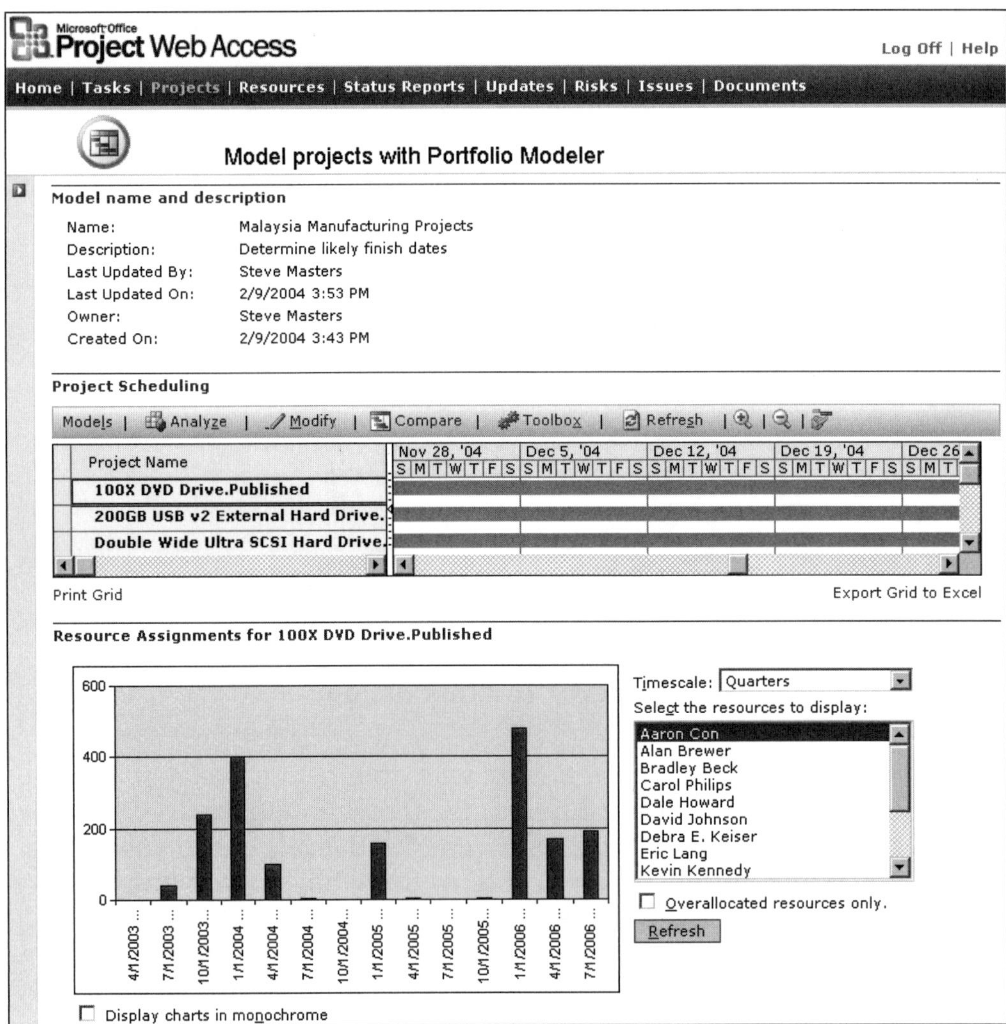

**Figure 15-39: Portfolio Model after making
changes in the Property Toolbox**

Analyze Your Model

Clicking the *Analyze* button on the toolbar displays another version of the Model Projects with Portfolio Modeler page shown in Figure 15-40. The Model Name and Description section displays vital statistics for the model. The Summary Statistics section displays data for the shortest possible schedule and the revised schedule that the system is proposing in the model. For both scenarios, the following information displays:

- Start Date
- Finish Date
- Resource Utilization
- Total work
- Resource Overhead

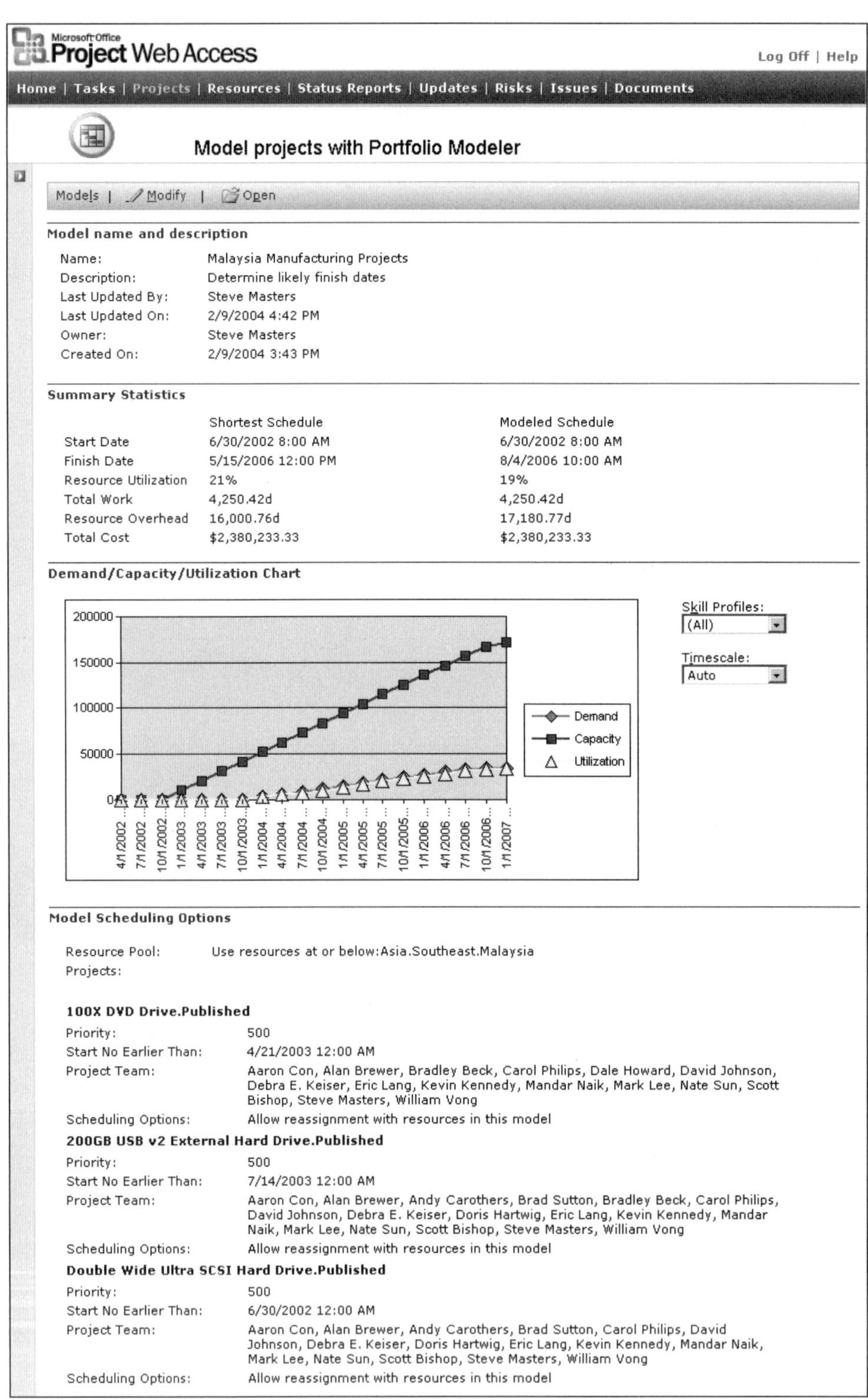

Figure 15-40: Analyze Model results

Resource utilization refers to the percentage of resource demand versus the available capacity. Resource overhead refers to spare capacity in the model. In other words, resource overhead is the total availability of all resources less the workload prescribed in the projects contained in the model. In the example, the modeled schedule finishes more than a month later than the shortest possible scenario. A manager, given these alternatives, might base a decision to go with the modeled schedule in order to preserve greater resource availability for other work.

Notice in the figure that the shortest schedule for the three projects is from 6/6/02 to 5/15/06. The modeled schedule will not finish until 8/4/06. This is the result of resolving resource overallocations in the selected projects and is probably the most realistic schedule for the three projects. This information has met my objective for creating the model, which was to determine the most likely finish date for the three Malaysia manufacturing projects.

The Demand/Capacity/Utilization Chart section displays a chart that maps demand, capacity, and utilization for the projects in the model. You can filter the display by selecting values from the *Skill Profiles* pick list, or by changing the Timescale of the display to days, weeks, months, quarters, or years. The Timescale selection defaults to Auto.

The Model Scheduling Options section enumerates the teams on each project based on the selected scheduling options.

Comparing Models

I created two different versions of my Malaysia Manufacturing model. One model reassigns resources in the model's pool, which allows the system to substitute available resources for overallocated resources. The other model uses the current resource assignments, but the system may delay tasks to level resource overallocations in the model's projects. Now I want to compare the results of these two models to determine which model gives me the earliest finish dates for the projects in the model.

To compare models, open one of the models to compare and then click the *Compare* button on the Portfolio Modeler toolbar. The system displays the page shown in Figure 15-41. Select the models that you want to compare and then click the *OK* button. I selected both of my Malaysia Manufacturing models.

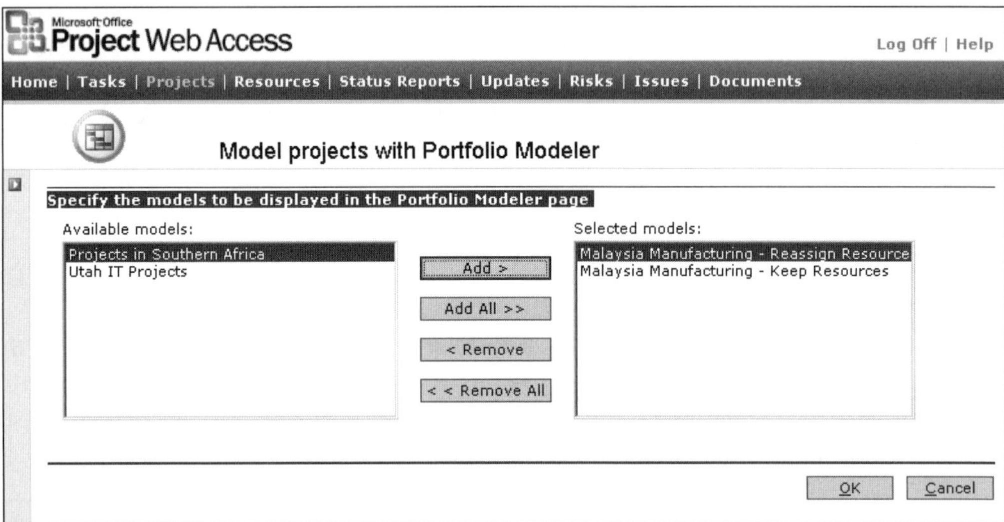

Figure 15-41: Select models to compare

The system displays the Portfolio Modeler page with the combined details of your selected models. Scrolling further down the page reveals the Resource Assignments section, which now responds to all versions of the schedules in the grid, as shown in Figure 15-42. Use the compare models page the same way you used it for a single model by selecting a project in the grid and then selecting one or more resources in the Resource Assignments section.

Notice in the figure that I scrolled the Gantt Chart to reveal the finish dates of each project in the two models. The model that reassigns resources from the model's pool shows a significantly earlier finish date for each project than the model that keeps the resource assignments. In fact, the difference in finish dates ranges from as little as six months to as much as a year. This difference is significant enough to cause me to run the Resource Substitution Wizard on each of the three projects in the models to accomplish the earlier finish date on each project.

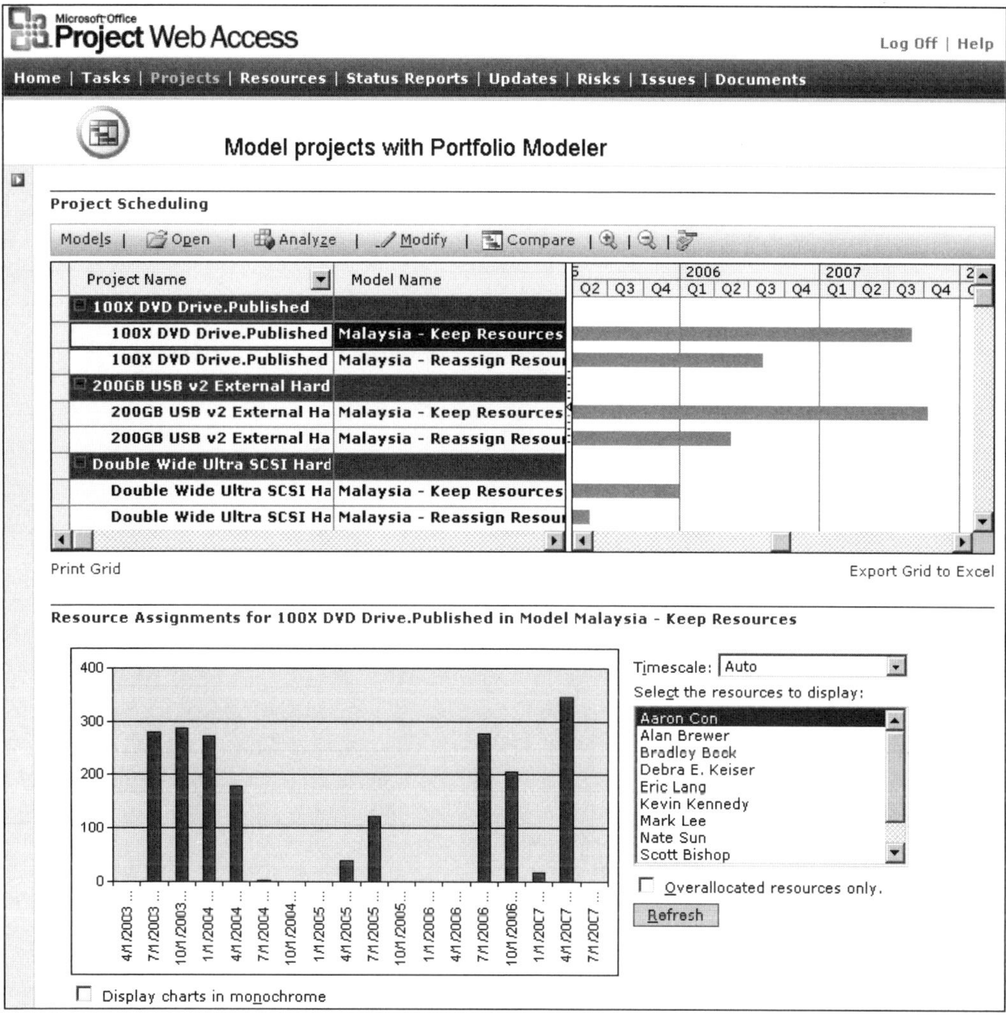

**Figure 15-42: Compare two
portfolio models**

Warning: The Portfolio Modeler can answer high-level what-if questions, but you cannot take the results of the model and update your projects with these results. Unfortunately, you cannot use the output from the Portfolio Modeler outside of the Portfolio Modeler's interface.

Index

A

B

C

D

E

F

I

L

M

O

P

S

U

V

W